Rationality Through Reasoning

The Blackwell/Brown Lectures in Philosophy

The Blackwell/Brown Lectures in Philosophy present compact books distilling cutting-edge research from across the discipline. Based on public lectures presented at Brown University, the books in the series are by established scholars of the highest caliber, presenting their work in a clear and concise format.

Forthcoming books by Philip Pettit

Rationality Through Reasoning

John Broome

WILEY Blackwell

Blackwell Publishing was acquired by John Wiley & Sons in February 2007. Blackwell's publishing program has been merged with Wiley's global Scientific, Technical, and Medical business to form Wiley-Blackwell.

Registered Office
John Wiley & Sons Ltd, The Atrium, Southern Gate, Chichester, West Sussex, PO19 8SQ, UK

Editorial Offices
350 Main Street, Malden, MA 02148-5020, USA
9600 Garsington Road, Oxford, OX4 2DQ, UK
The Atrium, Southern Gate, Chichester, West Sussex, PO19 8SQ, UK

For details of our global editorial offices, for customer services, and for information about how to apply for permission to reuse the copyright material in this book please see our website at www.wiley.com/wiley-blackwell.

Library of Congress Cataloging-in-Publication Data

9781405117104 (HB)
9781118656051 (PB)
Broome, John, 1947–
  Rationality through reasoning / John Broome.
     pages cm
Includes bibliographical references and index.
  ISBN 978-1-4051-1710-4 (cloth) – ISBN 978-1-118-65605-1 (pbk.)   1. Reasoning.
2. Practical reason. I. Title.
  BC177.B76 2013
  153.4'3–dc23

2013012754

A catalogue record for this book is available from the British Library.

Cover design by Simon Levy Associates.

Set in 10/12 pt Sabon by Toppan Best-set Premedia Limited

1   2013

For Derek Parfit

Contents

Preface

Long ago, Derek Parfit generously asked me to respond to a paper of his in a symposium at the 1997 Joint Session of the Aristotelian Society and the Mind Association. Writing my response was the beginning of my work on the subject of this book. Traditionally, the two papers in a symposium were published in the *Aristotelian Society Supplementary Volume* under the same title. But sharp-eyed readers may have noticed that, whereas Parfit's paper was entitled 'Reasons and motivation', mine was entitled 'Reason and motivation'. By that time, I had already concluded that rational motivation was less about reasons than many philosophers assume, and more about figuring out by reason what you ought to do and then coming through reason to do it.

The last stage brings a difficulty. If you come through reason to do a particular act, reason supports your doing it. But how could it support your doing an act unless it is one you ought to do? And it might not be one you ought to do; even if you have figured out by reason that you ought to do this act, you may have made a mistake. A solution came to me as I walked along Dag Hammarskjölds väg in Uppsala, one snowy day early in 1998. I was in Uppsala on the first of several long visits to the Swedish Collegium of Advanced Study. SCAS has always been exceptionally generous to me and given me the very best opportunities for working. Each visit has advanced my work on the subject of this book. That first time I realized that, when you come through reason to act, reason need not support your acting simpliciter. Instead, reason – rationality – requires of you that, if you believe you ought to do something, you do it. The condition is within the scope of what reason requires. Reason supports your making the conditional true, not your acting. This insight that the requirement of rationality has a 'wide scope' was not original; I soon discovered that Jonathan Dancy had mentioned it twenty years earlier in his paper 'The logical conscience'. But it provided a foundation for this book. Later, a long correspondence with Niko Kolodny helped me to refine it.

Through the following years I slowly disentangled some of the relevant concepts. First, I disentangled rationality from normativity in general. Many philosophers think of rationality as a sort of enforcer for normativity: it is your rationality that makes you do what you have a reason to do, or at least what you believe you have a reason to do. I now think that rationality is much less tightly connected with normativity than that. Second, I disentangled reasoning, which is something a person does, from rationality, which is a property of a person and her mental states. During these developments, I benefited from many discussions with those of my research students who were interested in aspects of the subject: first Andrew Riesner and later Julian Fink, Stephen Kearns, Yair Levy, James Morauta, Toby Ord, and Gerard Vong.

The last five years of my work on the book have mainly been occupied with trying to understand reasoning. My account of reasoning has gone through several revolutions, each correcting an initial mistake of mine. At first I was deceived by a similarity between the contents of instrumental practical reasoning and the contents of theoretical reasoning by modus ponens. I thought that the two were somehow fused together. I have now concluded that their similarity is only superficial. A second mistake was to assume that, when reasoning is correct, it is made correct by requirements of rationality. I now realize that reasoning is made correct by permissions, not requirements. Correct reasoning is not reasoning you are required to do by rationality, but reasoning you are permitted to do by rationality. This seems intuitively obvious, but I understood it properly only as a result of facing up to an objection to my previous account of reasoning that was shown me by Kieran Setiya. A third mistake was to assume that reasoning – at least when it is conscious and something we do – has to be conducted in language. This may be true, but a discussion with Paul Boghossian persuaded me it is best not to assume it. Boghossian also made me realize I should take more seriously the well-known difficulties of rule-following, which are associated with my view that reasoning is a rule-governed operation.

I gave three Blackwell-Brown Lectures in 2003. I was honoured to receive the invitation. This book exists because of it. The lectures drew together my work up to that point. It turned out to be an earlier point in the development of the book than either I or my publishers had anticipated. Still, from then on I possessed a draft book.

I have been honoured by subsequent invitations that have given me the opportunity to garner advice from philosophers in different parts of the world. I want to mention three in particular. First, I gave four Wedberg Lectures in Stockholm in 2004, where I benefited from the commentary of the four excellent discussants, Lars Bergström, Torbjörn Tännsjö, Folke Tersman and Åsa Wikforss. Second, there was a conference on my work in Canberra in 2007, with valuable papers from Geoffrey Brennan, Garrett Cullity, James Dreier, Andrew Reisner, Wlodek Rabinowicz, Nicholas Southwood and Daniel Star.

Third, I gave two Whitehead Lectures at Harvard in 2011, where again I received very useful comments.

Many institutions have supported me with their generosity during the long writing of this book. I have mentioned SCAS already. My visits there have alternated with visits to the Research School of Social Sciences at the Australian National University. Any philosopher who has spent time at the RSSS knows what wonderful stimulation is to be found there. My home universities – first St Andrews and now Oxford – have been very kind with the leave they granted me from teaching. For a whole three years, my research on this book was funded by a Major Research Fellowship from the Leverhulme Trust. Not only did the Trust finance me for all that time, but it has shown remarkable forbearance during the subsequent years while the book remained unfinished. I do hope it will think the result is worth the wait.

I have to express ironical thanks to another institution: the UK Research Excellence Framework. The REF is stupid in some ways. It demands that philosophy should have a demonstrable impact on society within fifteen years, whereas the actual impact of philosophy on society is wide and deep but takes decades or centuries to develop. However, the REF did have the merit of setting me a deadline. For its sake, this book had to go to press by the end of 2012. It went, with all the imperfections it still contains. I could have worked much longer on trying to eliminate each one. I am pleased I did not, and now I can even blame them on the REF.

Over the years I have been helped by a great number of philosophers who gave me their time. I am not adequately acknowledging my debts simply by including them in the great long list below. Many have sent me extensive comments and continued to do so for years. But when so many have helped me to a greater or lesser extent, what else can I do? I am worried, too, that I have probably forgotten to list some people whose contribution has been important. If you are one of those, please forgive my lapse of memory.

I have already mentioned Derek Parfit, who started me on this track, influenced the turnings I took, and also near the end sent me long comments about the whole book. Parfit's own work was the stimulus for mine. Several chapters of my book implicitly or explicitly engage with it. I often obstinately disagree with Parfit, but I hope he will recognize that I am much more on his side than against it. Really, he has always been my mentor.

I have also already mentioned my students at Oxford. I have learnt a great deal from them, and some have taken the trouble to comment extensively on my writing. More senior friends and colleagues, with whom I have had many conversations about topics in this book, include Gustaf Arrhenius, Michael Bratman, Geoffrey Brennan, Krister Bykvist, Roger Crisp, Jonathan Dancy, Brad Hooker, Douglas MacLean, Wlodek Rabinowicz, Nicholas Southwood, John Skorupski and Ralph Wedgwood.

I know of several philosophers besides Parfit and my students who have read drafts of the whole book and sent me comments. They include Josée Brunet, Roger Crisp, Garrett Cullity, Mark Schroeder and Ralph Wedgwood. Each has contributed greatly. I must mention Brunet in particular. She spent a year in Oxford, during which she worked carefully through my draft and regularly gave me thoughtful advice. She was a great help.

Now the great long list. Besides those I have mentioned already, each of the following philosophers has helped me, mostly through written comments. Some have helped me a great deal: Norbert Anwander, Nomy Arpaly, Robert Audi, Dennis Badenhop, Thomas Baldwin, Sophie Botros, Selim Berker, John Bishop, Sarah Broadie, Anne Burkard, Erik Carlson, Ruth Chang, Matthew Chrisman, Ursula Coope, Louis deRosset, Malte Engel, Pascal Engel, David Estlund, Daan Evers, Nancy Cartwright, Garrett Cullity, Bill Child, Janice Dowell, Gerald Dworkin, Edward Elliot, Kit Fine, Antonio Gaitán-Torres, Jan Gertken, Margaret Gilbert, Katrin Glüer-Pagin, Kalle Grill, Dorothy Grover, Olav Gjelsvik, Caspar Hare, Anandi Hattiangadi, Tim Henning, Pamela Hieronymi, John Horty, Kent Hurtig, Nadeem Hussain, John Hyman, Benedikt Kahmen, Benjamin Kiesewetter, Christine Korsgaard, Richard Kraut, Arto Laitinen, Daniel Laurier, Leon Leontyev, Micah Lewin, Sten Lindström, Christian List, Errol Lord, John Maier, Julia Markowits, Cynthia MacDonald, Graham MacDonald, David McCarthy, Adam Morton, Kevin Mulligan, Jennifer Nagel, Carsten Nielsen, Sven Nyholm, Jonas Olson, Peter Pagin, Herlinde Pauer-Studer, Adam Perry, Philip Pettit, Christian Piller, Eugen Pissarskoi, Andreas Pittrich, Dag Prawitz, Robert Pulvertaft, Joseph Raz, Henry Richardson, Michael Ridge, Simon Robertson, Jacob Ross, Abe Roth, Kieran Setiya, Nicholas Shackel, Thomas Schmidt, Oliver Schott, François and Laura Schroeter, Nick Shea, Peter Simons, Holly Smith, Michael Smith, Nicholas Smith, Daniel Star, Daniel Stoljar, Bart Streumer, Jussi Suikkanen, Pär Sundström, Sigrun Svarvasdottir, Lucas Swaine, Sergio Tennenbaum, Judith Thomson, Teru Thomas, Valerie Tiberius, John Turri, Gijs van Donselaar, Bruno Verbeek, Jay Wallace, Clas Weber, David Wiggins, Dominic Wilkinson, Stephen Winter and Michael Zimmerman.

I am very grateful to Yair Levy for checking the proofs of this book with great diligence, and for creating the index.

I am especially grateful to my wife Ann for her forbearance. She has now patiently sat out the writing of seven books.

1

Introduction

1.1 Motivation

When you believe you ought to do something, your belief often causes you to intend to do what you believe you ought to do. How does that happen? I call this 'the motivation question'. I shall try to answer it in this book.

It is also true that, when you believe you ought to do something, your belief often causes you actually to do it. We could also ask how that happens. This question raises the mind–body problem. When you believe you ought to do some bodily act, and this belief causes you to do the act, a state of your mind causes a physical movement. One part of the mind–body problem is to understand how a state of mind can have a physical effect like that. I wish to set this problem aside, and I do that by focusing on your intention rather than your action. The motivation question is about your mind only. When your belief causes you to intend to act, your intention will in turn generally cause you to act, but that is not my concern.

The motivation question has an easy answer: most people are disposed to intend to do what they believe they ought to do, perhaps not every time, but often. They have the 'enkratic disposition', as I shall call it. This is a genuine answer to the question, and correct as far as it goes. It has a real content. It tells us that the explanation of why you often intend to do what you believe you ought to do lies within you: you are constituted that way. We can no doubt add that you have this disposition as a result of natural selection.

However, this easy answer is very thin. It leaves a lot to be explained. How does the enkratic disposition work, exactly? In what way does it bring about its effect?

One possible answer is that some causal process within people, whose details have no philosophical interest, tends to make them intend to do what they believe they ought to do. But this answer is unsatisfying. Some people have the enkratic disposition more strongly than others, and some may not have it at all; some are strongly disposed to intend to do what they believe they ought to do, and others are not. We can classify people accordingly. Let us call the ones who have the disposition strongly 'sheep', and the others 'goats'. Unless we are Calvinists, we shall not be satisfied with merely classifying people. We should expect it to be at least partly up to people themselves whether they are goats or sheep. We should expect that people by their own efforts can actually bring themselves to intend to do what they believe they ought to do. And we should be able to explain how they can do so. It is not enough to say it just happens because of some causal process within them.

Rationality and reasoning

We can call in rationality to help answer the motivation question. We can say that rationality requires people to intend to do what they believe they ought to do, and that it requires them to be disposed to do so – to have the enkratic disposition. No doubt this is true, and it follows that the goats are not fully rational. This is a criticism to throw at the goats, but it is still 'merely classificatory', to use Thomas Nagel's term.[1] It gives us an explanation of why rational people are disposed to intend to do what they believe they ought to do, which is that they would not be classified as rational if they did not. But it gives us no explanation of how, in rational people, this disposition works.

In *Ethics and the A Priori*, Michael Smith undertakes 'to explain how it can be that our beliefs about what we are rationally justified in doing play a proper causal role in the genesis of our actions'.[2] (Smith is interested in desires rather than intentions.) His explanation is that

> In rational creatures . . . we would . . . expect there to be a causal connection between believing that it is desirable to act in a certain way and desiring to act in that way. . . . For the psychological states of rational deliberators and thinkers connect with each other in just the way that they rationally should.[3]

But this does not explain how our beliefs play a proper causal role in the genesis of our actions. It explains only why rational creatures are causally disposed to act in ways they believe are desirable. The explanation is that otherwise they would not count as rational.

Elsewhere, Smith mentions 'the capacity we have, as rational creatures, to have a coherent psychology'.[4] This is getting somewhere. Exercising a capacity is something we do; it does not just happen. So Smith is suggesting that we may ourselves bring it about that we desire to do what we believe we ought to do. But we still need to be told how we do that.

Calling in rationality is definitely a step towards the explanation we are looking for. It points us towards reasoning. We know that people have a particular means of coming to satisfy some of the requirements of rationality, and that is reasoning. Reasoning is something we do. It is a mental activity of ours that can bring us to satisfy some of the requirements of rationality.

For example, suppose you believe it is raining and that if it is raining the snow will melt. Plausibly, rationality requires you to believe what follows by modus ponens from beliefs of yours – in this case that the snow will melt – at least if you care about what follows. Suppose you do care whether the snow will melt; perhaps you are planning to ski today. But suppose you do not yet believe the snow will melt. (You have just woken up. You have noticed the rain, and you know that rain causes snow to melt, but you have not yet thought about the snow.) So at present you do not satisfy this requirement of rationality. But you can bring yourself to satisfy it by undertaking a process of reasoning. This process will set out from your initial beliefs and it will conclude with your believing the snow will melt. In doing this reasoning you are mentally active, and you bring yourself to satisfy a requirement of rationality.

Now suppose you believe you ought to oil that squeaky hinge. I have already assumed that rationality requires you to intend to do what you believe you ought to do. You can bring yourself to satisfy this requirement, too, by a process of reasoning. The process will start from your initial belief that you ought to oil that squeaky hinge and conclude with your intending to do so. So reasoning can bring you to intend to do what you believe you ought to do.

Your ability to reason constitutes part of your enkratic disposition. No doubt you often intend to do what you believe you ought to do automatically, without reasoning. But this does not always happen automatically, and when automatic processes fail, sometimes you achieve the result through the activity of reasoning. I call this type of reasoning 'enkratic reasoning'.

We have arrived at a more interesting answer to the motivation question. You have an enkratic disposition, and this disposition sometimes works through the philosophically interesting process. This process is enkratic reasoning, which is something you do. You have the ability to bring yourself, through reasoning, to intend to do what you believe you ought to do. I hope to justify this answer.

In one way, it is a very attractive answer to the motivation question, because it tells us that we can motivate ourselves by our own activity. But many moral philosophers will find it unattractive in a different way.[5] In moral contexts, these philosophers think a truly virtuous person does what she believes she ought to do automatically and without thinking. She does not reason about it. Indeed, they think a truly virtuous person often does what she ought to do without even forming the belief that she ought to do it. I do not deny these views. I say only that we *can* motivate ourselves through reasoning. Those of us who are not truly virtuous may find we need to do it often when morality makes demands on us.

I also need to stress at the outset that I am not concerned particularly with morality. 'Ought' is not particularly a moral word, and I do not treat it as one. It is a general normative word; chapter 2 examines its meaning. The motivation question as I mean it is about how people are motivated by normative beliefs in general. It is not particularly about moral motivation.

1.2   This book

The task of justifying my answer to the motivation question is large. As part of it, I need to present an account of reasoning in general. Since reasoning is a means by which we can bring ourselves to satisfy some of the requirements of rationality, I need as a preliminary to investigate rationality. Rationality in turn has connections with normativity: with ought and reasons. This book therefore starts with an examination of normativity, goes on to rationality and concludes with reasoning.

My initial motivation in writing this book was to answer the motivation question. However, this question itself takes up only this short chapter and the last one. In between, there is a lot of argument that I hope may prove independently useful. I have tried to answer, or at least contribute to answering, quite a number of fundamental questions within the philosophy of normativity. What are reasons? What is their relation to ought, and to rationality? Is there a logic of ought? What is rationality? Is rationality normative? How is it connected to our process of reasoning? What is the process of reasoning? What is practical reasoning in particular? When is reasoning correct? And so on.

My answer to each question is no doubt contentious to some extent. Since my answer to the motivation question is built on all of these answers together, it is the most contentious thing in the book. So even if you doubt my answer to the motivation question, I hope you may nevertheless be persuaded by some of my subsidiary arguments.

Chapters 2–4 describe the fundamental features of normativity. Chapters 2 and 3 are about ought, which I take to be the most fundamental feature. They do not try to define ought. Instead they distinguish various meanings of the word 'ought' and pick out the one that I call 'central'. This is the ought I consider most fundamental and the one that plays a role later in the book.

I identify it through the principle I call 'Enkrasia': that rationality requires you to intend to do what you believe you ought to do. The central ought is the ought mentioned in this principle.

Chapter 4 goes on to reasons. It defines a reason in terms of ought. Indeed, it defines reasons of two sorts, which I call '*pro toto* reasons' and '*pro tanto* reasons'.

Chapters 5–11 contain my account of rationality. They begin by rejecting in chapters 5 and 6 the common opinion that rationality consists in responding correctly to reasons or to beliefs about reasons.

My own account of rationality depends on the notion of a requirement of rationality. Next therefore, in chapters 7 and 8, I describe the nature and logic of requirements in general. Chapter 8 considers the vexed question of the logical scope of requirements.

Chapter 9 describes some synchronic requirements of rationality. It concentrates particularly on Enkrasia and the instrumental requirement that you intend what you believe to be a means to an end that you intend. Chapter 10 continues the description of rationality by describing some diachronic requirements. It concludes with a discussion of some particular permissions of rationality (negations of requirements) that I call 'basing permissions'. These are crucial to my later account of correct reasoning.

Chapter 11 considers the question of whether rationality is normative: whether, when rationality requires something of you, that fact constitutes a reason for you to do what it requires. I believe rationality is normative, but the chapter explains that I cannot demonstrate that this is so.

Chapters 12–16 are about reasoning. Chapter 12 rejects the common view that reasoning necessarily involves a normative belief. More exactly, it rejects the view that reasoning necessarily involves the belief that you ought to have a particular attitude, such as a particular belief or a particular intention. No normative beliefs are involved in my first-order account of reasoning, which follows in the next chapter.

The basics of the first-order account are in chapter 13. This chapter argues that reasoning is a mental process in which you operate on the contents of your attitudes, following a rule. It explains how reasoning is an activity – something you do – and it identifies reasoning as correct if the rule it follows corresponds to a basing permission of rationality.

Chapter 13 uses theoretical reasoning as its example; chapter 14 extends the first-order account to practical reasoning. It examines correctness in more detail.

My account of reasoning does not assume that we necessarily reason using language. But there is a case for thinking that we do, so that we have to express our attitudes in language in order to reason with them. That condition places some constraints on our reasoning. Chapter 15 considers what they are.

Chapter 16 returns finally to enkratic reasoning. It explains that enkratic reasoning fits my account of reasoning in general. If my account is right, therefore, enkratic reasoning is indeed something we can do to bring ourselves to intend to do what we believe we ought to do.

Metaphysics

You will not find in this book any discussion of the metaphysical nature of normativity.

True, my answer to the motivation question does have a metaphysical motivation. Some philosophers find it puzzling that a person can be motivated by a belief, so they are puzzled about the enkratic disposition. They find it puzzling that you can be caused to intend some action by the belief that you ought to do it. Their puzzlement has led some of them to be noncognitivists about normativity. They have concluded that the belief that you ought to do something cannot be an ordinary belief. They think it must be some other sort of mental state, in which motivation is already embedded.[6]

In this book I shall try to account for the enkratic disposition in a way that is not puzzling. My account leaves it open whether or not the belief that you ought to do something is an ordinary belief, but it removes one reason for thinking it is not. So it is intended to remove one of the grounds for noncognitivism. This is a modest metaphysical aim.

It is true too that my language is metaphysically presumptuous; it is realist. For example, I shall say that one sort of reason is an explanation of a deontic fact, and by a deontic fact I mean the fact that someone ought to do something or other. 'Fact' and 'explanation' are realist words. But our normative language just is presumptuous in this way, and I see no point in being squeamish about it.

Part of the job of metaphysics is to account for what we know about normativity. In this book I aim to provide some data for metaphysics to account for, by identifying some of the things we know. If it should all turn out false, or true only in a fiction,[7] so we do not know these things after all, that would be disappointing. But I trust the metaphysicians to do better than that.

Notes

1 Nagel, *The Possibility of Altruism*, p. 109.
2 p. 35.
3 p. 36.
4 *Ethics and the A Priori*, p. 4.

5 See, for example, Rosalind Hursthouse's *On Virtue Ethics* and Nomy Arpaly's *Unprincipled Virtue*, pp. 51–63.

6 For example, in Allan Gibbard's noncognitivist theory, set out in his *Thinking How to Live*, the belief that you ought to do something is a sort of intention.

7 In *Ethics: Inventing Right and Wrong*, J. L. Mackie argues that all ethical statements are false. In *The Myth of Morality*, Richard Joyce agrees, but argues that they should be taken as fictional. I do not know of anyone who takes either view about normative statements in general.

2
Ought

2.1 The meaning of 'ought'

'You ought to look both ways before you cross the road.' 'Protesters ought not to be allowed to clutter up the streets of London.' 'Everyone ought to know her own name.' 'The plural of "mouse" ought to be "mouses".' 'Grapefruits ought to be sweet.' 'John ought not to have said such cruel things.' – The word 'ought' appears everywhere.

Along with its synonym 'should', it is our workaday normative word. It can have a solemn – sometimes even a moral – meaning, but more often we use it lightly. I once advised a guest that he ought to eat a mangosteen because mangosteens taste delicious. I was speaking correctly. 'Ought' is certainly not particularly a moral word.

'Ought' appears frequently in this book because I am writing about rationality, and one of my topics is the relationship between rationality and normativity. Already in chapter 1 I have described one feature of the relationship using 'ought': I said that rationality requires you to intend to do what you believe you ought to do. I shall start the book's work by clarifying what I mean by this word.

I shall not try to define its meaning;[1] I assume you already know what 'ought' means. But its meaning varies with the context, and sometimes the word is ambiguous even within a single context. In this book 'ought' nearly always has one particular meaning, and I need to distinguish that one from others. That is the aim of this chapter and the next.

'Ought' differs from most English verbs in having no nominalization. Some authors use 'obligation' to play this role, but that is misleading: although you ought to look both ways before crossing the road, you have no obligation to do so. Still, I need a nominalization, and I shall give myself one by violating grammar. I shall use 'ought' as a noun as well as a verb. The noun means what the gerund 'oughting' would mean if it existed.

I aim to identify my meaning of 'ought', and I shall proceed by successively refining the meaning. I shall introduce successive distinctions among possible meanings: between normative and non-normative oughts, between owned and unowned oughts, between qualified and unqualified oughts and between objective and prospective oughts. Each time I shall locate my meaning on one side of the distinction. In the end it will be narrowed to my precise meaning.

I shall call this the 'central' ought. It is central in a number of respects that will appear in this chapter. In chapter 4 I shall define reasons in terms of this ought. This is to give it a central place in the philosophy of normativity as a whole.

These two chapters on ought are not just about meaning. In order to identify my particular ought, I have to survey some of the landscape of normativity, to sort out what different oughts there are. This involves some substantive normative theory at a very basic level. In particular, I shall identify one essential feature of ought as I mean it.

2.2 Normative and non-normative oughts

'Ought' is used both normatively and non-normatively. It is used normatively in the sentence

You ought to look both ways before crossing the road.

It is used non-normatively in the following sentences, at least when they have their most natural settings:

The plural of 'mouse' ought to be 'mouses',
We ought to have heard from the landing module ten minutes ago,
and These raspberries ought to ripen in June.

You might suspect there is some continuity between normative and non-normative meanings. In some sentences, 'ought' even seems to lie on a borderline between the two. An example is this:

Christine ought to know her seven-times table by the age of nine.

One implication of this sentence is the non-normative one that Christine would know her seven-times table by the age of nine if her skills were to develop typically. On the other hand, the sentence also seems to carry some of the implications that go with the normative ought. It seems to imply someone is at fault – perhaps Christine or perhaps her teachers – if Christine does not know her seven-times table by the age of nine.

Even some of my examples of non-normative meanings can appear to lie on the borderline of the normative. The 'mouses' example could suggest a complaint against English grammar: that it is not as it normatively ought to be. Examples like this may suggest there is no sharp boundary between normative and non-normative oughts. But actually there is no continuity, and there is a sharp boundary. These examples are ambiguous rather than border-line cases.

Suppose you believe children ought not to be taught arithmetic till they are teenagers, so you think no one ought to know their tables till they are fourteen. You certainly do not think Christine ought normatively to know her seven-times table by the age of nine. However, suppose you know that Christine is going through a standard education. You know that, if her skills developed typically in those surroundings, she would know her seven-times table by the age of nine. You can agree that, in a sense, she ought to know her seven-times table by the age of nine; she would know it if she developed typically.

Suppose you glory in the idiosyncrasies of English. You recognize that the plural of 'mouse' would be 'mouses' if grammar were simplified in one way. So you can agree that the plural of 'mouse' ought in one sense to be 'mouses'. But you do not think this simplification ought normatively to obtain, so in another sense you do not think the plural of 'mouse' ought to be 'mouses'.

My description of these examples exhibits 'ought' used in two quite different senses, a normative one and a non-normative one. 'The plural of "mouse" ought to be "mouses"' and 'Christine ought to know her seven-times table by the age of nine' are ambiguous. The 'ought' in them may have either sense, or it may waver between one and the other sense. But it is not on any borderline.

I say 'ought' in one sense is normative, but I cannot give a rule for identifying this sense. I could not explain the term 'normative' except in terms of 'ought'. 'Normative' means 'to do with ought', but this ought has to be a normative one, of course. So this definition gets us nowhere if we cannot already identify the normative ought. I simply have to assume you know a normative ought when you meet one. I do assume that: I assume that you, like most people, understand normative oughts well.

I could alternatively say that 'normative' means 'to do with reasons', and this may be helpful to many people. But there are normative and non-normative senses of 'reasons' too, and you have to be able to identify the normative ones. So this ultimately gets us no further forward. Moreover, in chapter 4 I shall define normative reasons in terms of normative oughts, so the definition of normativity as 'to do with ought' is more fundamental.

The terminology in this area is confusing because so many words have both normative and non-normative senses. Even the word 'normative' has a non-normative (in my sense) sense. For instance, it may be used to mean 'to do with norms', where 'a norm' refers to an established practice or alternatively to a rule or requirement.[2] When I need to make the distinction, I shall tendentiously call normativity as I mean it 'true normativity'. I think it is what 'normativity' means to most moral philosophers, if not to some other philosophers and to many non-philosophers. True normativity does not necessarily stem from morality. I shall mention other potential sources of normativity in section 2.4.

'Ought' as I use it is normative. The central ought is a truly normative ought.

Natural normativity

True normativity can be confused with other sorts. In her *Natural Goodness*, Philippa Foot introduces the concept of *natural normativity*. She introduces it in the context of natural history. She says:

> We are, let us suppose, evaluating the roots of a particular oak tree, saying perhaps that it has good roots because they are as sturdy and deep as an oak's roots should be. . . . Oak trees need to stay upright because, unlike creeping plants, they have no possibility of life on the ground, and they are tall, heavy trees. Therefore oaks need to have deep, sturdy roots: there is something wrong with them if they do not. . . . The good of an oak is its individual and reproductive life cycle, and what is necessary for this is an Aristotelian necessity in its case. Since it cannot bend like a reed in the wind, an oak that is as an oak should be is one that has deep and sturdy roots.[3]

Foot takes the notion of 'Aristotelian necessity' from Elizabeth Anscombe: an Aristotelian necessity is 'that which is necessary because and in so far as good hangs on it'.[4] Foot says the good of an oak is to complete its life cycle: to survive for a few hundred years, acquire nutrition, reproduce, and so on. For this it needs deep, sturdy roots. So an oak should have deep, sturdy roots. If I understand Foot right, '*A* should *F*' in this sense simply means that *F*ing is necessary for the good of something of *A*'s species.

Foot more often uses 'should' where I use 'ought to', but these expressions are generally synonymous. In deference to her, I shall switch to 'should' in this discussion of her argument.

Foot uses the term 'natural normativity' for what is referred to by 'should' in 'An oak should have deep, sturdy roots'. I cannot object to her use of this term. An oak's having deep, sturdy roots could fairly be called 'a norm', and that is enough to justify the term 'normativity'. However, in the context of an oak, natural normativity is not what I call true normativity. To say an oak should, in the sense of natural normativity, have deep, sturdy roots is only to say it needs deep, sturdy roots to complete its life cycle. This is not a truly normative statement. You might agree that an oak should in this sense have deep, sturdy roots, but you might nevertheless think that, in the truly normative sense of 'should', it is not the case that an oak should have deep, sturdy roots. There is no inconsistency in that.

Foot uses 'should' with the same meaning when speaking of human beings: 'a human being should F' means that Fing is necessary for the good of a member of the human species. Whereas the good of non-human living things is to complete their life-cycle, human beings have a much broader and more complex good. It includes living cooperatively, in caring relationships with each other. Being virtuous is necessary for this good. Each human being should be virtuous, therefore, where 'should' has the same meaning as it has in 'an oak should have deep, sturdy roots'.

Foot hopes to derive the conclusion that each human being should be virtuous, where 'should' is truly normative. But this conclusion cannot be drawn. Her premise is that each human being should be virtuous, where this is a matter of natural normativity. This means simply that being virtuous is necessary to the good of human beings. No truly normative conclusion follows.

Remember that 'the good of human beings' is to be understood in the same way as 'the good of an oak'. The good of an oak is completing its life-cycle; it is not a truly normative notion. The good of a human being is more complex but nevertheless a matter of the way human beings live their lives. It is not a truly normative notion either. So the claim that being virtuous is necessary to the good of human beings is not truly normative.

That human beings should in the sense of natural normativity be virtuous leaves it an open question whether they should in the truly normative sense be virtuous. The answer to the question is no doubt 'yes', but this conclusion cannot be derived from Foot's natural normativity.

Foot intends to exhibit a continuity between the non-normative and the normative. I think she fails in her intention. Her 'should' starts with a non-normative definition, and never becomes truly normative.

2.3   Owned and unowned oughts

Compare the sentences

Alison ought to get a sun hat.
and   Alex ought to get a severe punishment.

Intuitively, these sentences differ in their logical structure. As I put it, the first ascribes ownership of an ought to Alison, whereas the second does not ascribe ownership of an ought to Alex. I cannot accurately describe the sort of ownership I am referring to.[5] I could use other words. I could say that Alison is responsible for her getting a sun hat, or that she is at fault if she does not get a sun hat, but the words 'responsible' and 'fault' have various connotations that might lead you to misunderstand me. I could say that getting a sun hat is required *of* Alison; this is perhaps the most accurate way of conveying the idea of ownership.

The word 'owned' has irrelevant connotations, but I hope they are so obviously irrelevant that this word will not be misleading. I hope you will just recognize the way in which oughts can be owned. It is well recognized within philosophy. In deontic logic, owned oughts are commonly referred to as 'personal obligations'.[6] In a valuable discussion, Lloyd Humberstone identifies ownership as a special sort of agent-relativity, which he calls 'agent-implicating'.[7]

Some 'ought' sentences ascribe ownership and others do not, but we cannot tell which from their grammar. The Alison and Alex sentences have exactly the same grammar, yet one ascribes ownership and the other does not. Indeed, grammatical English does not provide any unambiguous way of ascribing ownership of an ought, except by some roundabout sentence that says explicitly whom the ought is owned by. This is a weakness in English grammar.

Its source is the fact that 'ought' is an auxiliary verb. This means it combines with a lexical verb to form a single, compound verb; in both the Alison and Alex sentences, the compound verb is 'ought to get'. A consequence is that constructions using 'ought' do not offer as many argument-places as we logically need for expressing ownership. We need places for two terms: one to denote the owner of the ought and one to be the subject of the lexical verb. But we are supplied with only one place, because a compound verb has only one subject. 'Ought' has no subject of its own, distinct from the subject of the lexical verb. Consequently, only the context set by the surrounding words tells us that 'Alison ought to get a sun hat' ascribes ownership but 'Alex ought to get a severe punishment' does not.

It may be good enough in ordinary life to rely on the context, but not in philosophy. I shall need to make ownership explicit, and I shall do so by once more inflicting some violence on English grammar. I shall treat 'ought' as a lexical verb rather than an auxiliary. The sentences:

    Alison ought to get a sun hat.

and Alison expects to get a sun hat.

differ in their grammar, because 'ought' is an auxiliary whereas 'expects' is a lexical verb. But I shall treat the first as having the same grammar as the second.

'Expects' can be used in various constructions. 'Alison expects to get a sun hat' has the same meaning as:

> Alison expects Alison to get a sun hat.
> and   Alison expects that Alison will get a sun hat.

We would not in practice say these things because we do not repeat a name unnecessarily, but they are grammatical sentences. Parallel sentences containing a second, different subject are common. For instance:

> Alison expects Alex to get a severe punishment.
> Alison expects that Alex will get a severe punishment.

In all the 'expects' sentences above, the subject of 'expects' is Alison. For that reason, each sentence, including 'Alison expects to get a sun hat', ascribes ownership of the expectation to Alison.

I shall make 'ought' follow the model of 'expect'. I stipulate that all of

> Alison ought to get a sun hat.
> Alison ought Alison to get a sun hat.
> and   Alison ought that Alison will get a sun hat.

are sentences, and that they all have the same meaning. The second and third sentences are ungrammatical in English, but they conform to my deviant grammar in which 'ought' is a lexical verb. I shall use the 'ought that' construction frequently. In all three sentences, 'Alison' is the subject of 'ought', and I stipulate that all these sentences ascribe ownership of the ought to Alison. In general, I stipulate that the subject of 'ought' always names the owner of the ought.

I am able to make this stipulation because my artificial grammar makes available a second argument-place for the subject of the verb that follows 'ought'. In the examples above the same name occupies both places, but that is not necessary. For instance, I can say:

> The judge ought that Alex will get a severe punishment.

My stipulation implies that the sentence I started with,

> Alex ought to get a severe punishment,

ascribes ownership of the ought to Alex. That is not part of the sentence's meaning in English, so my stipulation changes the meaning of some sentences. But having made this stipulation, I shall stick to it throughout this book, except where I explicitly cancel it. This should not cause confusion, because I shall avoid sentences of this form that might plausibly be understood not to ascribe ownership.

The ordinary meaning of 'Alex ought to get a severe punishment' is expressed in my language by:

> Some\one ought that Alex will get a severe punishment.

('There is a person N such that N ought that Alex will get a severe punishment' – I assume the ought is owned by someone.)

The propositional ought

An expectation is a relation between the owner of the expectation and a proposition. Treating 'ought' on the model of 'expects' implies that an owned ought is a relation between the owner and a proposition. This is a by-product of my stipulations. Is it desirable?

So as not to be distracted by grammar, let us use symbols. Let 'O' denote the owned ought relation as I conceive it. Call this relation the 'propositional ought'. The sentence 'NOp' says that this relation holds between N as owner and the proposition p. 'Alison O that Alison will get a sun hat', for example.

Some authors have assumed that when an ought is a propositional operator it must be unowned.[8] That was a confusion. An owned ought may be a propositional operator that is indexed to a person. So please do not assume that a propositional ought must be unowned. Indeed, I have just defined a propositional ought as a sort of owned ought.

An alternative is to treat an owned ought as a relation between an owner and a property.[9] Let 'Ø' denote this relation. Call it the 'property ought'. The sentence 'NØF' says that this relation holds between N as owner and the property F. 'Alison Ø the property of getting a sun hat', for example.

As a formal matter, owned oughts could be expressed either way. However, I prefer the propositional ought because it covers a wider range of deontic situations. For every property F there is a corresponding proposition FN, that N has the property F. Any sentence expressed in terms of the property ought therefore has an equivalent expressed in terms of the propositional ought. Instead of 'NØF', we may say 'NO (FN)', meaning just the same. But not every proposition has a corresponding property. For example, no property of the judge corresponds to the proposition that Alex gets a severe punishment.

So 'The judge O Alex gets a severe punishment' has no equivalent expressed in terms of the property ought.

Authors who prefer the property ought think that the generality provided by the propositional ought is spurious. They think there are no genuine deontic situations that cannot be described in terms of the property ought. 'The judge O Alex gets a severe punishment' could not describe a genuine situation, they think.

They think a situation like this may seem genuine only because a different, genuine situation is mistaken for it. The supposedly genuine situation is often described in English using the formula 'see to it that'. In the example:

The judge ought to see to it that Alex gets a severe punishment.

This could be put in terms of either the propositional ought or the property ought, by either

The judge O the judge sees to it that Alex gets a severe punishment.
or   The judge Ø the property of seeing to it that Alex gets a severe punishment.

So the propositional ought is not required.

This trick with 'see to it that' does not always work convincingly. Suppose the minister of education is responsible for the proper running of the schools, but she spends her days on the golf course and pays no attention to the schools. Suppose, however, that civil servants in the education department make sure that the schools are properly run. In that way, the minister's responsibility is discharged.[10]

What is her deontic situation? Is it that the minister ought to see to it that the schools are properly run? No, because she sees to nothing of the sort and yet her responsibility is discharged. Perhaps the situation can be correctly described only in terms of the propositional ought:

The minister O the schools are properly run.

This sentence has no equivalent in terms of the property ought.

This example suggests that the propositional ought cannot be dispensed with. But that is not the end of the argument. Judith Thomson has a different account. She would describe the deontic situation by saying that the minister ought not to let it be false that the schools are properly run.[11] If she is right, the situation can be described as follows in terms of the property ought:

The minister Ø the property of not letting it be false that the schools are properly run.

The minister does indeed have the property of not letting it be false that the schools are properly run, so if this is what she ought to achieve, she achieves it.

Perhaps Thomson's formula 'not to let it be false that' can be successfully applied to any owned ought. Perhaps, 'N ought that p' is always equivalent to 'N ought not to let it be false that p'. If so, any owned ought could be treated as a relation between the owner and a property. Whenever it is the case that NOp, there would be a property F such that p is the proposition that the owner N has the property F. The generality of the propositional ought could be reproduced with the property ought.

This may be true but it requires further testing. I remain cautious, and in any case I do not see what is gained by this manoeuvre. It is no objection to the propositional ought, and for safety I prefer to stick with the propositional ought.

Some authors hold the theory that an owned ought can always be treated as a relation between an owner and an act-type.[12] An act-type – for example, buying a sun hat – is a property of the actor. So this theory can be seen as a special case of the theory that an owned ought can always be treated as a relation between an owner and a property.

The more special theory is clearly false as it stands. Clearly, you ought never to commit murder, yet never committing murder is not an act-type. The theory must be extended to include non-act-types, such as never committing murder, along with act-types.

Even with that extension, the theory is implausible. It seems that any of the following claims could be true: you ought not to believe in fairies; you ought to be at work by nine; you ought not to prefer your own lesser good to your greater; you ought to believe in God; you ought to know your own name; you ought to intend to keep a promise when you make it; and so on. In none of these cases is what you ought an act-type or a non-act-type.

You might say that actually none of these claims could be strictly true. The strict truth must be different, and always involve an act. For example, the strict truth might be that you ought to get to work by nine rather than that you ought to be at work by nine. The strict truth might be that you ought to bring it about that you believe in God rather than that you ought to believe in God. And so on.

I doubt that a manoeuvre like this is always possible. For example, it seems it could be false that you ought to bring it about that you believe in God (because, say, God punishes anyone who brings it about that she believes in God), but nevertheless true that you ought to believe in God (because, say, there is strong evidence of God's existence). In any case, the mere possibility of this sort of manoeuvre does not show that the original claims cannot be true.

But suppose it could not be true that you ought to F – where this ought is owned by you, remember – unless there was something you could do to achieve your Fing. Even if that were so, it still would not follow that all those claims above are false. For instance, it would not follow that it is false that you ought not to believe in fairies. It would follow only that this is false if there is nothing you can do to bring it about that you do not believe in fairies.

I know no satisfactory arguments against those claims above. I therefore do not assume that, when you ought to F, your Fing must be an act. I assume there are things you ought to believe, or not believe, or know, or intend, or hope for, and so on. At this point I place no restriction on 'F'; it might be any verb phrase. Of course, any substantive deontic theory will make restrictions. It will specify what each particular person ought to achieve.

Unowned oughts

Some 'ought' sentences in English appear to refer to oughts that are not owned by anyone. When a disease strikes a person down in her prime,[13] we sometimes say

Life ought not to be so unfair.

This sentence does not conform to my stipulation that the subject of 'ought' is always the owner. It is plainly not meant to ascribe ownership of the ought to life. If it describes an owned ought, there must be someone who ought that life is not so unfair. Who would that be? God seems the only candidate; yet even an atheist might sincerely say 'Life ought not to be so unfair'.

This example suggests we have the concept of an *unowned ought*. I do not insist this is so; it does not matter for my argument. But I shall allow for the possibility of unowned oughts. I shall make an unowned ought explicit by using a construction of the form

It ought to be the case that life is not so unfair.

(This construction violates my stipulation that the subject of 'ought' is the owner. I waive that stipulation for this one particular construction.) As I did with an owned ought, I take an unowned ought to be a property of a proposition. 'It ought to be the case that life is not so unfair' ascribes this property to the proposition that life is not so unfair.

Although I do not insist there are unowned oughts, I do insist there are owned ones. In '*Ought* and moral obligation', Bernard Williams denied that.

At least, this is the interpretation he himself later put on this paper.[14] I shall assume it is the correct interpretation.

Under this interpretation, when Williams wrote 'Ought and moral obligation', he thought that all 'ought' sentences describe unowned oughts. He would have thought, for instance, that 'Alison ought to get a sun hat' means simply that it ought to be the case that Alison gets a sun hat. He agreed that a person may stand in a special relation to an ought. But he said that, when she does, it is because the person plays a special part in the ought's explanation. It is not a feature of the ought itself. For example, if you have promised to F, it ought to be the case that you F, and it is your promise that explains why this unowned ought obtains. The explanation is the promise, which belongs to you, but the ought does not belong to you.

The view that no oughts are owned is mistaken. I shall present one argument against it on page 24. Here I present another.

Take this example.[15] Suppose Alf has promised his mother he will do more homework over the year than Beth, and Beth has promised her mother that she will do at least as much homework over the year as Alf. For the sake of argument, let us assume that promises generate moral obligations. As Williams would see the situation, it ought to be the case that Alf does more homework than Beth, and it ought to be the case that Beth does at least as much homework as Alf.

This leads to a problem. The proposition that Beth does at least as much homework as Alf is just the proposition that Alf does not do more homework than Beth. So according to Williams, it ought to be the case that Alf does more homework than Beth, and it ought to be the case that Alf does not do more homework than Beth. Something both ought and ought not to be the case.

I call a situation like this a 'deontic conflict'. I am inclined to think the meaning of 'ought' makes deontic conflicts impossible.[16] Williams himself agreed that the meaning of what he called the 'practical ought' (in contrast to the 'moral ought') does so,[17] and I shall explain on page 28 that this is the concept I am concerned with. We should not accept the existence of a deontic conflict unless we have no alternative.

But in this example we have a much better alternative. It makes much better sense to see the situation as one where two people have opposing owned oughts than as one where two unowned oughts conflict. We should see the situation this way: Alf ought that Alf does more homework than Beth, and Beth ought that Alf does not do more homework than Beth. There is no deontic conflict there.

You might think that this account of the situation also leads to a problem. Two doubts might be raised against it. One is that it may seem to conflict with the principle that ought implies can. But actually it does not. True, it cannot be the case that Alf and Beth both do as they ought. However, each of them separately can do as he or she ought. Suppose that each is only moderately conscientious, so that neither will actually do more homework than the other is able to. However much homework Beth actually does, Alf can do more, and however much Alf actually does, Beth can do at least as much. Whichever one fails to fulfil his or her promise, it will be from lack of will rather than lack of ability.[18]

The second doubt is that perhaps Alf and Beth cannot have opposing oughts as I assumed they do. This will be impossible if normativity is 'agent-neutral' in the sense that was established by Derek Parfit.[19] According to an agent-neutral normative theory, whatever one person ought, everybody ought. It therefore cannot be the case that one person ought that p when another ought that not p. Utilitarianism is agent-neutral in this sense, because it claims that everybody ought to promote whatever will achieve the most good.

In the example, I chose promise-making as a way of generating opposing oughts. Plausibly each person ought to keep her own promises. But it does not matter how plausible the particular example is. What matters is whether it can ever be the case that one person ought that p and another ought that not p. Most non-neutral normative theories will lead to opposing oughts like this.

However, a fully agent-neutral normative theory will never do so. So for all I have said, an agent-neutralist is free to insist that no oughts are owned. However, this is not what agent-neutralists typically think. They typically think all oughts are owned in common rather than not owned at all. Utilitarians think that everybody ought to promote whatever will achieve the most good; they do not think that nobody ought to do this, and simply that it ought to be the case that everyone does it. Thomas Nagel introduced the distinction between agent-neutrality and agent-relativity (under a different name), and I shall explain on page 68 that he takes agent-neutrality to be common ownership rather than non-ownership. I shall explain on page 24 that he has a good reason to do so.

Ownership and agency

John Horty's *Agency and Deontic Logic* proposes a different sort of reduction of owned oughts to unowned oughts.[20] 'N ought that p', in my language would be analysed as 'It ought to be the case that N sees to it that p'. In effect, Horty reduces an owned ought to an unowned ought plus agency. This is a common idea. Many authors use the formula 'ought to do' to refer to owned oughts, in contrast to 'ought to be', which they use for unowned oughts.[21] Horty nicely formalizes the idea.

Where I say 'Alf ought that Alf does more homework than Beth', marking ownership with the expression 'ought that', Horty would say 'It ought to be the case that Alf sees to it that Alf does more homework than Beth'. 'It ought to be the case that' marks an unowned ought, and 'sees to it that' marks agency. That is how his analysis goes.

Let a be the proposition that Alf does more homework than Beth. I say 'Alf ought that a and Beth ought that not a'. Bernard Williams would say 'It ought to be case that a and it ought to be the case that not a'. This implies a deontic conflict. Horty would say 'It ought to be the case that Alf sees to it that a, and it ought to be the case that Beth sees to it that not a'. This does not imply a deontic conflict as I defined it.

It does imply a weaker sort of deontic conflict.[22] It is an analytical truth that, if someone sees to it that p, then p. So it is analytically impossible for both Alf to see to it that a and for Beth to see to it that not a. In my example, Horty's reduction implies that two things ought to be case when it is analytically impossible for both of them to be the case. We should not accept this type of conflict if there is a better alternative. And there remains the better alternative of recognizing owned oughts.

As it happens, the conflict cannot arise within Horty's formal theory, because his assumptions rule out examples like mine. But I think my example is a genuine possibility, so it is a genuine objection to his reduction of owned oughts.

In any case, I think it is clear that the reduction is mistaken. Ownership cannot be reduced to agency, because agency is quite different from ownership. Suppose it ought to be the case that the deck-hand sees to it that the hatch is closed. We can ask of whom it is required that the hatch is closed – whose responsibility it is, and who should be blamed if the hatch is not closed. There may be an answer to this question, and it may not be 'the deck-hand'. It might be 'the captain'. Perhaps the deck-hand is simply required to obey orders and no order has yet been issued. The deck hand is the agent who will see to it that the hatch is closed, if it is, yet the deck-hand is not the owner of the ought. The ought does have an owner all the same; it is the captain.

In a paper written with Nuel Belnap,[23] Horty himself explores a quite different account of ownership within deontic logic – one that accords better with the intuitive idea of ownership. As an alternative to reducing ownership to agency, that paper combines this more intuitive account of ownership with a formal account of agency. Applied to my example, and using my grammar, the combined theory would say 'Beth ought that Beth sees to it that Alf does not do more homework than Beth'. I think it is correct to separate ownership from agency.[24]

Owned oughts are central

In this chapter I am picking out the central ought that concerns me in this book. In this section I have distinguished owned from unowned oughts. For me, owned oughts are central because they play a central role in our practical rationality, and this book is about rationality.

One central feature of practical rationality is a principle I call 'Enkrasia'.[25] Very roughly formulated, it is:

> *Enkrasia, very roughly.* Rationality requires of you that, if you believe that you ought to F, you intend to F.

Enkrasia is important in this book. This statement of it falls short of precision in a number of respects. I shall describe two of them next.

Suppose you believe that someone ought that you learn astral navigation, but you believe it is the mate's job rather than yours to get you this training. Then you may be entirely rational even if you do not intend to get it yourself. In general, if you believe that someone ought that you do something, but you do not ascribe ownership of the ought to yourself, you may be entirely rational even if you do not intend to do that thing. So if Enkrasia is to be correct, it must specify that your belief ascribes ownership to you. Because of my grammatical stipulation, that is in fact specified in the formulation above. But I can stress the point by formulating Enkrasia with 'ought that': rationality requires of you that, if you believe that you ought that you F, you intend to F.

Next suppose you believe that the mate ought to learn astral navigation. Indeed you believe it is the mate's own responsibility to learn; you believe the mate ought that the mate learns astral navigation. Suppose also that you are the mate, but you do not know that; the previous mate has recently fallen overboard and the post has devolved on you, but no one has told you yet.

In a sense, you believe you ought to learn astral navigation, since you are the mate and you believe the mate ought to learn astral navigation. In a sense, your belief ascribes ownership of the ought to you. Nevertheless, you may be entirely rational even if you do not intend to learn astral navigation.

So if Enkrasia is to be correct, it must specify that you *self*-ascribe ownership of the ought. This does not just mean that you ascribe ownership to yourself. It means that you are in a position to express your ought-belief using the first-personal pronoun 'I'. You must be able to say 'I ought to learn astral navigation'. So long as you do not know you are the mate, you cannot express your belief this way. Many philosophers have claimed that practical rationality is essentially first-personal. This appears to be what they generally mean to say.[26] Page 161 mentions a second way in which practical rationality is first-personal.

We can incorporate the need for self-ascription into Enkrasia by employing the reflexive pronoun 'you yourself'. 'You yourself' corresponds in indirect speech to 'I' in direct speech.[27] We end up with:

> *Enkrasia, roughly.* Rationality requires of you that, if you believe that you yourself ought that you F, you intend that you F.

Yet other conditions need to be added before Enkrasia is stated exactly correctly. Furthermore, the formula also needs to be generalized a bit. The full, sharpened version is set out on page 170, and its controversial nature is explored there, but this rough version is good enough for now.

In it, 'you' stands for a generic person. In more formal statements I shall use the schematic letter 'N' instead, but I try not to use a letter for a person when I am writing less formally. Unfortunately, English does not contain a generic verb that I can use informally instead of the schematic letter 'F'. Instances of 'You ought to F' include 'You ought to be careful in the dark', 'You ought to know the capital of Idaho', 'You ought to wear a hat when it is sunny', 'You ought to believe what I tell you and do as I say', and 'You ought not to break the law just because you would benefit from doing so'. I shall also use 'You ought to F' to cover instances that strictly it does not cover, such as 'You ought not to dive here' and 'You ought either to leave Henry or stop mistrusting him'. No generic sentence in English has a meaning anything like as wide as I need. So I shall have to use that annoying 'F' throughout this book. I am sorry about that.

The rough formula for Enkrasia specifies that what you believe is that you yourself ought that you F, rather than that you yourself ought that you yourself F. Why not? Because that second pronoun does not need to be reflexive. So long as you self-ascribe ownership of the ought, rationality requires you to have the intention.

In English, when a pronoun can be reflexive, it generally is. So in informal contexts, the 'yourself' in 'you yourself' is generally redundant. When I can safely omit it, I often shall.

The requirement Enkrasia is a central feature of our rationality because it constitutes one of the main bridges between theoretical and practical rationality. We spend a lot of time deliberating about what we ought to do. Since this process brings us to acquire new beliefs – beliefs about what we ought to do – it is an exercise of our theoretical rationality. But we generally deliberate with a practical purpose. The beliefs that emerge engage our practical rationality. Specifically, they engage with the requirement Enkrasia, which is a part of our practical rationality. If we are practically rational, we end up intending to do what our theoretical deliberation brings us to believe we ought to do.

This explains why there have to be owned oughts. Only they engage with practical rationality through Enkrasia. I argued earlier that owned oughts cannot be reduced to unowned ones. I recognized on page 20 that my argument did not apply to any agent-neutral normative theory. But even an agent-neutral normative theory must aim to be practical, and this means its oughts must be owned. In an agent-neutral theory, if they are owned by someone they must be owned by everyone. I explained on page 20 that agent-neutralists do indeed think that oughts are owned in common by everyone.

Enkrasia and defining the central ought

Enkrasia constitutes the principal criterion by which I identify the central ought: this is the ought that Enkrasia applies to. Since Enkrasia applies to the owned ought, the owned ought is central. I use the same test several times in this chapter and the next.

The central ought is the ought that Enkrasia applies to. This is a sort of definition, but it only defines the central ought for someone who already understands 'ought'. It is not an attempt to define ought, but to pick out a particular ought. It is like defining aquamarine as the colour of the sea over white sand; it works only for someone who already understands colour.

Why do I not go further and define the central ought as *whatever* relation Enkrasia applies to? Why do I not define it as the relation such that rationality requires of you that, if you believe that you yourself stand in this relation to your *F*ing, you intend to *F*? This definition would work even for someone who does not understand 'ought'. It is roughly Ralph Wedgwood's definition of what he calls 'the practical ought'.[28] Wedgwood defines the practical ought through what he calls 'Normative Judgement Internalism' ('NJI'). A simple version of NJI is

> Necessarily, if one is rational, then, if one judges 'I ought to φ', one also intends to φ.[29]

This is close to my rough version of Enkrasia, and the qualifications Wedgwood adds to this simple version are similar to the ones I add to the rough version of Enkrasia in order to arrive at the full version on page 170. Wedgwood defines the practical ought as the relation that NJI applies to. Why do I not take this step?

Because I do not believe the central ought applies to acts only. Among other things, it applies to mental states of yours that you cannot expect to control by means of your intentions. Probably you ought to believe you are mortal, but probably you do not believe this belief is controlled by your intentions. Suppose, then, that you believe you ought to believe you are mortal, but you do not believe that intending to believe you are mortal would cause you to believe you are mortal. You would not be failing in rationality if you did not intend to believe you are mortal.

However, you would be violating the rough version of Enkrasia. This reveals one inaccuracy in that version. A condition included in the full version says, in effect, that Enkrasia requires nothing of you when you believe you ought to *F*, unless you believe your *F*ing is controlled by your intentions. If you do not believe your *F*ing is controlled by your intentions, Enkrasia is an empty requirement. I am speaking now of this full version.

In cases where you believe your *F*ing is controlled by your intentions, I could define ought as the relation that Enkrasia applies to. That would identify a particular relation. But in other cases, it would identify nothing, because in those cases Enkrasia is empty. Enkrasia applies to any relation in those cases. So Enkrasia can determine the meaning of 'ought' in every case only if you are independently able to project the meaning from cases where Enkrasia has content to cases where it is empty. You must be able to identify the same meaning in the two different sorts of case. Otherwise it would be like defining the meaning of '5 o'clock' on the sun by defining it on Earth and saying the meaning is just the same on the sun. The upshot is that you must already have a meaning of ought ready. If you have more than one, Enkrasia can be used to pick out the central one.

How can Wedgwood go further and actually define ought? Because he does not apply the practical ought to anything that is beyond the direct or indirect control of intentions. He extends the NJI to cover anything than can be 'part of one's ideal plan for what to do', rather than simply what one can intend.[30] The indirect effects of one's intentions can be part of one's ideal plan, but many mental states are still beyond the scope of the NJI. The practical ought does not apply to them.

2.4   Qualified and unqualified oughts

It can happen that you ought morally to do one thing, and ought rationally to do something else, and ought prudentially to do some third thing. Various oughts of different sorts can apply to you at the same time, and may conflict with each other. At least, that is a common opinion. It suggests there is a moral ought, a rational ought, a prudential ought, and so on. As well as that, we have an all-things-considered ought. Out of this plethora how do I pick the central ought?

That is easy. The central ought is the all-things-considered one. This is what we normally refer to with the word 'ought', unqualified. However, 'all-things-considered ought' is a misleading expression. Suppose I say that the holiday was fun, all things considered. I mean that the holiday was fun, and that this judgement of mine is based on all the relevant considerations. 'All things considered' refers to the judgement, not the fun. I would not be attributing some special property of all-things-considered funness to the holiday. Similarly, there is no special sort of all-things-considered ought. When I make a judgement about ought, I might use the expression 'all things considered' to say that my judgement takes every relevant consideration into account.

So instead of 'all-things-considered ought', I shall say 'unqualified ought' or just 'ought'. I shall call the moral ought, rational ought, prudential ought and so on 'qualified oughts'. In this section, I shall explain why I treat the unqualified ought as central.

To start with, I prefer a different terminology for qualified oughts. Rather than saying 'You morally ought to F', I prefer to say 'Morality requires you to F'. Similarly, I use 'rationality requires', 'prudence requires' and so on. I deal only with requirements that are owned. To make their owner explicit I shall sometimes say 'Morality requires of you that . . .', 'Prudence requires of you that . . .' and so on.

Chapter 7 contains a full account of requirements. For my purposes here I need to give them only a brief explanation.

Requirements

Each of the terms 'morality', 'rationality' and 'prudence' have a sense in which they denote a property. If you are rational, you have the property of rationality; if you are prudent, you have the property of prudence, and so on. But these terms each have another sense in which they denote what I call a *source of requirements*. In this sense, they are analogous to the law, which is another source of requirements. The law requires you to pay your taxes. Similarly, morality requires you to be kind to strangers, rationality requires you not to believe contradictions, and prudence requires you to eat lots of vegetables. There are many other sources of requirements too. Fashion is one; convention another. Fashion requires you not to wear socks with sandals; convention requires you to offer your right hand rather than your left when you wish to shake hands.

In one wide sense of 'normative', requirements of any sort are normative. 'Normative' can mean 'to do with norms', and a requirement may be called a norm. However, I do not use 'normative' in this sense, and a requirement is not necessarily normative in my sense. To say it is normative in my sense is to say it helps determine what you ought to do. This is what I called 'true normativity' on page 11.[31] More exactly, to say a requirement on you to F is normative is to say that the requirement constitutes a reason for you to F. I should not really be using this definition at this point in the book, since I shall not define a reason till chapter 4. But I can safely assume you will understand it in any case.

In this book, by 'a normative requirement' I mean a requirement that is normative. I have used this term differently in the past;[32] I apologize for changing my terminology. When the requirements issued by a source are normative, I shall call the source itself 'normative'.

For each source of requirements, it is an important question whether it is normative. I call this 'the Normative Question' about the source, in honour of Christine Korsgaard, who first gave this name to the Normative Question about morality.[33] It is often hard to answer. For instance, chapter 11 in this book considers whether rationality is normative, and does not reach a firm conclusion.

The Normative Question is complicated by the fact that requirements can be normative in a derivative way. For instance, the fact that convention requires you to offer your right hand for shaking hands is often normative. In many circumstances, it constitutes a reason to offer your right hand rather than your left, because you might cause offence if you do not. In many circumstances, morality requires you not to cause offence. So this requirement of convention has normativity derived from morality.

It is also complicated by the fact that a source may be normative in some contexts and not others. Take morality, for instance. It seems obvious that morality is normative, but according to an influential school of thought known as 'evidentialism', it is not normative for beliefs. Evidentialists think that only evidence or the lack of evidence can be a source of a normative requirement to believe or not believe something.[34] There do seem to be immoral beliefs. For example, it seems that morality requires you not to believe white people are superior to black people, because this belief can lead you to behave wrongly. But according to evidentialism, this moral fact does not constitute a reason not to believe whites are superior to blacks. If an evidentialist accepts that morality requires you not to believe whites are superior to blacks, she must deny that morality is normative for beliefs.

If a requirement on you to F is normative, it helps to determine whether or not you ought to F. The determination is straightforward when there is no conflict of normative requirements. When there is a conflict, whether or not you ought to F is determined by its resolution. The resolution of conflicts is considered in section 7.5. In any case, it is plain that, just because you are under a normative requirement to F, it does not follow that you ought to F. You might also be under a normative requirement not to F.

Qualified oughts and the central ought

Now back to qualified oughts. Whereas the word 'require' is not inherently normative, the word 'ought' in this context at least strongly suggests normativity. To say 'You rationally ought to F' instead of 'Rationality requires you to F' carries a strong suggestion that this requirement of rationality is normative. But there is a question whether that is so. So the 'ought' terminology begs a question that the 'requires' terminology does not beg. That is why I prefer the 'requires' terminology.

If you choose to deal in qualified oughts, remember that, if you qualifiedly ought to F, it does not follow that you ought to F. The source of the qualified ought may not even be normative. For instance, from the fact that you conventionally ought to F it definitely does not follow that you ought to F. And take a source that we may assume to be normative, say prudence. From the fact that prudence requires you to F, it does not follow that you ought to F. Another normative source may require you not to F. If so, whether or not you ought to F depends on the resolution of a conflict.

The 'ought's in constructions such as 'morally ought' and 'rationally ought' cannot be detached from their adverbs. In that respect they are like 'successful' in 'potentially successful'.

Many philosophers use 'ought' as a specifically moral word. By 'You ought to F' they mean what I mean by 'Morality requires you to F'. I think their usage is not standard English, but I cannot deny them the right to their own terminology. Moreover, if morality is normative, as no doubt it is, their 'ought' is normative. So I recognize their usage as a normative sense of 'ought' that is not my own. It is not the central ought.

My test for the central ought is that the rational requirement of Enkrasia, set out on page 170, applies to it. It clearly applies to the unqualified ought. Rationality requires of you that, if you believe you unqualifiedly ought to F, you intend to F. Enkrasia is the connection between beliefs and the practical attitude of intending. For this reason, Bernard Williams calls the unqualified ought the 'practical ought'.[35]

On the other hand, Enkrasia does not apply to any qualified ought, so no qualified ought is the central one. Take the moral ought as an example. It is not the case that rationality requires of you that, if you believe you morally ought to F, you intend to F. Even if you believe you morally ought to F, you might at the same time not believe you unqualifiedly ought to F. In that case, if you do not intend to F, you may nevertheless be rational. So Enkrasia does not apply to the moral ought.

Here in summary is the picture I have painted in this section of the structure of normativity. There are various sources of requirements. The requirements that issue from some of these sources are normative. Separate normative requirements, issuing from different sources together determine unqualified oughts: what you ought to do, ought to believe, ought to be, and so on. Normativity has components that all come together in the central ought.

Notes

1 Other philosophers have undertaken that task. One is Ralph Wedgwood in 'The meaning of "ought" ' and *The Nature of Normativity*. Another is Matthew Chrisman in 'On the meaning of "ought" '.
2 See p. 26.
3 *Natural Goodness*, p. 46.
4 *Natural Goodness*, p. 15.
5 There is a further account in my 'Williams on *ought*'.
6 For example, see Paul McNamara, 'Agential obligation', Christen Krogh and Henning Herrestad, 'Getting personal', and Jacob Ross, 'The irreducibility of personal obligation'.
7 See Humberstone's 'Two kinds of agent-relativity'. This paper contains references to earlier treatments of owned oughts.
8 Gilbert Harman seems to have made this assumption in his review of *The Significance of Sense* by Roger Wertheimer. As I interpret Bernard Williams, it is what he assumed in '*Ought* and moral obligation'. See my discussion in 'Williams on *ought*'.
9 For instance, James Forrester in *Being Good and Being Logical*, chapter 4, and Anthony Price in *Contextuality in Practical Reason*, chapter 2.
10 This example is modelled on one that appears in Christen Krogh and Henning Herrestad, 'Getting personal'.
11 Thomson, *The Realm of Rights*.
12 For example, Gilbert Harman in his review of *The Significance of Sense* by Roger Wertheimer.
13 Thanks here to Louise Kleszyk.
14 This interpretation appears in a lecture Williams gave in Oxford in 2002. (In the lecture he repudiated the view.) An alternative interpretation appears in Ralph Wedgwood's *The Nature of Normativity*, pp. 91–3. My paper 'Williams on *ought*' discusses the interpretation, and quotes the relevant sections of Williams's 2002 lecture
15 Other examples with the same effect appear in Peter Geach's 'Whatever happened to deontic logic?', Christen Krogh and Henning Herrestad, 'Getting personal', and Jacob Ross, 'The irreducibility of personal obligation'.
16 See the discussion on p. 128.
17 '*Ought* and moral obligation', p. 119. Williams believes there are other concepts of *ought* that permit deontic conflicts. See his 'Ethical consistency'.
18 Caspar Hare and William Lycan impressed on me the need to make sure each protagonists is able to succeed.
19 Parfit, *Reasons and Persons*, p. 143. I consider the definition of 'agent-neutral' in section 4.5. The context there is reasons, but the definition can be carried over to oughts.
20 See particularly sections 3.3 and 3.4.
21 Horty himself uses these expressions. Wilfred Sellars also uses them in 'Language as thought and as communication', but he means to make a different distinction. Sometimes when you ought to F, you are in a position to believe you ought to F, and to respond to your belief by

forming the intention of F*ing*. Only when this is so would Sellars call the 'ought' an 'ought to do'. But sometimes it can happen that you ought to F even though you are not in a position to believe this is so. For example, you may lack the concept of F*ing*. Then Sellars calls the 'ought' an 'ought to be'.

22 I am very grateful to Michael Bench-Capon for pointing this out to me.

23 Horty and Belnap, 'The deliberative stit', section 5.4.

24 I draw valuable support for this view from the arguments in Paul McNamara's 'Agential obligation'.

25 I have received extensive advice about the name 'Enkrasia' from my classically educated friends – among them Sarah Broadie, Roger Crisp, Richard Holton, Benjamin Kiesewetter and Jens Timmerman. The adjective 'enkratic' is a Greek work, but the corresponding noun in Greek is 'enkrateia' rather than 'enkrasia'. 'Enkrateia' implies mastery over temptation, but my invented word 'enkrasia' does not carry any such implication.

26 For example, Bernard Williams, *Ethics and the Limits of Philosophy*, p. 67, and Tyler Burge, 'Reason and the first person'. Christian Piller first made this point to me. See his 'Normative practical reasoning', p. 202.

27 See particularly Hector-Neri Castañeda, 'On the logic of attributions of self-knowledge to others'.

28 Wedgwood, *The Nature of Normativity*, Chapter 4.

29 *The Nature of Normativity*, p. 32.

30 *The Nature of Normativity*, p. 97.

31 A useful account of the distinction is in Nicholas Shackel's 'Two kinds of normativity'.

32 For example, in my 'Normative requirements'.

33 Korsgaard used this name in *The Sources of Normativity*, lecture 1.

34 For instance, see Jonathan Adler, *Belief's Own Ethics*.

35 '*Ought* and moral obligation', p. 118.

3

Objective, Subjective and Prospective Oughts

3.1 Sidgwick's View

We have not yet reached the end of classifying oughts. A number of particular arguments suggest that further distinctions need to be made between different sorts of oughts. This chapter reviews some of these arguments. I shall show that only one succeeds in making a real distinction. When I come to that one, I shall identify which side of the distinction the central ought lies on.

In this chapter, I shall concentrate mostly on oughts that are applied to acts rather than to mental states or other things. This is simply so I have to use the schematic letter 'F' less often.

The first argument I shall consider distinguishes objective and subjective oughts. Suppose you believe you ought to do something, but you do not do it. Intuition tell us you are going wrong in some way; you are not being true to your beliefs. So it seems that, if you believe you ought to do something, in some sense or other you ought to do it. But the second 'ought' in that sentence cannot have the same sense as the first. If it did, it would mean your belief is infallible: whenever you believe you ought to do something, you ought to do it. That cannot be so. The two 'ought's must therefore have different senses, which we may call 'objective' and 'subjective' respectively. The conclusion emerges that:

> *Sidgwick's View.* If you believe you ought objectively to do something, you ought subjectively to do it.

I attribute this view to Henry Sidgwick, but it is widely shared.[1]

The argument I gave for it is fallacious.[2] It sets out from this:

> *Intuitive Premise.* If you believe you ought to do something, but do not do it, you are going wrong.

From this we could at most conclude that you ought in some sense not to be in the position of believing you ought to do something and not doing it. Put differently:

> *Wide-Scope View.* You ought that, if you believe you ought to do something, you do it.

I call this 'the Wide-Scope View' because the first ought has a wide scope. It governs the conditional proposition that, if you believe you ought to do something, you do it.

The argument for Sidgwick's View depends on the further conclusion that:

> *Narrow-Scope View.* If you believe you ought to do something, you ought to do it.

I call this 'the Narrow-Scope View', because the second ought has a narrow scope; it governs the unconditional proposition that you do it. The two 'ought's in the Narrow-Scope View cannot have the same sense, because that would imply your belief is infallible. Once we recognize the 'ought's must have different senses, the Narrow-Scope View takes us to Sidgwick's View.

But the Narrow-Scope View simply does not follow from the Intuitive Premise. To think it does is an example of the so-called 'modal fallacy' or 'modal scope fallacy'.[3] It is easy to be trapped by this fallacy, because the grammar of English almost forces it on us. Start from the Wide-Scope View. It is not implausible that this does indeed follow from the Intuitive Premise, so let us assume for the moment that it does. My formulation of the Wide-Scope View is ungrammatical, and we might naturally want to express it grammatically. To do so, we might adopt the nearest grammatical sentence, which is: 'You ought, if you believe you ought to do something, to do it'. But in this sentence, the condition 'if you believe you ought to do something' is grammatically a parenthesis within the sentence as a whole; it is not contained within the scope of 'ought'. Grammar consequently allows us to move it to the front of the sentence without changing the sentence's meaning. We get the Narrow-Scope View: 'If you believe you ought to do something, you ought to do it'. So in trying to express the Wide-Scope View grammatically, we end up actually expressing the Narrow-Scope View.

So long as we avoid fallacy, from the Intuitive Premise we can at most infer the Wide-Scope View. The Wide-Scope View does not imply that your ought belief is infallible, even if the two 'ought's in it have the same meaning. So the Wide-Scope View gives no support to Sidgwick's View. The argument for Sidgwick's View is fallacious, and we have so far no grounds for thinking that 'ought' has an objective and a subjective sense.

This does not show that Sidgwick's View is false, but it does remove the only reason I know to believe it. Moreover, it offers the Wide-Scope View as a better alternative. In my statement of the Wide-Scope View, the two 'ought's have different scopes, but they need not have different senses. We should not multiply senses unnecessarily. I think Sidgwick's View mistakes a difference in scope for a difference in sense.

I can also offer a separate argument against Sidgwick's View. Suppose you have conflicting ought beliefs: you believe you ought to do something and you believe you ought not to do it. According to Sidgwick's View, you ought subjectively to do this thing and you ought subjectively not to do it. So Sidgwick's View converts your conflict of beliefs about oughts into a conflict of actual subjective oughts. But it is not plausible that actual oughts – even subjective ones – can conflict in this way.[4] At least one of your conflicting beliefs is no doubt mistaken, but a mistaken belief should not create a conflict of actual oughts.

Sidgwick's subjective oughts are in a way relative; they are relative to the person who is their subject. So, when a single person has conflicting ought beliefs, there will be conflicting oughts that are each relative to this one person. But it seems paradoxical for two oughts to conflict when they are each relative to the same thing.

The problem with subjective oughts is that they are relative to the wrong thing, a person. There is nothing wrong with relative oughts in general. Wide-scope oughts are also relative in a way. The Wide-Scope View can be thought of as saying that, relative to your belief that you ought to do something, you ought to do it. Suppose again that you have conflicting beliefs: you believe you ought to do something and you believe you ought not to do it. Then, relative to your first belief you ought to do this thing, and relative to your second belief you ought not to do it. This is not paradoxical at all, because the two oughts are relative to two different things, your two different beliefs.

The Wide-Scope View is decidedly preferable to Sidgwick's View, but I do not accept the Wide-Scope View either. Rather than the Wide-Scope View, I have already said that I accept the requirement Enkrasia, which is stated roughly on page 23 and more precisely on page 170. Here is a different rough formulation of it, adapted to the language of this section:

Enkrasia, very roughly. Rationality requires of you that, if you believe you ought to do something, you intend to do it.

It differs from the Wide-Scope View in two ways. One is that Enkrasia has 'you intend to do it' where the Wide-Scope View has 'you do it'. This is because of the principle that rationality supervenes on the mind, which is introduced on page 89 and discussed again on pages 151–2.

The other difference is that Enkrasia has 'rationality requires of you' where the Wide-Scope View has 'you ought'. Chapter 11 explains why I make that change. Is not a requirement of rationality just a subjective ought? It is true that it can be treated as a qualified ought of the sort I described in section 2.4; we could say 'you rationally ought' instead of 'rationality requires of you'. However, there is nothing subjective about it; it applies to everyone everywhere, whatever their beliefs may be.

In this section I have found no real distinction between different sorts of ought.

3.2   The need to decide

Another argument purports to make a distinction between objective and subjective oughts.

Suppose you have to decide between two particular acts. But suppose that, after gathering evidence, you conclude you are not in a position to believe rationally that you ought to do the first of the acts, nor that you ought to do the second. Suppose the moment is now upon you when you must decide. You are determined to make your decision rationally. You think you can do so only by applying the requirement Enkrasia, that rationality requires you to intend to do what you believe you ought to do. But you cannot apply Enkrasia unless either you believe you ought to do the first of the acts, or you believe you ought to do the second. Yet you are not in a position to hold either of those beliefs rationally. So it will seem to you that you cannot make your decision rationally.

However, you might plausibly think that, whatever predicament you find yourself in, there must always be some rational way of dealing with it. If that is so, you might conclude you must after all be able to hold one of those two beliefs rationally: either that you ought to do the first of the acts, or that you ought to do the second. Since you have to decide now, you cannot collect more evidence. So whichever of the two beliefs you rationally hold, it will have to be based on your present evidence. Yet you believe already that you are not in a position to hold either of those two beliefs rationally on the basis of your present evidence. So you find yourself with inconsistent beliefs.

You could resolve the inconsistency by taking the view that two senses of 'ought' are in play. In researching the evidence as a preliminary to making your decision, you have been trying to work out what you ought to do in a relatively objective sense. Having failed, you might think a different question then arises: what ought you to do in a more subjective sense that takes into account your unsatisfactory epistemic position? You may think you must be able to answer this different question rationally. Here you distinguish between a more objective and a more subjective sense of 'ought', which resolves the inconsistency. This may seem to be grounds for thinking your distinction is genuine.

However, your thinking is badly mistaken. It assumes that if you are to make a decision to act rationally, the decision must be based on a belief that you ought to do the act. That is false.

Buridan's ass, standing between two equally good stacks of hay, did not understand this point. The evidence available to it indicated that it was not the case that it ought to eat the left stack nor the case that it ought to eat the right one. Being rational, it therefore could not believe that it ought to eat the left stack, nor that it ought to eat the right one. It thought it could not rationally decide to eat either stack unless it believed it ought to eat that stack. Wishing to be rational, and holding this view about rationality, it died. Plainly its view about rationality is false.

It is false for two reasons. First, you can make a decision rationally even if it is not determined by any requirement of rationality. And second, even when a decision to act is determined by a requirement of rationality, the requirement need not be Enkrasia, which applies only when you believe you ought to do the act.

The first reason applies to the predicament of Buridan's ass. Its two options were equally good. Often we face a similar predicament. Often, too, we face a choice between two options that are incommensurate in value; this often happens when they promote values of very different sorts. When two options are equally good or incommensurate, it is not the case that you ought to choose one, and not the case that you ought to choose the other. Given that, it is likely that rationality does not determine a particular choice for you. Yet you may rationally make a choice.

In other cases it may as a matter of fact be the case that you ought to do a particular one of the acts available to you, but you are not in a position to believe rationally that it is the case. We are often rationally uncertain about what we ought to do. We may be uncertain about the relevant empirical facts, and we may be uncertain about what is the right deontic theory to apply. For example, we may be uncertain about what moral principles are correct.

Dealing properly with uncertainty is a part of the business of rationality. So we may expect some guidance from rationality about what to do when we are uncertain about what we ought to do. It may give guidance about what to believe in the face of uncertainty, and also about what to intend.

Enkrasia is only one among several requirements of rationality that apply to intentions. Another is the Instrumental Requirement set out on page 169, and there are others too. Enkrasia requires you to intend to F when you believe fully that you ought to F. We can expect there to be a requirement that sets out a rational connection between an intention and a partial belief about what you ought to do. I am sorry to say I do not know what that requirement is. I was once tempted to think it was:

> Rationality requires of you that, if you assign a probability of more than one half to the proposition that you ought to F, then you do not intend not to F.

Krister Bykvist persuaded me that this is false. You may assign a probability greater than one half to the proposition that you ought to F, but also believe that Fing might – though less probably – be a very wrong thing to do. In that case, you might rationally play safe and intend not to F.

Still, the formula illustrates the sort of requirement we can expect to find.[5] If such a requirement exists, it means that rationality sometimes requires you to intend to F even when you do not fully believe you ought to F. This is the second reason why you may rationally decide on an act even when you do not believe you ought to do that act.

So the argument that began this section is mistaken. We have not yet found a reason to distinguish between objective and subjective oughts.

3.3   Objective and prospective oughts

Another argument for distinguishing different sorts of oughts applies only in special situations. These are situations where you ought to do what will have the best consequences.[6] They are situations where consequentialism, as I shall use the term here,[7] applies. Some philosophers believe consequentialism always applies; others that it sometimes applies; others again that it never applies. Philosophers in the third group think that consequentialism is always false. They will not be impressed by the argument of this section.

Some philosophers claim that a similar argument can be developed even where consequentialism does not apply.[8] But I am not convinced this can be correctly done, and I prefer to be more cautious.

Let us suppose you are facing a situation where consequentialism applies. You have a choice between a number of alternative acts you might do. ('Act' may include refraining from acting.) Consequentialism says you ought to do an act if and only if every alternative act would have worse consequences, and you ought not to do an act if and only if some alternative act would have better consequences. One effect of this definition is to rule out deontic conflicts: if you ought not to do some act, it is not the case that you ought to do it.

The definition of consequentialism leaves it unspecified what is meant by 'consequence'. Different interpretations of this word give different versions of consequentialism. One interpretation takes the consequence of your doing an act to be the state of the world as it would be if you did the act. I call this state the 'outcome' of your doing the act, and I call the version of consequentialism that results from this interpretation 'outcome consequentialism'.

Another interpretation takes the consequence of your doing an act to be the prospect for the world that would result from your doing it. I call the resulting version of consequentialism 'prospect consequentialism'. By a *prospect*, I mean a portfolio of possible outcomes, each associated with a probability. Suppose you give money to a beggar. It may save her life and allow her to bring up her children, one of whom might later discover how to create boundless energy by nuclear fusion. Or the beggar might spend the money on heroin, and as a result die young. Or the money might save her life, and she might later become depressed and murder her mother. And so on; all sorts of outcomes might result from your gift. As a result of your gift, a probability will be associated with each of these possible outcomes, so your gift creates a prospect. Had you done something else, and not given the beggar this money, you would have created a different prospect.

Prospect consequentialism assumes that prospects have degrees of goodness. I think we should accept this assumption.[9] The goodness of a prospect will be a mathematical expectation of some sort. This means it will depend on probabilities, and plenty of questions may be asked about these probabilities. How subjective should they be, and how related to the evidence? Some of these questions are pursued in section 3.4. Here I can circumvent them by using an example based on objective chances.[10]

On your way home late at night, you find all your cards and money have been stolen apart from just enough cash – £35 – to buy your ticket home. Before you buy the ticket, you notice a casino where you can play roulette. The roulette wheel has 37 numbers. If you bet £1 on a number, you lose the £1 if the number does not come up, and you win £35 (and get your stake back) if it does come up. You work out that, by spreading your £35 over 35 of the numbers, you have a good chance – 35/37 to be precise – of gaining £1. You also have a 2/37 chance of losing all your money. You can refrain from betting, and if you do bet, you can spread your money over any collection of 35 numbers you choose. But for some reason, a bet spread over 35 numbers is the only sort available to you.

If you win, you can use the £1 you gain to buy a bar of chocolate in the station vending machine, and you will still be able to buy the ticket home. Let us assume this would be a better consequence for you than getting home without chocolate. If you lose, the consequence will be dire. You will have to sleep out on the street in the rain, and will miss an important meeting in the morning. Let us assume this would be a much worse consequence for you than getting home without chocolate. Assume the consequences for anyone else, including the owner of the casino, are negligible.

You have 667 alternatives to choose from: not betting at all, betting on all but 0 and 1, betting on all but 0 and 2, betting on all but 1 and 2, and so on. What do the two versions of consequentialism imply about what you ought to do?

Suppose the number 20 comes up. If you place a bet that includes that number, you will get home and have some chocolate. If you refrain from betting, you will get home without chocolate. If you place a bet that does not include 20, you will not get home. Outcome consequentialism implies you ought to bet, since there are some alternatives to not betting – making any bet that includes 20 – that lead to a better outcome than not betting leads to.

The argument is not that betting leads to a better outcome than the alternative to betting leads to. Consequentialism is defined on the basis of a number of specified alternatives. In the example, the alternatives are the 667 I mentioned. Betting is not one of them. However, not betting is one of them. Outcome consequentialism tells us that you ought not to take this alternative if there is an alternative that will lead to a better outcome. In the case where the number 20 comes up, there are several better alternatives. Therefore you ought not not to bet. That is to say, you ought to bet.

For the same reason, if any other number comes up, you ought to bet. You do not know what number will come up, but you do know for sure that you ought to bet. It follows that, for sure, it is not the case that you ought not to bet. Those are implication of outcome consequentialism.

What does prospect consequentialism say? Whatever bet you place, the resulting prospect gives you a 2/37 chance of not getting home, and a 35/37 chance of getting home and having chocolate. Not betting gives you a certainty of getting home, but without chocolate. Let us assume the latter is the best prospect. So according to prospect consequentialism, you ought not to bet.

The two versions of consequentialism therefore contradict each other. One says you ought not to bet; the other that it is not the case that you ought not to bet. On the face of it, this is a demonstration that both versions cannot be true, or at least that they cannot both apply to the example.

However, if you see merit in both versions, you might think that each can tell us the truth about what you ought to do, but in different senses of 'ought'. You might say that outcome consequentialism tells us what you ought objectively to do, and prospect consequentialism what you ought prospectively to do. I take the term 'prospective' from Michael Zimmerman, though my meaning is not quite the same as his.[11] In the example, you might say that prospectively you ought not to place a bet, but objectively it is not the case that you ought not to place a bet.

Prospect consequentialism and the prospective ought

Take a situation where consequentialism applies. We now have two versions of consequentialism that specify what you ought to do in this situation, in two different senses. Is either of those senses the central one? The central ought is the one to which Enkrasia on page 170 applies. So we need to check whether Enkrasia applies to either of the two consequentialist oughts.

If we were to accept prospect consequentialism, we would think that Enkrasia applies to its ought: the prospective ought. We would think that, if you formed your belief about what you ought to do on the basis of prospective consequentialism, you would not be rational unless you intended to do what you believed you ought to do. In the example, if you formed your belief correctly, you would believe you ought to refrain from betting, and we would think you less than fully rational if you did not intend to refrain from betting.

Prospect consequentialism does not imply that you ought to work out what you ought to do on the basis of prospect consequentialism.[12] Many examples suggest it is not always a good idea to make decisions by working out what prospect consequentialism says you ought to do, and deciding to do that. Most prospect consequentialists recognize that point. Some of them think that, instead, you ought to form your intentions on the basis of well-chosen rules. Some may even think you ought to have a false theory about what you ought to do, and make your decisions on the basis of that.

This does not suggest that prospect consequentialism's ought does not fit Enkrasia. If you form a belief that you ought to do something on the basis of prospect consequentialism, a prospect consequentialist might wish you had not done so. But she would nevertheless think you are failing in rationality if, having done so, you do not then intend to do what you believe you ought to do.

Prospect consequentialism is therefore a theory about the central ought, to which Enkrasia applies.

Outcome consequentialism and the objective ought

By contrast, if we were to accept outcome consequentialism, we would not think that Enkrasia applied to its ought: the objective ought. We would not think that, if you formed your belief about what you ought to do on the basis of outcome consequentialism, you would not be rational unless you intended to do what you believed you ought to do. In the example, if you formed your belief correctly, you would believe you ought to place a bet. But we would think you might rationally not intend to place a bet.

I would expect an outcome consequentialist in that situation to intend to refrain from placing a bet, just as any sensible person would. The objective ought of outcome consequentialism is not meant to fit Enkrasia, so it is not the central ought.

Is it a genuine ought nevertheless? It is not meant to be directly practical. G. E. Moore, who adopted outcome consequentialism, thought you could never know what you ought to do.[13] That makes his ought impractical in one way. The fact that Enkrasia does not apply to it makes it impractical in another way. An ought that is not supposed to be directly practical is misleading. We mostly take ought to be practical, and in particular we assume Enkrasia applies to it. I would prefer to reject this ought altogether, and so take outcome consequentialism to be false.

Still, the objective ought can be defended on grounds of hindsight. In the example, suppose you believe you ought to refrain from betting, and you do refrain. Suppose you nevertheless watch the wheel, and see that the number 20 comes up. You might then think you ought to have placed a bet that included 20. Your thought seems true in some sense, and it is plausible that its content refers to the objective ought.

So there may indeed be a genuine objective ought. If so, it is certainly not the central ought. If there is a genuine distinction between the prospective ought and the objective one, the central ought is the prospective one.[14]

An outcome consequentialist could adopt the account of subjective oughts that appears in Sidgwick's view on page 31: that you ought subjectively to do what you believe you ought objectively to do. Could an outcome consequentialist plausibly claim that Enkrasia applies to the subjective ought defined this way? She could not. Suppose you have correct beliefs about what you ought objectively to do. In the betting example, you believe you ought objectively to bet. So on Sidgwick's view you ought subjectively to bet. If Enkrasia applied to this subjective ought, you would not be rational if you did not intend to bet. But that is not plausible. You might quite rationally not intend to bet.

To summarize this section: where consequentialism applies, it gives us some grounds for distinguishing two sorts of ought. One may be called objective.

If it exists, it is not the central normative concept, and it is not directly practical. The other is the prospective ought, and it is relative to probabilities. It is the central ought.

3.4   Valuing prospects

My example in the last section contained objective chances. I assumed implicitly that you, the subject, are able to value prospects on the basis of those chances. You can consequently form rational beliefs about what you ought to do. But objective chances are a very special sort of uncertainty, and we need a more general account of the value of prospects.

We chiefly need this account when we are working out concretely what a person ought to do. That is not a topic for this book. However, I have claimed that the prospective ought is the central ought, on the grounds that Enkrasia applies to it. My claim was based on objective chances. I need to be sure the prospective ought satisfies Enkrasia more generally. Since that depends on how prospects are valued, I cannot ignore the question of valuation.

We may take it for granted that the value of a prospect is an expected value of some sort. That it is to say, it is the weighted average of the value of the prospect's possible outcomes, weighted by the outcomes' probabilities. The question is: what probabilities?

There are two schools of thought about this. According to one, probabilities are given by the available evidence.[15] According to the other, they are subjective probabilities of some sort, given by the belief-states of the person who is making the valuation. Let us try out these schools of thought on an example.[16]

You are offered a gambling opportunity. An urn contains three balls. Each is either white, dark red, or light red. No other information is available about the contents of the urn. One ball will be drawn from the urn at random. You can bet the ball will be white, or you can bet it will be red; those are the only bets offered. If you win your bet, you gain £1; if you lose, you lose £1. Alternatively, you can refrain from betting. For simplicity, I assume you are risk-neutral about money,[17] which means a prospect can be valued according to the mathematical expectation of your winnings in money.

You have three alternatives, each leading to a prospect: bet on white, bet on red, or do not bet. There is no difficulty valuing the third. The alternative of not betting gives you a certainty of zero: neither gaining nor losing. What about the other two? Let us start by valuing them on the basis of the evidence.

Here is one way to do so. The evidence is that the prospect created by betting on white is better than zero if two or three balls are white (and otherwise worse). The prospect created by betting on red is better than zero if no ball or one ball is white (and otherwise worse). So the evidence is that, for sure – whatever the number of white balls – one or the other of those prospects is better than zero. Zero is the value of the prospect created by not betting. If we apply prospect consequentialism to the prospects valued this way, we must conclude that you ought prospectively to bet.

The argument for this conclusion is not that the prospect created by betting is better than the prospect created by its alternatives. Betting is not one of the three alternatives I mentioned, so prospect consequentialism does not require us to evaluate it. The argument is that you ought not not to bet. Not betting is one of the alternatives that needs to be evaluated, and for sure there is one prospect better than the prospect created by not betting. To say you ought not not to bet is to say you ought to bet.

Enkrasia implies that you are not fully rational if you believe you ought to bet and you do not intend to bet. Since it is the truth that you ought prospectively to bet, we may assume that you may rationally believe that is so. Yet it is plain that you may rationally not intend to bet. So you could be fully rational if you believe you ought prospectively to bet and you do not intend to bet. We learn that, if the prospective ought is evaluated this way, Enkrasia does not apply to it. It is therefore not the central ought.

How else could we evaluate prospective oughts on the basis of the evidence? In the calculation I have just gone through, I treated the value of the prospect created by betting on red, and the value of the prospect created by betting on white, as uncertain. These values depended on the proportion of red to white balls in the urn. Perhaps that was a mistake. The idea of prospect consequentialism is surely that all uncertainty should be taken account of within the value of a prospect. The value should not itself be uncertain.[18]

Unfortunately, the evidence in the urn example does not allow us to embed all uncertainty within the value of a prospect. There is no evidence about the number of white balls in the urn except that it is not less than zero and not more than three. So the evidence gives us no probabilities for the number of white balls. When there is no evidence, the principle of insufficient reason is sometimes supposed to stand in its place. This principle tells us to assign an equal probability to each of the possibilities. But in the example the possibilities can be individuated in different ways, and each way yields different probabilities. Is one possibility that there are two white balls and one red ball in the urn? Or are there two possibilities here: one that there are two white balls and one light red one, and another that there are two white balls and one dark red one? Individuation of possibilities is arbitrary, which means we cannot apply the principle of insufficient reason.

Since the evidence does not give us probabilities, and values depend on probabilities, should we say that the prospect you create by making a bet does not have a value? That seems a reasonable view to take, and it would fix the problem with Enkrasia. Since neither prospect has a value, it would not be true that, for sure, one of these prospects is better than not betting. So we could not conclude that you ought prospectively to bet.

However, this way of valuing leads to a different problem. Let us adjust the prizes in the game. Let us suppose you always gain by betting: if you bet and win you gain £3, and if you bet and lose you gain £1. If we stick to the view that the prospects created by making a bet do not have a value, it would still not be true that, for sure, one of these prospects is better than not betting. So we still could not conclude that you ought prospectively to bet. Yet in this case you plainly ought to bet, since you can only gain by doing so.

We must therefore drop the view that the prospects have no value. How else could we value them on the basis of the evidence? We could return to the idea that each has a value, but it is uncertain what the value is. But this time we could treat the value as a function of the probability distribution of the number of white balls in the urn, whereas before we treated it as a function of the number of white balls in the urn. The probability distribution is unknown. Each possible distribution determines a value for the prospects. The prospects have unknown values determined this way.

This means that, in the adjusted game, the prospect created by betting on white has a value somewhere between £1 and £3, and so does the prospect created by betting on red. For sure, the value of these prospects is greater than zero, so it follows you ought prospectively to bet. This is the correct conclusion for the adjusted game.

Return now to the original game. On this new way of valuing, it is not certain that there is a prospect with a value greater than zero, because it is possible that betting on white and betting on red each create a prospect with a value of zero. There are some probability distributions that have this effect. One that does so assigns the same probability (a quarter) to each of the following possibilities: no white balls in the urn, one white ball in the urn, two white balls in the urn and three white balls in the urn.

Since there may be no prospect with a value greater than zero, the value of the prospect created by not betting, we cannot conclude that you ought prospectively to bet. Enkrasia may therefore apply to the prospective ought evaluated this way. If prospects are to be valued on the basis of the evidence, this is the only way of doing so that allows Enkrasia to apply to the prospective ought.

But it is a dubious way to make the valuation. It abandons the principle that the value of a prospect cannot itself be uncertain. Once that is abandoned, we could return to the first way of valuing prospects, which I described on pages 41–2. The difference is that, following the first way, we take the value of a prospect to be a function of the number of white balls in the urn, which is unknown. Following the new way of valuing prospects, we take the value of a prospect to be a function of the probability distribution of the number of white balls in the urn, which is unknown. The former way is actually preferable in one respect. It does not assume there is an unknown probability distribution over the number of balls in the urn, whereas the latter way does. There is no evidence about this distribution. Since probabilities are supposed to derive from evidence, there should be no probabilities where there is no evidence.

I conclude that Enkrasia can be made to apply to the prospective ought, evaluated on the basis of evidence, but the only way of achieving this result is dubious. So what about valuing prospects on the basis of subjective probabilities instead?

According to a Bayesian sort of subjectivism, you should attribute subjective probabilities to events, whether or not you have any evidence about these probabilities. If you follow this prescription, you will attribute some probability distribution to the number of white balls in the urn. This distribution will fix a determinate value on the prospect created by betting on white, which is simply the expected value of your winnings based on your probability distribution. Similarly it will fix a determinate value on the prospect created by betting on red. The value of one of these prospects will be minus the value of the other.

According to prospect consequentialism, if betting on white has a positive value, you ought to bet and you ought to bet on white. If betting on red has a positive value, you ought to bet and you ought to bet on red. If both bets have zero value, it is not the case that you ought to bet, and not the case that you ought not to bet. Enkrasia applies to prospective oughts evaluated this way. So the prospective ought evaluated this Bayesian way is the central ought.

Prospective oughts on this Bayesian account are subjective only within limits. Your subjective probabilities must be constrained by the evidence. In the example, you have evidence that tells you the probability of winning a bet, given the number of white and red balls in the urn. What you prospectively ought to do must take account of the evidence. But evidence does not always determine all the probabilities. It may leave a gap, and if it does Bayesians fill the gap with subjective probabilities.

There are many arguments for and against this sort of Bayesianism. I will leave the debate at this point. We have learnt that the prospective ought is the central ought if prospects are valued in the Bayesian way, because then Enkrasia will apply to it. If prospects are valued differently on the basis of evidence only, it is not so clear that the prospective ought is the central ought.

3.5   Summary

The word 'ought' has a number of meanings. In this chapter and the previous one, I picked out one meaning that I treat as central. It is the meaning I use in this book. I identified it by applying a particular criterion: it is the ought that satisfies the rational requirement of Enkrasia.

The central ought is normative, owned, unqualified and prospective.

Notes

1 See Henry Sidgwick's *Methods of Ethics*, p. 207. Sidgwick's view is actually expressed in terms of rightness rather than ought. He thinks it is subjectively right for you to do what you believe is objectively right. In *Reconsidering the Moral Significance of Ignorance*, lecture 1, Michael Zimmerman quotes several very prominent philosophers expressing much the same view.

2 My way of dealing with this argument comes from Jonathan Dancy in 'The logical conscience'.

3 See the account on Norman Swartz's web site: http://www.sfu.ca/~swartz/modal_fallacy.htm.

4 See p. 128.

5 Bykvist proposes one in 'Objective versus subjective moral oughts'.

6 This section has been strongly influenced by Michael Zimmerman's writings, including 'Is moral obligation objective or subjective?', *Living With Uncertainty* and *Reconsidering the Moral Significance of Ignorance*.

7 It is the conjunction of teleology and maximizing consequentialism as I used those terms in my *Weighing Lives*, chapter 3.

8 These philosophers include Michael Zimmerman in the writings mentioned in note 6.

9 See the argument in my *Weighing Goods*, section 6.1.

10 This example has the shape of one in Frank Jackson's 'Decision-theoretic consequentialism', and of the mineshaft example in Derek Parfit's *On What Matters*, pp. 159–60.

11 Zimmerman, *Living With Uncertainty*.

12 James Morauta helpfully reminded me of this point.

13 *Principia Ethica*, p. 149.

14 Allan Gibbard similarly sets aside the objective ought in *Wise Choices, Apt Feelings*, p. 42. Thanks to Toby Ord for pointing this out to me.

15 This school is championed by Michael Zimmerman in the writings mentioned in note 6.

16 It is modelled on an example in Michael Zimmerman's *Reconsidering the Moral Significance of Ignorance*.

17 See my *Weighing Goods*, particularly section 6.5.

18 Thanks here to Wlodek Rabinowicz.

4

Reasons

4.1 Introduction and preliminaries

Much of the recent philosophy of normativity has been devoted to reasons. Joseph Raz says 'The normativity of all that is normative consists in the way it is, or provides, or is otherwise related to reasons.'[1] John Skorupski identifies all of thinking as the domain of reasons, and says that all other normative concepts are reducible to the concept of a reason.[2]

This book is devoted to rationality, not reasons. Many philosophers assume that reasons and rationality are closely linked together. In chapters 5, 6 and 11 I shall argue that the link is less close than they think. Because I need to make that argument, and because one purpose of this book is to explore more generally the connection between rationality and normativity, I need to investigate what reasons are. That is the task of this chapter.[3]

In one respect, I can do better for reasons than I did for ought in chapter 2. I left ought undefined, but I shall go so far as to define reasons of two different sorts, in terms of ought.

Like 'ought', 'reason' has several meanings. Its ambiguity has led to some confusion in the philosophy of normativity, so I need to start with some remarks about this word's meaning.

First there is the verb 'to reason', whose gerund is 'reasoning'. Reasoning is an important topic in this book from chapter 12 onwards. Then there are two distinct nouns 'reason': a mass noun (a noun that has no plural) and a count noun (a noun that has a plural).

The singular of the count noun is 'a reason' and the plural 'reasons'. The count noun itself has several meanings. First, it can refer to what is sometimes called an 'explanatory reason'. This meaning appears in 'The reason stars twinkle is movements in the intervening air'. 'A reason' in this sense is more or less synonymous with 'an explanation of'.

Sometimes the explanation of why a person does something has a particular character: roughly, it involves the person's rationality in a distinctive way that

I shall not try to describe. Then we say the person does what she does *for* a reason. We might say 'The reason for which Hannibal used elephants was to terrorize the Romans'. The reason for which a person does something is called a 'motivating reason'. In general, a motivating reason is whatever explains or helps to explain what a person does in the distinctive way that involves her rationality.

Explanatory and motivating reasons are not normative, and they are not the topic of this chapter. This chapter is about what are called 'normative reasons'. Whereas motivating reasons explain or help to explain why a person does something, normative reasons explain or help to explain why a person ought to do something, or to believe something, or to hope for something, or to like something, or in general to F, where 'F' stands for a verb phrase. I shall define normative reasons precisely later, but this rough statement is enough to distinguish them from motivating reasons.[4] Sometimes a person does what she ought to do, and does it for the reasons that explain why she ought to do it. When that happens, her normative reasons are also her motivating reasons.

There are even several distinct normative meanings of 'a reason'. In sections 4.2 and 4.3 I shall define two of them.

The mass noun 'reason' also has several different meanings. In one of them, it is synonymous with 'rationality', which is a major topic of this book from chapter 5 onwards.

Section 4.4 investigates the different sense of the mass noun that appears in 'Tight-rope walkers have reason to concentrate' and in the expression 'most reason'.

Some philosophers use the mass noun to refer to reasons taken together.[5] The term 'practical reason' is often used to refer to the body of practical reasons. This usage, which I believe to be a recent innovation, adds to the already confusing state of our vocabulary. For example, it has led some authors to misunderstand David Hume's famous remark that ''Tis not contrary to reason to prefer the destruction of the whole world to the scratching of my finger'.[6] They think Hume meant to say that this preference is not contrary to the reasons, so he has no reason not to have this preference. But that was not his meaning.[7]

In this book I do not use the mass noun 'reason' at all, except when discussing the ideas of other philosophers who use it.

Explanation

Since I shall call on the notion of *explanation*, I need to make three clarifying remarks about it.

First remark. 'Explain' in common usage has various senses. In one of them, Darwin explained why evolution occurs. In another, *The Origin of Species* explains why evolution occurs. In a third, natural selection explains why it occurs. I shall stick to the third sense. As I use 'explain', an explanandum is explained by an explanans, rather than by a description of the explanans or by a describer of it.

'Explanation' is correspondingly ambiguous in common usage. It may refer to an act of explaining, to a description of an explanans or to the explanans itself. I shall stick to the third sense. For me, natural selection is an explanation of why evolution occurs, but *The Origin of Species* is not. 'An explanation' is another term for an explanans.

My meaning for 'explain' is very common. However, some philosophers seem not to have noticed it (and it is not recognized by the *Oxford English Dictionary*), so it needs emphasis. If you misunderstand this word you will misunderstand this chapter. 'Explain' as I use it denotes the relation that holds between an explanans and its corresponding explanandum. This explaining relation is simply the inverse of the because relation. To say that X explains Y is simply to say that Y is so because X is so. To say that natural selection explains evolution is to say that evolution occurs because natural selection occurs.

To say that X explains Y is also to say, in different words, that X makes Y so; the relation of explaining is the relation of making so. To say that natural selection explains evolution is to say that natural selection makes evolution so.

Second remark. Grammar allows various sorts of things to stand in the explaining relation to one another. For example, in saying that natural selection explains evolution, I was saying that one *process* explains another. But if we choose, we may harmlessly regiment our language by taking both explanans and explanandum to be *facts*. In the regimented language, we would say that the fact that natural selection occurs explains the fact that evolution occurs. In other words, evolution occurs because natural selection occurs.

Third remark. Although I shall not try to describe the nature of the explaining relation, I do need to say something about the individuation of explanations. Suppose Joanne broke a slate a while ago, and as a result the roof leaks. It rained last night, and today the carpet is wet. When we enquire why the carpet is wet, you might say the explanation is that it rained last night. I might say it is that Joanne broke a slate. Someone else might say it is that the roof leaks. We respectively make these statements: 'The explanation of why the carpet is wet is that it rained last night', 'The explanation of why the carpet is wet is that Joanne broke a slate', and 'The explanation of why the carpet is wet is that the roof leaks'. Read literally, no two of our statements can be true together. Still, our explanations are not rivals, and we would not feel we were contradicting each other. Nor would you be inclined to draw back from your assertion, and say only that the fact it rained last night is *an* explanation of why the carpet is wet. That would tend to suggest it is only a putative explanation, which might turn out not to be the explanation at all. So our use of the article 'the' is confusing. What is going on?

I suggest we think there is really one big explanation of why the carpet is wet. It is a complex fact that includes as parts all the separate facts the three of us described. Each of us is picking out a part to stand in for the whole. We call it *the* explanation because it is standing in for the one big explanation. We are employing a sort of synecdoche[8] or more exactly a *pars pro toto*. Which part we pick out will depend on our context: our background knowledge, our interests in the matter and so on.

Whether or not this suggestion about individuation is right, I think we should not fuss about the confusing state of the articles 'an' and 'the' attached to 'explanation'. It is generally a mistake to look for *the* canonical explanation of some fact. For one thing, most facts have more distal and more proximal explanations, and nothing picks one out from the others as canonical. We may accept several different facts as the explanation, and prefer one to another simply on the basis of context.

4.2 *Pro toto* reasons

Now I come to explanations of deontic facts. I use the term 'deontic fact' to include any fact that N ought that p – to use my special grammar from section 2.3 – where N is a person or other agent and p is a proposition. For convenience I shall assume p is the proposition that N Fs, where 'F' is a verb phrase. Examples of deontic facts are the fact that the prime minister ought to tell the truth, that Sonia ought to know how to behave at a funeral, and that Karl ought not to believe in Father Christmas. 'Ought' has the central meaning picked out in chapters 2 and 3: it is normative, owned, unqualified, prospective and so on.

Suppose you ought to F. And suppose the explanation of this fact is X. Then X is the reason why you ought to F. This is only because, in one sense of 'reason', 'the reason why' means the same as 'the explanation of why'. This sense of 'reason' is not normative. The relation of being the reason why holds between X and the fact that you ought to F. The latter fact is normative, but the relation is not normative in itself. It is the ordinary relation of explanation, which holds in many normative and non-normative situations.

However, in 'X is the reason why you ought to F', the 'reason why' is so closely attached to the normative 'ought' that the two tend to slide into each other. We slide from 'X is the reason why you ought to F' to 'X is the reason for you to F', meaning exactly the same thing by it. The 'reason why' (meaning explanation) bumps into the normative 'ought', yielding a normative sense of 'a reason' that combines the meaning of both.

In this sense, a reason for you to F can be defined as an explanation of why you ought to F. So we have a reason defined in terms of ought and explanation. I do not expect my picturesque etymology of this sense of 'a reason' to be taken seriously. But the sense itself is undoubtedly genuine.

Later, I shall define a second normative sense of 'a reason'. I shall distinguish a reason in this first sense by calling it 'a *pro toto* reason'. So:

> *Definition.* A pro toto *reason* for N to F is an explanation of why N ought to F.

In other words, a *pro toto* reason for you to F is something that makes it the case that you ought to F.

All the complications of the concept of *explanation* are inherited by the concept of *a* pro toto *reason*, and it is not my business to sort them out. An explanation need not be full or complete, and what counts as an explanation may depend on the context. For instance, it may depend on our background knowledge. All this is true of a *pro toto* reason, too. So long as something explains why you ought to F, it is a *pro toto* reason for you to F. A *pro toto* reason therefore need not be a unique canonical reason. As I explained on page 49, it may be a *pars pro toto*.

For example, suppose you ought to visit Mr Reed. The explanation might be that he is the best dentist around. If that is indeed the explanation, it is a *pro toto* reason for you to visit him. In a different context, the explanation might be that you ought to visit the best dentist around. This would be a *pro toto* reason for you to visit Mr Reed, in that context. We now have two alternative *pro toto* reasons, but they do not compete with each other.

A fuller explanation would be the conjunctive fact that you ought to visit the best dentist around and Mr Reed is the best dentist around. This too is a *pro toto* reason. It actually entails that you ought to visit Mr Reed. It is a necessarily *pro toto* reason. But even a necessarily *pro toto* reason is not a canonical reason. In some contexts, the conjunctive fact I stated would not adequately explain why you ought to visit Mr Reed. For instance, we might need an explanation that explains why you ought to visit the best dentist around.

I have defined the *property* of being a *pro toto* reason: a *pro toto* reason for you to *F* is an explanation of why you ought to *F*. Since various sorts of things can be explanations, various sorts of things can be *pro toto* reasons. For example, Mr Reed's skill at dentistry might be a *pro toto* reason to visit him. If we choose to regiment explanations by taking all of them to be facts, we shall correspondingly take *pro toto* reasons to be facts. If we do, we shall take the reason in this case to be the fact that Mr Reed is skilled at dentistry.

This reason is a non-normative fact. Reasons may alternatively be normative facts. In some circumstances, the normative fact that you ought to visit the best dentist around might be a *pro toto* reason to visit Mr Reed.[9] But whether the reason is a normative or a non-normative fact, it has the normative property of being a *pro toto* reason.

This property is complex, incorporating the two elements of ought and explanation. The next section explains that the same is true of a *pro tanto* reason too. Do not forget the element of explanation. Joseph Raz says:

> 'We can think of [the reasons for an action] as the facts statements of which form the premises of a sound inference to the conclusion that, other things being equal, the agent ought to perform the action.'[10]

In his 'Enticing reasons', Jonathan Dancy identifies an error in this claim. Dancy points out that, by Raz's criterion, conclusive evidence that you ought to perform an action would be itself a reason to perform the action. That is not necessarily so. Facts that merely entail that an agent ought to perform the action are not necessarily reasons for her to perform it; to be reasons they must explain why she ought to perform it.[11] If a newspaper publishes an article saying that a minister ought to resign, that is evidence that she ought to resign. If the newspaper is extremely reliable it may be conclusive evidence. But it is not a reason for the minister to resign.

4.3   *Pro tanto* reasons

Besides *pro toto* reasons, there must be reasons of at least one other normative sort. We often say there is a reason for you to *F*, when it is not the case that you ought to *F*. In these cases, the reason evidently does not explain the fact that you ought to *F*, since there is no such fact. It is therefore not a *pro toto* reason. Reasons of this sort are often called '*pro tanto* reasons'. I shall now set out to describe and ultimately define a *pro tanto* reason.[12] In this section and the following two, 'a reason' unqualified always refers to a *pro tanto* reason.

We attribute weights to reasons, and say that one reason is outweighed by another. This part of our vocabulary about reasons is metaphorical, and taken directly from mechanical weighing. Moreover, the explanation we give of a deontic fact is often governed by an analogy with mechanical weighing. We often say you ought to do something because the balance of reasons is in favour of your doing it. When an explanation takes this form, I shall call it a 'weighing explanation', and specifically a 'normative weighing explanation'. A reason that participates in a weighing explanation is a *pro tanto* reason.

How does a mechanical weighing explanation go? Suppose a balance tips to the left. A typical weighing explanation of why it does so will go like this. There is at least one object in the left-hand pan, and there may be one or more objects in the right-hand pan. Each object has a weight. The combined weights of the objects in the left-hand pan exceed the combined weights of the objects in the right-hand pan. That is why the balance tips left. (In the theory of mechanics, the word 'weight' refers to a force, which is a vector. I am not using it that way, but colloquially, to refer to a scalar magnitude.)

Suppose you ought to F. If there is a weighing explanation of why, it takes an analogous form. There is at least one reason for you to F, and there may be one or more reasons for you not to F. Each reason has a weight. The combined weights of the reasons for you to F exceeds the combined weights of the reasons for you not to F. That is why you ought to F.

In this analogous explanation, the fact that you ought to F is the explanandum, and analogous to the fact that the balance tips left. A reason for you to F is analogous to an object in the left-hand pan, and a reason for you not to F is analogous to an object in the right-hand pan.

The analogy is not perfect. For one thing, the weight of an object has a precise numerical magnitude, whereas the weight of a reason will rarely be such a precise thing as a number. It is likely to be an entity of some less determinate sort. Weights will not therefore combine by simple addition. For another thing, the weights of reasons will often be influenced by their context, and in particular by so-called 'organic' interactions between different reasons.

These are some features that are essential to a weighing explanation of why you ought to F. The explanation must include one or more *pro tanto* reasons, either for you to F or for you not to F. Each of these reasons must be associated with something that is identified as its 'weight'. The reasons and their weights play a characteristic role in the explanation. The role is that the weights of the reasons on each side are combined together in some way, and whether or not you ought to F is determined by the combined weights on either side.

Defining a *pro tanto* reason

That gives me enough material for defining a *pro tanto* reason. I have described a normative weighing explanation, and the characteristic role that *pro tanto* reasons play in one. A *pro tanto* reason is whatever plays this role in a normative weighing explanation.

That is not enough. I need to define specifically a *pro tanto* reason for N (you, say) to F. To do that, I need to add more detail to the definition.

Suppose you ought to F and this fact has a weighing explanation. In the explanation, the reasons for you to F play one role, and the reasons for you not to F play another. Let us call these respectively the 'for-F role' and the 'against-F role'. On pages 54–5 I shall come to the question of how we can identify these two roles.

Suppose alternatively that you ought not to F and this fact has a weighing explanation. In this explanation, the reasons for you not to F play the for-not-F role and the reasons for you to F play the against-not-F role. We may call the latter once again the 'for-F role' in this explanation.

Sometimes it is not the case that you ought to F, and also not the case that you ought not to F. Various explanations might account for this conjunctive normative fact. For example, it may be that your Fing has no normative significance. On some occasions the conjunctive fact has a weighing explanation. It would take this form: there are reasons for you to F and reasons for you not to F, each having a weight, and the reasons on neither side outweigh those on the other. This could be because their weights exactly balance. More often the reasons' weights will not be determinate enough to balance exactly, but still neither side outweighs the other. In this sort of case, the reasons on opposite sides are said to be 'incommensurate'.

In a weighing explanation of why it is not the case that you ought to F and not the case that you ought not to F, the reasons for you to F and those for you not to F play opposite but symmetrical roles. Again, we may call them respectively the 'for-F role' and the 'against-F role'.

Now we have enough roles for a definition:

> *Definition.* A *pro tanto reason* for N to F is something that plays the for-F role in a weighing explanation of why N ought to F, or in a weighing explanation of why N ought not to F, or in a weighing explanation of why it is not the case that N ought to F and not the case that N ought not to F.

This is a functional definition. It is like the definition of a missile's guidance system as something that plays a particular, specified role in an explanation of why the missile goes where it goes. The difference is that the function of a reason is not a causal one, because a normative weighing explanation is not a causal explanation. A reason has a normative function.

Counting in favour

T. M. Scanlon says:

> I will take the idea of a reason as a primitive. Any attempt to explain what it is to be a reason for something seems to me to lead back to the same idea: a consideration that counts in favor of it. 'Counts in favor how?' one might ask. 'By providing a reason for it' seems to be the only answer.[13]

I do not take the idea of a reason as primitive. I have defined it in terms of ought and explanation and the various roles within a weighing explanation.

The 'counts in favour' formula is very commonly offered as a way of explaining what a reason is.[14] I agree that a reason is a consideration that counts in favour of something. But my definition goes further and specifies what is the relevant sort of counting in favour.

As Scanlon implies, there are several ways of counting in favour. The fact that it is windy counts in favour of Woods's winning the tournament. But this is the wrong sort of counting in favour; the fact that it is windy is not a reason for Woods to win the tournament. The sense we need for a reason is connected to ought, and my definition specifies just what the connection is.

Still, although my definition picks out one sense of 'counts in favour', you might think it relies on our prior understanding of counting in favour in this sense. It defines a reason as something that plays the for-F role in a weighing explanation, and you might think that this role is nothing other than counting in favour of F. You might suspect that we could not identify the for-F role except through a prior understanding of counting in favour.[15]

That is not so. Notice first that a *pro tanto* reason can be defined without any reference to the for-F role. A reason is anything that plays the less specific characteristic role I described in a weighing explanation: it is something that has a weight, where the weights of reasons combine in some way to determine whether or not you ought to F.

The doubt is about my definition of a reason for you to F specifically. That definition refers to the for-F role in a weighing explanation. But it still does not rely on a prior understanding of counting in favour. The for-F role can be identified from the structure of the explanation itself.

Remember that I am only defining what a reason is; I am not trying to identify substantively what particular things are reasons for what. I am defining a reason by its role in a weighing explanation, so I can take it as given that we have before us a weighing explanation of why you ought to F. In it, the things that play the role of reasons fall into two opposing groups. The explanation of why you ought to F is that the combined weight of those in one group exceeds the combined weight of those in the other group. Since you ought to F, the reasons that play the for-F role are evidently the ones in the group that has the greater combined weight. In a weighing explanation of why you ought to F, the for-F role is the winning one, and that is how it can be identified. Similarly, in a weighing explanation of why you ought not to F, the for-F role is the losing one. In either case, we can identify this role without calling on any prior understanding of counting in favour.

This method of identifying the for-F role does not work for explanations of why it is not the case that you ought to F and not the case that you ought not to F. These are explanations of the third type mentioned in my definition. In these explanations like the others, the things that play the role of reasons fall into two opposing groups. But neither group wins over the other, so we cannot use the criterion of winning to identify the for-F role. The doubt is therefore more pertinent to weighing explanations of this type.

However, for this type, we can identify the for-F role as the same role as the for-F role in other weighing explanations. I assume we are able to re-identify the same role in weighing explanations of different sorts. I can put this differently. The for-F role is the role of counting in favour. I assume that, once you have learnt the concept of counting in favour, you can apply it outside the context where you learnt it.

So I agree that, in this one type of explanation, you need a prior understanding of counting in favour in order to identify the for-F role. But you do not need a prior understanding to identify that role in general. My definition of a *pro tanto* reason does not assume a prior understanding of counting in favour.

Examples of weighing explanations

I need some examples of weighing explanations. Since I do not in this chapter aim to say what particular things are reasons for what, I do not wish to assert that any particular weighing explanations are genuine. I shall simply assume that my examples are genuine for the sake of argument.

Here is the first. Suppose you ought to bring some wine to the party, and suppose the explanation of why is this. You promised to bring some wine, and you ought to keep your promises unless significant harm will result from doing so. In this case, suppose the only harm that will result is the cost to you in money and inconvenience of buying the wine, and this is not significant.

We can understand this as a weighing explanation. In favour of your bringing some wine is your promise. Against is the cost. Your promise plays the for-bringing-wine role in the explanation. It is therefore a *pro tanto* reason to bring wine. The cost plays the against-bringing-wine role. It is therefore a *pro tanto* reason not to bring wine. The promise is a reason of greater weight than the cost.

We could alternatively have taken the reasons to be facts: the fact that you promised to bring wine and the fact that your bringing wine has some cost in money and inconvenience. Treating *pro tanto* reasons as facts is a harmless regimentation.

Here is the second example. Suppose you are choosing between Montreux and Marrakesh as places to visit. Suppose that you ought to choose Montreux, on the grounds that it is a pleasant resort and not so far away as Marrakesh, though less exotic. The explanation of why you ought to visit Montreux is a weighing one. In favour of visiting Montreux are its pleasantness and proximity. Each plays the for-Montreux role in the explanation. They are *pro tanto* reasons for you to visit Montreux. Against visiting Montreux is the exoticness of the alternative, Marrakesh. That plays the against-Montreux role. It is a *pro tanto* reason for you not to visit Montreux. The reasons for visiting Montreux outweigh the one for not doing so.

The explanation could be filled out in more detail. Montreux's pleasantness consists in its beautiful views, cosy restaurants, opportunities for lake cruises and other pleasant features. Its nearness means your journey will add less carbon dioxide to the atmosphere. On the other hand, the exoticness of Marrakesh consists in teeming bazaars, belly-dancing and opportunities for camel rides. One reason for visiting Montreux is the beautiful views. Another is the cosiness of the restaurants. A reason for not visiting Montreux is that going instead to Marrakesh will allow you to take a camel-ride. And so on.

Call these 'particular reasons', and the ones I previously mentioned – pleasantness, proximity and exoticness – 'general reasons'. The particular and general reasons are not rivals to each other. That is to say, if we recognize the particular reasons we do not have to deny the existence of the general reasons, and vice versa. These two sets of reasons figure in explanations that are not rivals to each other. One explanation is just a more detailed spelling-out of the other. Nor are general reasons further reasons to be added to the particular ones. They are resultant reasons, resulting from combining the particular reasons.

I explained in section 4.1 that there may be various explanations of the same fact, which are not rivals to each other. I suggested that we can think of them as parts of one big explanation. One explanation may be deeper than another, in that it explains the other. Several of them may be weighing explanations, and each of those ones will pick out different sets of *pro tanto* reasons.

We should not expect to find a canonical weighing explanation, and correspondingly we should not expect to find canonical reasons.

Buck-passing

Here is another weighing explanation of why you ought to visit Montreux. Visiting it would be good to a degree, and visiting Marrakesh would be good to a lesser degree. Visiting Montreux would therefore be better than the alternative.

This is again not a rival to the explanations I have already given. If I am right about the relationship among explanations, it is another part of the one big explanation of why you ought to visit Montreux. It is genuinely explanatory. It tells us that what you ought to do is determined by the goodness of the alternatives. It is a substantive claim that this is so, either always or in this particular case – I call this claim 'teleology', and it can be denied.[16] It implies, for instance, that the pleasantness of Montreux contributes to the goodness of visiting Montreux, and that what makes the pleasantness a reason to visit Montreux is that it contributes to the goodness of doing so. These are substantive claims.

In this explanation, the goodness of visiting Montreux plays the for-Montreux role, and the goodness of the alternative plays the against-Montreux role. According to my definition, the goodness of visiting Montreux is a *pro tanto* reason to visit it; the goodness of the alternative a *pro tanto* reason not to visit it. The former reason has the greater weight.

T. M. Scanlon says:

> The fact that a resort is pleasant is a reason to visit it or to recommend it to a friend, and the fact that a discovery casts light on the causes of cancer is a reason to applaud it and to support further research of that kind. These natural properties provide a complete explanation of the reasons we have for reacting in these ways. . . . It is not clear what further work could be done by special reason-providing properties of goodness and value, and even less clear how these properties could provide reasons.[17]

I have explained how the goodness of visiting Montreux constitutes a reason for visiting it: it plays the appropriate role in a weighing explanation. I also described the work it does in the explanation: among other things, it implies pleasantness is good, and that teleology is true in this case. Scanlon seems to assume there is one canonical – he calls it 'complete' – explanation of why you ought to go to Montreux. But actually there are various explanations, at various levels of depth and detail. The explanation involving goodness is a thin one, but nevertheless an explanation.

Scanlon's main aim at this point in *What We Owe to Each Other* appears to be to argue for the priority of the right over the good, to use John Rawls's terminology.[18] I do not deny that the right is prior to the good; indeed I once argued that it is.[19] It is not at issue here. Visiting Montreux has the property of being good, which is explained by its more general properties of being a visit to a pleasant place and being a visit to a nearby place. It is also explained by its more particular properties of being a visit to a place that has beautiful views, being a visit to a place that has cosy restaurants, and so on. Each of these properties constitutes a reason to visit Montreux and is also a good property of visiting Montreux: each property has the normative property of being a reason and the evaluative property of being good. The argument leaves it open whether it is good because it is a reason, or a reason because it is good.

Is there always a weighing explanation?

If you ought to *F*, is that necessarily because the *pro tanto* reasons for you to *F* outweigh those for you not to *F*? To put the question another way: if you ought to *F*, is there necessarily a weighing explanation of why?

Certainly, when you ought to *F*, there are likely to be explanations of why you ought to *F* that are not weighing explanations. For example, suppose you ought to take your medicine now, and that is because you ought to take it at eight o'clock, and it is eight o'clock now. This explanation is plainly not a weighing one. True, the fact that you ought to take your medicine at eight o'clock and the fact that it is eight o'clock now combine to determine that you ought to take your medicine now. But these facts are not associated with weights that combine in the way they do in a weighing explanation. So they are not *pro tanto* reasons for you to take your medicine now.

However, even when there is a non-weighing explanation of why you ought to *F*, there may also be a weighing explanation. There is likely to be one in this example. There is likely to be a weighing explanation of the fact that you ought to take your medicine at eight o'clock rather than some other time, and this will constitute a weighing explanation of why you ought to take it now.

Still, some normative theories imply there are deontic facts that have no weighing explanation. At least, they seem to on the face of it. Moral theories that give a place to rigid deontic rules provide examples. Here is one.

Suppose you (a president) ought not to invade another nation. Suppose this is because you have no mandate from the UN and a rigid deontic rule says you ought not to invade a nation without a mandate from the UN. Then the fact that you ought not to invade seems not to have a weighing explanation.

But that is arguable. Intuitively it seems that, although you ought not to invade, there may nevertheless be *pro tanto* reasons for you to invade.[20] Perhaps invading would remove an evil dictator, say. Intuitively, it also seems that there may be *pro tanto* reasons for you not to invade. Perhaps the invasion will cause a dreadful civil war, say. According to my definition on page 53 of a *pro tanto* reason, where there are *pro tanto* reasons there is a weighing explanation. So if the definition is correct and the intuitions are correct, there must be a weighing explanation.

How could there be, when the deontic fact is determined by a rigid deontic rule? We could say that the rule is an extremely weighty *pro tanto* reason, that in practice will outweigh any reasons that are ranged against it. But that would not do justice to the idea that it is rigid. That idea implies it cannot possibly be outweighed, not merely that it will not in practice be outweighed.

But we could go further and say the rule is a *pro tanto* reason that has an infinite weight. This means it cannot possibly be outweighed by any other reason, except perhaps another rigid rule. This gives room for the intuition that other reasons may exist. It is a way to reconcile a rigid deontic rule with a weighing explanation.

It is awkward in some ways to accept the existence of *pro tanto* reasons that cannot be outweighed. First, it requires infinite weights. This strains the analogy between normative weighing explanations and mechanical ones. Second, it is awkward to call a reason '*pro tanto*' when it cannot be outweighed. Third, it may be intuitively awkward to think of a rigid deontic rule as merely a *pro tanto* reason that has an infinite weight. But perhaps we could live with these awkwardnesses. So moral theories that allow for rigid deontic rules do not provide incontrovertible examples of deontic facts that have no weighing explanation.

Next I have a different sort of putative example. Suppose you ought not to have contradictory beliefs. In particular, you ought not both to believe Mallory conquered Everest and believe Mallory did not conquer Everest. What explanation might there be for this deontic fact? Different philosophers have different views.

Some think there is a strong standing reason for you not to have contradictory beliefs. This is a reason against your having both the beliefs I mentioned. However, they think there might also conceivably be a reason for you to have a particular pair of contradictory beliefs. For instance, if in some way you could do good by having them, that would be a reason for you to have them. These philosophers think there is a weighing explanation of why you ought not both to believe Mallory conquered Everest and believe he did not. Against having both these beliefs is the standing reason against having contradictory beliefs. In this case there may happen to be no reason on the other side, for having both these beliefs. But in principle there could be, and this is enough for there to be a weighing explanation. In identifying an explanation as a weighing one, we should not insist that there actually are reasons on both sides. It is enough if there might possibly be reasons on both sides.

However, some philosophers – 'evidentialists' – think that what you ought or ought not to believe is determined only by your evidence. They think that any benefits that may arise from having or not having beliefs do not constitute reasons for having or not having them. Many evidentialists think you ought never to have contradictory beliefs. Moreover, they think there could not possibly be any reason for you to have a pair of contradictory beliefs, because your evidence could not possibly support your having them.

Of course, these evidentialists think there is an explanation of why you ought not both to believe Mallory conquered Everest and believe he did not; they do not think this is an inexplicable fact. But the explanation cannot be a weighing one. A weighing explanation must allow the possibility of reasons on either side, and they think there could not be any reason on the side of having both these beliefs. The explanation – whatever it is – is a *pro toto* reason according to my definition in section 4.2. It is not a *pro tanto* reason.

Whether or not it is true, this version of evidentialism makes sense. It shows it is at least conceptually possible for deontic facts to have no weighing explanation.

Permissible and obligatory

Here is one objection to my definition of a reason. The definition implies that, when the reasons for you to F outweigh the reasons for you not to F, then you ought to F. That means it is not permissible for you not to F. But sometimes, when the reasons for you to F outweigh the reasons for you not to F, it is permissible for you not to F and it is not the case that you ought to F. So it is said.

One type of example appears in Jonathan Dancy's paper 'Enticing reasons'. According to Dancy, the reasons for you to F may fall into two classes: enticing reasons and others. The others are 'peremptory', whereas the enticing reasons merely make Fing attractive. Suppose there are no non-enticing reasons either for you to F or for you not to F, but there is an enticing reason for you to F. Then, taking all the reasons together, the reasons for you to F outweigh those for you not to F. But still, says Dancy, it is perfectly permissible for you not to F. So it is not the case that you ought to F.

I think he is wrong. In so far as there is a class of reasons that may be called 'enticing', they can lead to oughts just like any other reason. I once advised a guest that he ought to try a mangosteen, on the grounds that mangosteens taste delicious. That they taste delicious would have to count for Dancy as an enticing reason. Nevertheless, I spoke correctly; it was the case that my guest ought to have tried a mangosteen. I did not think he was obliged to eat a mangosteen, and I thought it would have been understandable for him not to do so. For one thing, he might not have believed me when I told him he ought to. Still, had he believed me, and had he still declined to try a mangosteen, I would have thought that a mild lapse of rationality on his part.

Supererogation provides another type of example.[21] Sometimes the reasons for you to F outweigh those for you not to F, but it is permissible for you not to F because Fing would involve a big sacrifice. It is therefore not the case that you ought to F. So it is said.

Cases of supererogation vary. Take a prudential case to start with. Suppose it would be a great experience for you to watch the sun rise over the mountains; you would carry the memory with you all your life. You got to bed very late last night, and it would take a supreme effort to get up with the dawn, but nevertheless the balance of reasons is in favour of your doing so. In this case, I think you ought indeed to get up. If you correctly believe this, it would be a weakness on your part not at least to intend to get up, and I shall argue on pages 173–4 that this weakness is a failure of rationality. It is excusable and perhaps permissible in some sense, but nevertheless you ought to do what the balance of reasons favours.

Moral cases may be different. Suppose your guests would very much enjoy a visit to the nearby cathedral, but they cannot get there unless you take them. However, you have an impending deadline, and your time is precious to you. It may seem that the balance of reasons is in favour of taking your guests to the cathedral, but that doing so would be supererogatory and it would be permissible not to.

If that is how it seems, I think the true situation must be different. It may well be that the reasons are incommensurate, so that the balance of reasons is not in favour of taking your guests to the cathedral. There is a moral reason in favour of taking your guests to the cathedral and a prudential reason against it. These reasons cannot be precisely weighed against each other, and the result is that it is not the case that you ought to do it and not the case that you ought not to. I am using 'ought' in its central sense. We might say you ought morally to do it, meaning that morality requires you to. But it is not the case that you ought in the central sense to take your guests to the cathedral, and it is permissible – in the corresponding central sense – not to do so.

Reasons of other sorts

I have defined *pro toto* reasons and *pro tanto* reasons, but I do not claim that all reasons can be classed as one or the other. A *pro tanto* reason is something that plays a particular role in a weighing explanation of a deontic fact. But the explanation of a deontic fact is often not a weighing explanation, or at least not a straightforward one, and there are other roles to be played in explanations. Things that play those roles might be reasons of other sorts.

It is easy to identify other roles. For example, suppose you ought to F, even though you have promised your friend not to F. Part of the explanation may be that your friend has released you from your promise. Your promise would have been a *pro tanto* reason not to F, but the fact that your friend has released you cancels this reason. The fact that your friend has released you plays a particular, cancelling role in the explanation.

However, this fact could not be called a reason either for you to F or not to F. So this example does not yield a different sort of reason. Nor do I know any clear examples that do. I shall simply leave open the possibility of other sorts of reason.

4.4   Most reason

Instead of 'There is a reason for you to F', philosophers often write 'There is reason for you to F'. Some philosophers seem to omit or include the article 'a' indiscriminately, as though they intend no change of meaning.[22] For them, this use of 'reason' as a mass noun is just a stylistic variation, and we need not fuss about its grammar.

However, if we do pay attention to the grammar, we find it implies a substantial difference in meaning between 'There is a reason for you to F' and 'There is reason for you to F'. The first of these sentences asserts the existence of something that is a reason. The second does not; it does not quantify over things that are reasons. Like 'There is glory in victory', which ascribes the property of gloriousness to victory, it ascribes a particular property to your Fing.

What property? Not the property of being a reason, of course. The sentence says that your Fing has a sort of normative attraction.[23] This is only a metaphorical description of the property, but it is the best I can find. In 'There is reason for you to F' – read literally and not as a variant of 'There is a reason for you to F' – the mass noun 'reason' refers to a normative attraction.

'You ought to F' also ascribes a sort of normative attraction to your Fing. The difference is that 'reason' refers to a weaker, *pro tanto* attraction. There can be reason for you to F and also reason for you not to F, whereas it cannot be the case that you ought to F and also ought not to F.

Sometimes an author intends us to take the literal meaning of the mass noun seriously. In *The Possibility of Altruism*, Thomas Nagel defines a reason in terms of reason in this sense. He writes:

Every reason is a predicate R such that for all persons p and events A, if R is true of A, then p has prima facie reason to promote A.[24]

Nagel says explicitly that this is a definition.[25] In it, the first occurrence of 'reason' is a count noun and the second a mass noun. It would be no definition at all if the second 'reason' did not refer to something different from the first one. It must refer to what I have called normative attraction. The term 'prima facie' is Nagel's way of expressing the *pro tanto* nature of this attraction.

I see the appeal of treating reason as more primitive than a reason, and defining a reason in terms of it. When there is reason for you to F, your Fing has normative attraction. The reason there is for you to F explains why. Philosophers of normativity are primarily interested in normative things such as the normative attraction of your Fing. So it is natural to define a reason (which may be a non-normative entity such as a non-normative fact) as what explains a normative property. This is exactly what I have done in this chapter; the only difference is that I started from the normative attraction of ought rather than reason.

True, Nagel's definition does not say that a reason *explains* the existence of reason; only that a reason implies the existence of reason. But I think that is a mistake – the same mistake as Dancy identifies in Raz's definition of a reason quoted on page 51. According to Nagel's definition, any conclusive evidence that there is reason is a reason. But that is false. Nagel should have recognized that a reason must explain the existence of reason, as well as implying it.

The locution 'most reason' contains the same mass noun 'reason'. (The locution 'no reason' may contain either a count noun or a mass noun. Think of 'There is no bank in High Street' and 'There is no milk in the fridge'. 'Bank' is a count noun, 'milk' a mass noun.) Just as we can treat 'There is reason' as a stylistic variant of 'There is a reason', we can treat 'most reason' as a mere *façon de parler*, and not fuss about what it refers to; we can take 'There is most reason for you to F' to mean exactly the same as 'The reasons for you to F outweigh the reasons for you not to F'.

But in many philosophical writings, 'most reason' must have a less deflationary meaning. Many philosophers use this expression in place of 'ought'. They say 'You have most reason to F' instead of 'You ought to F'. Indeed, they sometimes define ought this way.[26] Whereas I have defined a reason in terms of ought, they define ought in terms of reason.

The deflationary meaning of 'most reason' is not available to these philosophers. They take 'You have most reason to F' to mean the same as 'You ought to F', which cannot mean the same as 'The reasons for you to F outweigh the reasons for you not to F'. The fact that you ought to F is not the same as the fact that the reasons for you to F outweigh the reasons for you not to F. If indeed you ought to F, and if this fact has a weighing explanation, then it is true that the reasons for you to F outweigh the reasons for you not to F. But the latter fact explains the former one, so it cannot be the same fact. A fact cannot explain itself. Ought is the explanandum and reasons the explanans.

This need not stop anyone from defining 'You ought to F' to mean 'There is most reason for you to F'. Reason, like ought, is a sort of normative attraction, which is explained by reasons. It is an explanandum for which reasons are an explanans.

And I think it makes sense to define ought as most reason. We might take normativity to be structured as follows. First, reasons explain reason, the normative attraction. Then the quantitative aggregation of reason determines whether or not you have most reason to F, which is the same as whether or not you ought to F. So reasons explain ought through explaining reason. Metaphysically, we might take ought, the normative attraction, to be nothing other than the aggregate or resultant of reason.[27]

I take normativity to have a different structure in which reasons explain ought directly, through a weighing explanation or in some other way. I prefer my structure for two reasons. The first is that it is more metaphysically economical: I do not even postulate the existence of reason as normative attraction. Reason in this sense plays no part in this book.

The second is a problem with the aggregation of reasons that afflicts the alternative structure. The problem does not arise in cases where you ought to F and there is a weighing explanation of why. In that case, each reason for you to F or not to F creates reason for you to F or not to F. Aggregating all this reason determines that there is most reason for you to F, and it follows that you ought to F. But when there is no weighing explanation of why you ought to F, it is not the case that the reasons for you to F outweigh the reasons for you not to F. So if you have most reason to F, that cannot be because of the aggregation of reason.

Take the example of evidentialism again, from page 60. An evidentialist may believe that you ought not to have contradictory beliefs, but that this fact is not explained by the weighing of reasons. According to this evidentialist, therefore, it cannot be explained by the aggregation of reason.

I think the evidentialist might still with propriety say you have most reason not to have contradictory beliefs. In general, we might say you have most reason to F even when there is no weighing explanation of why you ought to F. I think it is acceptable to use 'most reason' in this non-aggregative way, even though the quantitative term 'most' suggests aggregation.

The problem is that this usage separates the concept of *most reason* from the concept of *reason*. At first sight, the concept of *most reason* seems to be built from the concept of *reason* through aggregation. But if *most reason* is used in a non-aggregative way, it must be an independent concept. If ought is identified with most reason, it is not defined in terms of reason at all. Once again, reason seems to have no useful place in the structure of normativity.

4.5 Ownership of reasons

I have defined a reason for N to F as an explanation, or a particular part of a weighing explanation, of a deontic fact. A deontic fact is a fact of the form that N ought to F. 'Ought' has the central meaning specified in chapter 2, which implies that the ought is owned by N. The reason for N to F explains or partly explains this fact, and we may say that this reason is itself owned by N.

However, some 'ought' sentences in ordinary English do not ascribe ownership to the person named by the sentence's subject. 'Alex ought to get a severe punishment' is an example. (Here I suspend the stipulation I made on page 14 that the subject of 'ought' names the owner of the ought.) The same analysis of a reason can be applied to these cases: a reason for N to F is an explanation, or a particular part of a weighing explanation, of the fact that N ought to F. But when the ought does not belong to N, nor does the reason. The sentences 'There is a reason for Alex to get a severe punishment' and 'The cruelty of the crime is a reason for Alex to get a severe punishment' do not ascribe ownership of the reason to Alex.

Section 2.3 explained that English does not distinguish grammatically between 'ought' sentences that ascribe ownership and ones that do not. With reasons, we are grammatically better off: a sentence that ascribes ownership of a reason has a different grammar from one that does not. When 'There is a reason for N to F' ascribes ownership, the preposition 'for' governs 'N'. When this sentence does not ascribe ownership, it governs 'N to F'. The difference is invisible on the surface, but there is a test to detect it. When 'for' governs just 'N', the phrase 'for N' can be shifted to a different place in the sentence without changing the sentence's meaning. When 'There is a reason for N to F' ascribes ownership, it means the same as 'For N, there is a reason to F'. When the sentence does not ascribe ownership, the shift is not possible.

We even have an explicit way of ascribing ownership. We may say 'N has a reason to F', which explicitly ascribes ownership to N. So we may say

Alison has a reason to get a sun hat.

when the reason is owned by Alison, but we may not say

Alex has a reason to get a severe punishment.

because the reason is not owned by Alex.

Strictly, it is not correct to say that a reason may be owned by someone. Suppose you have a reason to allow extra time for your journey, and that reason is the fact that it is Friday afternoon. Plainly the fact that it is Friday afternoon does not belong to you. The very same fact may be a reason for many other people to do various things. They could not all own this fact. But we are used to the idea of a person's having a reason, and it does no harm to say that she owns it.

This 'have a reason' locution has been pressed by some philosophers into a different service. When those philosophers say you have a reason to F, they mean there is a reason for you to F and furthermore this reason is epistemically accessible to you.[28] Their usage is not standard English. Suppose Alex knows very well there is a reason for him to get a severe punishment. It would still be incorrect to say 'Alex has a reason to get a severe punishment', since the reason does not belong to Alex. Still, this epistemic use of 'has a reason' is no doubt valuable for philosophical purposes, and I do not object to it.

Nagel: agent-relative and agent-neutral reasons

How is the ownership of reasons connected with the well-recognized distinction between agent-neutral and agent-relative reasons?[29] I take agent-neutral and agent-relative reasons to be two sorts of owned reasons. I take an agent-neutral reason to be – speaking roughly – a reason that is owned by everyone, whereas an agent-relative reason is one that is owned by someone but not everyone. Either sort is owned, but agent-neutral reasons are owned by everyone.

To say this more precisely, I shall adapt the deviant grammar of section 2.3. There I used it for oughts; here I shall use it for reasons. Take this ungrammatical schema:

a is a reason owned by N that p.

When, for some a and some p, this is true for every person N, then a is an agent-neutral reason that p. When, for some a and some p, it is true for some person N but not for every person N, then a is an agent-relative reason that p. It is relative to those people for whom it is true. This is how I define agent-neutrality and agent-relativity.

The distinction was introduced by Thomas Nagel, though he originally used different terminology.[30] Nagel's definitions of agent-neutrality and agent-relativity are built on his particular definition of a reason. Nevertheless, given what he takes a reason to be, they are extensionally almost equivalent to mine. Every reason that is agent-neutral by Nagel's definition is agent-neutral by mine, and almost every reason that is agent-relative by Nagel's definition is agent-relative by mine.

To show this is so, I shall temporarily accept Nagel's definition of a reason (and temporarily switch to his notation, so that 'p' denotes a variable ranging over people). To repeat his definition, it is:

> Every reason is a predicate R such that for all persons p and events A, if R is true of A, then p has prima facie reason to promote A.[31]

Nagel clearly means to imply that, when a predicate R is a reason and R is true of A, so that p has reason to promote A, then R is a reason p has to promote A.

When a predicate R is a reason, Nagel goes on to define it to be an agent-relative reason if it contains a free occurrence of the 'agent-variable' p, and an agent-neutral reason if it does not.

Let R be a predicate that contains no free occurrence of 'p'. If R is a reason, it is agent-neutral by Nagel's definition. If it is a reason, the definition of a reason ensures that, whenever R is true of A, everyone has a reason to promote A, and that reason is R. Everyone has this same reason, so it is agent-neutral by my definition too.

Here is an example of Nagel's own.[32] Let R be the predicate 'will prolong G. E. Moore's life', which contains no free occurrence of 'p'. Let A be the event of Moore's removing himself from the path of an oncoming truck. If R is a reason, and if R is true of A – if Moore's removing himself from the path of an oncoming truck will prolong Moore's life – the definition of a reason ensures that everyone has a reason to promote A, and that reason is R. This R is an agent-neutral reason by both Nagel's definition and mine.

By contrast, let R be the predicate 'will prolong p's life', which contains a free occurrence of 'p'. Let us assume that this R too is a reason. That is to say, let us assume that, for all persons p and events A, if R is true of A, then p has a reason to promote A. Now, let A be the same event as before: Moore's removing himself from the path of an oncoming truck. In the present case, the antecedent clause in the formula, 'R is true of A', is true only in the one case when the agent-variable p takes on the particular value Moore. That is because the event A of Moore's removing himself from the path of an oncoming truck will prolong Moore's life, but no one else's. Only when the antecedent clause is true can we derive the consequent. So we can conclude only that Moore has a reason to promote A, and that reason is R. No one else has that reason. So this R is an agent-relative reason by both Nagel's definition and mine.

Virtually every reason that is agent-relative by Nagel's definition is agent-relative by mine. There may be one type of exception. Let R be the predicate 'will prolong the life of someone who lives on the same planet as p'. If this is a reason, it is agent-relative by Nagel's definition. But it is a reason to promote the event of Moore's removing himself from the path of an oncoming truck, and it is a reason that is had by everyone who lives on the same planet as Moore. As a matter of contingent fact, those may be all the people there are. If so, the reason is agent-neutral by my definition, since it is owned by everyone there is. My definition allows a reason to be contingently agent-neutral in this way, but Nagel's does not. Nagel appears to value this feature of his definition.[33]

From his definition of an agent-neutral reason, Nagel correctly draws the conclusion that agent-neutral reasons are 'reasons for anyone to promote what they apply to'.[34] This is a correct statement of the conclusion provided 'for' is understood in the way that implies ownership; the intended parsing must be '(reasons for anyone) to promote . . .'. Agent-neutral reasons as Nagel defines them are agent-neutral reasons as I define them. Agent-neutrality is common ownership.

True, in the very next sentence Nagel says the opposite. He says 'They are not reasons *for* particular individuals, but simply for the *occurrence* of the things of which they hold true'.[35] That is to say, agent-neutral reasons are reasons for no one. In my terms, they are unowned reasons. But Nagel here misstates his own theory. His definition implies that agent-neutral reasons are reasons for everyone, as I explained. Moreover, his subsequent arguments rely on this conclusion. Later, he says, for instance:

> If one acknowledges the presence of [an agent-neutral] reason for something, one has acknowledged a reason for *anyone* to promote or desire its occurrence.[36]

Nagel appears to be deliberately non-committal over this point, apparently because he thinks it does not matter. He says:

> For the purpose of my argument, however, it is not necessary to distinguish between [agent-neutral] reasons as reasons for things simply to occur, and as reasons for *anyone* to want and promote those things to which they apply.[37]

Still, the truth is that agent-neutral reasons as he defines them are reasons for everyone, not reasons for no one.[38]

Why Nagel's definition?

Nagel takes the notion of ownership for granted, even in his definition of a reason. The definition includes the expression '*p* has prima facie reason to promote *A*'. The context makes it clear that he is not using 'has' in any epistemic sense. He must mean it to express ownership.

Consequently, he could have defined agent-neutrality and agent-relativity as I did. He could have defined an agent-neutral reason as one that everyone has. If he particularly wanted to exclude reasons that are agent-neutral contingently, he could have defined an agent-neutral reason as one that everyone necessarily has. He could have defined an agent-relative reason as one that is had by someone but not by everyone, or not necessarily by everyone.

Instead he based his definitions on the internal structure of the reasons: on the structure of the predicates that are, for him, the reasons. The structure of a reason – specifically, whether or not it contains a free agent-variable – determines who owns it. So Nagel's definition is based on what determines or explains ownership rather than on ownership itself.

Yet it is the ownership of reasons, rather than the structure of reasons, that is important for Nagel's purposes. *The Possibility of Altruism* argues that reasons to promote an event are always owned in common by everyone. Since Nagel could have defined agent-neutrality as common ownership, he would have done better to do so.

Let me generalize the lesson. Philosophers of normativity are mainly interested in the normative state of the world. They want to know people's normative properties and relations. For instance, they want to know when a person ought to do something. But in recent decades many philosophers of normativity have concentrated on reasons, which are not normative properties of people but things that explain the normative properties of people. Many reasons are non-normative facts or (on Nagel's view) non-normative predicates. Attending particularly to reasons can distract you from the normative properties you aim to study. That seems to have happened to Nagel.

Notes

1   Raz, *Engaging Reason*, p. 67.
2   Skorupski, *The Domain of Reasons*, p. 1.
3   This chapter grew from my paper 'Reasons'.
4   In *The Moral Problem*, Michael Smith gives a very useful account of the distinction.
5   In 'How does coherence matter?', p. 232, Niko Kolodny explicitly adopts this practice, and recognizes that it is 'somewhat stipulative'.
6   *Treatise*, book 2, part 3, section 3.
7   As I shall explain on pp. 194–5.
8   As Brad Hooker pointed out to me. Compare David Lewis, 'Causal explanation', p. 215.
9   In 'Reasons as right-makers', Laura and François Schroeter deny that normative facts could be reasons. Their account of reasons is close to mine in many ways. This is one of the differences, and I do not attach much importance to it. They argue on grounds of common

sense that a reason is always a substantive descriptive fact. My common sense is evidently different from theirs.

10   Practical Reason and Norms, p. 187.
11   Stephen Kearns and Daniel Star deny this point in their 'Reasons'. My response is in my 'Replies'.
12   I believe Susan Hurley's *Natural Reasons*, pp. 130–5, first made this valuable term popular.
13   *What We Owe to Each Other*, p. 17.
14   Examples are Joseph Raz's, *Practical Reason and Norms*, p. 186, Jonathan Dancy's *Ethics Without Principles*, chapter 2, and Derek Parfit's *On What Matters*, chapter 1.
15   I am very grateful to Kit Fine for patiently pursuing this point with me.
16   See my *Weighing Lives*, section 3.1, or my *Weighing Goods*, chapter 1.
17   *What We Owe to Each Other*, p. 97.
18   *A Theory of Justice*, p. 24.
19   *Weighing Goods*, chapter 1. I took a less committed line in *Weighing Lives*, p. 32.
20   Seana Shiffrin urged this intuition on me.
21   This point was made to me separately by David McNaughton and Michael Smith. I thank Michael Ridge for pointing out to me a major error in my previous treatment of supererogation, which was not consistent with enkrasia.
22   Thomas Nagel does this in chapter 7 of *The Possibility of Altruism*, despite his definition of a reason quoted below. Another example is John Skorupski's *The Domain of Reasons*.
23   See the discussion of 'moral forces' in John Horty's 'Reasoning with moral conflicts'.
24   *The Possibility of Altruism*, p. 47.
25   p. 48.
26   One example is in Ingmar Persson, 'A consequentialist distinction', p. 354.
27   In 'Reasons as right-makers', Laura and François Schroeter argue that ought (they use 'right') is the aggregate of reasons themselves, which they take to be 'reason-giving facts in their reason-giving roles'. I do not see how a property such as ought or rightness can be the aggregate of facts in a role.
28   For example, Robert Audi, in *The Architecture of Reason*, pp. 53–4, and John Skorupski in *The Domain of Reasons*, p. 108. Michael Woods adopts this way of speaking in 'Reasons for action and desires', but recognizes it is not standard English.
29   On this topic I have found Michael Ridge's article 'Agent-neutral vs agent-relative reasons' very helpful.
30   pp. 90–1. The terms 'agent-relative reason' and 'agent-neutral reason' were introduced by Derek Parfit in *Reasons and Persons*, p. 143.
31   *The Possibility of Altruism*, p. 47.
32   p. 91.
33   See the footnote on pp. 120–1.
34   p. 91. Original italics.
35   p. 91. Original italics.
36   p. 119. Original italics.
37   p. 91. Original italics. Nagel repeats the same point in a footnote on p. 120.
38   Derek Parfit interprets Nagel this way, too, in *Reasons and Persons*, p. 143.

5

Responding to Reasons

5.1 Rationality and responding to reasons

This chapter examines a common account of rationality and argues that it is inadequate. It initiates an investigation of rationality that will occupy this and the next six chapters.

From the beginning I face a problem of terminology. I shall explain in chapter 7 that 'rationality' is not always the name of a property, but that often it is. This chapter and the next are about this property. We attribute the property of rationality to all sorts of things: to people's attitudes, to their actions, to the actions of governments, to traffic systems and so on. I assume that the rationality of other things is always derived in some way from the rationality of people. But in any case, these chapters are about specifically the rationality of people.

I shall investigate necessary and sufficient conditions for a person to possess this property. Like many properties, it comes in degrees: you can be more rational and less rational. But unlike most it has a maximum degree. It is possible to be fully rational – rational to the highest degree.

In identifying conditions for possessing rationality, it is easiest to start by identifying conditions for being fully rational. That is what I shall do. The degree to which someone is rational will then be the degree to which these conditions are satisfied. In investigating conditions for full rationality, I do not want to add 'fully' every time I write 'rational'. I shall therefore use the word 'rational' to mean fully rational. By 'not rational' I mean not fully rational. I shall maintain this practice throughout the book.

Many philosophers think of rationality as responding correctly to reasons. This chapter examines that view and rejects it. Chapter 6 examines the related view that rationality consists in responding correctly to beliefs about reasons.

The view that rationality consists in responding correctly to reasons must imply at least that:

Equivalence. Necessarily, you are rational if and only if you respond correctly to reasons.

As I shall put it: rationality is equivalent to responding correctly to reasons.

Some philosophers go further. They think that rationality can be *reduced* to reasons through Equivalence or some related formula.[1] They may have in mind a metaphysical reduction or a conceptual one. One purpose of this chapter is to argue that neither sort of reduction is possible. I shall argue that Equivalence and its variants are false. It will follow *a fortiori* that rationality cannot be reduced to reasons by this route.

Another purpose of the chapter is simply to explore a part of the relation between rationality and reasons. I shall look for what truth there is in Equivalence and its variants. Equivalence can be factored into two converse propositions, and I shall consider both. One is that rationality entails responding correctly to reasons:

Entailment. Necessarily, if you are rational you respond correctly to reasons.

The other is:

Sufficiency of reasons. Necessarily, if your respond correctly to reasons you are rational.

Responding correctly to reasons

I need to start by elucidating the notion of 'responding correctly to reasons'.

First, the reasons it refers to are normative ones. Furthermore, they are reasons that are owned by you; to be rational you do not need to respond to reasons that are not yours. So 'reasons' refers to your normative reasons. These are the reasons I described in section 4.5.

Next, what does 'correctly' mean? It is simply a placeholder. Equivalence claims there is *some* way of responding to reasons such that, necessarily, you are rational if and only if you respond to reasons that way. 'Responding correctly' means responding in that way, whatever it is.

What way of responding to reasons is correct, then? How must you respond if you are to be rational? Suppose you have a reason to F; must you F if you are to be rational? Not necessarily. Suppose you also have a reason not to F, as you may. If you had to F in order to respond correctly to a reason to F, to respond correctly to your two opposing reasons, you would have both to F and not F. You could not respond correctly to both reasons, therefore. But we must not interpret 'respond correctly' in a way that makes it impossible for you to respond correctly to opposing reasons. If we did, Equivalence would entail that you cannot be rational, since you inevitably encounter opposing reasons. We cannot have that.

Let us go more carefully. Suppose you ought to F. I take it for granted that, if this is so, there is some explanation of why it is so. The explanation may be what I described in section 4.3 as a weighing explanation. In that case, you ought to F because on balance your reasons require you to F. More briefly: your reasons require you to F.

In section 4.3 I allowed for the possibility that there is no weighing explanation of why you ought to F. Even so, when you ought to F, there must be some explanation of why. In section 4.2 I said we count this explanation as a reason for you to F; I called it a '*pro toto* reason'. So in this case too, we may say your reasons require you to F, if we take the liberty of allowing 'your reasons' to refer to one reason only. Taking all cases together, we may conclude that you ought to F if and only if your reasons require you to F.

This allows us to say that to respond correctly to reasons you must F whenever your reasons require you to F. This interpretation of responding correctly to reasons makes it possible for you to respond correctly even when your reasons are opposed. Exactly equivalently, we could say that to respond correctly to reasons you must F whenever you ought to F.

I prefer the latter formulation in terms of ought, because it more clearly displays its meaning. However, a formula that contains the word 'reasons' is perhaps more perspicuous when I am discussing responding to reasons. So in this chapter and the next I shall use 'your reasons require' rather than 'ought', despite my preference. The two have the same meaning,[2] so you are free to translate one into the other whenever you want. You may even do so in statements that describe a person's belief. 'You believe your reasons require you to F' means the same as 'You believe you ought to F'. My use of 'believe' is transparent in that respect.

Why is this not a reduction of ought to reasons, which I said in chapter 4 does not exist? Because 'require' has substantive content, as chapter 7 explains.

That you F whenever your reasons require you to F is a necessary condition for you to respond correctly to reasons. There is at least one other necessary condition. Even if you F whenever your reasons require you to F, you might not be responding correctly to reasons; it might just be a coincidence. Some appropriate connection must hold between your reasons and your Fing.[3] It may need to be an explanatory one. Alternatively, a counterfactual connection may be enough. For instance, the necessary condition might be that you would not have Fed had your reasons required you not to F.

I shall therefore add a clause to my formulae requiring an appropriate explanatory or counterfactual connection. But since it does not matter for my argument, I shall not try to specify just what sort of connection would be appropriate.

I shall assume we have now arrived at necessary and sufficient conditions for you to respond correctly to reasons.[4] You respond correctly to reasons if and only if, whenever your reasons require you to F, you F and an appropriate explanatory or counterfactual connection holds between your reasons and your Fing. This is an analysis of 'you respond correctly to reasons'.

Given my analysis, Equivalence comes down to:

> *Equivalence analysed.* Necessarily, you are rational if and only if, whenever your reasons require you to F, you F and an appropriate explanatory or counterfactual connection holds between your reasons and your Fing.

The Entailment Condition is:

> *Entailment analysed.* Necessarily, if you are rational then, whenever your reasons require you to F, you F and an appropriate explanatory or counterfactual connection holds between your reasons and your Fing.

This implies

> *Core Condition.* Necessarily, if you are rational, you F whenever your reasons require you to F.

The explanatory or counterfactual connection will not be important in this chapter or the next, so I shall chiefly concentrate on the Core Condition.

5.2 The quick objection

There is a quick objection to Equivalence. It can happen that your reasons require you to F but you do not believe your reasons require you to F. Furthermore, this can happen even if you are rational. Suppose it does. Since you do not believe your reasons require you to F, you may rationally fail to F. Therefore, even though your reasons require you to F, you may be rational even if you do not F. So the Core Condition is false. Therefore, Equivalence is false because it entails the Core Condition. So far as your rationality is concerned, ignorance of what your reasons require constitutes an excuse for not doing what your reasons require.

Many philosophers find this Quick Objection convincing. As a result, few accept exactly Equivalence. Instead, they assume that a rational person's response to reasons is filtered through her cognitive attitudes in some way. They think rationality is equivalent to responding correctly to your beliefs about reasons, or to the reasons you believe there to be, or what you see as reasons, or something of that sort. I shall come to modified views like this in chapter 6.

Before that, I need to deal with two possible responses to the Quick Objection. The first is this. A premise of the Quick Objection is that it can happen that your reasons require you to F, and you are rational, yet you do not believe your reasons require you to F. The response is to say that a rational person necessarily has correct beliefs about what her reasons require.

This would not be plausible if reasons were facts external to the person, because even a rational person can make mistakes about external facts. But one theory about reasons is that they are all attitudes of the person herself. At first it seems more plausible to claim that a rational person necessarily has correct beliefs about what her attitudes are.

However, even that claim cannot be true in general. Even a rational person must have attitudes that she herself does not believe she has. Otherwise, for each of her beliefs she would have the higher-order belief that she has that belief. She would have an infinite hierarchy of beliefs, which is impossible. So it is really not plausible to claim that a rational person necessarily has correct beliefs about her reasons, even if her reasons are attitudes of hers.

However, the theory that reasons are attitudes leads to a second, more plausible response to the Quick Objection. This is the subject of the next section.

5.3 Attitudinal reasons

This second response is to argue that ignorance of what your reasons require does not always excuse you from responding correctly to them. Some reasons may impose *strict liability*, as I shall put it. By this I mean that, necessarily, if you are rational you respond correctly to these reasons, whether or not you believe they exist, and whether or not you believe they are reasons. If you do not respond correctly to them, automatically you are not rational.

The most plausible candidates for reasons that impose strict liability are what I shall call 'attitudinal reasons'. Attitudinal reasons are reasons that consist in attitudes. It seems plausible (though I shall later deny it) that there are such reasons. Here are some examples:

Attitudinal reasons

R1. If you believe *p*, your belief is a reason for you not to believe not *p*.

R2. If you intend to *F*, your intention is a reason for you not to intend not to *F*.

R3. If you believe *p* and you believe that if *p* then *q*, your two beliefs are together a reason for you to believe *q*.

R4. If you intend to *F* and you believe your G*ing* is a means implied by your F*ing*, your intention and belief are together a reason for you to intend to *G*.

Note: throughout this book I use the terms 'belief' and 'intention' to refer to attitudes and not to the contents of attitudes.

R1 to *R4* each assert that an attitude of yours or a combination of your attitudes is a reason. But we might equally well take the reason to be the fact that you have the attitude or combination of attitudes. That would be to adopt the harmless regimentation that I mentioned on page 51; it would make no difference. Either way, I count them as attitudinal reasons.

Each attitudinal reason is matched by a corresponding necessary condition for rationality:

Conditions of rationality

C1. Necessarily, if you are rational, you do not believe *p* and believe not *p*.

C2. Necessarily, if you are rational, you do not intend to *F* and intend not to *F*.

C3. Necessarily, if you are rational then, if you believe *p* and you believe that if *p* then *q*, you believe *q*.

C4. Necessarily, if you are rational then, if you intend to *F* and you believe your G*ing* is a means implied by your F*ing*, you intend to *G*.

I have stated these conditions only approximately. For example, you might be rational even if you do not believe everything that follows by modus ponens from what you believe; you do not need to believe every trivial and pointless consequence of what you believe.[5] These conditions can be derived from requirements of rationality that are stated in chapter 9. (Section 9.4 also defines exactly what I mean by the expression 'means implied by' in *R4* and *C4*.) Whereas in chapter 9 I have formulated the requirements as accurately as I can, I have been less particular about *C1–C4* and the corresponding putative reasons described in *R1–R4*. They are only meant as illustrative examples, and need not be exact.

I hope it is obvious that there are necessary conditions like these, if not exactly these, for being rational. You could not be fully rational whilst having contradictory beliefs, say, or whilst failing to intend a means you believe is implied by an end you intend. *C1–C4* are weaker than the requirements stated in chapter 9; on page 135 I shall explain that a necessary condition for rationality is weaker than a corresponding requirement of rationality. Niko Kolodny denies that there are any 'rational requirements of formal coherence as such', but he does not deny that there are necessary conditions for rationality.[6] He argues that the necessary conditions can be explained on some basis other than rational requirements.

If attitudinal reasons exist, they impose strict liability just because each corresponds to a necessary condition of rationality. If you have an attitudinal reason to *F* but do not *F*, you fail to satisfy the corresponding condition, so you are not rational. You have contradictory intentions or contradictory beliefs, or you do not believe what follows by modus ponens from the contents of your beliefs, or in some other way you are not rational. That is so whether or not you believe you have a reason to *F*.

Ignorance is no excuse

If there are indeed attitudinal reasons, they impose strict liability. But how can a reason impose strict liability? Surely ignorance of a reason must excuse you from responding correctly to it. The answer lies in the nature of attitudinal reasons themselves. You can respond correctly to an attitudinal reason without believing it exists or, if you do believe it exists, without believing it is a reason. Given that you can do so, neither the fact that you do not believe it exists nor the fact that you do not believe it is a reason constitutes an excuse for not responding correctly to it.

How can you respond correctly to an attitudinal reason without believing it exists? You often respond to an attitude without believing it exists. You may respond to a belief of yours that it is raining by putting up your umbrella. To do so, you do not need to have a second-order belief that you believe it is raining.

I am not suggesting your attitude of belief in that case constitutes a reason. But here is an example of responding correctly to an attitude that constitutes a reason according to *R1*. Suppose you believe it is raining, but then you look out of the window and see the rain has stopped. You now believe it is not raining. We are assuming this belief constitutes a reason for you not to believe it is raining. Typically, you will indeed no longer believe it is raining once you acquire the opposite belief. Some automatic, unconscious process generally ensures that, when you come to believe a proposition, you stop believing its negation if you previously did. The operation of this process counts as responding correctly to your reason, which is your belief that it is not raining. For the process to work, you do not have to believe the reason exists. In this case, you do not have to believe you believe it is not raining.

You may respond correctly to any attitudinal reason like this, through automatic processes. But sometimes your automatic processes let you down; you do not respond automatically. Even then, you may respond correctly nonetheless, through a conscious process of reasoning. Suppose, as you wake up one morning on a cruise, you hear gulls from your cabin, so you believe there are gulls about. Suppose you also have a standing belief that, if there are gulls about, land is nearby. According to *R3* on page 76, these beliefs constitute a reason for you to believe land is nearby. But if they have not come together in your mind, you may not yet believe land is nearby. However, by a piece of conscious reasoning, you can reason your way to believing it. This reasoning will involve calling to mind the proposition that there are gulls about, and the proposition that, if there are gulls about, land is nearby. But it need not involve any second-order belief that you believe these propositions.

At least, that is my own view about reasoning. Others disagree: they think reasoning must involve second-order beliefs, at least if it is to be full-blown, critical reasoning.[7] My view is defended later in this book, from chapter 12 onwards.

It does not matter here in any case. The question is whether you can respond correctly to an attitudinal reason without believing it exists, and the answer is that you can. You can do so through automatic processes. It is also at least arguable that you can do so through conscious reasoning without believing the reason exists. We can add that, *a fortiori*, if you do believe an attitudinal reason exists, you can respond correctly to it without believing it is a reason.

All this shows how attitudinal reasons can impose strict liability. For them, ignorance is no excuse.

Responding correctly to attitudinal reasons

Attitudinal reasons are not subject to the Quick Objection, since they may impose strict liability. So if attitudinal reasons exist, they might provide support for the Core Condition on page 74 by removing one objection to it.

They would not directly support the Core Condition exactly. Even if attitudinal reasons exist, it does not follow that they are all the reasons there are. If there are reasons of other sorts, the Core Condition is not true in general, because the Quick Objection will apply to those reasons.

Nevertheless, the Core Condition might be true if it was limited to attitudinal reasons only. That is, it might be true that:

Limited Core Condition. Necessarily, if you are rational, you *F* whenever your attitudinal reasons require you to *F*.

Entailment and Equivalence might be true if they were similarly limited:

Limited Entailment. Necessarily, if you are rational, you respond correctly to attitudinal reasons.

Limited Equivalence. Necessarily, you are rational if and only if you respond correctly to attitudinal reasons.

Rationality might be equivalent to responding correctly to attitudinal reasons. So attitudinal reasons offer a limited defence of Equivalence.

Conflicting attitudinal reasons

I now set out to demolish this defence. On pages 81–2, I shall argue that there are no attitudinal reasons. But since that conclusion is controversial, I shall first argue that Limited Equivalence is false even if attitudinal reasons exist. I said it *might* be true if attitudinal reasons exist; now I shall show that actually it is not.

At this point I shall make no objection to Limited Entailment.[8] I shall object to the converse factor in Limited Equivalence, which is:

Limited sufficiency of reasons: Necessarily, if you respond correctly to attitudinal reasons, you are rational.

My argument starts by recognizing that your attitudinal reasons may oppose each other; you may have an attitudinal reason to *F* and an attitudinal reason not to *F*. I shall give an example soon. When your reasons are opposed, you respond correctly to them so long as you do not go against the balance of reasons. Inevitably, even if you respond correctly in this way, you will act in a way that one or other of your attitudinal reasons opposes. But I explained on page 77 that, if you act in a way that is opposed by an attitudinal reason, inevitably you are not rational. So, although you respond correctly to your attitudinal reasons, you are not rational. Therefore rationality is not equivalent to responding correctly to attitudinal reasons.

Here is the argument more briefly. To be rational, you have to satisfy particular, rigid conditions of rationality. But responding correctly to reasons is not a good method of satisfying rigid conditions. Reasons can oppose each other, so responding correctly to them cannot guarantee that you satisfy any particular condition of rationality.

Example

I shall explain this point in detail, using an example. Unfortunately, it will prove complicated to work all the way through. You may feel you can skip this detailed argument.

Suppose you intend to G, and you believe that your Hing is a means implied by your Ging. According to $R4$ on page 76, this intention and belief together constitute an attitudinal reason for you to intend to H. But suppose also that you intend not to H. According to $R2$ on page 76, this intention constitutes an attitudinal reason for you not to intend to H. So you have an attitudinal reason to intend to H and another not to intend to H.

To respond correctly to your attitudinal reasons in this case, you must go with the balance of them. Let us say that the balance is in favour of your not intending to H. Then you respond correctly to your attitudinal reasons if you do not intend to H. Suppose that indeed you do not intend to H. Then $C4$ on page 76 tells us you are not rational, because you intend to G and you believe your Hing is a means implied by your Ging, but you do not intend to H. So you respond correctly to your attitudinal reasons but you are not rational. Therefore, rationality is not equivalent to responding correctly to attitudinal reasons.

That is only the beginning of the argument. It shows that you can respond correctly to your attitudinal reasons to F and not to F and yet not be rational. But the conclusion we need in order to reject Limited Sufficiency of Reasons is that you can respond correctly to *all* your attitudinal reasons together and yet not be rational. Implicitly I assumed you are responding correctly to all your other ones, but that might be impossible. The argument requires two of your attitudinal reasons to be opposed, which the example shows is possible. But suppose it is possible only if you fail to respond correctly to some other attitudinal reason. Then, even if you respond correctly to the two particular opposing reasons, you do not respond correctly to all your attitudinal reasons together.

So a reply to the argument so far is to claim that your attitudinal reasons are linked together in such a way that no two of them can be opposed unless you fail to respond correctly to some other one of them. Call this 'the network theory'.

Is it true? I think not. So far as I can see, every one of your attitudinal reasons might be opposed by another. Then, when you respond correctly to all your attitudinal reasons, you will inevitably fail to satisfy some of them. Because each one imposes strict liability, that means you are not rational.

I can illustrate with the same example. The two attitudinal reasons I mentioned are opposed. According to the network theory, therefore, you must have some other attitudinal reason that you do not respond correctly to – one that I have not yet mentioned. An obvious candidate is this: your intention to G and your belief that your Hing is a means implied by your Ging, might together constitute a reason for you not to intend not to H. Since you do intend not to H, you are apparently not responding correctly to this reason.

But actually you may be responding correctly. This reason not to intend not to H may be opposed by another attitudinal reason. For instance, suppose you believe you ought not to H, and this belief constitutes a reason for you to intend not to H. Then the balance of reasons might favour your intending not to H, so you are responding correctly to these reasons too.

According to the network theory, then, there must be yet another attitudinal reason that you are not responding correctly to. Perhaps it is this: your belief that you ought not to H and your belief that your Hing is a means implied by your Ging might together constitute a reason for you not to intend to G. Since you do intend to G, you are apparently not responding correctly to this reason.

But again, actually you may be responding correctly. This reason not to intend to G may be opposed by another attitudinal reason. Perhaps it is opposed by a belief that you ought to G. And so on. So far as I can see, every one of your attitudinal reasons might be opposed by another.

I conclude that Limited Sufficiency of Reasons, and consequently Limited Equivalence, are false.

There are no attitudinal reasons

The example shows how responding correctly to attitudinal reasons does not guarantee rationality. A reason can be outweighed, so you may respond correctly to reasons without satisfying each reason. But to be rational you must satisfy each requirement of rationality. As I put it, reasons are slack, whereas requirements of rationality are rigid.

This removes the appeal of attitudinal reasons. Why should we think there are such things? They seem at first to underlie rationality, but they do not do so successfully. Moreover, there is a good argument for thinking there are none.

To be sure, your attitudes may constitute reasons for you. If you believe the World Trade Center was demolished by the CIA, your belief may be a

reason for you to change the web sites you read. But attitudes do not constitute reasons that correspond to conditions of rationality in the way I have
described.

Here is why. Take *R3* on page 76 as an example. For '*p*' substitute 'Carbon
dioxide is poisonous' and for '*q*' 'Emissions of carbon dioxide are harmful'.
There are various pieces of evidence for the proposition *q*, and others against
it. Each of these pieces of evidence constitutes a *pro tanto* reason either for or
against believing *q*. Just for the sake of argument, let us assume that the evidence falls just short of being conclusive, so, by a small margin, these evidential
reasons do not require you to believe emissions of carbon dioxide are harmful.

Now suppose there is no evidence for the proposition *p*, that carbon dioxide
is poisonous, but nevertheless you believe it. Suppose you also believe that if
p then *q* – that, if carbon dioxide is poisonous, emissions of it are harmful.
According to *R3*, these beliefs of yours constitute a reason to believe *q*. Since
the evidential reasons fall just short of requiring you to believe *q*, we may
assume this attitudinal reason tips the balance. Therefore all your reasons
together require you to believe emissions of carbon dioxide are harmful.

That is not credible. Your evidential reasons do not require you to believe
emissions of carbon dioxide are harmful, and it is not credible that your beliefs
could add to these reasons. You cannot, by means of your beliefs, bootstrap
a new reason into existence, to add to the evidence.

I can reinforce the example. *R3* entails that, if you believe *p* and you believe
that if *p* then *p*, these beliefs constitute a reason for you to believe *p*. That
cannot be so. We can take it for granted that you believe the tautology that
if *p* then *p*. Given that, *R3* entails that believing a proposition gives you a
reason to believe it. Any belief you have gives you a reason to have it. That
cannot be so; it would be absurd bootstrapping.[9]

I conclude *R3* is false. Similar bootstrapping arguments will work against
the other putative attitudinal reasons. For instance, intending to do something
does not create a reason to do it, to add to whatever other reasons there are
for doing it or not doing it. This argument is made on page 184. I conclude
there are no attitudinal reasons.

It follows that Limited Equivalence, Limited Entailment and the Limited
Core Condition are all empty. The Quick Objection to the Core Condition
emerges undefeated.

5.4   Sufficiency of reasons

The Quick Objection is an objection to Entailment. The other factor of
Equivalence, set out on page 72, also deserves attention. It is:

Sufficiency of reasons. Necessarily, if your respond correctly to reasons you are rational.

I rejected Limited Sufficiency of Reasons on page 81. But despite the terminology, Sufficiency of Reasons is a weaker claim. I have not yet given any reason to doubt it.

Reasons of rationality

It would be true if your reasons require you to satisfy each condition of rationality – if your reasons require you not to have contradictory beliefs, to believe what follows by modus ponens from things you believe, and so on. Sufficiency of reasons would follow.

But why might your reasons require you to satisfy each condition of rationality? It might be because rationality is itself normative. When *F*ing is a necessary condition of rationality, the fact that *F*ing is a necessary condition of rationality might itself constitute a reason for you to *F*. In chapter 11 I shall consider whether this is indeed so. I shall not produce a satisfactory argument to show it is, but I nevertheless find it plausible.

If rationality is normative, that means you have a reason to satisfy each condition of rationality. Call each of these reasons a 'reason of rationality'. Even if there are reasons of rationality, it does not follow that your reasons require you to satisfy each condition of rationality. You might also have a reason not to satisfy some particular condition of rationality, and that reason might not be outweighed by your reason of rationality to satisfy it. For instance, there might be a large benefit to be gained by having a pair of contradictory intentions, whereas having this particular pair might be a minor infringement of rationality. In that case, your reasons will not require you not to have this pair of contradictory intentions. You might then respond correctly to all your reasons, and yet not be rational, because you will have a pair of contradictory intentions. So even if there are reasons of rationality, they are not enough to make Sufficiency of Reasons true.

The further reason I called on in this example – the benefit of having a pair of contradictory beliefs – is 'state-given'. I take this term from Derek Parfit, who contrasts state-given reasons with object-given ones. My meaning is not quite the same as Parfit's.[10] A state-given reason to be in a particular state is one that derives from the properties of the state itself, whereas an object-given reason derives from the properties of the state's object or content. The benefit of having contradictory beliefs is a feature of the state of having contradictory beliefs, rather than a feature of the beliefs' contents. Some philosophers deny that state-given reasons exist. But reasons of rationality are themselves state-given, so if there are no state-given reasons there are no reasons of rationality, and this whole case for Sufficiency of Reasons will fail.

Rationality through worldly reasons

In any case, philosophers who support Sufficiency of Reasons do not usually do so on grounds of the normativity of rationality, and they do not rely on reasons of rationality. Instead, they think that your mind will be automatically coherent internally if it is properly adjusted to the world.

Facts about the world constitute reasons to have some particular attitudes. For instance, the fact that there is evidence for p is a reason to believe p, and the fact that you ought to F is a reason to intend to F. We might call these 'worldly reasons'. The only reasons excluded from this category are reasons of rationality; attitudinal reasons, if they exist, count as worldly reasons.[11] All the reasons I shall mention in the rest of this section are worldly ones, and I shall not usually bother to add the adverb 'worldly'.

Some philosophers think that, if you have all the attitudes your worldly reasons require you to have, and none of the attitudes they require you not to have, this is enough to ensure you satisfy all the conditions of rationality. Support for this idea can be found in Joseph Raz's 'The myth of instrumental rationality' and in several of Niko Kolodny's writings.[12] I shall draw on Kolodny's arguments, but I do not mean to imply that either of these authors would support Sufficiency of Reasons, or any particular condition of rationality such as C1–C4.

This idea is implausible at first sight. You may have reasons of various sorts to have or not have particular attitudes. Many of them seem unconnected with rationality. It would be surprising if they necessarily conspired together to ensure that, if you have or do not have all the attitudes your reasons require you to have or not have, you would turn out to satisfy all the requirements of rationality. It seems that on some occasions you might even have strong reasons not to be rational. For one thing, irrationality can make you impervious to threats.[13]

One way of responding to this problem is to make specific assumptions about the nature and working of reasons, to ensure they do imply rationality. For beliefs, this strategy can be made to work reasonably well. For example, it can support the claim C1 that, necessarily, you are not rational if you have contradictory beliefs. It may plausibly be argued that, if you have a pair of contradictory beliefs, at least one of them must be a belief that those reasons require you not to have. This argument is made by Niko Kolodny in 'How does coherence matter?'.

Kolodny claims that, for any proposition, either your reasons require you not to believe it, or they require you not to believe its negation. As I shall put it: there are no optional pairs of beliefs. This claim can be given an evidentialist defence.

Evidentialism is the view that all reasons for belief are constituted by evidence. Let us add to this the further plausible assumption that these reasons work as follows. Evidence has weight. Let us assume that whenever the evidence for a proposition does not outweigh the evidence for its negation, your reasons require you not to believe the proposition. This will be so when the evidence for the proposition is less weighty than the evidence for its negation, or equally as weighty as the evidence for its negation, or incommensurate with the evidence for its negation. In all these cases, we assume that your reasons require you not to believe the proposition, and this seems very plausible.

It follows from this assumption that, if your reasons permit you to believe a proposition, the evidence for it must outweigh the evidence for its negation. It then further follows that your reasons require you not to believe its negation. So if your reasons permit you to believe a proposition, they require you not to believe its negation. There are therefore no optional pairs of beliefs.

This evidentialist argument can be made consistent with the weighing model of *pro tanto* reasons described in section 4.3. We have only to assume that, for any proposition, there is a standing reason not to believe it, and this reason has some weight. Your reasons together will require you to believe the proposition if and only if your reason to believe it, constituted by the evidence for it, outweighs the reason for you not to believe it constituted by the evidence against it, together with the standing reason not to believe it.

Against this argument, a case could be made for thinking that there are some optional pairs of beliefs. For instance, this might be so if evidentialism is false, and not all reasons to believe are constituted by evidence. Suppose faith rather than evidence is a reason to believe a particular religious proposition. Then, it might be permissible to believe this proposition and also permissible to believe its negation. Yet even then it would not be rational to believe the proposition and also believe its negation. This fact cannot be explained by Kolodny's argument.

In any case, the claim that there are no optional pairs of beliefs is strong compared with the claim C1 that you are necessarily not rational if you have contradictory beliefs. It seems a pity to take on such a strong commitment for the sake of such a relatively weak result.

Nevertheless I recognize the argument as reasonably convincing for the case of contradictory beliefs. But whereas it is reasonably plausible that there are no optional pairs of beliefs, it is not at all plausible that there are no optional pairs of intentions. Your intentions are not tightly constrained by your reasons.

Often these reasons leave you free to intend something or alternatively to have the opposite intention. So no similar argument will support the claim C2, that, necessarily, you are not rational if you have contradictory intentions.

Suppose you are going on holiday. Your reasons do not require you to take your binoculars with you, and they do not require you not to; suppose the benefits of having binoculars with you are incommensurate with the pain of having to carry them. Consequently, you reasons do not require you to intend to take your binoculars, and they do not require you to intend not to.

Suppose that actually you have both intentions. This is possible.[14] Each intention is a complex disposition, and those dispositions can coexist. Each might already have been partially manifested in your actions. You might already have retrieved your binoculars from behind the golf-clubs, ready for taking them. But you might also have planned to take some extra clothing in your suitcase, seeing as you will not have the weight of your binoculars.

Having these contradictory intentions is not rational, just as it is not rational to have contradictory beliefs. You could not be fully rational whilst possessing contradictory intentions; this is the claim contained in C2 on page 76. I admit that I have little more than intuition to support this claim,[15] but nevertheless I take it to be plainly true. In 'The myth of practical consistency', Niko Kolodny recommends us to abandon it, but that seems to me a desperate measure.

Yet having both intentions is not contrary to your worldly reasons. (It is of course contrary to a reason of rationality if there are such things.) Your worldly reasons do not require you not to intend to take your binoculars, and nor do they require you not to intend not to take them.

You might think they require you not to have both intentions together, because having both may lead you to take some actions that will inevitably be wasted. In my example, you have already taken some actions. But it is not necessarily true that they are wasted. Even if you do not take your binoculars on holiday, it may nevertheless have been beneficial to get them out from behind the golf-clubs, because they are now more quickly available for identifying passing birds. And your planning to take extra clothing may have reminded you to take some things that you actually need. We may assume that one or the other of your contradictory intentions will evaporate before any harmful effects result. So having both of them is actually beneficial.

What about attitudinal reasons, which are worldly reasons as I defined them? According to R1 on page 76, your intention to take the binoculars is an attitudinal reason not to intend not to take them. I denied on page 82 that attitudinal reasons exist, but suppose for a moment that they do. The case for Sufficiency of Reasons cannot rest entirely on attitudinal reasons, because I have already argued in section 5.3 that Sufficiency of Attitudinal Reasons is false. You may have all the attitudes your attitudinal reasons require you to have, and none of the attitudes your attitudinal reasons require you not to have, and yet fail to satisfy some conditions of rationality.

In this example there are no other worldly reasons to support the case for Sufficiency of Reasons. The case would have to rest entirely on attitudinal reasons, which it cannot do.

Similar arguments apply to other practical conditions of rationality,[16] such as the instrumental condition C4. You cannot be fully rational if you do not intend a means that you believe is implied by an end you intend, even if you have no worldly reason to intend either the end or the means. In general, conditions of rationality apply to your attitudes, whether or not your reasons require you to have those attitudes. I conclude that Sufficiency of Reasons is false.

Notes

1   For instance, Niko Kolodny hopes to reduce rationality to responding correctly to reasons you believe there to be. This project is implicit in his 'Why be rational?' and explicit in his 'Why be disposed to be coherent?'.

2   See p. 128.

3   My thanks to Wlodek Rabinowicz for help here.

4   Selim Berker pointed out to me that a further condition may be necessary. Suppose your reasons do not require you to F and do not require you not to F. Suppose you F, and you would have Fed even if your reasons had required you not to. Then perhaps you are not responding correctly to reasons.

5   See the discussion in section 9.3.

6   Kolodny, 'How does coherence matter?'.

7   For instance, Tyler Burge in 'Reason and the first person'.

8   Thanks to Julia Markovits for making me realize this.

9   Thomas Nagel and Leon Leontyev independently pointed out to me that believing p may constitute indirect evidence of p; you would probably not believe p if you have no evidence for it. I take it this means believing p at one time may be a reason to believe p at a later time. But I do not think it means that believing p at one time is a reason for believing it at that time.

10 Parfit, *On What Matters*, p. 50. Parfit uses the term only for reasons that derive specifically from the goodness of the state itself.

11 See Niko Kolodny, 'The myth of practical consistency'.

12 Including his 'How does coherence matter?' and 'The myth of practical consistency'.

13 Examples appear in Derek Parfit's *Reasons and Persons*, pp. 12–13.

14 There is a discussion of the possibility of contradictory intentions on p. 156.

15 See section 9.1.

16 In section 4 of 'Rationality, normativity and commitment', Jacob Ross provides some very nice arguments against Sufficiency of Reasons. However, they assume conditions of rationality that are stronger than C1–C4, and that I hesitate to commit myself to.

6

Responding to Reason-Beliefs

6.1 The Enkratic Condition

Many philosophers accept the Quick Objection presented in section 5.2. It leads them to abandon the view that rationality consists in responding correctly to reasons. Instead they adopt a modified view. They think that rationality consists in responding correctly to your beliefs about reasons, or to reasons you believe there to be, or to what you see as reasons, or something of that sort. Can we find a modified view that is true? That is the question for this chapter.

I shall investigate in turn three alternative modifications to Entailment, which is set out on page 72. Each can be understood to claim that:

> *Belief Entailment.* Necessarily, if you are rational, you respond correctly to your reason-beliefs.

That is to say, rationality entails responding correctly to your reason-beliefs. The term 'reason-belief' is just a place-holder. Each alternative modification interprets the expression 'respond correctly to your reason-beliefs' differently. I shall accept Belief Entailment under some interpretations. But I shall not, under any interpretation, accept the stronger principle:

> *Belief Equivalence.* Necessarily, you are rational if and only if you respond correctly to your reason-beliefs.

Let us start with the Core Condition set out on page 74. An easy modification of it takes us to:

> *Direct Enkratic Condition.* Necessarily, if you are rational, you F whenever you believe your reasons require you to F.

This cannot be generally true, for the following reason. Suppose you believe your reasons require you to F, and you intend to F, but you are prevented from Fing by something outside your mind. You may be rational. For instance, suppose you believe your reasons require you to buy a ticket to Svolvaer, and you intend to do so, and you do all the right things to get one, but the travel agent makes a mistake and you end up buying a ticket to Svarlbard instead. You fail to do what you believe your reasons require you to do, but you might nevertheless be rational.

This is an application of the principle that rationality supervenes on the mind, as I shall put it.[1] If your mind has the same intrinsic properties (apart from the property of rationality) in one situation as it has in another, then you are rational in one to the same degree as you are rational in the other. It seems to be a conceptual feature of rationality that it depends only on the mind. I take it for granted.

If the travel agent had acted correctly and your mind had been just the same, you would have bought a ticket to Svolvaer. In that case, we may presume you would have been rational, since buying a ticket to Svolvaer is what you believe your reasons require you to do. Given the agent's actual behaviour, you buy a ticket to Svalbard. But the agent's behaviour cannot affect your rationality. Since your mind is the same in either case, you are rational in the original case too.

The consequence is that the Direct Enkratic Condition cannot be true unless the properties of your mind fully determine whether or not you F. It cannot be true if Fing is a bodily act, or a state such as living in Australia.

It might nevertheless be true in important cases. I shall come back to those in section 6.2. But to arrive at a general condition that can accommodate cases where your Fing is not determined by the properties of your mind, we need to modify the Core Condition some more. We can make it:

> *Enkratic Condition.* Necessarily, if you are rational, you intend to F whenever you believe your reasons require you to F.

This condition encounters no objection from the supervenience of rationality on the mind. True, when you believe your reasons require you to F, some external force may prevent you from intending to F, just as an external force may prevent you from Fing. For instance, a psychologist might have wired your brain so as to prevent you from intending to F. But then the external force has affected your rationality; the psychologist prevents you from being entirely rational. So this is not an objection to the Enkratic Condition.

I accept the Enkratic Condition. It follows from the principle of Enkrasia, which I adopted as far back as page 22. A rough version of it, expressed in this chapter's terminology, is:

> *Enkrasia, very roughly.* Rationality requires of you that, if you believe your reasons require you to F, you intend to F.

An accurate statement of Enkrasia appears on page 170. The Enkratic Condition is correspondingly roughly formulated; an accurate version may be derived from the accurate formulation of Enkrasia. But although the formulation above is only approximately true, it is good enough for this chapter. Enkrasia is a stronger claim than the Enkratic Condition. I shall explain the difference in chapter 7.

So I accept the Enkratic Condition. For the sake of argument, I am willing to strengthen it by adding an explanatory or counterfactual clause. We get:

> *Strengthened Enkratic Condition.* Necessarily, if you are rational then, whenever you believe your reasons require you to F, you intend to F and an appropriate explanatory or counterfactual connection holds between your belief and your intending to F.

This condition constitutes an interpretation of Belief Entailment on page 88. We have only to interpret 'you respond correctly to your reason-beliefs' to mean that, whenever you believe your reasons require you to F, you intend to F and an appropriate explanatory or counterfactual connection holds between your belief and your intending to F.

In this chapter, I am looking for what truth lies in the view that rationality consists in responding correctly to reason-beliefs. I have found that one part of this view, or more accurately an interpretation of one part of it, is true. Specifically, in the Strengthened Enkratic Condition, I have found a way to interpret Belief Entailment that makes it true. Rationality entails responding correctly to your reason-beliefs.

But that is as far as I can go. Rationality is not equivalent to responding correctly to your reason-beliefs. Many other conditions are necessary for rationality. I listed a few on page 76. To be rational, you must not have contradictory beliefs, you must intend what you believe is a means implied by an end that you intend, and so on. Chapter 9 lists many requirements of rationality, and each one entails a necessary condition for rationality. You may satisfy the Enkratic Condition without satisfying any of the others.

Furthermore, the Enkratic Condition is not even a very central part of rationality. The centre of rationality is such things as avoiding contradictory beliefs and intentions. Indeed, the Enkratic Condition is in some ways so different from those central conditions that a case can be made for thinking it is not a condition of rationality at all. I shall respond to that case on pages 173–4.

We have fallen far short of Belief Equivalence. But the argument is not yet finished. The next section continues to explore the connection between rationality and beliefs about reasons.

6.2   Meeting your own standards

At the end of section 6.1 I insisted that many other conditions are necessary for rationality besides the Enkratic Condition. That was my basis for rejecting Belief Equivalence. I earlier listed some of these conditions on page 76. However, I have no basis for them apart from intuition. I admitted that the formulation of some is only approximate. Moreover, there is a general reason to doubt conditions of this sort.

Take the claim that, necessarily, if you are rational you do not have contradictory beliefs. Dialetheists see nothing wrong with having some pairs of contradictory beliefs, because they believe that some contradictions are true.[2] They believe some propositions (such as the Liar) are special, in that both they and their negations are true. They have serious arguments to support their position. If a dialetheist believes p and believes not p, is she necessarily not rational? Plausibly not. Even if dialetheism is false, we might not think it irrational to believe it. And if you do believe it, plausibly you might rationally have particular beliefs that conform to it.

This suggests we might weaken the condition against contradictory beliefs. For example, we might make it:

Necessarily, if you are rational, you do not believe p and believe not p, unless you believe p is special.

To state this formula properly, 'special' would have to be defined. I would be happy to accept some weakened formula such as this.

But the example of dialetheists may suggest a more radical alteration to what I have been saying. Conditions of rationality such as the ones I mentioned on page 76 all impose strict liability in the sense I adopted in section 5.3. Each asserts that you are not rational if you fail to meet some condition, and this is so whatever your own beliefs are about the matter. It makes no difference whether or not you believe your reasons require you to meet the condition, or what you believe about the rationality of meeting it. In view of the example of dialetheists, this sort of strict liability may seem too unforgiving. We might look for more liberal conditions of rationality.

As an alternative to strict liability, we might think of rationality as meeting your own standards, so that you are not rational only if you fail by your own lights. The Direct Enkratic Condition on page 88 offers a way to capture this thought. I explained on page 89 that this condition is not universally true, because it is inconsistent with the supervenience of rationality on the mind. But we may restrict the range of verb phrases that can be substituted for '*F*' to ones that describe a particular state of mind. For instance, *F*ing might be intending to go to Venice, or not having contradictory beliefs. We get:

> *Restricted Direct Enkratic Condition.* When *F*ing is being in a particular state of mind, necessarily, if you are rational, you *F* whenever you believe your reasons require you to *F*.[3]

This restricted condition is consistent with the supervenience of rationality on the mind. It constitutes another interpretation of Belief Entailment, different from the one on page 90. We have only to interpret responding correctly to your reason-beliefs as *F*ing whenever you believe your reasons require you to *F*. (We would get a better interpretation if we strengthened the condition by adding an explanatory or counterfactual clause. That could easily be done, but for convenience in this section I shall suppress that clause.)

I shall treat *F*ing whenever you believe your reasons require you to *F* as also an interpretation of meeting your own standards. So for this section only, responding correctly to your reason-beliefs is just the same as meeting your own standards. The Restricted Direct Enkratic Condition is a way of saying both that rationality entails meeting your own standards and that rationality entails responding correctly to reasons.

In this section, I shall generally omit the word 'restricted'; I tacitly maintain the restriction to states of mind throughout the section.

One instance of the Direct Enkratic Condition is: necessarily, if you are rational, you do not have contradictory beliefs if you believe your reasons require you not to have contradictory beliefs. Another is: necessarily, if you are rational, you intend what you believe is necessary to an end that you intend, if you believe your reasons require you to intend what you believe is necessary to an end that you intend. And so on. The Direct Enkratic Condition gives us a liberal version of each of the conditions of rationality that I have mentioned. It tells us that, to be rational you must satisfy each of these conditions, provided that you yourself believe your reasons require you to satisfy it. For another example, it gives us this liberal version of the Enkratic Condition: necessarily, if you are rational, you intend to do what you believe your reasons require you to do, if you believe your reasons require you to intend to do what you believe your reasons require you to do.

Once we notice this consequence of the Direct Enkratic Condition, we might decide to give up all the separate conditions of rationality. We might replace each of them with the Direct Enkratic Condition on its own, which gives us a liberal version of each.

If all the conditions of rationality could be replaced by just this one, the result would be that:

> When F ing is being in a particular state of mind, necessarily, you are rational if and only if you F whenever you believe your reasons require you to F.

That is to say, rationality would be equivalent to meeting your own standards, and to responding correctly to your reason-beliefs. Belief Equivalence would be true.

However, this does not give us a successful argument for Belief Equivalence, for two reasons. First, even if the Direct Enkratic Condition were true, it could not replace all the other conditions of rationality. Second, the Direct Enkratic Condition is not true. I shall make these two points in turn.

First objection

Let us suppose for a moment that the Direct Enkratic Condition is true. I shall explain why it cannot replace all the other conditions of rationality.

Each of these other conditions asserts strict liability: that you are not rational if you do not conform to it, whatever you believe about the conditions themselves. Replacing each with the Direct Enkratic Condition removes strict liability. Whether or not you are rational depends on your own beliefs about conditions of rationality. Your rationality is judged by your own standards.

That is a nice liberal thought. But however liberal we wish to be, your rationality cannot be judged entirely by your own standards. The Direct Enkratic Condition itself asserts strict liability. If you believe your reasons require you to F but you do not F, this condition asserts you are not rational. It asserts this whether or not you believe your reasons require of you that, if you believe your reasons require you to F, you F.

So some strict liability is inevitable. Given that, we have no strong liberal motive to confine it to the Direct Enkratic Condition alone. And in any case, it is not really credible that all the particular conditions of rationality can be replaced by this one. For example, there is obviously something irrational about a person who does not intend a means she believes is necessary to an end she intends, even if she herself does not believe her reasons require her to intend a means she believes is necessary to an end she intends.

Rationality cannot be equivalent to meeting your own standards, because some people's standards are more in accordance with rationality than other people's are.

Objection to the Direct Enkratic Condition

I explained on page 89 that the unrestricted version of the Direct Enkratic Condition is false because it is inconsistent with the supervenience of rationality on the mind. The following two examples show that even the restricted version is false.

The first is built from Gregory Kavka's famous toxin puzzle.[4] You have been offered a very large prize for intending to drink a toxin at noon tomorrow. The prize is for having this intention now; to win, you need not actually drink the toxin tomorrow. Drinking it would be horrible. You believe your reasons require you to intend to drink the toxin, because that is the way to win the prize. But you do not intend to drink it. According to the Direct Enkratic Condition, you are not rational. But that is not necessarily so.

Suppose you believe that, whatever your intention now may be, you will not actually drink the toxin. You believe that, at noon tomorrow, you will realize nothing is to be gained by drinking it and, since doing so would be horrible, you will not drink it. Suppose this belief prevents you from intending to drink the toxin; believing you will not do something normally prevents you from intending to do it. That is why you do not now intend to drink the toxin. It is intuitively clear you might nevertheless be rational.

The second example is this. Suppose you do not believe God exists, but you believe your reasons require you to believe he does exist. According to the Direct Enkratic Condition, you are not rational. But that is not necessarily so.

Suppose you do not believe God exists because you believe on evidential grounds that he does not exist: you believe that, if God existed, the world would not be as bad as it is. Suppose, indeed, that you are unable to believe God exists. Nothing you could do – going regularly to church, or taking a course of religious instruction, or anything else – would bring you to believe he exists. However, you believe your reasons require you to believe God exists, on grounds of personal safety. You believe it is a good idea to believe he exists, just in case he does. Again, it is intuitively clear you might nevertheless be rational.

In each of these examples, you have a belief that is arguably false: in the one case, your belief that the reasons require you to intend to drink the toxin; in the other, your belief that the reasons require you to believe God exists. Two separate arguments can be raised against the truth of each of these beliefs.

One comes from the principle that ought implies can. As I told the stories, you cannot intend to drink the toxin, and you cannot believe God exists. If ought implies can, it follows that it is not the case that your reasons require you to intend to drink the toxin, and not the case that your reasons require you to believe God exists. So your belief is false in either case. Still, even if it is true that ought implies can in this context, you might rationally believe the opposite. Even if your belief is false, it might be rational.

The second argument is founded on the claim that there are no state-given reasons for intentions or beliefs. In the first example, the reason you believe you have for intending to drink the toxin is that having this intention will win you the prize. This is a merit of the state of intention, not a merit of the intention's object, which is drinking the toxin. So it is a state-given reason. In the second example, the reason you believe you have for believing God exists is that it would be safest to have this belief. This is a merit of the state of belief, not a feature of the belief's object, which is the proposition that God exists. So again, this is a state-given reason.

Derek Parfit denies there are state-given reasons for beliefs,[5] and his arguments would apply also to intentions. If he is right, your belief is false in each example. But even if he is right, you might rationally take a different view. Your belief may be false, but you might rationally hold it.

I conclude from the examples that the restricted version of the Direct Enkratic Condition is false. It can fail when you believe you have state-given reasons to have an intention or a belief.

What attraction does the Direct Enkratic Condition have in the first place? Why should we think you are necessarily not rational if you are not in a mental state that you believe your reasons require you to be in? Plausibly, you would indeed not be rational if your mental states were under your control. If you believe your reasons require you to be in a mental state, and you are able to put yourself in that state, then plausibly you are not rational if you do not do so. But actually many of your mental states, including many of your intentional attitudes, are not under your control. So the Direct Enkratic Condition is not attractive in that way.

We might be inclined to believe it even so. We might think a rational person simply has a psychological disposition to be in a mental state whenever she believes her reasons require her to be in it. Her disposition must be maintained by some causal process, but it need not be under her control. It could be an automatic process, but one that takes place in any rational person.[6]

The examples show this is not credible. In one of them, you believe you will not drink the toxin but you believe your reasons require you to intend to drink it. Given those beliefs of yours, no automatic process will cause you to intend to drink the toxin, however rational you may be. Indeed, an automatic process will prevent you from intending it: you cannot intend what you believe you will not do. In the other example, you believe that, if God existed, the world would not be as bad as it is, but you believe your reasons require you to believe God exists. No automatic process will cause you to believe God exists. Indeed, an automatic process is likely to prevent you from believing it; if you are rational, automatic processes tend to make your beliefs follow the evidence as you see it. In general, if you are rational, those automatic processes you are subject to normally follow your beliefs about the objects of your attitudes. They do not follow your beliefs about the attitudes themselves.

So we have to reject the Direct Enkratic Condition, even restricted to mental states. Its apparent attraction is spurious, and the counterexamples show it is false.

Scanlon's condition

It is easy to adjust the Direct Enkratic Condition to avoid the counterexamples. The condition ran into trouble over state-given reasons, so we must limit it to object-given reasons. We get:

> *Scanlon's Condition.* When *F*ing is having a particular attitude, necessarily, if you are rational then, if you believe your object-given reasons require you to *F*, you *F*.

This is not T. M. Scanlon's own formulation, but I have taken the liberty of attaching his name to it because I think it approximates a view he presents in his paper 'Structural irrationality'. He says 'it seems clearly irrational to fail to have an attitude one explicitly judges oneself to have conclusive reasons for',[7] and he makes it clear that he is thinking of object-given reasons only.[8] As Scanlon does, I have restricted the formula to attitudes rather than mental states in general. Scanlon may not intend it to apply even to all attitudes, but he does intend it to apply at least to beliefs and intentions. I shall apply it to beliefs and intentions only.

Because Scanlon's Condition is limited to object-given reasons, it is not subject to the objection I raised against the Direct Enkratic Condition. For all I know, it may be true. If it is, by adding an explanatory or counterfactual condition, we can derive from it a version of Belief Entailment. Rationality entails responding correctly your to reason-beliefs where, in this case, we take 'you respond correctly to your reason-beliefs' to mean that, whenever you believe your object-given reasons require you to F, you F and an appropriate explanatory or counterfactual connection holds between your belief and your Fing. With some strain, we could also take this to be meeting your own standards, so we could maintain the equivalence between responding correctly to your reason-beliefs and meeting your own standards.

In any case, if it is true, Scanlon's Condition can add some support to the idea that rationality entails responding correctly to your reason-beliefs. However, the support it can add is slight. It may be true, but it has few applications. This means that, although it evades my objection to the Direct Enkratic Condition, it is much more subject to my first objection to this version of Belief Entailment: that there must be other conditions of rationality besides this one. The problem is that the antecedent in Scanlon's condition, that you believe your object-given reasons require you to F, is rarely satisfied. People rarely have beliefs of this sort.

One difficulty is that almost no one has the conceptual equipment that is needed for having such a belief. Almost no one has the concept of an *object-given reason*. That is a philosopher's construct. However, this difficulty can be overcome. Your object-given reasons for and against believing a proposition are nothing other than your evidence for and against the proposition. So if you have a belief about your evidence for and against p, it is a belief about your object-given reasons for and against believing p, even if you do not recognize it as such. If you believe that your evidence requires you to believe p, we may say that you believe your object-given reasons require you to believe p. We are entitled to say this because we may give 'believe' a sense that is suitably transparent to the concepts through which you grasp the subject-matter of your belief. So if you have this belief about your evidence, Scanlon's Condition applies to you.

No doubt you sometimes have beliefs of that sort. Scanlon's Condition does have some applications, therefore. But more commonly you believe simply that your evidence shows that p, rather than that it requires you to believe p. Your belief is not about the attitude of believing p, but about the object of this attitude, which is the proposition that p. Our beliefs connect our object-given reasons with the objects of our attitudes more commonly than they connect them with the attitudes themselves.

This is especially clearly so when the attitude in question is an intention rather than a belief. Let us see how Scanlon's Condition applies to an intention. Let it be the intention to G, so let us substitute 'intend to G' for 'F' in the condition. Object-given reasons for and against intending to G are reasons for and against Ging. So to satisfy the antecedent in Scanlon's condition you would need to believe that your reasons for and against Ging on balance require you to intend to G. But this would be a very peculiar belief to have. Much more probably, your belief will not be about intending to G but about the object of the intention, which is Ging. You will simply believe that your reasons for and against Ging on balance require you to G. In short, you will believe your reasons require you to G.

Take the toxin case again.[9] Suppose as before that you believe your reasons require you to intend to drink the toxin, because of the prize to be had. But suppose you believe that, in the matter of actually drinking the toxin, your reasons are on balance against it. Would you believe that your reasons for and against drinking the toxin on balance require you to intend not to drink the toxin? Probably not. This would be a difficult belief to hold on to, given your other belief that all your reasons together require you to intend to drink the toxin. Much more probably, you will simply believe that your reasons require you not to drink the toxin.

In 'Structural irrationality', Scanlon recognizes all this.[10] He recognizes that, since Scanlon's Condition has so few applications, there must be other conditions of rationality too. There must also be conditions that apply when you have beliefs about the objects of your attitudes, rather than about the attitudes themselves. For the particular cases of beliefs and intentions, these conditions will be something like:

> *Evidential Condition.* Necessarily, if you are rational then, if you believe your evidence shows that p, you believe p.
> *Enkratic Condition.* Necessarily, if you are rational then, if you believe your reasons require you to G, you intend to G.

Again, these are not Scanlon's formulations, but I think they represent his views approximately. The second is none other than the Enkratic Condition, which I accepted on page 90. I mentioned there that it is only roughly true, and Scanlon himself points out one of its inaccuracies.[11] An accurate version can be derived from my precise formulation of Enkrasia on page 170.

Besides these two, there remain all the other conditions of rationality mentioned on page 76 and in chapter 9. All these must be added to Scanlon's Condition.

This is as far as the idea of rationality as meeting your own standards can take us. It is not far. Through Scanlon's Condition, we have found it can give a little extra support to Belief Entailment. Under suitable interpretations, we may say that rationality entails meeting your own standards, and that it entails responding correctly to your reason-beliefs. However, because Scanlon's Condition is at best one condition of rationality among many, rationality is not equivalent to meeting your own standards, and nor is it equivalent to responding correctly to your reason-beliefs. We have found no support for Belief Equivalence.

Scanlon's argument

I doubt Scanlon himself would accept this bleak conclusion. He does accept that Scanlon's Condition is not the only condition of rationality. Nevertheless, in 'Structural irrationality' he still appears to think of rationality as meeting your own standards.[12]

For one thing, although he does not think Scanlon's Condition subsumes all the other conditions of rationality, he does evidently regard it as more fundamental than others. He thinks it needs little justification, whereas he takes trouble to justify the others. To support Scanlon's Condition, he says simply that 'it seems clearly irrational to fail to have an attitude one explicitly judges oneself to have conclusive reasons for'.[13] This sort of irrationality is failing to meet your own standards.

Second, Scanlon's way of justifying the Evidential and Enkratic Conditions is by showing they are instances of meeting your own standards. He takes failing to meet them to be failing by your own lights. Speaking of the Enkratic Condition, he says:

> For an agent, the force of the . . . normative links between an assessment of the reasons for doing A at t and a decision to do A at t lies in the incompatibility that the agent who violates these links must feel between her various normative attitudes.[14]

'Must feel' indicates the agent herself must be conscious of the incompatibility. And if you fail to satisfy the Evidential Condition, he says, your 'irrationality consists simply in the conscious holding of attitudes that are directly incompatible'.[15] Again, I think he means to say you are conscious of their incompatibility. So, although Scanlon does not claim that the Evidential and Enkratic Conditions are instances of Scanlon's Condition, he does claim they are instances of meeting your own standards in some different way.

I disagree with both these views. Even if Scanlon's Condition is true, I do not think it is more fundamental than other conditions of rationality. Scanlon finds it obvious, but I do not. It may indeed be 'clearly irrational to fail to have an attitude one explicitly judges oneself to have conclusive reasons for'. But that is not your position when you fail to satisfy Scanlon's Condition. The judgement of yours that figures in Scanlon's Condition is about your object-given reasons only, not about all your reasons. Take the toxin case again.[16] Suppose you judge that your object-given reasons require you not to intend to drink the toxin, but that all your reasons together require you to intend to drink it. Suppose you manage to intend to drink it, perhaps by employing a clever psychotherapist. This is not obviously irrational. I do not deny it is irrational, but I insist the question is debatable. Failing to satisfy Scanlon's Condition seems less obviously irrational to me than failing to satisfy the Enkratic Condition.

Nor do I think Scanlon succeeds in showing that the Evidential and Enkratic Conditions are instances of meeting your own standards. I shall concentrate on his argument for the Enkratic Condition. Scanlon starts by claiming that intending to do A – at least if you arrive at this intention by deciding to do A – involves 'tak[ing] one's doing A as something that can provide reason to do or not do other things'.[17] I disagree already. I do not think intending involves having any normative attitude. An intention is a disposition of a particular sort to do what is intended. You may intend to do something even if you think you have no reason to do it. True, an intention often includes a disposition to do some instrumental reasoning on the way to doing what you intend. But my account of instrumental reasoning in chapter 14 of this book shows that it need not involve any normative attitudes at all. Philosophers tend to impute too much normativity to the content of attitudes and reasoning. One purpose of this book is to resist that tendency.

Let that pass. The quotation on page 99 mentions an incompatibility that an agent who violates the Enkratic Condition must feel among her normative attitudes. We can now see what those allegedly incompatible attitudes are. The first is that the agent believes her object-given reasons require her to do A. The other is more accurately the lack of an attitude. It is that, since the agent does not intend to do A, she does not take her doing A as something that can provide reason to do or not do other things. These are not directly incompatible attitudes; they are not attitudes with contradictory contents, for instance. Indeed, any incompatibility they have must be very indirect, since the content of the first, possessed attitude is about reasons for doing A, and the content of the second, lacked attitude is about reasons to do things other than A. Failing to satisfy the Enkratic Condition already involves the incompatibility, such as it is, between believing your reasons require you to do A and not intending to do A. The incompatibility Scanlon identifies seems no more direct or pressing than that.

Scanlon thinks the agent must herself feel the incompatibility. But, given that the incompatibility is very indirect, I see no reason to think she must feel it, any more than she must already feel the incompatibility between believing her reasons require her to do A and not intending to do A. If she does not feel one, she need not feel the other. So Scanlon's argument has not advanced us towards the conclusion that she must feel an incompatibility among her attitudes. We cannot conclude that this agent fails to meet her own standards.

6.3   Responding correctly to P-beliefs

The Quick Objection shows that rationality is not equivalent to responding correctly to reasons. It led us to consider instead the modified idea that rationality is equivalent to responding correctly to your reason-beliefs. The Quick Objection does not tell us just what the content of those beliefs must be. Sections 6.1 and 6.2 considered one sort of content; now I come to a different sort.

Suppose, out walking, you come to believe there is a puddle on the path ahead. Your belief has a non-normative content. But suppose that, if there were a puddle on the path ahead, that fact would constitute a reason for you to stop. Then what you believe would, if true, be a reason for you to stop. This section is about beliefs whose content is a proposition that would, if true, be a reason.

I need a term to distinguish beliefs of this sort, and for lack of a good one, I shall arbitrarily call them 'P-beliefs'. I include P-beliefs under the heading of 'reason-beliefs'.

You can respond to P-beliefs. For instance, you can respond to your belief there is a puddle ahead by stopping. You may do so automatically: as soon as you acquire the belief that there is a puddle on the path head, you automatically stop. In doing this, you may not form any normative belief, such as the belief that you have a reason to stop. You might not even have the concept of *a reason*. Yet you could still respond to your belief that there is a puddle on the path ahead, by stopping.

Since you can respond to P-beliefs, we may ask whether rationality is equivalent to, or entails, responding correctly to them. Derek Parfit says:

> We are rational insofar as we respond well to reasons or apparent reasons. We have some *apparent* reason when we have beliefs about the relevant facts whose truth would give us that reason.[18]

I think he means to say that rationality entails responding correctly to P-beliefs.[19] This section considers whether that is so.

Suppose you believe there is a puddle on the path ahead, and you respond by stopping. Do you respond *correctly* to your belief? Probably not. If there is a puddle on the path ahead, that is one reason for you to stop. But probably you have other reasons either to stop or not to stop. Perhaps you need to get back home, or perhaps you are enjoying the exercise. These are all *pro tanto* reasons. All of them together determine whether or not your reasons require you to stop. There is therefore no such thing as responding correctly to just one of them. You can respond correctly only to all of them together; you do so by doing what all of them together require. Consequently, we could not count you as responding correctly to a P-belief in just one of the reasons.

Could you ever respond correctly to a P-belief? The puddle does not provide an example, but are there any examples? A P-belief in a *pro toto* reason might provide one. A *pro toto* reason for you to *F* makes it the case that your reasons require you to *F*.[20] Suppose you believe a proposition *p*, and suppose that *p*, if true, would be a *pro toto* reason for you to *F*. Then, if you *F* (and if an appropriate explanatory or counterfactual connection holds between your belief and your *F*ing), perhaps we could count you as responding correctly to your belief. Moreover, it might be the case that, necessarily, if you are rational, you do.

An example

Here is a plausible example of that sort. Suppose, gazing at the horizon at night, you believe you see a red light. What you believe is that you see a red light. Plausibly, if you do indeed see a red light, this would be a *pro toto* reason to believe you see a coloured light. Therefore, if you respond to your belief that you see a red light by also believing you see a coloured light, plausibly you are responding correctly to your belief that you see a red light.

Moreover, it is also plausible that, necessarily, if you are rational you respond correctly to this belief. Rationality entails responding correctly to it, that is to say. I do not assert this is true; only that it is plausible. I cannot think of any more convincing example. So for the sake of pursuing the argument further, I shall assume it is true.

If it is, it illustrates another sort of strict liability. You are not rational if you do not respond correctly to this P-belief, and this is so whatever your normative beliefs may be. Section 5.3 examined strict liability in responding to a reason. Here we have strict liability in responding to a P-belief.

This strict liability is possible only if it is consistent with the supervenience of rationality on the mind.[21] This will be so only if the reason you believe to exist – that you see a red light – is (if it exists), not just a *pro toto* reason, but necessarily a *pro toto* reason for you to believe you see a coloured light.[22] Rationality could not entail responding correctly to a P-belief whose content would, if true, be merely contingently a *pro toto* reason; that would be inconsistent with supervenience. So from here on in this section I shall deal only with reasons that are necessarily *pro toto*. I assume that, if you see a red light, that is necessarily a *pro toto* reason for you to believe you see a coloured light.

Strict liability raises a further question. The claim is that you are strictly liable for responding correctly to a P-belief, whatever your normative beliefs may be. But might you not also have a normative belief that imposes a conflicting liability? Is that a problem?

In the example, you have the P-belief that you see a red light. I said that, plausibly, you are not rational unless you believe you see a coloured light. But suppose you also have the normative belief that your reasons require you not to believe you see a coloured light. Suppose you believe you will be punished if you believe you see a coloured light. According to the Direct Enkratic Condition on page 88, you are not rational if you believe you see a coloured light. So according to that condition you are inevitably not rational, whether or not you believe you see a coloured light. Is that a problem?

No, because I rejected the Direct Enkratic Condition in section 6.2. Rationality does not require you to believe what you believe you ought to believe. It is true that I gave no grounds for rejecting the Direct Enkratic Condition except when it is applied to a normative belief in a state-given reason.[23] So this solution may not be generalizable. But it works for the example because in the example your normative belief is a belief in a state-given reason.

It therefore seems that we can accept strict liability for this example. Since a P-belief is a reason-belief, this means we can endorse this weaker, existential version of Belief Entailment on page 88:

> *Existential Belief Entailment.* There are some reason-beliefs such that, necessarily, if you are rational and you have one of these beliefs, you respond correctly to it.

Rationality entails responding correctly to these particular reason-beliefs.

Practical reasons

But so far we have just one, contrived example that satisfies Existential Belief Entailment. Moreover, it is concerned with belief rather than action. Let us call a P-belief 'practical' if its content would, if true, be a reason to do some non-mental act. Can we find an example of a practical P-belief that satisfies Existential Belief Entailment?

Before I try one out, I need to make an adjustment to the notion of responding correctly to a P-belief. Suppose you have a practical P-belief. Its content would, if true, be a reason to do some non-mental act. Then it could not be the case that, necessarily, if you are rational you do this act. That condition would violate the supervenience of rationality on the mind. You might fail to do the act because of some obstruction outside your mind, which has nothing to do with your rationality. So if we insist that, to respond correctly to a practical P-belief, you must act, Belief Entailment will inevitably be false.

I have already been through this argument on page 89. There it led me to adjust the notion of responding correctly to a normative belief; here I shall correspondingly adjust the notion of responding correctly to a P-belief. To respond correctly to a P-belief whose content would, if true, be a *pro toto* reason to do something, you must intend to do that thing. You do not have to do it.

We are looking for an example of a practical P-belief such that rationality entails responding correctly to it. Derek Parfit proposes one.[24] Suppose you are due to have an operation next Tuesday. However, you have the chance of changing your appointment to Wednesday. Anaesthetics will be available on Wednesday but not on Tuesday. So if you change your appointment, you will suffer only slight pain on Wednesday, but if you do not change it, you will suffer agony on Tuesday.

To this non-normative fact, let us add others such as: the surgeon will be just as careful on either day; you have nothing else to do on Wednesday; Tuesday is equally as real as any other day of the week; if the calendar had been designed differently, a different day would have been Tuesday; and so on. Take the big conjunction of all these non-normative facts. I shall assume that enough facts are included in this conjunction to ensure that it necessarily constitutes a *pro toto* reason for you to change your appointment to Wednesday. Necessarily, if this big conjunctive fact obtains, it makes it the case that your reasons require you to change your appointment.

Suppose you believe the big conjunction. What you believe would, if true, necessarily be a *pro toto* reason for you to change your appointment. To respond correctly to this belief would be to intend to change your appointment. Furthermore, Parfit argues you would necessarily not be rational if you had this belief and did not intend to change your appointment. So this appears to be an example of what we are looking for. You have a practical P-belief and, necessarily, you are not rational if you do not respond correctly to it.

This is another assertion of strict liability. You are not rational if you fail to respond to your P-belief, whatever your own beliefs may be about the normative situation. This time I am not convinced. In this practical case, strict liability may lead to a conflict that cannot be satisfactorily resolved.

Suppose you have a normative belief that conflicts with your P-belief. Suppose you believe that your reasons require you not to change your appointment. That might be because you have some false, bizarre normative theory according to which you should avoid pain on Wednesdays much more than on Tuesdays. Then the Enkratic Condition[25] entails that you are necessarily not rational unless you intend not to change your appointment. Strict liability implies you are necessarily not rational unless you intend to change your appointment. But if you have both intentions they contradict each other, which means you are necessarily not rational according to condition C2 on page 76.

This leaves us with four possibilities: the Enkratic Condition is false, or condition C2 is false, or you are indeed necessarily not rational, or strict liability is false in this case. I shall dismiss all but the last of these possibilities.

On page 103 I mentioned a similar objection in the example of the red light. There, the conflict between your normative belief and your P-belief was generated by the Direct Enkratic Condition. I solved it by rejecting that condition. In our present practical example, the conflict is generated by the Enkratic Condition. This condition is on firmer ground. It is entailed by Enkrasia, which is defended in section 9.5. I think we should accept it. Condition C2 – that you cannot be rational if you have contradictory intentions – also seems obviously true. That is the first two possibilities knocked out.

The next possibility is that you are necessarily not rational. Can you be rational while holding such a bizarre normative theory as you do? I think so. There is no logical inconsistency among your beliefs; your belief that your reasons require you not to change your appointment is not logically inconsistent with your non-normative belief in the big conjunction. Moreover, your belief in a bizarre normative theory may be supported by all the evidence you have. Perhaps you acquired it as you grew up, through testimony from people you justifiably trusted. We are not entitled to impugn your rationality just because you hold a bizarre normative theory. You are not necessarily not rational, then.

We are pushed to the only remaining possibility: that strict liability is false in this practical example. You may rationally not intend to change your appointment, despite your P-belief. The content of this belief would, if true, make it the case that your reasons require you to change your appointment. But that is only because of the normative facts, and you do not believe those normative facts. Instead, you have a normative belief that entails the opposite: that your reasons require you not to change your appointment. You may hold this belief rationally. Consequently, you may not intend to change your appointment, and yet be rational.

A parallel argument could be brought to bear on any practical P-belief: you may be rational even if you fail to respond correctly to this belief.

When you have no conflicting normative belief

That need not be the end of the story. Derek Parfit has pointed out to me a way of going further. The problem revealed in the example is that your P-belief may conflict with a normative belief of yours. If you respond correctly to your normative belief, you will then not respond correctly to your P-belief. That is why you may be rational even if you do not respond correctly to your P-belief. But if you have no conflicting normative belief, you have no grounds for failing to respond correctly to your P-belief. We might conclude you are necessarily not rational if you do not respond correctly to your P-belief when you have no conflicting normative belief.

That may be true for the particular example of pain on Tuesday. In this example, it seems obvious that what you believe, if true, would necessarily be a *pro toto* reason for you to change your appointment. Given that, perhaps it takes a normative belief (which would have to be bizarre) to oppose its obviousness, and make it rational for you not to change it. I am not sure whether or not this is so.

If it is so, this still weaker version of Existential Belief Entailment may be true:

> *Conditional Existential Belief Entailment.* There are some reason-beliefs such that, necessarily, if you are rational, and you have one of these beliefs and no conflicting normative belief, you respond correctly to it.

Derek Parfit treats this condition as an important feature of rationality.[26] However, not every P-belief in a necessarily *pro toto* reason satisfies it. When you have a P-belief whose content would, if true, necessarily be a *pro toto* reason for you to *F*, it need not be obvious that this is so. It might be so only because of some fact that you do not believe and to which you have no easy access. In that case, you might rationally fail to respond correctly to your P-belief, even if you have no conflicting normative belief.[27]

Here is an example. You are shown a substance, which you believe to be sulphur, and are asked what its atomic number is. Giving the correct answer is the only way to avoid a painful punishment. You have the conjunctive belief that the substance is sulphur and that giving the correct answer to the question is the only way to avoid a painful punishment. Plausibly the content of this belief, if true, would necessarily be a *pro toto* reason to give the answer 16, since it is a necessary truth that the atomic number of sulphur is 16. Yet you do not intend to give that answer because you do not know the atomic number of sulphur. You do not respond correctly to your P-belief. Yet you might be fully rational; your ignorance of atomic numbers is not necessarily irrational.

Conclusion

This section has investigated the idea that rationality entails responding correctly to P-beliefs. I have reached the following conclusions.

First, to many of your P-beliefs, there is no such thing as responding correctly. You can respond correctly only if the content of your belief would, if true, constitute a *pro toto* reason. But the contents of many of your P-beliefs would, if true, be only *pro tanto* reasons. An example is your belief that there is a puddle in the path ahead.

Second, plausibly there are some P-beliefs such that, necessarily, if you are rational you respond correctly to them. They satisfy Existential Belief Entailment.

Third, it is doubtful that any of your practical P-beliefs are among those that satisfy this condition. In the example of pain on Tuesdays, your belief does not satisfy it.

However, fourth, it may be true that there are some practical P-beliefs that satisfy Conditional Existential Belief Entailment. In the example of pain on Tuesdays, your belief may satisfy this condition.

But, fifth, there are P-beliefs that do not satisfy this condition. In the sulphur example, your belief does not.

Finally (a point I have not made previously in this section), there are many other conditions of rationality besides responding correctly to P-beliefs. The Enkratic Condition is one; this is a condition on responding to normative beliefs. Another is that, necessarily, you are not rational if you have contradictory intentions. Others are set out on page 76. So rationality is far from equivalent to responding correctly to P-beliefs. Responding correctly to some of these beliefs may be a part of rationality, but it is not the whole of it.

6.4   Conclusion

In this chapter and the previous one, I have investigated many variations on the view that rationality consists in responding correctly to reasons. I hope I have done enough to scotch this view.

I first formulated it in section 5.1 as Equivalence, which I went on to reject in sections 5.2 and 5.3. In this chapter I moved on to Belief Equivalence, the view that rationality is equivalent to responding correctly to your reason-beliefs. I concluded there is some truth in one of its factors, Belief Entailment, which is the view that rationality entails responding correctly to your reason-beliefs. The Strengthened Enkratic Condition on page 90 constitutes one interpretation of Belief Entailment, and I take it to be true. In sections 6.2 and 6.3 I also found some truth in other interpretations of Belief Entailment.

However, there are necessary conditions for rationality that are not captured by Belief Entailment under any interpretation. For example, to be rational you must not have contradictory intentions. So rationality is not equivalent either to responding correctly to reasons, or to responding correctly to reason-beliefs.

A fortiori, rationality does not consist in responding correctly to reasons, or in responding correctly to reason-beliefs. Rationality must be an independent source of requirements in its own right. I now move on to developing that idea.

Notes

1   I adopt this expression from Ralph Wedgwood's 'Internalism explained'.
2   See 'Paraconsistent logic' by Graham Priest and Koji Tanaka and Zach Weber.
3   This formula is close to what Niko Kolodny calls the 'core requirements' on p. 524 of 'Why be rational?'. The differences are, first, that this formula states a condition of rationality rather than a requirement and, second, that Kolodny's formula is restricted to attitudes rather than mental states in general. In that paper, Kolodny hoped to reduce all of rationality to the core requirements, which is the ambition investigated in this section.
4   From Kavka's 'The toxin puzzle'.
5   *On What Matters*, vol. 1, p. 432.
6   There is a fuller discussion of this idea in section 12.3.
7   'Structural irrationality', p. 91.
8   'Structural irrationality', p. 90.
9   See p. 94.
10   p. 91.
11   'Structural irrationality', pp. 95–6.
12   Thanks to useful comments I have received on this subject from Krister Bykvist, Jonathan Dancy and Jussi Suikkanen.
13   'Structural irrationality', p. 91.
14   'Structural irrationality', p. 96.
15   'Structural irrationality', p. 99.
16   See p. 94.
17   'Structural irrationality', p. 95.
18   *On What Matters*, p. 5.
19   The quoted sentence might be read as saying that rationality is equivalent to responding correctly to P-beliefs. But that is not Parfit's meaning. In *On What Matters*, pp. 36 and 113, he explicitly denies that claim.
20   See section 4.2.
21   See p. 89.
22   James Morauta made this point to me. See his *Evaluating Intentions*, pp. 133–43.
23   Thanks to Robert Audi for pointing this out to me.
24   *Reasons and Persons*, p. 124. Parfit develops this example further in *On What Matters*, pp. 120–5.
25   p. 89.
26   *On What Matters*, pp. 111–18.
27   This point is made by Andrew Reisner in *Conflicts of Normativity*, chapter 2.

7

Requirements

7.1 Two sorts of requirement

At the end of chapter 6 I described rationality as a source of requirements. This chapter explains more exactly what that means. It continues the discussion of rationality, but it also explains what requirements in general are. It will be a rather technical chapter, because it is particularly concerned with the formal aspects of requirements.[1]

The verb 'requires' has a number of senses. The first appears in constructions where its subject denotes a property: 'Beauty requires hard work'; 'Staying healthy requires you to eat olives'; 'Success in battle requires good horses'; 'Crossing the Rubicon required determination'. Here I say 'requires' has the 'property sense'.

In other constructions the subject of 'requires' denotes a person or thing that has some sort of real or presumed authority: 'The minister requires the ambassador's presence'; 'The law requires you to drive carefully'; 'The bill requires payment'; 'Fashion requires knee-length skirts'; 'My conscience requires me to turn you in'.[2] In these case I say 'requires' has the 'source' sense. I call the minister, the law, the bill, my conscience and so on 'sources' of requirements.

A third sense appears in: 'Trees require water'; 'A will requires to be kept safe'; 'The patient requires constant attention'. In these constructions 'requires' is very close in meaning to 'needs'. This sense plays no role in this book, and I shall not mention it again.[3]

The first task of this chapter is to describe and distinguish requirements in the property sense and requirements in the source sense. This is particularly necessary because many terms can refer to either a property or a source of requirements. Each of the words 'morality', 'prudence' and 'rationality', which appear constantly in this book, are in this class. Each is the name of a property that people can possess: the property of being moral, of being prudent or of being rational. And also each can denote a source of requirements. We think of morality, for example, as having an authority to require things of us. So 'morality', 'prudence' and 'rationality' each have a property sense and a source sense. 'Rationality' in its source sense is synonymous with the mass noun 'reason' in one of its senses.[4]

'Success in battle requires . . .' and 'the minister requires . . .' display clearly in their subject which sense of 'requires' they use. But the expressions 'morality requires . . .', 'prudence requires . . .' and 'rationality requires . . .' do not. They are ambiguous because 'morality', 'prudence' and 'rationality' are ambiguous. Since the two senses of 'requires' have different logical properties, the ambiguity can lead to logical mistakes. That is why I need to start by separating the senses.

When I speak of requirements of rationality in chapter 9 and elsewhere in this book, I use the source sense. I describe the property sense in this chapter only to separate it from the source sense.

Nevertheless, I shall often need to refer to the property of rationality, so I have a further ambiguity to resolve. Even as the names of properties, 'rationality' and 'morality' are ambiguous.[5] They may refer to capacities or to attainments. If you say of human beings in general that they are moral animals, you probably mean they have a capacity for morality. The opposite of 'moral' in this sense is 'nonmoral'. Similarly, to say that human beings are rational animals is to say they have a capacity of rationality. The opposite of 'rational' in this sense is 'nonrational'. When I use 'rational' and 'moral' in this book I rarely use the capacity senses and I make it explicit when I do. Instead, I refer to attainments. The opposite of moral in my sense is 'immoral'; the opposite of 'rational' is 'irrational'.

7.2   Property requirements

Since in this book I use 'requires' and 'requirement' in the source sense, which I shall analyse in section 7.3, I do not need to commit myself to any particular analysis of the property sense. Still, it is important to get the two senses clear. Our intuitions about the meaning of 'requires' are influenced by both of them, and this can cause confusion if they are not clearly separated. In particular, I shall explain that the appeal of Standard Deontic Logic (SDL) for requirements comes from the property sense, whereas there is no reason to think the source sense conforms to SDL. So I shall start by mentioning some analyses that are available for the property sense. I think this sense is fluid and subject to context, so more than one analysis may be correct.

Interpretations

Start with an all-or-nothing property such as survival. 'Your survival requires you to have a functioning liver', in the property sense, means that your having a functioning liver is a condition that is required for you to have the property of survival. 'A condition that is required' can be interpreted in more than one way.

One interpretation treats it as a strictly necessary condition. Your survival requires you to have a functioning liver' means that, necessarily, if you do not have a functioning liver, you do not survive. Equivalently: necessarily, if you survive you have a functioning liver. I shall call this the 'modal' interpretation. In general under the modal interpretation of a property requirement, 'F requires of N that p' means that:

Modal Analysis. Necessarily, if N has the property F, then p.

We may say that the property F *entails* p. This is exactly the language I used in chapters 5 and 6, where I was investigating the property of rationality and conditions for possessing it. For example, Entailment on page 72 is the proposition that rationality *entails* responding correctly to reasons, as I put it there. In the language of this chapter, it is the proposition that rationality *requires* you to respond correctly to reasons, where 'requires' has the property sense interpreted modally.

The Modal Analysis has some problems. One is that the conditional sentence 'If you jump from an airborne plane, your survival requires you to have a parachute' seems true. But read literally with the Modal Analysis, it would mean that, if you jump from an airborne plane, then, necessarily, if you survive you have a parachute. That is not true. You can perfectly well survive without having a parachute; you have only to avoid jumping from an airborne plane. Even if you actually do jump from an airborne plane, you do not have to, so it is not necessarily the case that, if you survive, you have a parachute.

This problem has a standard solution. Colloquial English sentences, read literally, do not always give modal operators their logically correct scope. Compare the sentence 'If you jump from an airborne plane, you must have a parachute to survive'. This means that you must (if you jump from an airborne plane, have a parachute to survive). The scope of the 'must' includes the whole conditional, even though in the literal English it includes only the consequent. Similarly, the sentence 'If you jump from an airborne plane, survival requires you to have a parachute' means that survival requires of you that, if you jump from an airborne plane, you have a parachute. In other words, necessarily, if you survive, then, if you jump from an airborne plane, you have a parachute.

This is true, which explains why the sentence seems true. The lesson to be learnt is that we must not be too literal over the scope of 'requires'.

A second problem with the Modal Analysis is that, although it seems true that your survival requires you to have a functioning liver, it is not true that, necessarily, if you survive you have a functioning liver. There are possible worlds containing liver machines, in which you survive without a functioning liver. So it seems that 'Your survival requires you to have a functioning liver' does not mean the same as 'Necessarily, if you survive, you have a functioning liver'.

A fix for this second problem is to narrow the meaning of 'necessarily'. We should not take it to cover every metaphysical possibility, but instead limit it according to the context. In the case of survival, I take it to be some sort of practical necessity. I take 'Survival requires you to have a functioning liver' to mean that, in all practically possible worlds, if you survive you have a functioning liver.

An alternative fix is to adopt a subjunctive rather than modal interpretation of property requirements.[6] That is a way of focusing on nearby possibilities and ignoring remote ones. Under this interpretation, 'Survival requires you to have a functioning liver' means that you would not survive if you did not have a functioning liver. In general 'F requires of N that p', interpreted subjunctively, means that N would not have the property F if p were not so.

This analysis is incorrect as it stands. The truth of the subjunctive conditional is too contingent. Suppose you will soon be killed by a meteorite. The only thing that would save your life would be to move to some other place, but actually you are not going to move. Then you would not survive if you were not to twiddle your thumbs. But your survival does not require you to twiddle your thumbs. So the subjunctive analysis fails. It may be reparable by adding a further explanatory condition. The analysis of 'F requires of N that p' would then be:

> *Explanatory Analysis.* If p were not so, then N would not have F because p is not so.

This gives us an 'explanatory' interpretation of a property requirement.[7]

Under both the modal and explanatory interpretations, 'F requires of N that p' means that p is a condition that is required for N to have the property F. But if we switch attention to properties that come in degrees, a further interpretation becomes plausible. We may take 'F requires of N that p' to mean that p is a condition required for N to be Fer than she otherwise would be, or perhaps Fer than she is. I call this the 'comparative' interpretation.

Michael Smith adopts the comparative interpretation of property requirements in his paper 'Internal reasons'. He argues that a person is rationally required to have a desire of a particular sort (a desire she believes she would have were she fully rational) on the grounds that she would be more rational if she had this desire than if she did not.[8] (Smith does not use 'rational' for fully rational, as I do.)

The comparative interpretation comes in two versions: that p is a condition required for N to be Fer than she is, and that p is a condition required for N to be Fer than she otherwise would be. Furthermore, the expression 'condition required' can be understood in either a modal or an explanatory way. The result is that there are in the end four potential versions of the comparative interpretation. 'F requires of N that p' might mean any of:

(1) Necessarily, if N is Fer than she would be were p not so, then p.
(2) Necessarily, if N is Fer than she actually is, then p.
(3) Were p not so, then because p is not so, N would not be Fer than she would be were p so.
(4) Were p not so, then because p is not so, N would not be Fer than she actually is.

(1) cannot be the right analysis. Take a world where the antecedent of (1) – the proposition that N is Fer than she would be were p not so – is true for some p. p must be true at this world, because if it were false N would be exactly as F as she would be if p were false. So the antecedent of (1) entails p, which is the consequent of (1). (1) is therefore vacuously true for any p. It cannot express a requirement.

(3) encounters a different problem. Think about the property of longevity. Suppose there are two ways of getting to live longer: eating olives and exercising. If you were not to eat olives, then, because you do not eat them, you would not live longer than you would if you ate them. If you were not to exercise, then, because you do not exercise, you would not live longer than you would if you exercised. Therefore, according to the analysis (3), longevity requires you to eat olives and longevity requires you to take exercise. But intuitively this gets the meaning of 'requires' wrong. Since, by eating olives, you can live longer without exercising, it seems wrong to say that longevity requires you to exercise and wrong to say it requires you to eat olives. A similar problem afflicts (4).

You might think that, although the property of longevity raises this problem, not all properties do. The property of morality may not, for instance. Suppose you have two means of becoming more moral: you can give something to charity and you can keep a promise you have made. According to (3), morality requires you to give something to charity and morality requires you to keep your promise. You might think that is exactly right. Morality does indeed require both.

If you think this way, it is probably because you are influenced by the source sense of 'requires'. I shall describe this sense in section 7.3. It seems plausible that, in the source sense, morality really does require you to give something to charity and also require you to keep your promise. Moreover, I shall argue that, for morality, the source sense is often more natural than the property sense. So your intuition about morality's requirements may tell you about the source sense rather than the property sense. We should discount this intuition as a guide to the analysis of property requirements.

I conclude that the two explanatory analyses (3) and (4) are unsatisfactory for the comparative interpretation of property requirements. We are left with (2).

(2) has a small technical problem. If N is actually as F as she can be, she cannot be any Fer. In that case the antecedent in (2) is false at all worlds. This means (2) itself is true for every p; every proposition would be required by F according to the analysis. The fix is to elaborate the formula a little. We get:

> *Comparative Analysis.* Necessarily, if N is as F as she can be, or N is Fer than she actually is, then p.

The language is confusing. This formula means that p is true at every world where either N is as F as she can be or N is Fer than she is at the actual world. According to the Comparative Analysis, a property requires of you whatever is a strictly necessary condition for you to possess the property to a higher degree than you actually do, or to the highest degree.

The analysis does not preclude p's being true at the actual world. Suppose longevity requires you to look after yourself. According to the Comparative Analysis, this means that, at every possible world where you live longer than you are actually going to live, you look after yourself. This does not imply that you do not actually look after yourself. So you may actually satisfy this requirement.

Logic

Property requirements are friendly to deontic logic. Deontic logic is the logic of 'ought'. It is generally formalized using a propositional operator 'O', where 'Op' is intended to be read as 'it ought to be the case that p'. But it can be reinterpreted for requirements. We may read 'Op' instead as 'F requires of N that p'. Then if we give requirements either the Modal Analysis on page 111 or the Comparative Analysis above, they will conform to Standard Deontic Logic (SDL).

To see why, take the Comparative Analysis first. Take any possible world w and suppose it is the actual world. Define $I(w)$ to be the set of worlds where either N is as F as she can be or N is Fer than she is at w. $I(w)$ is non-empty.

According to the Comparative Analysis, it is true at w that F requires of N that p if and only if p is true at every world in $I(w)$.

This sets up exactly the standard semantics of SDL.[9] There is a relation that maps each world w into a non-empty set of worlds $I(w)$ such that Op is true at w if and only if p is true at every world in $I(w)$. (When 'Op' is read as 'It ought to be the case that p', $I(w)$ is the set of worlds where everything that ought to be the case at w is the case.) This semantics validates SDL, so SDL applies to requirements under the Comparative Analysis.

The standard semantics of SDL can also be set up on the basis of the Modal Interpretation. We make $I(w)$ the set of worlds where N has the property F. ($I(w)$ is independent of w in this case.) Then, according to the Modal Analysis, it is true at w that F requires of N that p if and only if p is true at every world in $I(w)$. SDL follows.

$I(w)$ needs to be non-empty, which in this case means it must be possible for N to have the property F. This is a precondition for the Modal Interpretation to be even credible. If N could not have the property F, the Modal Interpretation's antecedent 'N has the property F' would be false at every world. This would mean that the Modal Interpretation itself would be true for every p. Every proposition would be required by F, which cannot be so.

To make sense of the modal interpretation, we therefore have to make sure we adopt a notion of necessity that satisfies the second condition. That may require a rather wide sort of necessity. On the other hand, on page 112 I explained that we cannot have too wide a sort if the modal interpretation is to give us the correct truth-conditions for requirements. We need a suitable compromise. That should not be hard to find.

The Modal and Comparative Analyses of property requirements both ensure that these requirements satisfy SDL. Consequently they satisfy each of SDL's axioms and theorems. They satisfy Axiom D, which says that a property's requirements do not contradict each other: if F requires of N that p, F does not require of N that not p. They also satisfy Axiom K: if F requires of N that p, and if F requires of N that if p then q, then F requires of N that q. These axioms and other consequences of SDL will be examined in section 7.4.

On the other hand, under the Explanatory Analysis, property requirements do not satisfy SDL. Here is an example to show that Axiom K is not satisfied under this analysis. Your hotel is on fire and smoke is pouring into your room under the door. You are wrapped in the duvet, and about to jump from the window. If you were not to jump, because you do not jump you would die of smoke inhalation. So according to the Explanatory Analysis, your survival requires you to jump. If you were to jump without being wrapped in the duvet, because you do so, you would die of cold because of the freezing conditions. So according to the Explanatory Analysis, your survival requires of you that, if you jump, you are wrapped in the duvet. Given these facts, Axiom K implies that your survival requires you to be wrapped in the duvet.

However, were you not wrapped in the duvet, because you are not, you would notice that the duvet could be used to stop the smoke coming under the door. You would in fact survive by using it for that purpose. So according to the Explanatory Analysis your survival does not require you to be wrapped in the duvet. Axiom K is inconsistent with this analysis, therefore.

However, I think it is fair to say all in all that property requirements are friendly to SDL. For this reason, SDL can seem attractive as a logic of requirements.

7.3   Source requirements

'Requires' has a second sense.[10] The names 'morality', 'rationality', 'prudence' and the rest sometimes refer, not to properties, but to *sources* of requirements. When they are read that way, 'morality requires' and the rest follow the model of 'the law requires'. The law is a source of requirements, and 'the law' is not ambiguous in the way that 'morality' and the rest are; it is never the name of a property that can be possessed by a person. So 'the law requires' provides a useful model for picking out the second sense of 'requires'. This is the sense that appears in sentences of the form 'S requires of N that p', where S is a source of requirements. For reasons that will emerge, I think 'morality requires' and the rest are most naturally read with this meaning. But in any case this is the meaning I shall adopt in this book. I shall call it the 'source sense' and speak of 'source requirements'. From now on, when I use 'requires', it always has the source sense unless I say otherwise.

'Requires' in the source sense could be replaced with 'prescribes'. Instead of 'Rationality requires of you that . . .' we could say 'Rationality prescribes to you that . . .'. Exactly the same meaning could be conveyed by these two expressions, and the second has the advantage that it could not be confused with a property requirement. I use 'requires' only because it seems slightly more natural.

I cannot say what sort of thing sources of requirements are – what category the law, morality, rationality, prudence, convention, fashion, etiquette, honour, the rules of chess and all the rest fall under. I do not know a generic term for things of this sort.

I explained on page 27 that the requirements issued by a source are not necessarily normative. We do not necessarily have any reason to satisfy them. However, no doubt some sources do issue requirements that are normative. Morality and prudence (by which I mean self-interest) are presumably among them. Chapter 11 considers whether rationality is.

Formalities

How are we to represent source requirements formally? For each individual requirement there is a proposition that specifies what is required; I call it the 'required proposition'. If morality requires you to be kind to strangers, the required proposition is that you are kind to strangers. Any particular source issues a number of requirements. Since each can be specified by a proposition, the whole set of a source's requirements can be specified by a set of propositions. In accordance with colloquial English, I sometimes use the word 'requirement' to refer to the fact that something is required, and sometimes to what is required – to the required proposition.

We must allow for the possibility that the requirements a person is under depend on her circumstances. Here is how I shall do that formally using the semantics of possible worlds. There is a set of worlds, at each of which each proposition has a truth value. The values of all propositions at a particular world conform to propositional calculus. For each source of requirements S, each person N and each world w, there is a set of propositions $R_S(N, w)$, which is the set of things that S requires of N at w. Each member of the set is a required proposition. The function R_S I shall call S's *code* of requirements. Since I shall deal with only one source and one person at a time, I can usually drop the 'S' and the 'N' from the formula. The code is then the function R, whose value at w is $R(w)$.

This formulation of the code allows the requirements N is under at different worlds to differ. The set of worlds at which a particular requirement applies to N – the set at which a particular required proposition is required of N – is the *domain* of the requirement for N.

Take a requirement N is under at some particular world. To say N *satisfies* the requirement at that world is to say the required proposition is true at that world.

Now we have requirements founded on a code, we can define a property that corresponds to the source of the code. For N to have the property is for her to satisfy all the requirements that the source puts her under. For example, for her to be rational – to have the property of rationality – is for her to satisfy all the requirements of rationality she is under. She is rational at a world if and only if each of the things that rationality requires of her at that world actually obtains at that world. More formally, the proposition that she is rational is true at a world w if and only if every proposition in the set $R(w)$ is true at w.

I am sticking to my practice of using 'rational' to mean fully rational. But I shall relax the practice for this one paragraph, in order to mention degrees of rationality. Take two worlds where the requirements of rationality on N

are the same. Suppose that at one N satisfies all the requirements she satisfies at the other and some more as well. Then N is more rational at the first than at the second. This gives a sufficient condition for being more rational, but not a necessary one. N may also be more rational at one world than at another if the requirements she satisfies at the one are together more important than those she satisfies at the other. This criterion makes sense only if we have some sort of scale of importance for requirements. No doubt we do, but no doubt it is vague and incomplete. So the ordering 'more rational than' is no doubt vague and incomplete. Once we have this ordering – rough as it is – we could define N as rational, as opposed to fully rational, if she is sufficiently high up the ordering. But now I revert to using 'rational' to mean fully rational. In effect, I take 'sufficiently high' to include only the maximum.

We can similarly define properties such as morality and prudence. To generalize, I call the property that corresponds to a source S the 'S-property'. I write it 'F_S'. For N to have the S-property at w is for it to be the case that, for every required proposition r in $R_S(N, w)$, r is true at w.

Source requirements are local

The code of requirements comes first, and I have defined the corresponding property on the basis of the code.[11] It is not that the property comes first and the code aims at achieving the property.

To emphasize the point, notice this consequence of my semantics. Suppose the actual world is w. And suppose the requirements at this world are mutually consistent. Then there are worlds where all the requirements in $R(w)$ are satisfied. Take one of these worlds w'. The requirements at w' are $R(w')$, and nothing says that all the requirements in $R(w')$ are satisfied at w'. Let me put this in counterfactual terms, taking the requirements of prudence as an example. As things are, prudence requires some things of you. If you were to satisfy all those requirements of prudence, you might not then satisfy all the requirements of prudence you would then be under. That is to say, you might not then have the property of prudence. So satisfying all the requirements does not necessarily give you the property. It is also true that, if you were to have the property of prudence, you might not then satisfy all the requirements of prudence you are actually under.

These possibilities arise because the requirements you are under may not be the same at all worlds. If that was a problem, we could eliminate it by insisting that the requirements at all worlds are the same: that $R(w)$ is the same at all w. But should we do that? Is it a problem?

It is not; it is what we should expect. What prudence requires of you in your actual imprudent state may not be what it would require of you if you were prudent. Suppose you have just lost a lot of money at poker. Perhaps prudence requires you to borrow from your bank, in order to pay your poker debts. But were you prudent, you would not have lost that money in the first place, and prudence would not require you to borrow from the bank. This makes good sense.

Indeed, it is part of the point of switching our attention from the property sense to the source sense of 'requires'. We are interested in what prudence, or morality or something else, requires of you in the particular situation you are in. For this, it is not very relevant what you would do if you had the property of prudence, or morality or anything else. You may be very far from having the property, and because of that, what is required of you may be very different from what you would do if you had it. We may say that requirements in the source sense are *local*.[12] They are not concerned with the global property of being rational, or moral or anything else.

In practice our interests are local. We are more interested in coping with our actual imperfect situation than in how to be perfect. This makes the source sense of 'requires' more natural than the property sense.

Various symptoms of its naturalness will show up in section 7.4, and here is one now. A consequence of my semantics is that not all propositions that are necessary conditions for having the S-property need be in the code of S. For instance, not all propositions that are necessary conditions for your being moral need be required of you, in the source sense, by morality.[13] Suppose, for instance, that a necessary condition for being moral is that you are alive. Then morality requires you, in the property sense, to be alive, but it need not require you, in the source sense, to be alive. It seems unnatural to say that morality requires you to be alive, so this point gives support to my claim that the source sense is more natural than the property sense.

7.4 Logic for requirements?

My formulation of requirements is very undemanding. It allows the set of required propositions at a world to contain any number of propositions, related together or not. So no logical relations among required propositions is implied by the formulation. Requirements as I have described them do not necessarily conform to Standard Deontic Logic, and they are in no danger of running up against any of the well-known paradoxes of deontic logic.[14]

But should we not expect there to be some logic of requirements? I am not sure we should, and if there is one, I would expect it to be weak. A *logic* of requirements should arise from the meaning of 'requires' alone, and I doubt that much of a logic does arise from that meaning. There may indeed be deductive relations among requirements, but they are more likely to arise from the substance of particular sources of requirements than from the meaning of 'requires'.

Take 'morality requires' for example. We have various substantive theories about what morality requires. One example is the broad theory that may be called 'maximizing teleology'. According to maximizing teleology, morality requires you to do the best act out of those that are available to you. So what morality requires of you depends on the goodness of alternative acts. That is to say, it depends on an axiology, and an axiology has particular structural features. The relation of betterness is transitive, for instance. This structure will imply that particular deductive relations hold among the things that morality requires of you.[15] We may expect maximizing teleology and a non-teleological theory of morality to support very different inferences.

Still, I do not insist that there is no logic of requirements at all. If my semantics is to incorporate one, it will have to be injected directly into the semantics by imposing conditions on the structure of the code $R(w)$. I shall consider some conditions that might be imposed.

Axiom K

We might inject Axiom K, a fundamental axiom of SDL:

> *Axiom K.* ((S requires of N that p) & (S requires of N that $p \supset q$)) $\supset$ (S requires of N that q).

We could inject it by imposing on the code the condition that, for any world w, the set $R(w)$ is closed under implication by modus ponens. That is to say, whenever p and $p \supset q$ are in $R(w)$, then q is also in $R(w)$.

I do not recommend injecting Axiom K. I find it intuitively unattractive. Here is an example that shows why. Suppose that, since you have entered a marathon, prudence requires you to exercise hard every day, and it also requires of you that, if you exercise hard every day, you eat heartily. According to Axiom K, prudence requires you to eat heartily. But suppose that, despite what prudence requires, you take no exercise. You could exercise hard, but you do not bother. In that case, intuition suggests it is wrong to conclude that prudence requires you to eat heartily. It seems perfectly consistent to think that, since you take no exercise, prudence does not require you to eat heartily. So intuition suggests that Axiom K is wrong.

True, if you do not eat heartily, you fail to do something that prudence requires of you: either you do not exercise hard every day, or you do exercise hard every day but do not eat heartily. So your failure to eat heartily entails that you are not prudent. Necessarily, if you are prudent, you eat heartily. If we were reading 'requires' in the property sense under the modal interpretation, we would have to persuade ourselves that prudence requires you to eat heartily.

That does seem a peculiar claim to make when you take no exercise. This adds support to my claim that the property sense of 'requires' is not a natural one. At any rate, I am concerned with the source sense. Nothing suggests that eating heartily is within the code of prudence. So in the source sense, prudence does not require you to eat heartily.

To generalize, suppose some source requires you to F, and requires you to G if you F. Suppose you do not G. The fact that you do not G entails that either you do not F, or you do F but do not G. So the fact that you do not G entails that you do not satisfy one of the source's requirements. However, it does not follow that the source requires you specifically to G. Axiom K is unsatisfactory.

This axiom is the culprit in generating many of the paradoxes of deontic logic. We are better off without it.

Inheritance

Another axiom that might be injected is:

> *Logical Inheritance.* ((S requires of N that p) & ($p \supset q$) is logically valid) $\supset$ (S requires of N that q).

That is to say, if something is required, then all its logical consequences are required. This axiom is endorsed by Bas van Fraassen in his 'Value and the heart's command'. Van Fraassen's semantics is in other respects like mine,[16] so this axiom is worth considering. To inject it, we would impose on the code the condition that, for any world w, if p belongs to $R(w)$, and if $p \supset q$ is logically valid, then q belongs to $R(w)$.

Like Axiom K, the logical inheritance axiom leads to paradoxes. A similar example illustrates one.[17] Suppose prudence requires you to eat heartily and exercise hard every day. According to Logical Inheritance, prudence requires you to eat heartily. But suppose you take no exercise. Intuition suggests it is not the case that prudence requires you to eat heartily. It is not plausible that the code of prudence includes the requirement that you eat heartily. So we should reject Logical Inheritance.

Lou Goble disagrees. He says:

We might, for example, have a body of law; what the law requires reaches beyond the bare stipulations written in that body to include, one would think, also what those stipulations entail. If the law says there shall be no camping at any time on public streets, it does not seem much of a defense for a camper to plead that the law never said that there should be no camping on the streets on Thursday night.[18]

I agree it is not much of a defence, but I do not think the example supports Logical Inheritance. Suppose the law says there shall be no camping at any time on public streets and does not mention Thursday. Suppose you camp on the streets on Thursday night. When you are arrested, you will be charged under the law that says there shall be no camping at any time on public streets. You have no defence; you did indeed break this law. You will not be charged under a law that says there shall be no camping on the streets on Thursday night because there is no such law. The code of law does not include the proposition that you do not camp on the streets on a Thursday night. So long as we hold tight to the source meaning of 'requires', we should not think the law requires you not to camp on the streets on Thursday night.

Logical Equivalents

On the other hand, I do think we should inject the weaker axiom:

> *Substitution of Logical Equivalents.* ((S requires of N that p) & ($p \leftrightarrow q$) is logically valid) $\supset$ (S requires of N that q).

This is forced on us if we identify a proposition with the set of worlds at which it is true, since when p and q are logically equivalent they are then the same proposition. But I know of no objection to this axiom even under a different understanding of propositions. So we should assume that, for any world w, if p belongs to $R(w)$, and if p is logically equivalent to q, then q belongs to $R(w)$.

Axiom D

Another fundamental axiom of SDL is:

> *Axiom D.* (S requires of N that p) $\supset \neg$ (S requires of N that $\neg p$),

which says that S issues no contradictory requirements. This could be injected into the logic of requirements by imposing the condition that, for any w, when $R(w)$ contains p it does not contain not p.

It seems it must be possible for some sources of requirements to issue inconsistent requirements. For example, the rules of a game are a source of requirements, and the rules written out for a newly-invented game might contain a contradiction. So I do not think we should inject Axiom D into the logic of requirements generally. It cannot be a feature of the meaning of 'requires'.

On the other hand, Axiom D may well apply to some particular sources of requirements. For instance, I shall assume on pages 136–8 that rationality does not issue inconsistent requirements, so that *a fortiori* it does not issue contradictory ones. I take this to be a special feature of rationality and not a logical feature of requirement.

What about the law? Just as inventors of games can write contradictory rules, it is plainly possible for legislators to pass contradictory statutes. If they do, the result seems to be that the law issues contradictory requirements. But possibly that is not the result. For all I know, there may be some special feature of law that prevents it from being contradictory. If so, when there are contradictory statues, at least one of them must be invalid. But if the law cannot be contradictory, this is a special feature of the law and not a logical feature of requirement.

On page 128 I shall suggest that Axiom D applies to *normative* sources of requirements: a normative source does not issue contradictory requirements.

Necessary Detachment

One principle I accept is this:

> *Necessary Detachment.* ((Necessarily p) & (S requires of N that $p \supset q$)) $\supset$ (S requires of N that q).

It is a sort of detachment rule. From a requirement whose content is the conditional $p \supset q$, it allows us to derive a requirement with the unconditional content q. That is to say, we can detach the consequent q from its antecedent p. Detachment is allowed provided the antecedent is necessarily true.

This is only one of several possible detachment rules. Another would be:

> (p & (S requires of N that $p \supset q$)) $\supset$ (S requires of N that q).

Deontic logicians call this 'factual detachment'. There is little to be said for it and a lot to be said against it. A famous counterexample is this. It is no doubt true that morality requires of you that, if you murder your sister, you murder her painlessly. Suppose you are going to murder your sister. Factual detachment would allow us to derive the conclusion that morality requires you to murder your sister painlessly. That conclusion is obviously false: morality does not require you to murder your sister in any way at all.

Axiom K on page 120 is another detachment rule, analogous to what deontic logicians call 'deontic detachment'. I have already rejected this rule. But I accept Necessary Detachment, for reasons I am about to explain.

I am not yet in a position to inject it into my semantic structure, because I have so far said nothing about necessity within the structure. Suppose, first, that we were to take necessity to be truth at all worlds. Suppose, also, that we were to identify a proposition with the set of worlds at which it is true. Then Necessary Detachment would follow. Take a world w where S requires of N that $p \supset q$. Then $p \supset q$ is one of the required propositions at w. The proposition $p \supset q$ is the set of worlds where $p \supset q$ is true, which is to say the set of worlds where either p is false or q is true. Now suppose p is necessarily true, which we are taking to mean it is true at all worlds. Then the worlds where $p \supset q$ is true is just the set of worlds where q is true. So the proposition q is the same as the proposition $p \supset q$. Since the latter is one of the required propositions at w, so is the former. At w, S requires of N that q. We have achieved detachment.

Treating necessity as truth at all worlds gives us the S5 logic for necessity. But I do not think Necessary Detachment applies only to necessity understood that way. Here, for instance, is an application that I find appealing. Let us suppose this is a requirement of morality:

Morality requires of you that, if you have promised to F, you F.

Now suppose you have promised to F. That is a fact you can do nothing about; you cannot alter the past. Let us treat it as necessary. Then Necessary Detachment allows us to conclude that morality requires of you that you F. In general, we can derive from the above principle that

If you have promised to F, morality requires you to F.

I find this a satisfactory explanation of a feature of promising that has puzzled some philosophers. How are you in a position, merely by saying something, to impose a moral requirement on yourself? David Hume says:

> Since every new promise imposes a new obligation of morality on the person who promises, and since this new obligation arises from his will; 'tis one of

the most mysterious and incomprehensible operations that can possibly be imagin'd.[19]

The solution to the puzzle is that you are constantly under the conditional requirement that, if you have promised to F, you F. You do not bring this requirement on yourself by your will; it is an inescapable requirement of morality. Then, when you make a promise to F, it simply follows that you are required by morality to F. Nothing surprising happens: merely that a conclusion follows.

The requirement of morality is presumably not exactly as I specified it. My formula seems too strong for at least three reasons. One is that, if you have promised to do something morally wrong, your promise presumably does not make it the case that morality requires you to do it. The second is that, if you have made contradictory promises, my formula implies that morality requires contradictory things of you. So it implies that moral requirement can infringe axiom D. We could accept that axiom D does not apply to requirements of morality,[20] but perhaps an easier response is to think that the requirement as I specified it is too strong. The third is that there seem to be cases where you are not required to do what you have promised to do, either because doing it would be harmful, or because there is something morally more urgent that you should do.

To accommodate these points, perhaps the formula should contain some more conditional clauses. Or perhaps it should be replaced by something weaker than a strict requirement – by some sort of a *pro tanto* requirement perhaps. Requirements of morality are beyond the scope of this book, so I shall not try to work out the right formula here.

Provided some appropriately weaker version of the requirement can be found, the rule of Necessary Detachment provides a good solution to a puzzle about promising. But in applying Necessary Detachment to promising, I did not treat necessity as truth at all worlds. Even if you have promised to F, there are worlds where you have not promised to F. However, there are systems of tense logic in which a past event counts as necessary.[21] We may call this sort of necessity 'unalterability'. Because it leads to attractive results such as this one for promising, I propose extending Necessary Detachment to unalterability.[22]

For my purposes I do not need to go so far as adding to the semantics all the details that will make room for unalterability. Although I propose extending Necessary Detachment to unalterability, and I shall investigate some of its consequences, my argument in this book does not depend on it. I would withdraw my proposal if it turned out to lead to unsatisfactory consequences.

Transmission

I have already rejected:

> *Necessary Inheritance.* $((S$ requires of N that $p)$ & necessarily $(p \supset q)) \supset$ $(S$ requires of N that $q)$.

This is stronger than logical inheritance, which I rejected on pages 121–2.

However, I have not yet rejected the weaker principle that, if a source requires something of you, it requires of you whatever is a necessary *means* to that thing:[23]

> *End to Means Transmission.* $((S$ requires of N that $p)$ & necessarily $(p \supset q)$ & q is a means to $p) \supset (S$ requires of N that $q)$.

I do not recommend injecting this principle either. Suppose that prudence requires you to see your doctor, and the only way of doing so is to take a day off work. (The importance of seeing your doctor outweighs the bad consequences of taking a day off work.) According to End to Means Transmission, prudence requires you to take a day off work. But suppose you have no intention of seeing your doctor, and you will not do so even if you take a day off work. You will simply sit around feeling anxious. Then it is implausible that prudence requires you to take a day off work.[24]

7.5 Ought

What ought you to do? I mean: what ought you to do all things considered? I argued in section 2.4 that the answer to this question is determined by requirements that issue from various sources. Sometimes only one source is relevant. For example, prudence generally requires you to look both ways when you cross the road, and there is generally no opposing requirement. Sometimes more than one requirement is involved, and they may conflict. The law may require you to shop your daughter to the police, whereas morality may require you not to do so.

Not all requirements necessarily contribute to determining what you ought to do. The ones that do I call 'normative'. A normative requirement to *F* constitutes a reason to *F*. Sources that issue normative requirements are normative sources.

Some sources are normative in their own right; morality and prudence or self-interest are presumably among them. Epistemic requirements are presumably normative in their own right when it comes to determining what you ought to believe. Other sources derive normativity from a different source. For example, the law often derives normativity from prudence, because it is often prudent to obey the law. You may also be under requirements that are not normative at all. For example, the requirements of an unjust political party are generally not normative, even for members of the party.

Whether or not you ought to F is determined in some way by the interaction of normative requirements you are under: requirements to F or requirements not to F. If you find yourself under a normative requirement to F, and under none not to F, then you ought to F. If you find yourself under a normative requirement not to F, and none to F, then you ought not to F. If you find yourself under no normative requirement either to F or not to F, then it is not the case that you ought to F and not the case that you ought not to F.

Those cases are easy. Whether or not you ought to F is not so straightforward when you find yourself under one or more normative requirements to F, and one or more not to F. The resolution of this conflict may be that you ought to F, or that you ought not to F, or that it is not the case that you ought to F and not the case that you ought not to F.

Different substantive normative theories say different things about how a conflict is resolved. According to some, the requirements that issue from one particular source dominate all others. For instance, morality may dominate, so that conflicts between requirements of morality and other requirements are always resolved in favour of morality. Or morality may somehow subsume other requirements.[25] Either way, the result will be that, necessarily, if morality requires you to F, you ought to F.[26] According to other theories, the resolution of conflicting requirements will emerge from some weighing or balancing of them. Each requirement is a *pro tanto* reason, which weighs against others. We do not have to pursue these issues.

Deontic logic

Take some normative source of requirements – self-interest say. There will be a range of Fs that are not the concern of any other normative source. Over this range, whether or not you ought to F will be determined by what self-interest requires of you. You ought to F if and only if self-interest requires you to F. Over this range, logical features of ought must match those of the requirements of self-interest. Then take another normative source. Over the range of Fs that are not the concern of any normative source besides this one, logical features of ought must match the logical features of this other source's requirements. And so on. The upshot is that ought behaves like normative requirement. Its logical features must match those of requirements from each normative source.

This explains how I was able in chapters 5 and 6 to express oughts by the expression 'your reasons require'. The requirements of normative sources, taken together, determine what you ought to do. What you ought to do has the logical features of the requirements that issue from a single normative source. So we can treat the normative sources of requirements as together one big source. We could say 'the normative sources require . . .'. But since the requirements issued by each source are reasons, the expression 'the reasons require . . .' is a good one to use instead.

I said in section 7.4 that the logic of requirement is very thin. The same goes for deontic logic – the logic of ought. My rejection of principles such as Axiom K and End to Means Transmission goes for ought as well as for requirement. Nor should we expect there to be a substantial deontic logic. What you ought to do may be determined in complex ways, which it takes a substantive deontic theory to describe. There is no reason to expect the result to resemble a logic.

Nevertheless, the logic of ought need not be as thin as the logic of requirement in general. It may be that ought has logical features of its own, determined by the meaning of 'ought'. If that is so, those must also be features of normative requirements, not because they are requirements but because they are normative. I mentioned on pages 119–20 that deductive relations might hold among requirements that issue from a particular source, not because of the logic of requirement but because of substantive features of the source. These would fall into that category; they hold because the source has the substantive feature of being normative.

What features might these be? A good candidate is Axiom D on page 122. Many authors think there cannot be inconsistent oughts. J. J. Thomson says

> I think myself that it was . . . patently incorrect to think that 'I ought to give C a banana' and 'I ought to give D a banana' can both be true compatibly with my having only one banana; I think we simply do not use the English word 'ought' in such a way that this is so.[27]

Thomson rules out inconsistent oughts; *a fortiori* she rules out deontic conflicts. Since she thinks this is a matter of the meaning of 'ought', we can treat it as a feature of logic. It gives us:

Axiom D for Ought. (N ought that p) $\supset \neg$ (N ought that $\neg p$).

I am inclined to agree with Thomson. If she is right, no source of normative requirements can issue contradictory requirements. For example, there can be no moral conflicts: morality cannot require you to do something and also require you not to do it.

Normative transmission

Many authors also think there must be some sort of transmission of normativity from an end to a means, which should be reflected in deontic logic. On page 126 I rejected the specific principle of End to Means Transmission for requirements. I reject the corresponding deontic principle for the same reason as I gave there.

I assume there is some true normative transmission principle, though I do not know what it is.[28] But I am not impressed by a reason several philosophers offer for thinking there has to be one. When a rational person is motivated to pursue an end, she is motivated to take a means to it. That is to say, there is transmission of motivation from end to means. These philosophers think that is best explained by normative transmission.[29]

Thomas Nagel is one. He says:

> Reasons are transmitted across the relation between ends and means, and that is also the commonest and simplest way that motivational influence is transmitted.[30]

But this is a bad explanation. A person may be motivated to pursue an end even when she has no normative reason to pursue it. Yet even then, if the person is rational, her motivation is transmitted from end to means. This cannot be explained by transmission of normative reasons.

If you insist on explaining transmission of motivation Nagel's way, you will end up imputing to the person the belief that she has a normative reason to pursue her end. For example, Christine Korsgaard says:

> For the instrumental principle to provide you with a reason [to take the means to an end], you must think that the fact that you will an end *is a reason* for the end. . . . [This] means that your willing the end gives it a normative status for you, that your willing the end in a sense makes it good.[31]

There is no need to be so extravagant with normativity. The best way to explain transmission of motivation is through the Instrumental Requirement of rationality set out on page 159. It directly links intending an end to intending a means. Neither normativity nor normative beliefs are involved.

Notes

1   This chapter grew from my paper 'Requirements'.
2   This last, nice example comes from Ali Abedi.

3   I am not sure what sense Roderick Chisholm has in mind in his well-known work on require-
     ments, presented in his 'The ethics of requirement' and 'Practical reasoning'. His example
     from Kant, 'Virtue requires being rewarded' (p. 119 in the reprinted version of 'Practical
     reason') seems closest to this third meaning, but I find it hard to make good sense of this
     sentence. It certainly uses neither the property sense nor the source sense, either of which
     might be displayed in 'Virtue requires you to be honest towards strangers'. I believe that
     Chisholm and I are dealing with different subjects.
4   See p. 47.
5   My thanks to Olav Gjelsvik for pointing this out to me.
6   This suggestion was put to me by Berit Brogaard and Joe Salerno.
7   A similar analysis is defended by Julian Fink in 'A constitutive account of "rationality
     requires"'.
8   Smith, 'Internal reasons', p. 115.
9   See 'Deontic logic' by Paul McNamara.
10   Kit Fine has pointed out to me that my account of source requirements is closely parallel to
     his account of essence presented in his 'Essence and modality'. I have not been able to work
     out whether there are simply parallels, or whether my account of requirement is an actual
     instance of his general account of essence.
11   Niko Kolodny recommended this order of priority to me.
12   I borrow this term from Niko Kolodny in 'Why be rational?'. However, I give it a slightly
     different meaning, as Benjamin Kiesewetter pointed out to me.
13   I first learnt this point from Sven Danielsson's 'What shall we do with deontic logic?'. Dan-
     ielsson applies it to *ought* rather than *requires*. He says: 'There are weighty reasons for giving
     up the idea that we ought to do what we necessarily do if we do what we ought to do'.
14   A full formalization of the system appears in Berislav Žarnić's 'A logical typology of norma-
     tive systems'.
15   One theory of this sort appears in John Horty's *Agency and Deontic Logic*, particularly in
     chapter 3.
16   As Krister Bykvist pointed out to me.
17   I was pointed towards this example by advice from James Higginbotham and Jacob Ross.
     Inheritance also leads to Ross's Paradox; see Alf Ross, 'Imperatives and logic'.
18   Goble, 'Normative conflicts and deontic logic'.
19   Hume, *Treatise*, book 3, part 2, section 5.
20   But see p. 128.
21   For a nice account, see Horty's *Agency and Deontic Logic*, chapter 2.
22   Here I am simply following the lead set by Patricia Greenspan in 'Conditional oughts and
     hypothetical imperatives'. I differ from Greenspan in that I reject Axiom K whereas she
     accepts it.
23   Kieran Setiya makes this claim about ought, rather than requirement, in his 'Cognitivism
     about practical reasoning'.
24   I have recently received from Benjamin Kiesewetter a powerful defence of End to Means
     Transmission in his paper 'Instrumental normativity'.
25   Torbjörn Tännsjö argues in *From Reasons to Norms: On the Basic Question in Ethics* that
     all practical reasons are moral.
26   Chapter 4 of Samuel Scheffler's *Human Morality* is a useful discussion of whether this is so.
27   Thomson, *The Realm of Rights*, p. 83, quoted by John Horty in 'Reasoning with moral
     conflicts'. Thomson's view is not universally shared. In 'Values and the heart's command',
     Bas van Fraassen argues that deontic conflicts and moral conflicts are possible. He does not
     distinguish between the two. In 'Reasoning with moral conflicts', John Horty does distinguish
     the two. He appears to agree with van Fraassen about moral conflicts, but he seems to think

there can be no conflicts among all things considered oughts. For the reason given in this section, I do not see how that is possible.

28 In 'Instrumental reasons', Niko Kolodny offers one that I can find no fault with.
29 Besides Nagel, another example is Sergio Tenenbaum. See his 'Minimalism about intention'.
30 *The Possibility of Altruism*, p. 33.
31 Korsgaard, 'The Normativity of Instrumental Reason', pp. 245–6.

8

Conditional Requirements

8.1 Application and content

Most requirements are conditional in some way. Prudence requires you to wear a warm coat, conditional on its being winter. Morality requires you to keep your promises, which means it requires you, conditional on your having promised to do something, to do it. Rationality requires you to intend appropriate means to any end that you intend, which means it requires you to intend the means conditional on your intending the end. And so on. In this chapter I shall consider in what different ways a requirement can be conditional. I shall be particularly concerned with the requirements of rationality, and in what way they are conditional.

First, a requirement may have a conditional content. When a requirement of prudence, for example, has conditional content, then prudence requires of you that if p then q, for some propositions p and q. The content – if p then q – may be a material conditional, or a conditional of some other sort. I shall mostly assume we are dealing with material conditionals. However, I shall mention other sorts on pages 141–3.

Alternatively, a requirement might be conditional in its application rather than in its content. By this I mean simply that it requires something of you if some condition is satisfied. For instance, it may be that, if p, then prudence requires q of you. A requirement may be conditional both in application and in content: its application may be conditional on some condition, and its content conditional on some other condition.

When a requirement is conditional in its content, it is commonly said to have a wide scope, because what is required is the compound proposition that if p then q. When the requirement is conditional in application, it is commonly said to have a narrow scope, because what is required is simply q.

You might at first think that a narrow-scope requirement would follow from the corresponding wide-scope one. If it is required of you that if p

then q, does it not follow that, if p obtains, it is required of you that q? It does not. That would be factual detachment, which I rejected on pages 123–4.

The question sometimes arises whether a particular conditional requirement is conditional in its content or in its application. It may be clear for some p and q that prudence requires of you that q conditional on p, but there may be a question whether prudence requires of you that if p then q, or alternatively whether the situation is that, if p, prudence requires of you that q. The question is whether the requirement has a wide or a narrow scope.

As an example, here is a specific question about scope. Suppose prudence requires you to use a mosquito net, conditional on being in tropical Africa. Is the position that, if you are in tropical Africa, prudence requires of you that you use a mosquito net? Or instead, does prudence require of you that, if you are in tropical Africa, you use a mosquito net? In the former case the requirement has a narrow scope; in the latter a wide one.

Here is a way to think about the question. There are three different things you can do with a requirement. You can infringe it, satisfy it or avoid it.[1] If you are in tropical Africa and you do not use a mosquito net, you infringe the requirement, and that is so whether it has a wide or a narrow scope. If you are in tropical Africa and you use a mosquito net, you satisfy the requirement, whether it has a wide or a narrow scope. But suppose you are not in tropical Africa. In that case, do you avoid the requirement, or do you satisfy it? This is the question that separates the two possibilities. If the requirement has a wide scope, you satisfy it; if it has a narrow scope, you avoid it.

In section 8.2, I shall answer the question of scope for the conditional requirements of rationality, as far as I can. This turns out to be hard to do, because it is hard to identify satisfactory criteria for answering it. We can work out the consequences of the two alternative answers, to see which we can most easily live with. However, we are not in a position to work out many consequences because the logic of requirements is so thin.

Furthermore, the question is complicated by the fact that both sorts of requirement may obtain simultaneously. It may be true both that a source requires of you that if p then q, and also that, if p is true, the same source requires of you that q. Nothing rules out that possibility.

Properties corresponding to conditional requirements

One putative approach to answering the question about scope will definitely not work. It will do no good to think about the *property* that corresponds to the source of requirements we are investigating. The requirements of, say, rationality determine the boundaries of the property of rationality according to the definition on page 118. They determine when you are rational and when you are not rational. You might think we could start by working out what implications wide-scope and narrow-scope requirements have for the property of rationality. It might turn out that one gives a better account of the property than the other. But actually that is not so.

At least, it is not so if the content of the wide-scope requirement is a material conditional. It turns out in that case at least that wide-scope and narrow-scope requirements have exactly the same implications for the corresponding property. The proposition that you are rational comes out exactly the same, whichever way a conditional requirement of rationality is formulated. Either way, you are rational at exactly the same worlds. So in determining the scope of the requirement, we can learn nothing from the property.

Let me put this more precisely. Take the code of some source S. This code defines the S-property corresponding to the code, in the manner described on page 118. Now change the code by replacing a wide-scope requirement that $p \supset q$ with a narrow-scope requirement that q, which applies only if p if true. In more detail, do this as follows. Change the code only at worlds where it requires $p \supset q$. At those worlds, delete the requirement that $p \supset q$, and at those of them where p is true, add the requirement that q. Make no other changes. It turns out that the property that corresponds to the code is unchanged by this operation. That is proved in the appendix to this chapter.

Given this fact, you might wonder why the question of scope is important. Should we not simply be interested in the property – in what makes a person rational, for instance? But I explained on page 119 that we have a good reason to be interested also in what the code requires of you in your particular circumstances. You may be far from possessing the associated property – rationality, for instance. The property may not be very relevant at all.

8.2   Conditional requirements of rationality

Jurisdiction

Before coming to rationality, it will be helpful to start with law. The law requires you to drive on the left, conditional on your being in Britain. Is this requirement conditional in application or in content? Is the position that, if you are in Britain, the law requires you to drive on the left? Or is it that the law requires of you that, if you are in Britain, you drive on the left?

That is easy to answer. This requirement is conditional in application. The law requiring you to drive on the left is a British law, so it can apply only to people in Britain. In this legal case, the domain of the requirement is obviously limited by the jurisdiction of the particular legal system.

The position is that, if you are in Britain, the law requires you to drive on the left. If you are in Britain and drive on the left, you satisfy the requirement. If you are in Britain and drive on the right, you infringe the requirement. If you are not in Britain you avoid the requirement; you are outside its domain.

Rationality also has a sort of jurisdiction. It applies to some things, such as people, and not to other things, such as stones. I do not need to specify exactly where the boundary of its jurisdiction lies.[2] Perhaps I may safely say the jurisdiction consists of all beings that have a rational capacity, whilst deliberately leaving it unspecified what a rational capacity is. But whatever the jurisdiction turns out to be, it provides a limit to the domain of requirements of rationality.

Because of rationality's limited domain, all my formulae that say 'Rationality requires of N that . . .' are implicitly prefixed by the condition 'If N is within the jurisdiction of rationality'. Requirements of rationality are conditional in their application to that extent.

Scope

Many are not conditional in application to any further extent. They apply to anyone who is within the jurisdiction of rationality. For those requirements, 'Rationality requires of N that . . .' may be prefixed by 'Necessarily, if N is within the jurisdiction of rationality'. For instance, the plausible requirement not to have contradictory intentions may be formulated:

> *No Contradictory Intentions.* Necessarily, if you are within the jurisdiction of rationality, rationality requires of you that you do not intend to F and intend not to F.

This requirement entails the necessary condition of rationality C2 on page 76, that, necessarily, if you are rational you do not intend to F and also intend not to F.

All the conditions C1–C4 on page 76 are entailed by necessary requirements of rationality in the same way. Any necessary requirement entails a corresponding necessary condition. The converse is not true; I explained on page 119 that not all conditions that are necessary for possessing the property of rationality are necessarily required by rationality. So the requirement is strictly stronger than the condition.

Nearly all necessary requirements of rationality are conditional in their contents. They have a wide scope. No Contradictory Intentions can be rewritten to show its conditional content:

No Contradictory Intentions. Necessarily, if you are within the jurisdiction of rationality, rationality requires of you that, if you intend to *F*, you do not intend not to *F*.

Another example is Enkrasia, which I adopted on page 23. I repeat it here, adding the prefix, but simplifying it in other respects:

Enkrasia, very roughly. Necessarily, if you are within the jurisdiction of rationality, rationality requires of you that, if you believe you ought to *F*, you intend to *F*.

In contrast to the wide-scope formulation, Niko Kolodny in 'Why be rational?' defends this narrow-scope version of Enkrasia:

Narrow-Scope Enkrasia. Necessarily, if you are within the jurisdiction of rationality, and if you believe you ought to *F*, rationality requires of you that you intend to *F*.

In the rest of this chapter I shall review some considerations that may favour wide-scope or narrow-scope formulations of rational requirements. I shall focus particularly on Enkrasia because much of the debate has focused on it.

My overall conclusion will be modest. I shall defend wide-scope requirements such as Enkrasia, but I shall not deny narrow-scope ones such as Narrow-Scope Enkrasia. Both could be true. They could both be true even holding constant the meaning of 'requires'. But it is also possible that one is true under one sense of 'requires' and the other under another sense. Colloquial English is not very precise in matters of scope; I mentioned an example on page 111. I am committed to the source sense of 'requires', but even within the source sense there may be a choice about how to tighten up its meaning in logical respects. It can be tightened in a way that gives the requirements of rationality a wide scope; perhaps it can alternatively be tightened in a different way.

Nevertheless, I shall offer good reasons for attending to wide-scope requirements rather than narrow-scope ones, and that is what I shall do in the rest of this book.

Inconsistent requirements

Intuition suggests that some sources of requirements do not issue inconsistent requirements, and rationality is plausibly one of them. The main concern of rationality is consistency among a person's attitudes, so we should not expect it to issue inconsistent requirements. But it turns out that narrow-scope formulae, including Narrow-Scope Enkrasia, are more prone to inconsistency than are wide-scope ones. This is one reason for doubting narrow-scope formulae.

I shall give an example based on Narrow-Scope Enkrasia and No Contradictory Intentions. To avoid begging the question, we could equally well use this narrow-scope version of this requirement:

> Necessarily, if you are within the jurisdiction of rationality, and if you intend to F, rationality requires of you that you do not intend not to F.

Suppose you believe you are facing a deontic conflict: for some F, you believe you ought to F and also believe you ought not to F. Then, according to Narrow-Scope Enkrasia,

> Rationality requires of you that you intend to F.

and

> Rationality requires of you that you intend not to F.

Put these two requirements together with the requirement that you do not have contradictory intentions, in either the wide-scope or the narrow-scope form. The conclusion emerges that the requirements you are under cannot all be satisfied together. This is a consequence of the narrow-scope formulation of Enkrasia.

It does not mean you cannot be rational; Narrow-Scope Enkrasia does not have such a strong consequence as that. The requirements that apply to you at the actual world cannot be satisfied together, but there may be other worlds where all the requirements that apply to you at those worlds are satisfied. It would be a world where you do not believe you are facing a deontic conflict. Still, it remains intuitively implausible that rationality would ever place you under inconsistent requirements. If it does not, we have to reject Narrow-Scope Enkrasia.

One point could be made in its defence. Notice that in my example you are actually not rational. Since at the actual world you are under conflicting requirements, at least one of those requirements is inevitably not satisfied at the actual world. Therefore, at the actual world you do not have the property of rationality. This is not a consequence of the narrow-scope formulae particularly. It would be true even if we switched to the wide-scope formulae. That is guaranteed by the theorem described on page 134: when a narrow-scope formula entails you are not rational, so does the corresponding wide-scope one.

Either way, so long as you believe you ought to *F* and also believe you ought not to *F*, you are not rational. This does not imply that rationality specifically requires you not to have this pair of beliefs. It implies that if you have this pair of beliefs, you must be failing to satisfy some requirement of rationality or other.

Given that you are not rational, we might be less bothered by the fact that rationality imposes inconsistent requirements on you. We might think that, given that you are not rational, a conflict within rationality cannot be avoided. That is the point that could be made in defence of Narrow-Scope Enkrasia.

It is not a good one. If you were rational you would already satisfy all the requirements you are under. Requirements matter most for people who are not rational, and the requirements they are under should contribute to making them rational. The only way you can achieve rationality is by either not having the belief that you ought to *F* or not having the belief that you ought not to *F*. But these beliefs do not even figure in the requirements you are under according to Narrow-Scope Enkrasia. According to that formula, the requirements you are under are, first, to intend to *F* and second, to intend not to *F*. So Narrow-Scope Enkrasia seems particularly inappropriate.

Wide-scope Enkrasia avoids this complaint. According to it, rationality requires you either not to believe you ought to *F* or to intend to *F*, and it also requires you either not to believe you ought not to *F* or to intend not to *F*. Even when we add that rationality requires you not both to intend to *F* and intend not to *F*, it remains possible for you to satisfy all three requirements. One way to do so is by not believing you ought to *F*; another is by not believing you ought not to *F*. Doing one or the other is necessary if you are to be rational. So fulfilling the requirements you are under would at least contribute to your rationality to this extent.

Narrow-Scope Enkrasia makes it inevitable that the requirements of rationality will be inconsistent with each other in some circumstances. My wide-scope formulation of Enkrasia does not do that. This suggests the narrow-scope formulation is incorrect, since intuition suggests that rationality should not issue inconsistent requirements. However, I do not claim this as a conclusive demonstration that the narrow-scope formula is false. Perhaps we should accept that rationality sometimes issues inconsistent requirements.

Asymmetry

Next an argument that Mark Schroeder deploys in his 'The scope of instrumental reason' against the wide-scope formulation of various requirements.[3] When a wide-scope requirement holds, what is required of you is a conditional proposition that if *p* then *q*. If this is a material conditional or any other conditional that contraposes, it is equivalent to the proposition that if not q then not p. So Substitution of Logical Equivalents implies it is also required of you that if not q then not p. Wide-scope requirements have this sort of symmetry: they can be read backwards or forwards. But sometimes the situation is not symmetrical.

Take as an example the wide-scope formulation of Enkrasia.[4]

> Rationality requires of you that if you believe you ought to F, you intend to F.

Contraposing gives:

> Rationality requires of you that if you do not intend to F, you do not believe you ought to F.

Enkrasia, then, is symmetrical between believing you ought to F and not intending to F. But so far as rationality is concerned, the relation between believing you ought to F and not intending to F is asymmetrical. It would be rational for you to intend to F because you believe you ought to F, but irrational for you not to believe you ought to F because you do not intend to F.

The Instrumental Requirement of rationality, which is stated on page 159, provides another example of asymmetric rational relations between attitudes. Roughly, rationality requires you to intend what you believe is a means implied by an end that you intend. Suppose you intend an end e. It would be rational to intend m because you believe m is a means implied by e, but not rational not to believe m is a means implied by e because you do not intend m.

How should this asymmetry be accounted for? The first thing to notice is that it does not have to be accounted for within the requirement of rationality itself. Take the case of Enkrasia again. You are necessarily not rational if you believe you ought to F but you do not intend to F. This fact is symmetrical between believing you ought to F and not intending to F. It can be accounted for by Enkrasia in either its wide-scope or its narrow-scope formulation. The relation between the belief and the non-intention also has asymmetrical features, but nothing says those features also have to be accounted for by Enkrasia. Many requirements of rationality apply to you at any time, and some other one of those requirements may break the symmetry.

For instance, some requirements require particular relations to hold among your cognitive states, including your beliefs. The Modus Ponens Requirement on page 157 is an example. Suppose you have beliefs – call them 'grounding beliefs' – whose contents entail by modus ponens that you ought to F, and suppose you care about whether you ought to F. Then the Modus Ponens Requirement tell us you are not rational if you do not believe you ought to F.

Enkrasia tells us you are not rational if you believe you ought to F but do not intend to F. Those two requirements together tell us that, given your grounding beliefs, you can be rational only if you believe you ought to F and you intend to F. Consequently, your situation is not symmetrical between intending to F and not believing you ought to F. Your grounding beliefs break the symmetry.

There are no doubt other requirements of this sort, besides the Modus Ponens Requirement. No doubt one or more requirements connect a belief that you ought to F with your evidence that you ought to F; I do not try to specify those requirements in this book. So there are a number of states you might be in – call them 'grounding states' – that ensure you are not rational unless you believe you ought to F. Being in any of these states breaks the symmetry.

However, that does not explain the whole asymmetry. The situation is asymmetrical even if you are not in any grounding state. Suppose you are not in any state that determines you are not rational unless you believe you ought to F. But suppose that actually you do believe you ought to F. And suppose you do not intend to F. You do not satisfy Enkrasia, so at present you are not rational on that account. You can come to satisfy Enkrasia either by starting to intend to F or by ceasing to believe you ought to F. However, if you cease believing you ought to F because you do not intend to F, you are not rational. On the other hand, if you start intending to F because you believe you ought to F, you may be rational. That is an asymmetry that still needs to be accounted for.

Actually, that description of the asymmetry is not quite accurate. Suppose your lack of an intention to F causes you by some unconscious process to consider whether, indeed, you ought to F. Suppose that, once you start considering, you notice you have no grounds for believing you ought to F, and consequently you drop your belief. You might be rational, even though you drop the belief because you do not intend to F.

What makes this consistent with your being rational is the fact that the 'because' is purely causal. On the other hand, you will definitely not be rational if your lack of belief is *based on* – as opposed to merely caused by – your lack of an intention. So the asymmetry is this: you may rationally have an intention to F based on a belief that you ought to F, but you may not rationally lack the belief that you ought to F on the basis of your not intending to F.

Basing prohibitions

I account for this asymmetry by means of a further requirement of rationality:

Rationality requires of you that you do not not believe you ought to *F* on the basis of your not intending to *F*.

There is no symmetrical, reciprocal requirement. This requirement is separate from Enkrasia; it rules out one particular way of satisfying Enkrasia. It is an example of a 'basing prohibition of rationality'. I shall examine basing prohibitions in section 10.4. I should admit immediately that I do not know how to give a proper analysis of *basing*.

It is important to recognize that there are basing prohibitions. Besides rational requirements such as Enkrasia, which are synchronic and require particular combinations of attitudes to obtain or not obtain at any time, there are also rational requirements that require some particular attitude, or lack of an attitude, not to be based on other particular attitudes or lacks. They are asymmetric, and they explain the asymmetry we have been exploring.

There are basing prohibitions but no positive basing requirements.[5] For instance, if you believe you ought to *F*, there is no requirement that you have an intention to *F* that is based on this belief. To be rational, just having the intention is enough. Suppose you have always intended to *F*, but you have only recently formed the belief that you ought to *F*. Your intention is not based on your belief, but nevertheless you may be rational.

For this reason, the asymmetry cannot be accounted for by making adjustments to positive requirements such as Enkrasia. It depends on a separate prohibition. It gives no reason to favour one version of Enkrasia over another.

That is my account of the asymmetry. There are wide-scope synchronic requirements of rationality, and also basing prohibitions of rationality.

Alternative accounts of the asymmetry

What alternative accounts of the asymmetry are available? We are taking it for granted that rationality requires you to intend to *F*, conditional in some way on your believing you ought to *F*. Is there a way of understanding the nature of the conditionality that accounts for the asymmetry?

Narrow-scope requirements are not symmetrical in the way wide-scope ones are, so they seem promising candidates. Narrow-Scope Enkrasia on page 136 is not symmetrical, for example. But remember the asymmetry we need to account for is an explanatory one. Consequently, a narrow-scope requirement could not account for it adequately if it was understood as a material conditional. Material conditionals do not represent an explanatory connection. But we might understand Narrow-Scope Enkrasia as some other sort of conditional statement, rather than a material conditional.

'If' sometimes implies an explanatory connection. The sentence 'If the moon shines he will come' can imply that if the moon shines he will come because it shines. We could even make an explanatory connection explicit by adding a clause to Narrow-Scope Enkrasia

> Necessarily, if you are within the jurisdiction of rationality, and if you believe you ought to F, then because you believe you ought to F, rationality requires of you that you intend to F.

This makes good sense.

However it does not account for the full extent of the asymmetry. It does not express the negative requirement not to lack the belief that you ought to F on the basis of your not intending to F. That needs to be a separate requirement. Since we need a separate requirement, and since the second requirement on its own is enough to account for the asymmetry, the narrow-scope requirement has in this respect no advantage over the wide-scope one.

There are various other ways of understanding conditional requirements. One is A. W. Price's in *Contextuality in Practical Reason*. Price argues that, when a conditional requirement has the sort of asymmetry we are dealing with, the 'if' it contains should not be understood as a connective that links propositions.[6] Price would formulate Enkrasia as 'Rationality requires you to (intend to F if you believe you ought to F)', where the brackets mark out a single verb phrase. Syntactically, the 'if' clause modifies the verb 'intend'. Semantically, according to Price, 'if' in this context 'signifies the relation of a ground to a consequent'.[7] Rationality requires of you that you have an intention to F that is grounded on your belief that you ought to F. That is his understanding of Enkrasia.

This proposal has two faults. First, it is not true that rationality requires your intention to be grounded on your belief. If you have the intention before you have the belief, and simply keep it when you acquire the belief, you would not fail of rationality on that account. Second, it does not capture the negative requirement that, if you do not believe you ought to F, your lack of belief must not be based on your not intending to F.

Dyadic requirements

Another treatment of conditional requirements takes 'rationality requires' to be a dyadic operator, following the model of dyadic deontic logic.[8] Instead of putting rational requirements in the form 'Rationality requires of you that p', as I have been doing, we put them in the form 'Rationality requires of you, conditional on p, that q'. 'Rationality requires of you, conditional on . . . , that . . .' expresses a new propositional operator, which operates on two propositions rather than one.

We could define the dyadic operator in terms of the monadic one. We could say that 'Rationality requires of you, conditional on p, that q' means the same as 'Rationality requires of you that if p then q', for some sense of 'if . . . then'. Or alternatively we could say it means the same as 'If p then rationality requires of you that q'. But we do not have to reduce the dyadic operator in this way. We could give it a different meaning by equipping it with a logic of some sort, and connecting it in some more complicated way with our intuitive understanding of rationality. Again, this would be to follow the model of dyadic deontic logic. We could make sure the logic is asymmetric in that it does not allow contraposition of p and q.

The dyadic operator treated this way is an artificial construction that offers a new flexibility in specifying requirements of rationality. Enkrasia could be formulated as:

> Rationality requires of you, conditional on your believing you ought to F, that you intend to F.

This is to be understood in the asymmetric, dyadic manner.

I say this is an artificial construction, but it may not be. The semantics given to the dyadic operator by deontic logicians is the same as Angelika Kratzer's semantics for deontic conditionals. That is supposed to be part of the semantics of 'if' in natural language.[9]

In any case, this formulation cannot account adequately for the asymmetry, for the same reason as before. The asymmetry exists because of a negative requirement of rationality: if you do not believe you ought to F, your lack of belief must *not* be explained in one particular way. Enkrasia, even understood dyadically, does not account for this fact.

Nothing in this whole discussion of asymmetry gives support to a narrow-scope formulation of Enkrasia.

Diachronic requirements

Till now, I have been considering synchronic requirements only: requirements concerned with the relations among contemporaneous mental attitudes. In 'Why be rational?' Niko Kolodny says he is talking about requirements on processes rather than states, but the particular requirements he mentions in that paper are not on processes. I believe he is actually thinking of diachronic requirements on attitudes. He may have in mind a formula such as this:

> *Diachronic Narrow-Scope Enkrasia.* If you believe at one time that you ought to F, there is a later time such that rationality requires of you that at that later time you intend to F.

Compare the wide-scope version:

> *Diachronic Wide-Scope Enkrasia.* Rationality requires of you that, if at one time you believe you ought to *F*, there is a later time at which you intend to *F*.

I mention the wide-scope version because it would be possible to derive Narrow-scope Diachronic Enkrasia from it. The axiom of Necessary Detachment set out on page 123 would permit the derivation. To make it, we would have to treat events that occur before a particular time as necessary relative to that time. I do not need to spell out how the derivation would go. On page 124 I explained how we might derive a moral requirement to do a particular act from a general moral requirement to keep promises you have made. This present derivation would follow the same pattern.

So if I accepted the wide-scope version of this diachronic formula, I would accept the narrow-scope version too. However, actually I accept neither. The two diachronic versions of Enkrasia are both false. It is possible to believe at one time you ought to *F*, and fail to intend at any later time to *F*, and yet be rational.

How? Like this. Right up to a particular time *t*, you believe you ought to *F*, and up to that time you intend to *F*. Up to that time we may assume you are rational, because you satisfy the synchronic version of Enkrasia. Then, at that time, for some good reason you stop believing you ought to *F*. Perhaps you learn that *F*ing is dangerous. Simultaneously you drop your intention to *F*. There is nothing irrational about that; we may assume you remain rational, therefore. So you believe at *t* that you ought to *F* and at no later time do you intend to *F*, yet you are rational throughout.

This counterexample illustrates a general difficulty faced by diachronic requirements. They link attitudes at different times, and they are not plausible if the first attitude has vanished by the time the second appears. However, I do not deny all diachronic requirements of rationality;[10] chapter 10 mentions some I accept.

The normativity of rationality

One of the main theses of Kolodny's 'Why be rational?' is that rationality is not normative. I explained on page 27 what it means to say a requirement on you to *F* is normative: it means the requirement is a reason for you to *F*. To say rationality is normative means that all the requirements that issue from rationality are normative. Kolodny points out that, if Narrow-Scope Enkrasia (page 136) were true, and if rationality were normative, it would immediately follow that

Necessarily, if you are within the jurisdiction of rationality, and if you believe you ought to *F*, you have a reason to intend to *F*.

He argues that cannot possibly be so.

His argument is that this would amount to impossible bootstrapping. It is not possible that, merely by believing you ought to *F*, you can ensure that you have a reason to intend to *F*. Your belief might be false; it might not be the case that you ought to *F*. If not, how could you possibly have a reason to intend to *F*, just because of your false belief? Kolodny thinks the belief cannot bootstrap a reason into existence that way.

I accept this point. Kolodny's own argument for it is brief,[11] but I agree with his objection to bootstrapping.[12] On page 82 I too used a bootstrapping argument with a different purpose. From his bootstrapping argument, Kolodny draws the conclusion that requirements of rationality are not normative. I draw the alternative conclusion that we cannot rely on Kolodny's formulation of Enkrasia.

Enkrasia formulated in my wide-scope way leads to no parallel argument, because it does not entail bootstrapping. True, it can seem to be exposed to some risk of bootstrapping through Necessary Detachment.[13] From the wide-scope formulation on page 136, together with Necessary Detachment set out on page 123, we can derive:

Necessarily, if you are within the jurisdiction of rationality, and if you necessarily believe you ought to *F*, rationality requires you to intend to *F*.

If rationality is normative:

Necessarily, if you are within the jurisdiction of rationality, and if you necessarily believe you ought to *F*, you have a reason to intend to *F*.

So bootstrapping would be entailed if you necessarily believe you ought to *F*. But there is no real bootstrapping problem here, because it could not be necessary that you have this belief.

True, it could be necessary in a psychological sense: you might be psychologically unable to help having it. But we have no reason to accept Necessary Detachment for mere psychological necessity. Nothing suggests we should limit the possible worlds in our semantics to psychologically possible ones. Imagine, say, that you were psychologically unable to rid your mind of a particular pair of contradictory beliefs. We would still think that rationality requires you not to have this pair of beliefs. Now we have further good reason not to limit ourselves to psychologically possible worlds: if we did, we might be stuck with impossible bootstrapping through Necessary Detachment.

So it is easy to block the derivation of impossible bootstrapping from the wide-scope formulation of Enkrasia. But impossible bootstrapping can be derived from the narrow-scope formulation through modus ponens. That derivation cannot be blocked.

The upshot is that Kolodny's narrow-scope formulation bears the whole weight of his conclusion that rationality is not normative. I would not put so much confidence in it. To be sure, there is a genuine question over whether the requirements of rationality are normative. I shall consider it in chapter 11. But it is a strong and *prima facie* implausible claim to deny that rationality is normative. I think it unwise to close off this question simply by adopting the narrow-scope formulation of Enkrasia.

The bootstrapping argument shows that Narrow-Scope Enkrasia, in so far as it is true, is not normative. It may be true under some sense of 'require'; I do not deny that. But I have shown in this section that we have at least as good evidence for wide-scope Enkrasia as we do for Narrow-Scope Enkrasia. And we have as yet no grounds for thinking that wide-scope Enkrasia is not normative.

According to wide-scope Enkrasia, rationality requires of you that, if you believe you ought to *F*, you intend to *F*. For all we know as yet, this requirement might constitute a reason. If so, it would be a reason for you that, if you believe you ought to *F*, you intend to *F*. I use the ungrammatical construction I introduced on page 66, to make it explicit that the reason has a wide scope to match the wide scope of the requirement.

If we adopt whatever is the sense of 'require' that validates wide-scope Enkrasia, then for all we know as yet, every requirement of rationality in this sense could be normative. That is to say, it could be true that rationality is normative. So Kolodny has not demonstrated it is not. He has demonstrated only that some requirements of rationality, in a sense of 'require' that *may* be acceptable, are not normative.

I do not want to close off the question of whether rationality is normative, just by adopting a particular sense of 'require'. So from now on I shall work with wide-scope formulations and adopt whatever sense of 'require' goes with them.

Notes

1 Mark Schroeder makes this point in his 'The scope of instrumental reason'. Peter Vranas develops it more formally in 'New foundations for imperative logic'.

2 The question is considered in more detail in Julian Fink's 'A constitutive account of "rationality requires"'.

3 The same point appears in Niko Kolodny's 'Why be rational?' and in A. W. Price's *Contextuality in Practical Reason*, p. 81.

4   This is Niko Kolodny's application of the argument in 'Why be rational?'

5   Here I disagree with Jonathan Way's 'The symmetry of rational requirements'.

6   p. 67.

7   p. 93.

8   See, for instance, G. H. Von Wright, 'A note on deontic logic and derived obligation', or David Lewis, 'Semantic analysis for dyadic deontic logic'.

9   For the semantics of dyadic deontic logic, see David Lewis, 'Semantic analyses for dyadic deontic logic'. For Kratzer's semantics, see her *Modals and Conditionals*, pp. 66–8.

10 In 'Unifying the requirements of rationality', Andrew Reisner takes an entirely sceptical attitude to them.

11 It is in a footnote on p. 539.

12 See my 'Normative requirements'.

13 I take this point from Kieran Setiya's 'Cognitivism about instrumental reason'. Setiya derives the bootstrapping conclusion using the principle of End to Means Transmission, which I rejected on p. 126. But Necessary Detachment can serve instead to reconstruct his conclusion.

Appendix to Chapter 8

Theorem

Let R be a code of requirements on N. Define a different code R' as follows.

1) For worlds w where $(p \supset q)$ is not in $R(w)$, then $R'(w)$ is the same as $R(w)$.
2) For worlds w where $(p \supset q)$ is in $R(w)$ and p is false at w, $R'(w)$ is the same as $R(w)$ except that $(p \supset q)$ is removed.
3) For worlds w where $(p \supset q)$ is in $R(w)$ and p is true at w, $R'(w)$ is the same as $R(w)$ except that $(p \supset q)$ is removed and q is added.

Let F be the property that corresponds to R and F' the property that corresponds to R'. Then at all worlds, N has the property F if and only if N has the property F'.

Proof

In case 1, since $R'(w)$ is the same as $R(w)$, every proposition in $R'(w)$ is true at w if and only if every proposition in $R(w)$ is true at w. By the definition of the properties F and F', N has F at w if and only if N has F' at w.

Take case 2 and suppose first that N has F at w . By the definition of F, all propositions in $R(w)$ are true at w. Therefore all propositions in $R'(w)$ are true at w, since $R'(w)$ is the same at $R(w)$ with one proposition removed. So N has F' at w.

Take case 2 and suppose next that N does not have F at w. Since p is false at w, $(p \supset q)$ is true at w. Since N does not have F at w, some proposition in $R(w)$ other than $(p \supset q)$ is false at w. That proposition is in $R'(w)$, and it is false at w, so N does not have F' at w.

Take case 3 and suppose first that N has F at w. All the propositions in $R'(w)$ apart from q are in $R(w)$. Since N has F at w, all these propositions are true at w. q is also true at w for the following reason: p is true at w and, since $(p \supset q)$ is in $R(w)$ and N has F at w, $(p \supset q)$ is also true at w. So all propositions in $R'(w)$ are true at w. Therefore N has F' at w.

Take case 3 and suppose next that N does not have F at w. Either $(p \supset q)$ is false at w or some other proposition in $R(w)$ is false at w. If the latter, that proposition is in $R'(w)$, and it is false at w, so N does not have F' at w. If the former, since p is true at w and $(p \supset q)$ is false at w, q is false at w. But q is in $R'(w)$, so N does not have F' at w.

Therefore in all cases, N has F at w if and only if N has F' at w.

9

Synchronic Rationality

9.1 Introduction and method

I have already mentioned some requirements of rationality; for instance, I introduced Enkrasia on page 22. But I have not yet specified any of them precisely. Now I shall try to do better. In chapters 7 and 8, I described the meaning and logic of requirements in general. In this chapter and the next I shall specify a number of particular requirements of rationality and formulate them as precisely as I can. However, I cannot be sure that I have found exactly the correct formulation of all of them. Their details are always debatable.

I set these requirements out partly because I call on some of them elsewhere in the book. Another purpose is simply to explore rationality in more depth. I explained in section 7.3 that the property of rationality is defined by the requirements. So listing requirements is the way to describe rationality.

Strictly, my formulae are requirement-schemata. Each appropriate substitution for the schematic letters in one of them yields an individual requirement. I shall nevertheless call the schemata 'requirements'.

In this chapter, I shall describe some requirements of rationality that apply to the attitudes a person has at a single time. In chapter 10 I shall mention diachronic requirements, which connect together a person's attitudes at different times. There are other sorts of rational requirements, too. Suppose your attitudes satisfy all the requirements that apply to them. You would not be fully rational if they did so purely by coincidence.[1] To be fully rational, you must have dispositions that would lead you to satisfy the requirements in other circumstances too. Rationality requires you to have those dispositions. But I shall not try to formulate requirements on dispositions.

Rationality also regulates some of the processes whereby we come to satisfy the requirements on attitudes. One of these processes is the activity of reasoning. There are correct and incorrect ways to reason, and rationality

requires you, when you reason, to reason correctly. I shall consider requirements of correct reasoning in sections 13.7 and 14.2.

The requirements I set out in this chapter are examples only; they are
very far from a complete list of synchronic requirements. It is no objection to one of my requirements that there is another related one. For
instance, on page 159 I shall state something I describe as the Instrumental Requirement, but I do not mean to suggest it covers all of instrumental rationality. Later, on page 170, I shall mention another instrumental
requirement.

In this and later chapters, I mark requirements that I reject with an asterisk,
and others that I do not endorse with a question-mark.

Method

How can we identify requirements of rationality? I wish I could describe a
general method of doing so, but I am sorry to say I cannot. I shall defend a
number of requirements one by one, on particular grounds that seem appropriate. I follow Thomas Nagel's prescription:

> Rationality can be defined only in terms of adherence to rational requirements.
> One cannot discover or justify the principles which specify those requirements
> by deriving them from the concept of rationality, since it is precisely those
> requirements which define the concept, and they must be rendered plausible as
> requirements independently.[2]

Several philosophers have argued that rational requirements must be
somehow inherent in the nature of the mental states they are concerned with.
For instance, as people say, it is in the nature of beliefs that they aim at truth.
Since two contradictory beliefs cannot both be true, that may explain why it
is not rational to have contradictory beliefs. This seems plausible, but I do not
know how this general idea can be worked out in detail, to provide a criterion
for determining what rationality requires.

Other philosophers think that rationality serves some purpose, and we
can identify requirements of rationality by whether they contribute to achieving that purpose. I shall consider this idea in section 11.3, and reject it. A
specific version of it is that rationality serves the purpose of self-interest. I
see nothing to be said for that; nothing connects rationality particularly with
self-interest.

Since I reject these general approaches to rationality, I find myself forced
to appeal largely to our intuitions. But I can at least mention a few general
principles that provide some guidance.

Rationality supervenes on the mind: taking means to your end

One is that rationality supervenes on the mind: if your mind in one situation has the same properties as it has in another, then you are rational in one to the same degree as you are rational in the other. I adopted this principle on page 89.

It rules out some common views. For instance, it rules out the view that rationality requires you to take a means to your ends, when taking means involves a non-mental act. Suppose you fail to take a means to an end of yours through no fault of your own. Say you unexpectedly find yourself unable to make the necessary physical movements. Alternatively, although you are able to take the means, suppose something in the outside world prevents you from doing so; the slow-watch example on page 152 illustrates how that might happen. In these cases, what prevents you from taking means to your end is something outside your mind. According to the principle that rationality supervenes on the mind, you may nevertheless be rational. That is the right conclusion; these are not failures of your rationality. Therefore, rationality does not require you to take means to your ends.

On page 159 I shall set out what I believe to be a correct replacement for this view. Very roughly, rationality requires you to intend what you believe is a means implied by an end that you intend.

But surely, rationality must require more than just intending the means.[3] Surely it must require you actually to act, or at least try to act. Suppose you intend to catch a 12 o'clock plane, and believe you will not do so unless you get on the 9 o'clock bus. Suppose you intend to get on the 9 o'clock bus. But suppose you do not actually do so and do not try to do so. You stand around by the bus till 9 o'clock, and then it leaves without you. It seems you do not perform entirely rationally. It seems therefore that intending the means is not enough for rationality.

But this story is not really possible if nothing prevents you from getting on the bus. Up till the time the bus leaves, you intend to catch the 12 o'clock plane, and believe you will not do so unless you get on the bus. So if you are to be rational so far as your intention is concerned, you must intend to get on the bus right up to that time. That is implicit in the story. But an intention to get on the bus is a particular sort of disposition to do so. If you are disposed to do something, you do it unless something prevents you. So if you do not get on the bus, and nothing prevents you, you do not intend to.

To be sure, if you do not get on at a particular time, and nothing prevents you, it does not follow that you do not intend at that time to get on. At that time, you may intend to get on at a later time. But concentrate on what you believe to be the last possible moment when you could get on. If you are still off the bus at that time, and you do not then get on, and nothing prevents you, at that moment you do not intend to get on. At that moment you do not intend what you believe is a means implied by an end you intend. That is where you fail to be rational.

What if you do not believe there is a last moment when you could get on the bus? In this case, I am still sure that, if you do not get on the bus and nothing prevents you from doing so, then you do not intend to get on the bus. But in this case my view runs up against a technical problem. Suppose you believe you can get on the bus by initiating the act of doing so at any time before 08.59, but that initiating the act at 08.59 exactly is too late. Then it seems that, at any time before 08.59, you may intend to get on the bus by initiating the act of doing so at a later time that is still before 08.59. This seems possible even though you never actually get on the bus at all, and nothing prevents you from doing so. Yet I am sure that, if you never get on the bus and nothing prevents you, you do not intend to.

I do not know how to solve this problem. It seems to depend on an implausible precision in your attitudes. I assume it can be solved and I shall ignore it. I take it for granted that the bus story is impossible if nothing prevents you from getting on the bus.

If you have an intention and nothing prevents you, you perform the intended act. So, if nothing prevents you, you are not rational if you do not take the means to your intended end. That tempts us to the false conclusion that rationality requires you to take the means. But the reason you are not rational is that you do not intend the means, not that you do not take the means.

Now change the example to a case where something prevents you. Suppose your watch is slow. Consequently, you believe you have another five minutes when actually you have not. You take your time over saying goodbye, and when you turn round to get on the bus, it has gone. You do not get on the bus or even try to. The slowness of your watch prevents you from even trying. In a case where you are prevented from taking a means or trying to do so, you may be rational so long as you intend the means.

The principle that rationality supervenes on the mind means that nonmental acts are not subject to requirements of rationality. However, it can still make good sense to describe an act as rational or irrational. For example, to say that a particular act would be irrational may mean that, were you to do this act, because of that you would not be rational. Perhaps you would not do it without intending to, and perhaps you would be less than fully rational if you were to have this intention, given other attitudes that you have.

The guiding principle that rationality supervenes on the mind can be made a little more specific by adding another intuitive principle. What rationality requires of you is proper order in your mind. It requires your mental states to be properly related to each other. That is to say, it requires your mind to be coherent in particular respects.

Wide scope

I have already explained in section 8.2 that I shall adopt wide-scope formulations of requirements of rationality. This means that nearly all my requirements require some particular relation to hold among your attitudes. They do not require you to have or not to have any particular single attitude. One exception – perhaps the only one – is the requirement not to believe a contradiction: not to believe it is raining and not raining, for instance.

This does not mean we cannot describe a particular single attitude as rational or irrational. For instance, to say a particular attitude would be irrational may mean that, were you to have this attitude, because you have it you would not be rational. Perhaps rationality requires you not to have this attitude, given other attitudes that you have.

Synchronic requirements

The requirements described in this chapter are synchronic. They are concerned only with attitudes that exist at a single time. In the formal statements of them, the same time index 't' is attached to each attitude.

When you acquire a new attitude – for instance you learn something or you make a decision – many of your other attitudes may need to adjust correspondingly, to bring you into conformity with various synchronic requirements of rationality. These adjustments are likely to take time. In the meanwhile, you are not satisfying the synchronic requirements. So if they are genuine requirements, you are not rational. But we might think there is nothing irrational about you, so long as you adjust your attitudes to your new situation as quickly as you can. This might raise a doubt about the synchronic nature of the requirements. But it does not give me any doubt. I know I fail to be rational in many respects anyway, and I am happy to recognize this temporary respect, while my attitudes catch up.

Psychological limitations

There is a wider issue. That some of our attitudes take time to catch up is a limitation of our human psychology. Requirements of rationality as I formulate them generally take no account of this limitation. Should they? We have a choice, broadly, between two approaches to formulating requirements. One is to base them on the ideal. Ideally rational beings would instantly update their attitudes when things change. So if we take this approach, our requirements will not permit delay. The other is to formulate them in such a way that human beings, with their limitations, could satisfy them. If we take this more relaxed approach, we will have to allow for delay.

I am already pushed towards the first, stringent approach by the assumption I made on page 135 that most requirements of rationality are necessary within what I called the domain of rationality. They apply to you at all worlds where you are a rational being. This means that, if a requirement would apply to you were you a superior sort of rational being such as an angel, it applies to you as a human being.

I could still abjure the stringent approach if I chose. Just as I have already limited the domain of rational requirements to rational beings, I could limit it to rational human beings. I could assume requirements are necessary within that domain only. But that would make the requirements of rationality depend on the psychological abilities of human beings. That is an unsatisfactorily indefinite standard to work with. Who knows what human beings are capable of? So I shall by and large adopt the stringent approach. I find it natural to think of rationality as an ideal we may aim at but not attain.

However, in some cases, the stringent approach is too stringent even for me. The requirement Consistency below would be satisfied by an ideal being, but I shall explain that I find it implausibly strong.

9.2 Consistency

I shall start my survey of rational requirements with some requirements on beliefs. For beliefs, there is a further general principle that can guide us besides the ones mentioned in section 9.1. It is the principle that rational requirements on beliefs derive from deductive relations that hold among the beliefs' contents. The way deductive relations among contents feed through into requirements on beliefs is not straightforward, but since I only need examples, I shall choose relatively uncontroversial ones. They depend on logical validity, which I suppose is the least controversial sort of deductive relation.

Requirements of consistency first. I could claim that rationality requires you not to hold any beliefs that are logically inconsistent with each other:

> * *Consistency.* When p, q, r, . . . form a logically inconsistent set of propositions, rationality requires of N that N does not believe at t all of p, q, r, ...

But that would be extremely demanding. Suppose you believe the axioms of arithmetic, and you also believe the Goldbach conjecture. The axioms together with the conjecture may constitute a set of logically inconsistent propositions; mathematicians have not yet worked out whether or not this is so. If it is so, you have inconsistent beliefs, but we should not say on that basis that you are not rational. Despite a lot of devoted work, no one has yet discovered a counterexample to the Goldbach conjecture. That suggests you may at present rationally believe it, even if it is actually false.

Presumably an ideally rational being would not have logically inconsistent beliefs. It would be able to avoid them because it would know, among other things, whether the Goldbach conjecture is false. My stringent approach to rationality would therefore support Consistency. However, I am loth to adopt a requirement that goes so far beyond the abilities of human beings. Out of caution, I shall not do so.

I shall adopt much weaker consistency requirements instead. One is that rationality requires you not to have contradictory beliefs:

> *No Contradictory Beliefs.* Rationality requires of N that N does not believe at t that p and also believe at t that not p.

Even this may be too strong. On page 91 I raised the question of what to do about dialetheists, who believe there are some true contradictions. To allow for them and perhaps others, I would not object to weakening the formulae in some suitable way. I tentatively proposed a weaker version on page 91. I expect a similar case could be made for weakening most of the requirements mentioned in this chapter. But I shall ignore these rather special arguments. I assume they will demand only minor adjustments to my formulae.

A more wide-ranging objection can be drawn from Gilbert Harman's *Change in View*.[4] Everyone has some pairs of contradictory beliefs. Moreover, for most of us it is not worthwhile to weed out all of our contradictory beliefs. Surely rationality does not require us to do so. These points may seem inconsistent with No Contradictory Beliefs, but they are not. Together with No Contradictory Beliefs, they do imply that none of us satisfies all the requirements of rationality, so none of us is fully rational. But none of us fallible creatures can expect to be fully rational, and we should not resent a requirement that implies we are not. Moreover, just because rationality requires us not to have any particular pairs of contradictory beliefs, it does not follow that it requires us to search out all our pairs of contradictory beliefs and get rid of them.

Rationality also requires you not to believe any contradiction:

> *No Contradictions.* Rationality requires of N that N does not believe at t that p and not p.

This is a requirement of consistency, since a contradiction is inconsistent with itself.

This is a convenient point to mention a consistency requirement on intentions too. I first stated it on page 136:

No Contradictory Intentions. Rationality requires of N that N does not intend at t that p and also intend at t that not p.

Lars Bergström and Kent Hurtig have separately put it to me that some of my putative requirements of rationality are ones you cannot fail to satisfy. For example, it may be impossible for you to believe a contradiction. But rationality cannot require you to satisfy a condition that you cannot fail to satisfy. So they claim I am wrong to say these are requirements.

One issue here is interpretability.[5] A person whose attitudes violate too many rules of rationality cannot be interpreted as having attitudes at all. However, I think it is clear that you can fail to satisfy at least some of my requirements and still be interpretable.

For example, you might have contradictory beliefs.[6] Suppose you used to keep the whisky under the bed, but recently you started keeping it behind the fridge. When you instinctively go for whisky, you head for the bedroom, but if you first think about it, you go to the kitchen. A belief is a bundle of dispositions, and your conflicting dispositions may be enough to determine both that you believe the whisky is under the bed and that you believe the whisky is not under the bed.

You might also have contradictory intentions. You might form the intention of being in London on 23 February, to go to a seminar. Then, later, you might learn that there will be a tube strike in London on 23 February, and form the intention of not being in London that day, without noticing you already have the opposite intention. You may have both intentions for a while, until you notice the coincidence of dates. Each intention consists in a bundle of dispositions, and you may have dispositions that constitute each of them. For example, you may be disposed to say you will be in London on 23 February when you are chatting about forthcoming events in philosophy, and to say you will not be in London on 23 February when chatting about the state of public transport. You might go so far as to buy a train ticket to London, and on some other occasion also buy a ticket to go to a theatre in Penzance, both for 23 February.

So the objection applies to at most some of my requirements. In any case, even if you cannot fail to satisfy a requirement, that does not stop it from being a requirement. Suppose you train yourself to be super-rational, so it is psychologically impossible for you to have contradictory intentions. Rationality would still require you not to have contradictory intentions.

If the impossibility is not merely psychological but analytic or metaphysical, the objection is more convincing. For instance, I doubt that rationality requires you not to intend a contradiction, just because I doubt it is metaphysically possible for you to intend a contradiction. I cannot think what dispositions a contradictory intention would consist in.[7]

But you could believe a contradiction. A dialetheist may believe that the liar sentence 'This sentence is false' is true and also not true. She may be disposed to assert sincerely that it is true and not true. I said on page 155 that she may be rational in having this belief. If so, No Contradictions is false because it is too strong. But at any rate it is not false for the reason given by Bergström and Hurtig.

9.3   Deduction

Now a different sort of requirement that also derives from logical validity, but from deduction rather than consistency. I could claim that:

> ? *Deduction.* When s is logically entailed by p, q, r, . . . , rationality requires of N that, if N believes at t all of p, q, r, . . . , then N believes at t that s.

Like Consistency, Deduction is extremely demanding. Suppose you believe the axioms of arithmetic but you do not believe the Goldbach conjecture. The Goldbach conjecture may be logically entailed by the axioms of arithmetic. According to Deduction, you are not rational if it is. But that seems too harsh. For a reason I shall come to on page 159, I am not even sure that Deduction would be satisfied by an ideal being. So I do not accept Deduction.

Instead, I shall accept a requirement that derives from the simplest sort of logical deduction, modus ponens. Rationality requires you to believe what follows by modus ponens from things you believe:

> *Modus Ponens Requirement.* Rationality requires of N that, if N believes at t that p, and N believes at t that if p then q, and if N cares at t whether q, then N believes at t that q.

A technical note: p and q must be different propositions. If they were the same, the Modus Ponens Requirement would say that rationality requires of you that, if you believe at t that p, and some other conditions are true, then you believe at t that p. Rationality would require a tautology of you, which cannot plausibly be true.[8]

The Modus Ponens Requirement seems plausible. But why the caring clause? A cleaner version would be:

> ? Rationality requires of N that, if N believes at t that p and N believes at t that if p then q, then N believes at t that q.

What is wrong with that? It would be too demanding.

Gilbert Harman makes this point. He argues that rationality cannot require you to clutter your mind with all the trivial beliefs that follow from things you believe.[9] He does not reject the clean formula outright on the basis of this 'principle of clutter avoidance', because he recognizes that some beliefs do not take up space in your mind. For instance, no doubt you have believed for a long time that sheep do not live in the Atlantic Ocean, but this belief has probably not been taking up any space in your mind till now. Beliefs are dispositions, which need not occupy space. For this reason, Harman applies his 'principle of clutter avoidance' to what he calls explicit beliefs only, and not to all beliefs.

Still, his point applies to dispositional beliefs too. Robert Audi points out that you may be disposed to believe q, without actually believing it.[10] That is to say, the disposition to believe q is different from the dispositions that constitutes believing q. For example, you might be in a position to arrive at a belief in q through a quick process of reasoning, but not actually believe q because you have not done the reasoning. If you are rational, and if you believe p and you believe that if p then q, then you will certainly be disposed to believe q if you think about it. But you may not bother to do the reasoning that would give you this belief.

This point of Audi's takes us to the formula:

> ? Rationality requires of N that, if N believes at t that p and N believes at t that if p then q, then either N believes at t that q or N is disposed at t to believe that q if N thinks about it.

This may well be a genuine requirement of rationality. But the following example shows we can go further.

Suppose your route home is by South Street. You want to avoid a dangerous route, so you care whether South Street is dangerous. But suppose you do not believe South Street is dangerous, and you go home that way. There is nothing irrational in that. However, suppose you have beliefs whose contents entail by modus ponens that South Street is dangerous. Suppose moreover that you are disposed to believe South Street is dangerous, because you would quickly come to believe it if you thought about it. But suppose you have not done the reasoning, and you therefore do not actually believe South Street is dangerous. You are not entirely rational. Had you not cared whether South Street is dangerous, you might rationally have stuck with the mere disposition to have the belief. But since you do care, to be rational you need the actual belief.

The Modus Ponens Requirement generalizes this conclusion. What does 'N cares whether p' mean in the formula? It is meant to be a very weak condition. I would say you care whether p if you are seriously concerned about p, as you are in the example of South Street. But I would also say it if you only idly wonder whether *p*. I include any sort of interest in *p*. Caring whether *p* is a sort of mental state, which means the requirement is consistent with the supervenience of rationality on the mind.

We seem to have reached the Modus Ponens Requirement by taking account of a contingent limitation of our minds: there is a limit to how many beliefs we can have, and to how much time we can spend on reasoning out conclusions. Ideally rational beings do not have this limitation. So should the stringent approach to requirements that I adopted on page 154 lead me to omit the qualifying clause? Should I stick with the clean version?

I do not think so. An ideal being would bear no cost in acquiring a new belief by deduction. But if it would also get no benefit from doing so, I see no reason to think it would necessarily acquire it. Why would an ideal being have pointless beliefs? At any rate, it seems safest to include that clause in the Modus Ponens Requirement. For the same reason, I am not sure that an ideal being would satisfy Deduction.

9.4   Instrumental Rationality

The next requirement is the most fundamental instrumental requirement of practical rationality: that you intend what you believe to be a means implied by an end you intend. There are other instrumental requirements too; I shall mention some at the end of this section. But since this one is fundamental, I shall take the liberty of calling it *the* Instrumental Requirement.

Kant's formulation is:

> Who wills the end, wills (so far as reason has a decisive influence on his actions) also the means which are indispensably necessary and in his power.[11]

The words 'so far as reason has a decisive influence on his actions' show that Kant intended to state a condition of rationality. My own formula is:[12]

> *Instrumental Requirement.* Rationality requires of N that, if
> (1)   N intends at *t* that *e*, and if
> (2)   N believes at *t* that, if *m* were not so, because of that *e* would not be so, and if
> (3)   N believes at *t* that, if she herself were not then to intend *m*, because of that *m* would not be so, then
> (4)   N intends at *t* that *m*.

'*e*' and '*m*' are propositional letters; they stand for 'end' and 'means' respectively. The propositions *e* and *m* must not be the same. If they were, the

Instrumental Requirement would say that rationality requires of you that, if you intend at t that e, and some other conditions are true, you intend at t that e. It would say that rationality requires a tautology of you, which cannot plausibly be true.

Means implied

Conditions (1) and (4) of the Instrumental Requirement are straightforward, but (2) and (3) need a lot of explaining.

Their language is slightly compressed. By (2) I mean 'N believes at t that, if m were not so, e would not be so because m is not so'. (3) could be similarly expanded. These two conditions can be expressed more briefly using my technical term 'means implied by'. When I say that a is a means implied by b, I mean that, were a not so, because of that b would not be so. 'Means implied by' is not a happy expression, but I cannot think of a better one. Conditions (2) and (3) are equivalent to:

(2) N believes at t that m is a means implied by e, and
(3) N believes at t that her herself's then intending m is a means implied by m.

Compare (2) with Kant's expression 'the means which are indispensably necessary'. Kant should have said 'the means which he believes are indispensably necessary'; but I presume the omission of 'he believes' was just a slip. My condition (2) is weaker than Kant's in that mine does not require you to believe the means is indispensably necessary for the end.

Since (2) is weaker than Kant's equivalent, the Instrumental Requirement itself is stronger than Kant's formula. It is much more widely applicable than Kant's. To be sure, there are cases where you will believe a particular means is indispensably necessary to an end. For instance, unless you live in Paris, you probably believe that going to Paris is an indispensably necessary means of going to the Eiffel Tower. But cases like that are relatively rare. Much more often, you recognize more than one way to achieve your end. If you intend to get milk, no doubt you believe one means is to buy some from a shop, but you probably also believe another means is to find a cow in a field at night, and milk her. That would be such a bad means you will give it no attention. Nevertheless, you do not believe that buying milk from a shop is an indispensably necessary means of getting milk. So Kant's formula does not apply to you. On the other hand, you probably do believe that if you were not to buy milk from a shop, because of that you would not get milk. Therefore my formula probably does apply to you. Section 14.3 considers how you may arrive at a conditional belief of this sort, in the course of your practical reasoning.

Conditions (2) and (3) are even weaker than I have so far said. On page 160 I defined '*a* is a means implied by *b*', to mean that, were *a* not so, because of that *b* would not be so. This definition includes more than genuine means. Suppose that, were you to call your friend today, because of that you would not call her tomorrow.[13] On my definition, not calling your friend today counts as a means implied by calling her tomorrow. But it is not genuinely a means to calling her tomorrow.

This point provides no argument against the Instrumental Requirement. Suppose you intend to call your friend tomorrow; suppose you believe that, were you to call her today, because of that you would not call her tomorrow; and suppose you believe that, were you not to intend not to call her today, because of that you would call her today. (Perhaps you habitually call her every Sunday evening, and today is Sunday.) Then you are not rational unless you intend not to call her today, just as the Instrumental Requirement implies.

Instead, the point shows that the Instrumental Requirement is broader than it seems at first. It covers intending means you believe are implied by an end you intend, and it also covers intending means you believe are implied by preserving your intention to achieve that end.

The Instrumental Requirement is broader even than that. It covers other things that are not genuinely means. Suppose you intend to write a letter, and you cannot write adequately in any language but English. Then you no doubt believe that, if you were not to write the letter in English, because of that you would not write it at all. The Instrumental Requirement applies to you, as it should. It requires you, given your intention to write a letter, to intend to write it in English. However, writing a letter in English is not genuinely a means to writing a letter; it *is* writing a letter.

So the Instrumental Requirement is significantly more general than it may seem. But I shall mostly ignore this extra generality. I shall continue to use my technical term 'implied means' as I defined it, even though it includes more than genuine means.

Condition (3) describes a belief of *N*'s using the reflexive pronoun 'she herself' and the adverb 'then'. These are the equivalents in indirect speech of the indexical words 'I' and 'now' in direct speech. If *N* was to express her belief, she would say:

If I were not now to intend *m*, because of that *m* would not be so.

The indexical component in *N*'s belief is essential; without it the Instrumental Requirement would be false.[14] I hope this is obvious. The need for the reflexive pronoun is a second way in which practical reasoning is essentially first-personal; I mentioned the first way on pages 22–3. The need for 'then' is worth stressing here because it will be important in section 14.2. Suppose you believe at t that, were you not at some future time to intend m, then m would not be so. But suppose you believe at t that that time has not yet arrived. Then at t you might rationally not intend m.

Up to

Condition (3) is presumably what Kant meant by the words 'and in his power'. (He should have said 'and which he believes is in his power'.) But 'in his power' does not accurately express what Kant meant, or should have meant. To say the means is in a person's power is to say that the means would be so were the person to intend it. However, we need the converse: that the means would not be so were he not to intend it. This is better expressed by the colloquial expression 'up to him' than by 'in his power'.

I shall express (3) colloquially using the 'up to' phrase. Further, I shall use the expression 'm is up to you now' to mean that, if you were not now to intend m, because of that m would not be so. Condition (3) is then equivalent to:

(3) N believes at t that m is up to her herself then.

'Then' refers to the time of N's intention rather than her action.

Mine is a specialized use of 'up to'. When you say 'It is up to Karen to get on the plane', you normally mean that Karen's getting on the plane is something that has to be *done* – not merely intended – by Karen.[15] But I think mine is an acceptable meaning, now I have defined it.

Why does the Instrumental Requirement contain the condition (3)? Suppose you do not believe that m is up to you. Then you can be rational even if you intend e and believe m is a means implied by e, and yet you do not intend m. You may believe m is so anyway, without your intending it.[16]

For instance, suppose you intend to catch a particular plane tomorrow and believe your waking at six is a means implied by this end. But you know you are woken at six every morning by the braying of your neighbour's donkey. Then you do not need to intend to wake at six, because you believe that will happen anyway.

Waking at six is not an act of yours; it is something that happens to you. You might think we could eliminate the need for condition (3) by restricting m to propositions that describe acts of yours. But Frances Kamm describes more subtle examples that shows this is not so.[17] Suppose you intend an end, and believe some particular act of yours is a means implied by this end. But suppose you believe the means will be a side-effect of something else you intend. Then you may be rational even if you do not intend the means.

Here is an example, which is not Kamm's own. You are a doctor and you intend to relieve the pain of one of your patients by giving her morphine. You believe that, in order to relieve her pain, you will have to give her so much morphine that you will kill her as a side-effect. That is to say, you believe that relieving her pain and killing her share a common cause, which is giving her a lot of morphine. You do not believe killing her is a means implied by relieving her pain. You do not intend to kill her.

You also intend to admit a new patient to your hospital. Since there are no spare beds, and you cannot move living patients out of the hospital, you believe you can admit a new patient only by killing an existing one. So you believe that killing a patient is a means implied by the end of admitting a new patient, which you intend. But that is all right, because you believe you will kill a patient anyway, as a side-effect of your other intention to relieve her pain. You do not intend to kill a patient.

Intuitively, it seems you may be rational, and that is Kamm's view. So if you violate the Instrumental Requirement, that requirement is not correctly formulated. Do you violate it? First take e to be the proposition that you relieve the patient's pain and m the proposition that you kill the patient. Then you do not satisfy condition (2), since you do not believe that killing the patient is a means implied by relieving her pain. Therefore, although you do not intend to kill the patient, you do not violate the Instrumental Requirement this way.

Next take e to be the proposition that you admit a new patient to hospital and m the proposition that you kill a patient. Then you do not satisfy condition (3), since you do not believe that intending to kill a patient is a means implied by killing one: you believe you will kill a patient even though you do not intend to. True, you do believe that killing a patient is up to you in a colloquial sense, but you do not believe it is up to you in my specialized sense. Therefore you do not violate the Instrumental Requirement this way either, even though you do not intend to kill a patient.

Either way, you do not violate the Instrumental Requirement. But that is only because it contains both conditions (2) and (3). The example shows that both conditions are needed, even when m describes an act of yours.

The Instrumental requirement is genuinely practical

Compare the Instrumental requirement with a requirement I have not previously mentioned:

Bogus Instrumental Requirement. Rationality requires of N that, if
(1a)   N believes at *t* that *e* will be so, and if
(2a)   N believes at *t* that, if *m* is not so, *e* will not be so, and if
(3a)   N believes at *t* that, if she herself does not then intend that *m*, *m* will not be so, and if
(C)   N cares at *t* whether she herself then intends that *m*, then
(4a)   N believes at *t* that she herself then intends that *m*.

The Bogus Instrumental Requirement incorporates two steps of modus tollens. It is an extension of the Modus Ponens Requirement. It is plausible, and for the sake of argument in this section I shall assume it is a genuine requirement. In calling it 'bogus' I do not mean to say it is not a requirement of rationality. I mean to say it is not an *instrumental* requirement. Indeed, it is not a practical requirement at all. It is purely theoretical – a requirement on beliefs only.

Still, it is associated with the genuine Instrumental Requirement, because the three attitudes of intending something, believing you intend it, and believing you will do it are normally associated.[18] Normally you satisfy (1a) if you satisfy (1): you believe that *e* if you intend that *e*. Normally you satisfy (4) if you satisfy (4a): you intend that *m* if you believe you intend that *m*. Moreover, (2) presumably entails (2a) and (3) presumably entails (3a).

Suppose you satisfy (1), (2) and (3). Then normally you satisfy (1a), and you definitely satisfy (2a) and (3a). It is also fair to assume you satisfy (C). Therefore, if you satisfy the Bogus Instrumental Requirement you normally satisfy (4a), and hence normally (4). So if you satisfy the Bogus Instrumental Requirement, you normally also satisfy the genuine Instrumental Requirement.

This argument and variations on it are the source of the view that Michael Bratman calls 'cognitivism' about practical rationality.[19] Cognitivists claim that the Instrumental Requirement, which is practical, is actually derived from the Bogus Instrumental Requirement, which is theoretical, or from something like it. In that way, they give priority to the theoretical requirement. In general, they think practical requirements of rationality are derived from theoretical ones.

To generalize further, cognitivism is the view that a person's rationality supervenes on her cognitive attitudes: that if your cognitive attitudes are the same in one situation as they are in another, then you are rational in one situation to the same degree as you are rational in the other. It is a guiding principle of this chapter that rationality supervenes on the mind. Cognitivism makes the supervenience base narrower.

However, the genuine Instrumental Requirement is actually independent of the bogus one. To show this, I shall describe a case where you satisfy the Bogus Instrumental Requirement but breach the genuine Instrumental Requirement. It will be a case where you satisfy (1) without satisfying (1a). I could alternatively describe a case where you satisfy (4a) without satisfying (4).[20]

You have planned a complex world tour, which includes visiting Agra. You intend to visit Agra. However, you have temporarily forgotten this part of your plan. You still have the intention; an intention is a dispositional state, and the dispositions that constitute your intention are still in place. You are disposed to do what needs doing to get you to Agra, when it needs doing. You are disposed to remember your intention before you get to India and then do what is needed to put it into effect. But you have forgotten this intention. You do not believe you intend to visit Agra, and consequently you do not believe you will visit Agra. Let e be the proposition that you visit Agra. You intend e, so you satisfy condition (1). But you do not believe e, so you do not satisfy condition (1a). That means you satisfy the Bogus Instrumental Requirement by default.

Let m be the proposition that you buy a train ticket from Delhi to Agra. Suppose you satisfy (2): you believe that buying a train ticket from Delhi to Agra is a means implied by visiting Agra. And suppose you satisfy (3): you believe that your now intending to buy a train ticket from Delhi to Agra is a means implied by buying one. (Actually you are wrong about that; you will have time to buy the ticket later, after you remember your intention.) But suppose you do not satisfy (4): you do not intend to buy a train ticket from Delhi to Agra. Then you breach the Instrumental Requirement. Since you satisfy the Bogus Instrumental Requirement, it follows that the Instrumental Requirement is an independent requirement.

In the course of this argument, I assumed you have an intention without believing you have it. Possibly rationality requires you not to be in this state; possibly it requires you to believe you have those intentions you do have. I do not deny that. But it does not affect the argument since this requirement, if it exists, is not a requirement of theoretical rationality.[21]

The argument may be generalized.[22] The Instrumental Requirement cannot be derived from any theoretical requirement. You can intend something without believing you intend it, and you can believe you intend something when you do not intend it. Since a theoretical requirement regulates beliefs, it cannot regulate intentions when they are mismatched with beliefs in this way.

Faced with this conclusion, a cognitivist might now doubt that the Instrumental Requirement is truly a requirement of rationality at all. Roughly, it says you are not rational unless you intend what you believe is a means implied by an end that you intend. A cognitivist might claim this is so only when you believe you intend the end and believe you do not intend the means. If you have those beliefs you breach the Bogus Instrumental Requirement, so you are not rational on that account. If you do not have them you may be rational.

Intuitively, your attitudes are not properly aligned with each other if you do not satisfy the Instrumental Requirement. We may say they are not coherent. According to the cognitivist position I just described, there is nothing irrational about having incoherent attitudes unless you believe you have those attitudes.

How might this position be sustained? First, it might be a general truth that incoherent attitudes are not irrational unless you believe you have them. But that would be implausible. For one thing, it would mean that the Bogus Instrumental Requirement itself is incorrect, since it does not require you to believe you have the beliefs it mentions. Indeed, none of the requirements listed in this chapter would be correct. Furthermore, it would mean that you cannot fail to be rational if you have no second-order beliefs – beliefs about your attitudes. More generally, incoherence among your top-level beliefs – beliefs that you do not believe you have – would not be irrational. Suppose you have a pair of contradictory first-order beliefs but do not believe you have them. On this view, your contradictory beliefs would not be irrational. That is implausible.

Alternatively, it might be that incoherent intentions are not irrational unless you believe you have them, whereas the same is not true of beliefs. But to support cognitivism on that basis would be dogmatic. Why should incoherent intentions be rationally permissible, but not incoherent beliefs? Whereas it is intuitively a feature of rationality that it supervenes on the mind, I see no intuitive support for the idea that it supervenes on cognitive attitudes. It is intuitively very plausible that rationality requires coherence among intentions.

I see no good reason to doubt the Instrumental Requirement on grounds of cognitivism. It is an independent, practical requirement.

Means and implications

Conditions (2) and (3) of the Instrumental Requirement are stronger than the corresponding conditions (2a) and (3a) of the Bogus Instrumental Requirement. They need to be stronger because the Instrumental Requirement is an independent, practical requirement. They are needed to ensure that your beliefs are about means to your end rather than mere implications of your end. The Instrumental Requirement would not be a genuine requirement of rationality if its conditions were any weaker than they are.

Conditions (2) and (3) are stronger than (2a) and (3a) in two respects. Firstly, they contain subjunctive rather than material conditionals. Secondly, they contain 'because' clauses. Both these features are needed. If either feature was cut out of either condition, the Instrumental Requirement would not be correct. I shall explain why.

Cutting the features one at a time out of (2) would give us, respectively:

(2b)   N believes at t that, if m is not so, because of that e will not be so.

(2c)   N believes at t that, if m were not so, e would not be so.

As an illustration, let e be that you visit Agra, and m that you visit Fatehpur Sikri. Suppose you believe you will visit Fatehpur Sikri. Then you believe that the antecedent of the conditional in (2b) is false. You therefore believe the conditional is true, at least if we take it to be a material conditional. So you satisfy (2b). Yet you might not believe that visiting Fatehpur Sikri is a means of visiting Agra.

Suppose alternatively you believe that, if you were not to visit Fatehpur Sikri, you would not visit Agra. The two cities are close together, and both contain treasures of Moghul architecture. For those reasons, you believe you would never visit one without visiting the other. Then you would satisfy (2c). Yet again you might not believe that visiting Fatehpur Sikri is a means of visiting Agra.

Now suppose you intend to visit Agra, so you satisfy (1). Suppose you satisfy either (2b) or (2c) but you do not believe visiting Fatehpur Sikri is a means of visiting Agra. Suppose you believe that intending to visit Fatehpur Sikri is a means implied by visiting Fatehpur Sikri, so you satisfy (3). And suppose you do not intend to visit Fatehpur Sikri: you do not satisfy (4). You may yet be rational. You may rationally fail to intend to visit Fatehpur Sikri, seeing as you do not believe it is a means to any end that you intend. This shows that the Instrumental Requirement would not be correct if (2) was replaced by either (2b) or (2c).

One feature of this argument needs attention. I supposed you satisfy either (2b) or (2c) and you satisfy (3). It follows that you satisfy (2a) of the Bogus Instrumental Requirement on page 164, which is weaker than each of (2b) and (2c), and you satisfy (3a), which is weaker than (3). So the Bogus Instrumental Requirement kicks in. It tells us you are not fully rational if you believe you will visit Agra, and you do not believe you intend to visit Fatehpur Sikri. Yet in my examples I have assumed you intend to visit Agra and you do not intend to visit Fatehpur Sikri. So, if you satisfy the Bogus Instrumental Requirement, then either you intend to visit Agra without believing you will visit it, or you believe you intend to visit Fatehpur Sikri without actually intending to visit it. Yet I claimed you are rational. Is that possible? Could you be rational when you have that sort of disparity between your beliefs and your intentions?

I think so. But I do not need to defend that view of mine. My aim is to show that the Instrumental Requirement would not be a requirement of rationality if we replaced condition (2) with a weaker condition. To that end, I assumed you satisfy (1), (2b) or (2c), and (3), but not (4), and I claimed you might nevertheless be rational. But suppose that is not so. Suppose that, necessarily, you are not rational if you satisfy (1), (2b) or (2c), and (3), but not (4). It does not follow that rationality requires you to satisfy (4) if you satisfy (1), (2b) or (2c), and (3). I explained in section 7.3 that 'necessarily you are not rational if you *F*' does not imply 'rationality requires you not to *F*'.

And in this case, if indeed it is true that, necessarily, you are not rational if you satisfy (1), (2b) or (2c), and (3) but not (4), it is clear where you fail. You fail in intending to visit Agra without believing you will visit it, or in your believing you intend to visit Fatehpur Sikri without actually intending to visit it, or in not satisfying the Bogus Instrumental Requirement. There is no irrationality specifically in failing to satisfy (4) when you satisfy (1), (2b) or (2c), and (3). So rationality does not require you to satisfy (4) if you satisfy (1), (2b) or (2c), and (3).

A parallel argument would show that condition (3) in the Instrumental Requirement, like (2), cannot be weakened. But the parallel argument would have to be even more arcane. Since its conclusion is less important, I shall not set it out.

Unsophisticated content

Condition (3) requires you to have a second-order belief about an intention. So apparently you cannot satisfy condition (3) unless you have the concept of *intend*. But surely even unsophisticated people who do not have this concept must be constrained by instrumental rationality.

This does not constitute an objection to the Instrumental Requirement. Like other requirements, the Instrumental Requirement is only a necessary condition for rationality. It is still a genuine requirement even if it does not express the whole of instrumental rationality. Still, it would be poorly formulated if it did not apply to unsophisticated people. And it does, despite appearances. Here is why.

We already know that an instrumental requirement, even for an unsophisticated person, must contain a condition equivalent to (3). I have explained that no weaker condition will do: unless you satisfy a condition as strong as this, you may satisfy all the other conditions and yet rationally not intend *m*. So we cannot have a weaker condition for unsophisticated people.

And actually, an unsophisticated person may satisfy condition (3) without having all the concepts that are used in my statement of it. As I use 'believe', it is transparent to some of the concepts that are used in describing the content of the belief. Suppose you have a belief that you express by saying 'If I were not now to intend m, because of that, m would not be so'. I say of you that you believe your now intending m is a means implied by m. But 'means implied by' is a technical term invented by me. You do not have the concept of *means implied by* unless you have read this chapter with attention. Still, even if you do not have the concept, what I say is true. That illustrates the transparency of 'believe' as I use it.

If you are unsophisticated, you can have a belief with this same content. If you do, you will not express it by saying 'My now intending m is a means implied by m', nor by saying 'If I were not now to intend m, because of that, m would not be so'. Instead, you might say 'It is up to me now that m'. Still, you satisfy condition (3), and the Instrumental Requirement applies to you.

By using the versions of conditions (2) and (3) I introduced on pages 160 and 162, the Instrumental Requirement may be written in the less forbidding form:

> *Instrumental Requirement.* Rationality requires of N that, if
> (1) N intends at t that e, and if
> (2) N believes at t that m is a means implied by e, and if
> (3) N believes at t that m is up to her herself then, then
> (4) N intends at t that m.

Choice of means

The Instrumental Requirement generally requires you to intend some means – to intend that there is a means that you take – to an end that you intend. There are a few exceptional cases where you believe you can achieve your end without taking any means at all. But in other cases, you believe that, were you not to take some means, because of that the end would not be achieved. That is to say (applying the definition of an implied means from page 160), you believe that taking some means is a means implied by the end. The Instrumental Requirement therefore applies to taking some means.

You will often be able to identify a number of specific alternative means for achieving your end. That is to say, you believe that a disjunction m or n or p or . . . constitutes an implied means to the end. Then rationality requires you, if you intend the end and you believe the truth of the disjunction is up to you, to intend the disjunction.

In a case of this sort, there must a requirement of rationality that regulates your choice among the options. In particular, it seems intuitively that you must be required to choose what you believe is the best of the alternative means. I think that is indeed so. However, I am not sure how to formulate accurately the notion of the *best means*,[23] so I shall not try to set out this requirement formally.

However, I can describe one requirement that applies when you have a choice of means. It does not specify which means to choose, but it does require you to choose. When you believe you have a choice among alternative means to an end, you do not believe any particular one of them is implied by the end. However, as time passes, there is likely to come a moment when you believe you will not achieve the end unless you then intend one of the alternatives. You are not rational unless you have chosen one by that time.

A generalization of the Instrumental Requirement applies at that time:

> *Generalized Instrumental Requirement.* Rationality requires of N that, if
> (1)   N intends at t that e, and if
> (2)   N believes at t that, if none of m or n or p or . . . were so, because of that e would not be so, and if
> (3)   N believes at t that, if she herself were not then to intend m, because of that m would not be so, and if she herself were not then to intend n, because of that n would not be so, and if she herself were not then to intend p, because of that p would not be so, . . . , then
> (4)   N intends at t that m, or intends at t that n, or intends at t that p, or . . . .

The disjunction m or n or p or . . . may contain any number of disjuncts. It may contain just one, and then this requirement reduces to the simple Instrumental Requirement. So this is strictly a generalization. It is just as intuitively attractive as the ungeneralized requirement.

9.5   Enkrasia

Rationality requires you to intend what you believe you ought; it requires you not to be akratic. More accurately:

> *Enkrasia.* Rationality requires of N that, if
> (1)   N believes at t that she herself ought that p, and if
> (2)   N believes at t that, if she herself were then to intend that p, because of that, p would be so, and if
> (3)   N believes at t that, if she herself were not then to intend that p, because of that, p would not be so, then
> (4)   N intends at t that p.

In this section, I shall first of all explain this formulation. Then I shall come to general objections that may be raised against it. I postpone one further objection to Section 16.2.

To understand the formula's complexities, for a moment ignore conditions (2) and (3). Ignoring them leaves us with the rough formulation of Enkrasia that appears on page 23. For the sake of form, I have put 'N' for 'you' and added the temporal specification 'at *t*'. I have also put the general propositional letter '*p*' in place of the more specific 'you *F*'. This simply gives the formula some extra generality, as I explained on pages 15–18.

Condition (1) incorporates the two constraints on Enkrasia that I explained on page 22: the ought must be owned by *N*, and it must be self-ascribed by *N*.

Now look at conditions (2) and (3). Like condition (3) in the Instrumental Requirement, these conditions contain the indexical terms 'she herself' and 'then'. The reason is the one I gave on page 161. Since Enkrasia mentions self-ascription twice, it may be said to be essentially first-personal in two different ways.

If you are unsophisticated, and do not have the concept of *intend*, you might nevertheless satisfy (2) and (3). You might express the two beliefs described in (2) and (3) together, by saying 'It is up to me now whether or not *p*'. This gives us a more friendly way of expressing Enkrasia:

Enkrasia. Rationality requires of *N* that, if
(1)   *N* believes at *t* that she herself ought that *p*, and if
(2&3)   *N* believes at *t* that it is up to her herself then whether or not *p*, then
(4)   *N* intends at *t* that *p*.

But I need to keep conditions (2) and (3) separate in order to explain them.

Condition (3) is the same as condition (3) in the Instrumental Requirement. It requires you to believe that intending *p* is a means implied by *p*. If you believe *p* would be so anyway, you can be rational without intending it, even though you believe you ought that *p*. Suppose you have moved to Fiji, and consequently believe you ought to learn about Fijian culture. But suppose you believe this will happen anyway, since you are living in Fiji. Then you may be rational even if you do not intend to learn about Fijian culture.

Condition (2) excuses you from intending something when you do not believe that intending it would be effective. Suppose you believe you ought to believe in God, but you do not believe that intending to believe in God would bring you do so. You do not believe you have that sort of control over this belief. Then you might be rational even if you do not intend to believe in God.

In this example, you have beliefs whose contents are inconsistent with the principle that ought implies can. Does that not mean you are less than fully rational anyway, whether or not you intend to believe in God? Not necessarily. You may not believe that ought implies can. Perhaps ought actually does imply can, but this is a controversial principle, and you may be rational even if you do not accept it.

When you believe you ought to have a mental attitude, condition (2) will often excuse you from intending to have it. You will rarely believe your intentions control your attitudes, because they rarely do. If you intend to believe something, that will rarely cause you to believe it; if you intend to want something, that will rarely cause you to want it; if you intend to intend something, that will rarely cause you to intend it; and so on. So you will rarely satisfy condition (2). There are exceptions. Sometimes you have means available to influence your attitudes. You might be able to cause yourself to believe in God by going regularly to church and taking religious instruction. If you believe this will work, and you believe you ought to believe in God, then you are not rational unless you intend to believe in God.

Still, condition (2) means that Enkrasia is less often applicable to mental attitudes than to acts; it is less often applicable when you believe you ought to have a particular attitude than when you believe you ought to do a particular act. This is a limitation of the requirement.

Applied to mental attitudes, Enkrasia may seem unsatisfactorily indirect in any case. It connects a belief of yours that you ought to *F* with your intending to *F*. When *F*ing is being in a mental state, should we not expect a requirement of rationality to connect a belief of yours that you ought to *F* directly with your *F*ing? That would give us a version of what may be called Direct Enkrasia:

> * *Restricted Direct Enkrasia.* When *p* is the proposition that *N* is in a particular state of mind, rationality requires of *N* that, if *N* believes at *t* that she herself ought that *p*, then *p*.[24]

In section 6.2, I examined the Restricted Direct Enkratic Condition, which is an immediate consequence of this formula. I explained why it has to be restricted to states of mind; it is not true in general because of the general principle that rationality supervenes on the mind. So this formula is particularly adapted to states of mind, whereas Enkrasia itself is better adapted to acts. For states of mind, should we therefore adopt Restricted Direct Enkrasia instead of Enkrasia itself?

We should not, because Restricted Direct Enkrasia is false. It entails the Restricted Direct Enkratic Condition, which I showed to be false in section 6.2. In that section, I also examined a variant of this condition that I labelled 'Scanlon's Condition' on page 96. I did not deny Scanlon's Condition, but I explained that it has few applications. Versions of Direct Enkrasia have an initial appeal, but they are no real alternative to Enkrasia itself.

Objection: Enkrasia is not a requirement of rationality

So much for the formulation of Enkrasia. Even given its best formulation, Enkrasia is contentious. To many people, it does not seem it can be a matter of rationality that you intend what you believe you ought. Intending what you believe you ought seems very different from not having contradictory beliefs, or intending what you believe is a means implied by an end that you intend, or satisfying other requirements of rationality.[25]

I think the source of the worry is that satisfying Enkrasia may demand an effort. It often involves overcoming a strong pull in the opposite direction. You may believe you ought to do something that you hate doing. But intuitively rationality should not demand that sort of effort. Rationality is a matter of getting your attitudes into good order. That may demand a certain sort of ability, but it should not demand effort. A good example was put to me by Neil Pescod. You may be afraid to do what you believe you ought to do. For instance, you may believe you ought to enter a burning building to save someone's life, but be afraid to do so. If you do not intend to do something out of fear, is that irrational?

Since I have no general criterion for identifying requirements of rationality, I have no knock-down argument to overcome this worry, but I have some responses to it.

The first responds to the idea that satisfying requirements of rationality should not demand effort. That is not so if the requirements I have previously mentioned are genuine. Achieving some of those requirements may demand effort. Take the Instrumental Requirement, for instance. Suppose you intend to be a doctor, and have planned your life around that intention. Now you come to the moment in your medical training where you have to dissect a cadaver. Entering the room, you find your whole self in revolt against doing so. But you believe you will not be a doctor unless you do. To satisfy the Instrumental Requirement, you must either form the intention of dissecting the cadaver, or give up your intention of being a doctor. Either will require a great effort.

Take the Modus Ponens Requirement as another example. You may believe that you are a man and that if you are a man you are mortal. But you may find it very hard to bring yourself to believe you are mortal, or to give up either the belief that you are a man or the belief that all men are mortal.

A second response is this. Akrasia is a failure of some sort: *something* requires you not to be akratic. If it is not rationality, what is it? It cannot be morality – at least not always – since morality may not be involved at all.

Your ought belief may have nothing to do with morality. You may believe on grounds of prudence that you ought not to eat a doughnut.

Could the requirement issue from whatever source you believe your ought derives from? For instance, if you believe you ought not to eat the doughnut on grounds of prudence, could it be prudence that requires you not to be akratic on this occasion? That would be odd. You may believe the ought mentioned in Enkrasia derives from various sources, but it is always the same, central ought described in chapter 2. So it would be odd if Enkrasia issued from different sources in different cases.

Moreover, you may have no belief about what is the source of your ought. Perhaps your friend tells you that you ought to do something, and you believe her, but she does not tell you why. In that case, the requirement cannot issue from whatever source you believe your ought derives from. On other occasions too, you may believe your ought derives from more than one source. For instance, if you are a parent, you may believe that prudence and morality together determine that you ought not to climb dangerous mountains, although neither would on its own. Then the requirement not to be akratic cannot issue from either prudence or morality.

So the requirement must issue from a distinct source in at least some cases. Given that, it seems natural to expect that source to cover all cases. There are grounds for identifying it as rationality. Enkrasia is a matter of internal coherence among your mental attitudes; it is not a matter of the relation between those attitudes and the world. This is a characteristic of requirements of rationality. Moreover, I shall argue in chapter 16 that you can come to satisfy Enkrasia by means of reasoning. This too is characteristic of rationality.

I do not deny the possibility that some other source of requirements as well as rationality may also require you not to be akratic on some occasions. For instance, if you believe you ought to do something on moral grounds but you do not intend to do it, this may be a moral failure as well as a rational one.

Despite all this, you might still feel Enkrasia has a different nature from other requirements of rationality. You might want to ascribe it to some source of requirements that is different from rationality, but that is also concerned with coherence among your mental attitudes. Since I have no general criterion for rationality, I am not able to reject this idea outright. But in this book I hope to display enough similarity between Enkrasia and other requirements of rationality to make it appropriate to class them together.

Objection: akrasia is impossible

That objection was that you may rationally fail to satisfy Enkrasia. An opposite objection is that you cannot fail to satisfy Enkrasia at all. To put it another way: akrasia is impossible. R. M. Hare is one philosopher who takes this view.

Hare thinks that to believe you ought to F is partly to accept a first-person imperative, which he writes 'Let me F!'[26] And he thinks that to accept this imperative is to intend to F.[27] I take a middle course: I think you can fail to satisfy Enkrasia, but to do so is irrational.

Hare's conclusion arises from his theory of the metaphysics of ethics, which leads him to think that a belief that you ought to F cannot be an ordinary belief. I think his conclusion constitutes a *reductio ad absurdum* of his theory, and I think the same about any theory that implies akrasia is impossible.[28] In this book I do not wish to discuss the metaphysics of ethics. I shall simply take it for granted that akrasia is possible.

9.6   Bayesian requirements

So far in this book I have considered only 'all-out' beliefs and intentions, which you either have fully or not at all. I have not allowed for degrees of belief or intention. The Bayesian way of thinking offers an alternative approach to rational requirements, at least for beliefs if not intentions. Bayesian requirements apply in the first place to degrees of belief.[29] It may be possible to derive requirements on all-out beliefs from them, but if it is, those requirements are secondary according to the Bayesianism.

I have not adopted the Bayesian approach in this book for just one reason. From chapter 12 onwards, I shall investigate the process of reasoning, by means of which we can bring ourselves to satisfy requirements of rationality. I have some idea how we reason with all-out beliefs and intentions, which is explored in some detail in those chapters. But I am less clear how we could reason with degrees of belief. I shall sketch an approach to this question in section 15.2. But working it out in detail is more than I can cope with in this book.

Still, I do not deny Bayesianism. I shall give this one example of a Bayesian requirement, which I shall refer to later:[30]

> ? *Bayesian requirement.* When p, q and r are mutually contrary propositions such that (p or q or r) is necessarily true, rationality requires of N that N's degrees of belief in p, q and r respectively add up to one.

This is only an illustration. It may well not be correctly formulated.

Notes

1   This point is made forcefully by A. W. Price in *Contextuality in Practical Reason*, chapter 3, section V.

2 Nagel, *The Possibility of Altruism*, p. 20.
3 This point was put to me by Derek Parfit and is made in Garrett Cullity's 'Decisions, reasons, and rationality'.
4 pp. 15–16.
5 Thanks to Dorothy Grover for pointing this out to me.
6 See Nathan Salmon, 'Being of two minds'.
7 In 'Practical reason and the possibility of error', Douglas Lavin considers in much more detail whether you can be subject to a requirement that you cannot violate.
8 Lars Bergström made this point to me.
9 *Change in View*, p. 12. The clause 'if N cares at t whether q' is what Harman calls an 'interest condition' on p. 55.
10 'Dispositional beliefs and dispositions to believe'.
11 *Groundwork of the Metaphysic of Morals*, pp. 80–1.
12 My formulation owes a great deal to a discussion with Adam Morton. Without his help I would have made some bad mistakes.
13 Thanks to Wlodek Rabinowicz for this example.
14 I think Wlodek Rabinowicz first made this point to me. It is mentioned by Robert Binkley in 'A theory of practical reason', p. 443. Torbjörn Tännsjö showed me the need for 'now'.
15 Thanks to Peter Simons.
16 In his 'How to be a cognitivist about practical reason', Jacob Ross argues that (3) is too strong and a weaker condition will serve instead. I do not disagree.
17 'The doctrine of triple effect'.
18 The relations between these three attitudes are explored in section 15.4.
19 One variation on this cognitivist argument appears on pp. 21–2 of Jay Wallace's 'Normativity, commitment, and instrumental reason'. Wallace in effect employs a weaker version of (1a), that N does not believe that e will not be so, and a weaker version of (4a), that N does not believe that she herself does not then intend that m. The term 'cognitivist' comes from Michael Bratman, 'Cognitivism about practical reason'. Defences of it appear in Kieran Setiya's 'Cognitivism about instrumental reason' and Jacob Ross's 'How to be a cognitivist about practical reason'.
20 In 'Intention, belief, practical, theoretical', Michael Bratman uses cases of this second kind in arguing against cognitivism.
21 See the discussion in Wallace, 'Normativity, commitment, and instrumental reason', pp. 21–3, and Bratman's response in 'Intention, belief, practical, theoretical', section 4.
22 It is much more fully developed in Michael Bratman's 'Intention, belief, practical, theoretical' and 'Intention, belief, and instrumental rationality'.
23 My 'Practical reasoning' explores some of the difficulties of doing so. For one thing, it shows that decision theory does not offer a correct formulation.
24 Niko Kolodny calls this 'the core requirements' on p. 557 of 'Why be rational?'.
25 Ronald Dworkin, in particular, urged this point on me.
26 *The Language of Morals*, chapters 11 and 12.
27 *The Language of Morals*, p. 20.
28 Another example is the metaethical theory presented in Allan Gibbard's *Thinking How to Live*. My comments on this theory appear in my 'Comments on Allan Gibbard's Tanner Lectures'.
29 For an introduction, see Luc Bovens and Stephan Hartmann, *Bayesian Epistemology*.
30 On p. 198 and p. 277.

10

Diachronic Rationality

10.1 Persistence of Intention

Diachronic requirements of rationality connect your attitudes at one time with your attitudes at another. In this chapter I shall describe diachronic requirements of two different sorts: requirements of persistence and then basing prohibitions.

Under requirements of persistence, I start with persistence of intentions.[1] If you have an intention, and then you stop having it, that is irrational unless something licenses you to drop it. You must not just drop it. You could not manage your life if your intentions were liable to vanish incontinently. To bring some intertemporal coherence to our lives, we regularly decide at one time to do something at a later time. But making decisions will not actually achieve coherence unless we generally do as we decide. To decide is to form an intention, and to be effective that intention must persist until we put it into effect.

A failure of persistence is a sort of forgetting, so you might think it is a failure of memory rather than of rationality. Memory seems to be a separate faculty from rationality. However, you will at least agree that, if your intentions do not persist, it is a failing of coherence of a sort. Your mental attitudes at one time do not cohere properly with those at another. This at least puts forgetting in the same general area as a failing of rationality. Given that, it does not matter to me whether or not you would naturally classify it as a failing of rationality or of something else. In counting Enkrasia as a requirement of rationality, I am already accepting an expansive notion of rationality, which covers various aspects of coherence among your attitudes. I am happy to let it cover this part of memory too.

So I take the incoherence that would result from a failure of persistence to be a sort of irrationality. Indeed, I think rationality requires persistence. Here is how I formulate this requirement:

> *Persistence of Intention.* If t_1 is earlier than t_2, rationality requires of N that, if N intends at t_1 that p, and no cancelling event occurs between t_1 and t_2, then either N intends at t_2 that p, or N considers at t_2 whether p.

This needs explaining.

Considering

First an ambiguity to clear up. In Persistence of Intention, 'considers whether p' does not have its most ordinary meaning. It refers to considering for intention rather than considering for belief. Suppose you are deciding what your child's next present will be. You might say 'I am considering whether it will be a bike or a computer'. This is good English, though perhaps an uncommon turn of phrase. It exhibits the meaning that 'consider' has in Persistence of Intention.

The ambiguity can be eliminated if we confine our attention to propositions that N could express by 'I F' for some verb phrase 'F' – 'I buy a bike' or 'I avoid mosquito bites', and so on. For these cases, we may use an infinitival construction for the object of consideration, and the ambiguity is removed. We may say 'N considers whether to avoid mosquito bites', for example. For these cases, Persistence of Intention may be written:

> *Persistence of Intention, special form.* If t_1 is earlier than t_2, rationality requires of N that, if N intends at t_1 to F, and no cancelling event occurs between t_1 and t_2, then either N intends at t_2 to F, or N considers at t_2 whether to F.

In this section I shall deal only with special cases of this sort, simply to avoid the ambiguity of 'considers'. The argument applies equally to other cases.

Next point: the activity of considering whether to F takes a while, but t_2 is just a moment. When I say you consider at t_2 whether to F, I mean that either you begin at t_2 to consider whether to F, or you are already engaged at t_2 in considering whether to F.

'Consider' does not necessarily mean 'consider for the first time'. You may have previously considered whether to F – for instance when you first decided to F. Alternatively, you may have come to intend to F without any consideration.

Bootstrapping

Next you might ask why the requirement ends with a disjunction? What would be wrong with this simplified requirement?:

> * If t_1 is earlier than t_2, rationality requires of you that, if you intend at t_1 to F, and no cancelling event occurs between t_1 and t_2, then you intend at t_2 to F.

The answer is that it would lead to implausible bootstrapping, given two other principles that I accept.

The first of those is Necessary Detachment which I accepted on page 123. In applying this principle, let us treat past events as necessary in the way I proposed on page 125. Suppose you intend at some time to F, and suppose no cancelling event occurs between that time and a later one. From the perspective of the later time, those facts are in the past, and therefore necessary. Applying Necessary Detachment to the simplified requirement, we may conclude that rationality requires you to intend at the later time to F.

The second principle is Normativity of Rationality from page 192. This is the principle that, when rationality requires you to G, that fact constitutes a reason for you to G. In chapter 11 I shall express my belief in this principle, although I have no successful way of defending it. Given Normativity of Rationality as well as Necessary Detachment, the simplified requirement above entails that, if you intend to F at one time, and no cancelling event occurs before a later time, then you have a reason to intend to F at the later time. Furthermore, the fact that you intend to F at the earlier time explains why you have a reason to intend to F at the later time. That means this fact would itself be a reason to intend to F at a later time.

All this would lead us to conclude that intending something at one time constitutes a reason to intend it at a later time. That would be implausible bootstrapping.

The simplified requirement will therefore not do. Persistence of Intention needs that disjunction at the end. If you intend to F (and no other cancelling event occurs), you are required to keep your intention unless and until you consider whether to F, either again or for the first time. Once you begin to consider, you may immediately drop the intention without violating the requirement.

Moreover, we must include considering whether to F among the cancelling events mentioned in Persistence of Intention. Including it ensures that, once you have begun to consider whether to F, you may permanently (and not merely while you are considering) drop your intention to F without violating the requirement.

Does even Persistence of Intention allow too much bootstrapping? Let us apply to it the same argument as I applied to the simplified requirement. Along with Persistence of Intention, let us assume Necessary Detachment and Normativity of Rationality. We shall conclude that an intention to F at one time constitutes a reason either to intend to F at a later time or to consider at that later time whether to F. This is not in itself implausible bootstrapping.

However, it may well be the case that you have a separate reason not to consider at a later time whether to F. For example, you might have already carefully considered whether to F, and it would now be a waste of time to think again. Or you might have reached a time when you must act on your intention rather than deliberate.[2] If you have a reason not to consider whether to F, can we now derive implausible bootstrapping from Persistence of Intention?

We cannot. Let us assume for the sake of argument that, if you have a reason for either Aing or Bing and a reason for not Aing, those two reasons together constitute a reason for Bing. I do not endorse this pattern of deduction, but I do not deny it either. From it, we could derive the conclusion that your intending to F at one time, together with your reason not to consider later whether to F, constitute a reason to intend later to F. But that is not objectionable. So far as Persistence of Intention is concerned, if ever you do start to consider whether to F, the fact that you previously intended to F is not then any reason at all to continue intending it. The reason evaporates as soon as you begin to consider. It is therefore not a reason you could correctly take account of in the course of your consideration.

Cancelling events

Next, what are cancelling events in the case of intentions? I have already mentioned that one of them is your considering whether to F. I shall call this 'the first type' of cancelling event.

Other cancelling events license your dropping your intention without considering whether to F. Among them are events that are precipitated by your actually Fing. Fulfilling your intention obviously licenses you to stop having it, and it will normally cause you to stop having it without your doing any considering. However, a cancelling event has to be mental, because of the supervenience of rationality on the mind. So it cannot be the event of actually doing what you intend, when this is a non-mental act. I think it is the event of your coming to believe at some time that you would F even if you yourself did not then intend to F. I am stretching the meaning of that sentence a bit: I mean to include the event of your coming to believe you have already Fed. I may not have described the event exactly correctly, but I hope I am not far wrong. I shall call it 'the second type' of cancelling event.

Another event that would license your dropping your intention would be coming to realize you cannot fulfil it. The slow-watch example on page 152 shows how this could happen. When you realize you are too late to get on the bus, your realization licenses you to drop your intention of getting on. I think the cancelling event, set out accurately, is your coming to believe at some time that you yourself would not *F* even if you yourself then intended to *F*. Again, this may not be exactly the right description, but I hope it is not far off. I shall call this 'the third type' of cancelling event.

There are other cancelling events besides those three types. Your death is another one. But those three are the most important for my purposes.

Is forgetting a cancelling event? I take it that intending something at one time, and not intending it at a later time, when no cancelling event occurs in the meantime, just is forgetting. Forgetting is not itself a separate event that happens between the two times, and it is not a cancelling event. Indeed, Persistence of Intention is just the requirement that you do not forget an intention.

Putting it like that may cast doubt on Persistence of Intention. Forgetting does not intuitively seem irrational after a long time has elapsed. We could accommodate this intuition by incorporating a time limit into the requirement. But I prefer not to, because on page 154 I adopted a stringent approach to rational requirements. My requirements are mostly based on the attitudes of ideally rational beings, who do not forget. You might also doubt that forgetting is irrational even in the short term, because memory is a separate faculty from rationality. But I have already said on page 177 that I employ a notion of rationality that is broad enough to encompass this part of memory.

10.2   The rationality of doing as you decide

Now I come to the main lesson I want to draw from Persistence of Intention.[3] People generally do what they decide to do. There is a causal explanation of why: to decide to do something is to form the intention of doing it; then causal processes generally ensure that the intention persists, and in due course it causes you to do what you intend. But the progression from deciding to doing is not merely a causal process; it is a feature of our rationality that it generally goes through. When the progression breaks down on a particular occasion, and you do not do what you decide to do, that often means you are not entirely rational. What explains the rational nature of the progression?

Persistence of Intention explains a large part of it. In making a decision to *F*, you form an intention to *F*. Persistence of Intention tells us that rationality requires your intention to persist until some cancelling event occurs. Provided it persists long enough, it will cause you to *F* unless something prevents you from *F*ing. As I explained on page 151, this is just because your intention to *F* is a disposition to *F*. Persistence of Intention therefore makes a rational connection between a decision and a later action. If you violate this requirement, so your intention stops before any cancelling event, then the progression breaks down and you are not rational.

On the other hand, if you satisfy Persistence of Intention, your intention to *F* persists until some cancelling event occurs. Often this event will be precipitated by your *F*ing, which will cause a cancelling event of the second type I mentioned. If that is what brings your intention to an end, the progression from decision to action goes through, and you may be rational.

The progression can break down even if you satisfy Persistence of Intention. Sometimes a cancelling event occurs before you *F*. It may be a cancelling event of the first type: your considering – actually it will be reconsidering – whether to *F*. If an event of considering brings your intention to an end, the progression breaks down. Nevertheless, because you satisfy Persistence of Intention, you may be rational. Alternatively, you may not be rational; you may violate some other requirement. For instance, circumstances may make it irrational for you to reconsider your intention – perhaps you should be acting and not thinking, say. Or, when you do reconsider it, it may be irrational for you then to abandon it – perhaps you believe you ought to *F*, say.

Sometimes the cancelling event will be of the third type. Again, if this is what brings your intention to an end, you satisfy Persistence of Intention. So you may be rational even though the progression from decision to action breaks down. The slow-watch example on page 152 is a case where you are rational. Alternatively, this cancelling event may result from your violating some other requirement of rationality, and in that case you fail to be rational on that account.

There are other cancelling events that may occur before you *F*. For example, you may die. Since once again you satisfy Persistence of Intention, in this case too you may be rational even though the progression from decision to action breaks down. In all these cases, Persistence of Intention gives a good account of your rationality or irrationality. So this requirement goes a long way towards explaining the rational nature of the progression from decision to action.

But there is more to it than that. If you have an intention to *F* that persists, it will normally cause you to *F*, because it is a disposition to *F*. Often, this connection between intention and action also has a rational aspect; it is not merely causal. That is because, when you *F*, you often take some means to doing so. Not always: sometimes you *F* without taking any means; for instance, you may raise your arm without using a means. But most often, you will *F* by some means. Then your intention to *F* causes you to intend the means, and this causal connection has a rational aspect. If it fails, you are not rational.

Moreover, you often make this connection through a process of rational deliberation – that is, by reasoning.

I shall leave aside the reasoning process till chapter 14. Here I need only say that the rational aspect of taking a means is accounted for by the Instrumental Requirement on page 159. It, together with Persistence of Intention, constitute a full and satisfactory explanation of the rational nature of the progression from decision to action.

A rival view

Several authors offer a rival explanation in terms of reasons. They claim that intending to do something constitutes a reason to do it. So when you form an intention to F by deciding to F, you acquire a reason to F. If you do not F, you fail to do what you have this reason to do. They take that to be irrational. When the progression from decision to action breaks down, they think you fail to be rational because you fail to do what you have a reason to do.[4]

Christine Korsgaard explains on a similar basis the other rational aspect of the progression from decision to action: that you fail to be rational if you fail to take a means to your end.[5] When you intend to F, she thinks your intention is a reason for you to F. It consequently gives you a reason to take a means to F. If you do not take the means, you fail to be rational because you fail to do what you have a reason to do.

There are several flaws in this reasons-based account. One is that it implicitly assumes rationality consists in responding correctly to reasons – a view I claim to have scotched in chapter 5.

Another is that it does not explain what needs to be explained. It is a necessary truth that, if you decide to F, and do not later consider whether to F, and no other cancelling event such as your death occurs, and nothing prevents you from Fing, you fail to be rational if you do not F. This is so even if you ought not to F. As Sidgwick says:

> [Consider] resolutions to act in a certain way at some future time: we continually make such resolutions, and sometimes when the time comes for carrying them out, we do in fact act otherwise under the influence of passion or mere habit, without consciously cancelling our previous resolve. This inconsistency of will our practical reason condemns as irrational, even apart from any judgment of approbation or disapprobation on either volition considered by itself.[6]

That is what needs to be explained. But even if intending to F constitutes a reason to F, that cannot explain it. Even if it is a reason to F, your intention to F clearly does not make it the case that you ought to F. It can be at most only a *pro tanto* reason. It might be outweighed by opposite reasons so that, when you intend to F, it might nevertheless be the case that you ought not to F. All the same, you are definitely not rational if you intend to F (and no cancelling event occurs and so on) but you do not F. The fact – if it is a fact – that your intention is a reason cannot explain why that is so.[7]

It also cannot explain why you are not rational if you intend an end but do not intend a necessary means to it, even if you ought not to intend the means (which implies that you ought not to intend the end). If you ought not to take the means, whatever reason you may have to take the means is evidently outweighed. If your intending the end gives you a reason to take a means, that reason is outweighed. So it cannot explain why you are not rational if you do not take the means.

The third, most serious flaw in the reason-based account is that intending to do something simply is not a reason to do that thing. If it was, it would imply implausible bootstrapping.[8] Suppose you have no reason either for or against Fing, and you happen to decide to F. Now you intend to F, so according to the theory you now have a reason to F. Since you have no contrary reason not to F, the balance of your reasons is in favour of your Fing. You now actually ought to F, therefore. But that is implausible. It is implausible that just deciding to do something can make it the case that you ought to do it, when previously that was not the case.

A different example. Suppose you are wondering whether to visit Paris, but have not yet made up your mind. There are reasons in favour and reasons against. Whether or not you ought to go depends on the balance of reasons. Now suppose you make up your mind to go, so now you intend to go to Paris. Ought you to go or not, now? What does that now depend on?

Before answering this question, I need to exclude some complicating factors. Your decision can create reasons in various indirect ways. Once it leads you to make some investment in going to Paris, reasons to go there will begin to accumulate. If you have bought a non-refundable ticket, that adds to your reasons. Even if you have only got as far as calling the travel agent, that effort is still a small investment and may add to you reasons in favour of going. Some people value their resoluteness, and lose some of their self-esteem if they change their minds. For these people, every decision is automatically a sort of investment, and gives them a reason to carry it out.[9] Reasons like this are the complicating factors that I need to exclude. They are consequences of your intention, but we are interested in whether the intention itself is a reason. To exclude these factors, let us suppose you have made no investment of any sort. You have simply decided to go to Paris, and so far done nothing about it. Also, you attach no particular value to resoluteness. Ought you to go or not?

The answer is intuitively clear. If the balance of your antecedent reasons was in favour of your going to Paris, you ought to go there. You have made the right decision, and you ought to carry it out. If the balance was against your going to Paris, you ought not to go there. You have made the wrong decision and you ought not to carry it out. Your intention itself does not count one whit in favour of going to Paris. It makes no difference to what you should do. What you should do depends only on the antecedent reasons.

Suppose there is a slight balance of antecedent reasons against going, but you made a mistake in your judgement and wrongly decided to go. A few minutes later, having invested nothing in the decision, you discover your mistake. Should you change your mind? If your intention were a reason, there would automatically be a reason not to, and if the balance of antecedent reasons was slight enough, you should stick to your decision. But it is intuitively clear that you should change your mind. So your intention to go is not a reason to go.

My conclusion

My own theory accounts for the rational nature of the progression from decision to action, without postulating that an intention to F is a reason to F. If you intend to F but do not intend to take a means to F, you are not rational because you violate the Instrumental Requirement. You are not rational even if you have no reason to F in the first place. If you intend at one time to F but do not intend at a later time to F, you are not rational unless a cancelling event has occurred in the meantime. That is because you violate Persistence of Intention. You are not rational even if you have no reason to intend to F in the first place. So my theory explains what needs to be explained.

10.3   Diachronic requirements on beliefs

Diachronic requirements on beliefs play no part in this book, so I shall give them no more than a mention.

Just as you could not manage your life if your intentions were to vanish incontinently, you could not manage it if your beliefs were to vanish incontinently. For example, in getting about town, you have to rely on the persistence of your beliefs about where the various streets and shops are. So it seems there must be some persistence requirement on beliefs.

It may be:

> ? *Persistence of Belief.* If t_1 is earlier than t_2, rationality requires of N that, if N believes at t_1 that p, and no cancelling event occurs between

t_1 and t_2, and if N cares at t_2 whether p, then either N believes at t_2 that p, or N considers at t_2 whether p.

I do not insist that Persistence of Belief is correctly formulated, but I think there must be some requirement of rationality like it.

The formula is parallel to Persistence of Intentions except that it contains the clause 'if N cares at t_2 whether p'. The Modus Ponens Requirement on page 157 contains a similar caring clause. As you go through life, you constantly acquire beliefs that there is no point in retaining. For instance, you might happen to notice, and so come to believe, that at about 10 o'clock a bird alighted on your neighbour's pine tree. The caring clause registers the fact that you may rationally forget these pointless beliefs.[10]

Cancelling events for beliefs include considering whether p. They also include acquiring evidence against p, which might happen without your considering whether p. For instance, you might perceive that not-p.

Bayesianism recognizes other diachronic requirements on beliefs besides the persistence requirement. Bayesians are concerned with degrees of belief – credences – and how they are revised in response to evidence. One putative Bayesian requirement is:

> ? *Bayes's Rule.* If t_1 is earlier than t_2, rationality requires of N that, if N at t_1 has credence $c(p)$ in p, credence $c(q)$ in q and conditional credence $c(p|q)$ in p conditional on q, and if between t_1 and t_2 N learns only and with certainty that q, then N at t_2 has credence $c(p)c(p|q)/c(q)$ in p.

This is at best roughly formulated. The 'learns only' condition is standing in for something more complicated: a condition that all the adjustments to N's beliefs between t_1 and t_2 are based on her acquisition of the belief that q with certainty. I do not know how to formulate this condition exactly. I explained in section 9.6 that I shall not deal with Bayesian requirements in this book.

10.4   Basing prohibitions and basing permissions

I have already mentioned several prohibitions of rationality. They are requirements that you not be in some particular state. No Contradictory Beliefs on page 155 is one. I now come to a particular class of prohibitions that I call *basing prohibitions*. One example is this:[11]

> Rationality requires of N that N does not believe that Paul is lazy on the basis of believing that Paul is foreign and believing that some foreigners are lazy.

What is it for you to have an attitude 'on the basis of' other attitudes? I shall return to this question on page 188, but I can immediately say one thing. One part of it is that the based attitude is caused by the based-on attitudes.

This has consequences for the time-indexing of basing prohibitions. Causation can take time. In this book I am particularly concerned with causal processes of reasoning, which take time. It is possible that a based-on attitude may no longer exist by the time the based attitude has come into existence.

For example, suppose you believe that Paul is foreign and that some foreigners are lazy. Suppose that, by a process of fallacious reasoning that takes time, you come to believe that Paul is lazy. Suppose, oddly, that by the time you acquire this new belief, you have already ceased believing that Paul is foreign.

If we interpret the prohibition above as synchronic, applying only to contemporaneous beliefs, you do not violate it. But clearly you do violate a prohibition of rationality. So we must interpret this requirement as applying to attitudes that are not necessarily contemporaneous. We may interpret it like this:

> Rationality requires of N that N does not believe at some time that Paul is lazy on the basis of believing at some time that Paul is foreign and believing at some time that some foreigners are lazy.

Basing prohibitions are diachronic, then. Any basing prohibition can be expressed in the form of the general schema:

> Rationality requires of N that it is not the case that
> N has attitude A at some time and
> N has attitude B at some time and
> N has attitude C at some time and
> . . .
> N has attitude K at some time and
> N's attitude K is based on N's attitudes A, B, C . . .

I mentioned on page 141 another example of a basing prohibition:

> Rationality requires of N that N does not not believe that she herself ought to F on the basis of her not intending to F.

More transparently: rationality prohibits N from not believing that she herself ought to F on the basis of her not intending to F.

To fit this and prohibitions like it into the form of the general schema, I have to make an innovation in terminology. I call the absence of an attitude itself an attitude. If you do not believe the sea is wet, I say you have the attitude of non-belief towards the proposition that the sea is wet. I call this a 'negative' attitude.

A basing prohibition does not prohibit attitudes themselves. Without any irrationality, you might not believe you ought to F and at the same time not intend to F. Rationality prohibits you only from having the first of these attitudes on the basis of the second.

Types of basing

Now back to the question of what basing is. It is not simply causation. When an attitude of yours is based on others, it is caused by them, but the converse is not necessarily the case. One attitude can be caused by others, even if it is not based on them. Suppose you believe p and you believe that if q then p. These two beliefs of yours might cause you to think about whether q. As a result of thinking about it, you might come to believe q, on some grounds that are independent of p. Then your belief that q is caused by your belief that p and your belief that if q then p, but it is not based on them.

There is also a distinction to be made between two sorts of basing. Beliefs are often based on evidence or on what you take to be evidence. You might believe the weather will be good tomorrow on the basis of this evening's red sky. Attitudes can be evidence. For instance, if your friend intends to make a trip to the shops, that is evidence that she will do so, since intentions are often fulfilled. You might believe your friend will make a trip to the shops on the basis of this evidence. The same may work for your own intentions. If you intend to read Proust, that is some evidence that you will read Proust. You might believe you will read Proust on the basis of your intention as evidence.[12] I call this 'evidential basing'.

There must be another sort of basing. For one thing, presumably only cognitive attitudes such as believing or not believing can be based on evidence, and yet attitudes of other types, such as intentions, can have a basis. For another thing, when even a cognitive attitude is based on other attitudes, the basing is rarely evidential. Suppose you believe that the test paper is orange, and you believe that if the test paper is orange you are pregnant. Suppose you draw the conclusion that you are pregnant. Your evidence is the evidence you have for your premises, which is the colour of the test paper and the testimony of the instructions that came with it. It is not your belief that the test paper is orange and your belief that if the test paper is orange you are pregnant. The evidence would exist whatever your beliefs might be.

Nevertheless, your belief that you are pregnant is in some sense based on those beliefs of yours. It is based on them, as I shall put it, *inferentially* rather than evidentially.

In this book, whenever I mention basing, I always refer to inferential rather than evidential basing. Whereas evidential basing is central to episte-mology, inferential basing is more central to the study of rationality and reasoning.

I have now done everything I can to identify the sort of basing I am con-cerned with: it is causal, and it is inferential rather than evidential. I am sorry to say I cannot go so far as to give a full analysis of basing.[13] To this extent I have to take it as primitive. However, I can give examples of basing. Reasoning supplies one. If you derive one attitude from others by reasoning, it is based on those others.

There are other examples. Sometimes basing happens automatically and unconsciously. Suppose you had always believed platypuses are mammals, but in some way you came to believe that platypuses are not mammals. Probably an automatic process caused you at the same time to stop believing platypuses are mammals; automatic processes normally prevent you from having contra-dictory beliefs. Then your non-belief in the proposition that platypuses are mammals (a negative attitude) is based on your belief in the proposition that platypuses are not mammals. Yet you did not acquire the non-belief by reasoning.

Basing permissions

Prohibitions in one special class do not exactly fit the general schema above. These are prohibitions against attitudes that are not based on anything. For example, it seems plausible that rationality requires you not to believe any-thing on no basis at all. This could be true only if we allow a belief to be based on other things besides propositional attitudes; for instance, you might rationally have a belief based on a perception. But with that qualification, it seems plausible.

On the other hand it seems rationally permissible to have at least some baseless intentions. This is one of the notable asymmetries between beliefs and intentions. Suppose you are offered a choice between two identical bales of hay. It seems rationality permits you to intend on no basis to take the left-hand bale rather than the right-hand one.

This is an example of a *basing permission of rationality*. Basing permissions will play an important part in my account of reasoning, which starts in chapter 13. In general they can be written in the form of this schema:

Rationality permits N that
N has attitude A at some time and
N has attitude B at some time and
N has attitude C at some time and
. . .
N has attitude K at some time and
N's attitude K is based on N's attitudes A, B, C . . .

(I have once again taken a slight grammatical liberty in the construction 'permits N that'.)

A basing permission is nothing other than the negation of a basing prohibition. To say that rationality permits you that *p* means that rationality does not require of you that not *p*.

A permission in this form does not imply that N may permissibly have any of the attitudes A, B, C, . . . or K individually. That is because permission does not necessarily distribute over a conjunction. The logic of permission can be derived from the logic of requirement. If requirement satisfied the axiom of Logical Inheritance stated on page 121, then permission would distribute. (The proof is easy.) But on page 121 I rejected Logical Inheritance, and I reject the distribution of permission too.

The hay example illustrates another important point. Even if we suppose it is permissible to intend to take the left-hand bale on no basis, we shall definitely not suppose it is permissible to intend to take the left-hand bale on the basis of a belief that you ought not to take the left-hand bale. Suppose an attitude K may be permissibly based on a particular (perhaps empty) set of other attitudes. Extend that set by adding one or more further attitudes. It is not necessarily permissible to base K on the extended set.

Where do basing permissions come from? I explained on page 150 that I have no general method for identifying requirements of rationality. I have no general method for identifying permissions of rationality either. I do not apologize for this; working out what basing permissions there are is a large and difficult undertaking. Take basing permissions for beliefs, for instance. It seems it should be a relatively easy task to work these out. But a substantial part of the discipline of epistemology is concerned with just that. When is it permissible – or justified, as epistemologists say – to base one belief on others?

At least one claim seems plausible at first: that it is always permissible to base a belief on other beliefs if the content of the first belief is a logical consequence of the contents of the others. But even this is not so. Suppose the Goldbach Conjecture is a logical consequence of the Peano Axioms – no one knows whether this is so. Even if it is so, rationality does not permit you to believe the Goldbach Conjecture on the basis of believing the Peano Axioms.[14]

Evidently, remote logical consequences do not support basing permissions. But modus ponens certainly does. That is to say:

> *Modus Ponens Permission.* Rationality permits N that N believes q at some time on the basis of believing at some time that p and believing at some time that if p then q.

Basing permissions for beliefs go much further than this. For one thing, a large range of logical consequences beyond modus ponens will support basing permissions. For another, other principles of inference support basing permissions, too. Among them are inductive inference, inference to the best explanation and others.

I shall not offer any more examples here. Several examples of basing permissions for intentions appear in section 14.2 and later.

Notes

1   Many thanks to Andrew Reisner and also to Sergio Tenenbaum for advice on persistence requirements. Both these authors deny there are any – see Reisner's 'Unifying the requirements of rationality' and Tenenbaum's 'Minimalism about intention'.

2   In Michael Bratman's *Intention, Plans and Practical Reason*, chapter 5, there is a thorough account of when it is and is not rational to reconsider.

3   What follows is an improved version of the argument I developed in 'Are intentions reasons?'.

4   For example, see David Velleman's 'Deciding how to decide'.

5   Korsgaard, 'The normativity of instrumental reason'.

6   Sidgwick, *The Methods of Ethics*, p. 37.

7   In 'Are intentions reasons?' I called this argument the 'strictness test'.

8   This bootstrapping objection was raised by Michael Bratman in *Intention, Plans and Practical Reason*, pp. 24–7.

9   I owe this point to Howard Sobel.

10 Jennifer Nagel pointed out to me that pointless beliefs can be rationally forgotten. Christian Piller pointed out to me that a caring clause is a way to take account of Nagel's point.

11 I use this very specific example in order to avoid a problem pointed out to me by Branden Fitelsen. Thanks also to Jeff King, who showed me how I might avoid the problem in a different way.

12 This possibility is disputed by many philosophers who follow Elizabeth Anscombe's *Intention*, for instance by Kieran Setiya in 'Knowledge of intention'. I have no need to disagree with them at this point: it makes no difference to my argument if intentions cannot work as evidence in this way.

13 An idealized account appears in Ralph Wedgwood's 'The normative force of reasoning', p. 662. I cannot use it because, as Wedgwood recognizes, it makes it impossible for one attitude to be based on others in a way that is rationally prohibited. It would consequently make basing prohibitions otiose.

14 This point is made by Paul Boghossian in 'Blind reasoning', p. 269.

11
Rationality and Normativity

11.1 The Normative Question

I explained on page 26 that I do not use 'requires' as a normative term. If I told you that Catholicism requires you to abstain from meat on Fridays, I would not be saying anything against your eating meat on Fridays. When I say rationality requires this or that of you, my meaning is not normative. Nevertheless, it seems plausible that rationality actually is normative. Is it? I call this the 'Normative Question' about rationality.[1] This chapter considers the answer.

The Normative Question asks whether it is true that:

> *Normativity of Rationality.* Necessarily, if rationality requires N to F, that fact is a reason for N to F.

The reason mentioned in this formula may be *pro tanto*,[2] and it may be outweighed. In that way, the formula allows for the possibility that rationality is normative but defeasible. Suppose that, on some occasion, your having contradictory beliefs would be very beneficial – perhaps it would prevent a war. On this occasion it may not be the case that you ought not to have contradictory beliefs. Nevertheless, rationality requires you not to have contradictory beliefs even on this occasion, and this is a reason that counts against your having them.

Some philosophers go further and adopt:

> *Strong Normativity.* Necessarily, if rationality requires N to F, then N ought to F because rationality requires N to F.

Alternatively put: if rationality requires you to F, that fact is a necessarily *pro toto* reason for you to F. This claim is explicit in the writings of some philosophers,[3] and implicit in the writing of many. It is common to describe requirements of rationality using the normative term 'ought'. For example, saying 'You ought not to have contradictory beliefs' is a common way of expressing the requirement not to have contradictory beliefs. In the past I myself adopted this style of expression; I was implicitly assuming Strong Normativity.[4]

If you accept Normativity of Rationality but not Strong Normativity, you will think that the reasons generated by rationality sometimes conflict with reasons that issue from other sources of normativity, such as morality or prudence. But you will probably believe that conflicts of this sort are rare. Rationality is concerned with coherence among your attitudes such as your beliefs and intentions, whereas morality, prudence and other sources of normativity are rarely concerned with those things. Within its own domain, rationality is almost unchallenged. Examples of conflict between rationality and other sources of requirements tend to be far-fetched, like my example of preventing a war. So according to Normativity of Rationality, when rationality requires something of you, it will normally be the case that you ought to achieve that thing.

A weaker claim is:

> *Weak Normativity.* Necessarily, if rationality requires N to F, there is a reason for N to F.

According to Weak Normativity, that rationality requires you to F entails that you have a reason to F, but the fact that rationality requires you to F may not itself be the reason. Weak Normativity will come up in this chapter, but it is not a version of the claim that rationality is normative. It associates rationality with normativity, but it does not say that rationality is a source of normative requirements.

I shall conclude this chapter by confessing that, although I believe Normativity of Rationality, I have no argument for it. Fortunately, my account of reasoning does not depend on it.

11.2   More on rationality and reasons

Chapters 5 and 6 started an exploration of the connection between reasons and rationality, and this chapter continues it. Before coming to Normativity of Rationality, in this section I have a few rather miscellaneous remarks to make about the connection.

First, the word 'reason' and the word 'rational' are connected together etymologically and grammatically. They have the same Latin root, and 'rational' is the adjective that corresponds to the noun 'reason'. It has the meaning 'connected with reason'. A rational animal is one that has the faculty of reason. Since 'rationality' is the noun constructed from the adjective 'rational', which in turns corresponds to the noun 'reason', the meanings of 'rationality' and 'reason' (the mass noun) overlap considerably.

It would presumably be correct to use 'rational' with the different meaning of 'connected with reasons' – with what the count noun 'reasons' refers to.[5] A book about reasons would be a rational book in this sense, in the way that a book about mathematics is a mathematical book. This is at best a rare usage of 'rational', if it exists at all.

On the other hand, it is very common to forget the difference between the mass noun 'reason' and the count noun 'a reason'. I suspect this is why so many philosophers unhesitatingly associate rationality with reasons.[6] But whatever is the connection between rationality and reasons, it is not as obvious as these philosophers assume. It needs working out, and it may not be very close.

Hume

To illustrate the dangers, take a common reaction to David Hume's famous remark:

> 'Tis not contrary to reason to prefer the destruction of the whole world to the scratching of my finger.[7]

'Reason' here is the mass noun. 'Contrary to reason' may fairly be rendered in modern English as 'irrational'. (Hume himself does not use that word.) Hume is saying it would not be irrational to have the preference he describes. He is not saying there is no reason not to have that preference. We should not attribute such an extraordinary view to Hume. Some philosophers have been more shocked by Hume's remark than they need have been.[8]

At this point, Hume is saying nothing about reasons. He rarely uses the count noun 'reason' in a normative sense, and never in the section of the *Treatise* that contains the remark I quoted. It would obviously be very immoral to prefer the destruction of the whole world to the scratching of your finger, and therefore you ought not to have this preference. Since Hume had no less of a moral sense than the rest of us, I assume he would have agreed that the preference is contrary to morality and that you ought not to have it. There was no inconsistency in his also thinking that it is not contrary to reason, since he did not think morality arises from reason.[9]

Preferring the destruction of the world to the scratching of your finger is imprudent as well as immoral.[10] Hume makes it clear that he thinks prudence no more arises from reason than morality does. ''Tis as little contrary to reason to prefer even my own acknowledg'd lesser good to my greater', he says.[11]

Had Hume been willing to speak of normative reasons, I assume he would have agreed that morality and prudence give you normative reasons not to prefer the destruction of the world to the scratching of your finger. He would have agreed the preference is contrary to these reasons.

Does the Normative Question make sense?

In chapter 5, I have already considered and rejected one more developed idea – as opposed to an unhesitating association – that connects rationality with reasons. This is the idea that rationality consists in responding correctly to reasons. If you like this idea, you will accept Weak Normativity: you will think rationality would not require something of you unless there was a reason for you to achieve that thing. However, you will not accept Normativity of Rationality, because you will not think the fact that rationality requires something of you is itself a reason to achieve that thing. You will not think rationality is a source of normative requirements.

The idea that rationality consists in responding correctly to reasons leads some philosophers to think the Normative Question about rationality is not a sensible question to ask. The Normative Question about morality, put roughly, is the question of whether you have a reason to satisfy the requirements of morality. That is a sensible question. But if rationality consists in responding correctly to reasons, the Normative Question about rationality comes to little more than asking whether you have a reason to do what you have a reason to do. That is not a sensible question.

That is only a rough gesture at an argument. In his paper 'Humean doubts', James Dreier develops a long and careful argument along those lines.[12] He concludes 'There is no sense at all to be made of the question of whether we have any reason to follow the rules of rationality'.[13] I cannot do full justice to Dreier's argument here, but I shall sketch a version of it. I shall modify it to the extent of making it independent of the claim I reject, that rationality consists in responding correctly to reasons. Instead, I shall make it rest on a claim I take to be true: that responding correctly to beliefs about reasons is one part of rationality. Chapter 6 explains this claim in more detail.

Take a person who is irrational. She does not satisfy many requirements of rationality. Among other irrationalities, she does not respond correctly to her beliefs about reasons. Suppose she asks why she should satisfy the requirements of rationality. The only answer anyone could give her would have to be a reason for her to satisfy these requirements. If this answer is to influence her, she must believe it. If she does, she will then believe she has this reason. But this person does not respond correctly to her beliefs about reasons. So giving her this reason would not motivate her to do what it is a reason to do, which is to satisfy the requirements of rationality.

Dreier next assumes that any reason there is for a person to do something must be able to motivate the person to do that thing. This is one version of the doctrine known as 'internalism' about reasons. Since our irrational person could not be motivated by a reason to satisfy the requirements of rationality, this version of internalism implies that nothing could even be a reason for her to do so.

It seems we should conclude that our irrational subject has no reason to satisfy the requirements of rationality. For her, the Normative Question about rationality has the answer 'No'. However, Dreier draws a different conclusion from the argument:

> 'If you can't draw the practical inferences . . . then nothing counts as a reason for you. That is why [a requirement of rationality has] a kind of ground-level normative status.'[14]

Dreier's thinking seems to be that, if no answer can be given to the question of why one should be rational, it is unquestionable that one should be rational. Rationality has an unquestionable, ground-level normative status. Perhaps he thinks we must not question whether we have a reason to be rational because, if we do, no answer can be given us. In any case, he draws the conclusion that the Normative Question makes no sense.

In either case – whether the conclusion is that the Normative Question makes no sense, or that the answer to the Normative Question is 'No' – if the argument were sound, it would leave this chapter without much point. It would be silly to spend much space on trying to answer the Normative Question.

But the argument is not sound. Its assumption of strong internalism is false. Just because our irrational subject would not be motivated by a reason to be rational, it does not follow she has no reason to be rational. This book is an account of motivation, and it gives no support to that sort of internalism. The Normative Question is worth pursuing. It may have 'No' for an answer, but if so it will certainly take some work to establish it.

11.3   Is rationality derivatively normative?

Now I start to look for an answer to the Normative Question itself. Is rationality normative? In this section I shall consider whether rationality is *derivatively normative*. I say a source of requirements is derivatively normative when it is normative and when there is an explanation of why it is normative that stems from some different source of normative requirements. In other words, a source is derivatively normative when it is made normative by some different normative source.

Suppose a source S is normative. That means the requirements it issues are normative: whenever S requires you to F, the fact that it requires you to F is a reason for you to F. We may ask why this fact is a reason. If there is an answer that stems from some different source of normative requirements, then S is derivatively normative.

For instance, it is plausible that the law is derivatively normative. (This is only an illustration; I do not mean to take a stand on the normativity of law.) When the law requires you to F, that fact is a reason for you to F, and the explanation of why it is a reason plausibly stems from some other source. The explanation might be that you risk punishment if you break the law, and prudence requires you not to risk punishment. Or it might be that morality requires you to keep the law. Either way, the law is derivatively normative. Its normativity derives from morality or prudence, which are plausibly non-derivatively normative.

On the face of it, it is also plausible that rationality is derivatively normative. Rationality seems a good way of coming to satisfy normative requirements that issue from sources of normativity other than rationality. There are some things you ought to do, some things you ought to hope for, some things you ought to believe, some things you ought not to do, nor hope for, nor believe, and so on. There are some Fs such that you ought to F. These oughts derive from prudence, morality and no doubt other sources. Rationality seems plausibly a good means of your coming to F in many instances when you ought to F – of achieving much of what you ought to achieve, as I put it. Perhaps rationality is normative for this derivative reason. This section considers whether that is so.

The direct strategy

There are some big obstacles in the way of turning this plausible thought into a proper argument for Normativity of Rationality. The first is that, often when rationality requires you to F, Fing achieves nothing you have any reason to achieve, stemming from any source apart from rationality. For example, suppose you believe you ought to sell your car, but your belief is false and actually you have no reason to sell it. You can satisfy Enkrasia on this occasion by intending to sell your car. If you do, as a result you will probably sell it. But you have no reason to sell it. Satisfying enkrasia on this occasion achieves nothing you have any reason to achieve, stemming from any source beyond rationality.

This first problem is the most serious. If it were not for this problem, we could at least say that, whenever rationality requires you to *F*, you have a reason to *F*. That is the principle of Weak Normativity, set out on page 193. For some purposes we might be content with Weak Normativity; we might not need the stronger principle Normativity of Rationality. But the first problem stands in the way of defending even Weak Normativity on derivative grounds.

The second problem arises even when satisfying a requirement of rationality does achieve something you have a reason to achieve, stemming from some source other than rationality. The problem is that we still cannot conclude that the requirement is normative. Even if we were somehow able to overcome the first problem and so demonstrate Weak Normativity, the second problem would prevent us from demonstrating Normativity of Rationality.

I shall use a Bayesian example of the second problem, since Bayesians often support their requirements on derivative grounds. Just for the sake of argument, let us assume that the Bayesian Requirement on page 175 is correct. I repeat it here.

> ? *Bayesian requirement.* When *p*, *q* and *r* are mutually contrary propositions such that (*p* or *q* or *r*) is necessarily true, rationality requires of *N* that *N*'s degrees of belief in *p*, *q* and *r* respectively add up to one.

Bayesians point out that, if you do not satisfy this requirement, you risk being exploited. Someone could make a Dutch book against you.

A Dutch book is a group of bets that are offered to you. It is designed in such a way that you will accept each individual bet in the group, but that doing so will certainly lose you money. The details do not matter here. A Dutch book can be made against anyone who does not satisfy the Bayesian Requirement. The conclusion emerges that you have a prudential reason to satisfy this requirement. If you do not, you risk losing money.

The Dutch book argument is open to question, but I shall not question it here. Even if it is successful, it does not show that the Bayesian Requirement is normative. It shows you have a prudential reason to have degrees of belief that add up to one. It does not show that the fact rationality requires you to have degrees of belief that add up to one constitutes a reason for you to do so. It gives you a prudential reason for having degrees of belief that add up to one, independently of whatever rationality requires. Even if rationality did not require you to have degrees of belief that add up to one, you would still have just the same prudential reason to do so.

In this respect, rationality differs from law. The law requires you to pay taxes, and you risk punishment if you break the law. Therefore, you risk punishment if you do not pay taxes. That is a prudential reason for you to pay taxes. That much is parallel to the case of rationality: you have a prudential reason to have degrees of belief that add up to one, and you have a prudential reason to pay taxes. The difference is that, whereas in the case of rationality you have the prudential reason independently of what rationality requires, in the legal case you have the prudential reason only because the law requires you to pay taxes. If the law did not require you to pay taxes, you would have no prudential reason to do so. Consequently, the fact that the law requires you to pay taxes is a reason for you to pay taxes. Prudence makes it a reason.[15] The requirement to pay taxes is normative, and prudence explains why. But the fact rationality requires you to have degrees of belief that add up to one is not a reason to have degrees of belief that add up to one. At least, the Dutch book argument does not show it to be one.

The consequence of the two problems I have mentioned is that we cannot demonstrate that each requirement of rationality is derivatively normative. This blocks a direct demonstration that rationality is derivatively normative.

The indirect strategy through a rational disposition

But perhaps we might take an indirect approach. We might start with rationality as a whole, rather than individual requirements of rationality. We might be able to show that rationality as a whole is in some way derivatively normative. From that, we might be able to infer that its individual requirements are normative.

In the end I shall argue that this indirect strategy fails. This means I can develop it in a generous spirit. I shall make the best case for it that I can, helping myself to assumptions that I cannot justify properly, and using arguments that are frankly sketchy. Even after such a generous treatment, the strategy turns out to fail.

I see two different ways of implementing it. Each has a different interpretation of that vague expression 'rationality as a whole'. One interprets it as the property of rationality, which I defined on page 117. It is the property you have when you satisfy all the requirements of rationality. This is the property of rationality as an attainment rather than the capacity of rationality mentioned on page 110.

The other implementation interprets it as a rational disposition. By that I mean a disposition that causes you to satisfy many rational requirements. This is only a rough definition because of the vague term 'many', but it will serve for my purposes. It includes the capacity of rationality and also a disposition to exercise that capacity. The connection between a rational disposition and satisfying individual rational requirements is causal.

I shall start with the rational disposition, and come to the property of rationality later. Possessing a rational disposition is plausibly part of the best means of achieving much of what you ought to achieve. By 'best' I mean better than other means that are psychologically possible for you. In principle, there might be an alternative disposition that could form part of an even better means of achieving much of what you ought to achieve. On some occasions, a rational disposition will steer you wrong. The car-selling example illustrates how it will sometimes cause you to fail to achieve something you ought to achieve; it might cause you to sell a car when you ought not to. The alternative disposition would be like the rational disposition, but altered a little to correct some of those glitches. But the necessary alterations would often depend on circumstances in the outside world that are not represented in your mind. Therefore, this alternative would not be psychologically possible for you.

Simply because it seems plausible, I shall assume that a rational disposition is part of the best means of achieving much of what you ought to achieve. From this, I shall also assume that a further plausible conclusion can be derived: that you ought to have a rational disposition.

I am sorry to say I cannot offer a proper derivation of this conclusion. It is a matter of the transmission of normativity from ends to means. In this case the end is achieving much of what you ought to achieve, and the means – more exactly, part of the best means – is having a rational disposition. But I know no principle that correctly specifies how normativity is transmitted from ends to means.[16] To see how tricky transmission is, look back to page 129, where I rejected the principle of deontic transmission. At first it may seem obvious that, if you ought to pursue an end, you ought to take any necessary means to it. But actually that is false.

Nevertheless, normativity must be transmitted somehow from ends to means. The whole idea of derivative normativity is that you can have a reason to do something because it is a means of doing something else you have a reason to do. That is nothing other than transmission. We are dealing with what seems a plausible case of it. So, although I cannot derive the conclusion that you ought to have a rational disposition through any general principle I know, nevertheless I assume it is derivable.

I assume, then, that you ought to have a rational disposition, and this is on derivative grounds: because a rational disposition is part of the best means of achieving much of what you ought to achieve. The next step in the indirect strategy is to derive the conclusion that you have a reason to satisfy each individual requirement of rationality.

If we can bring off this derivation, a bonus is that we shall have derived the conclusion in a way that shows what the reason is. For each individual requirement, we shall have derived the conclusion that you ought to satisfy it from the fact that you ought to have a disposition to satisfy requirements of rationality. The reason must therefore be that it is a requirement of rationality. We shall have shown that, whenever rationality requires you to F, the fact that rationality requires you to F is a reason for you to F. If we can also show this is necessary, we shall have demonstrated Normativity of Rationality.

We would have done so on derivative grounds. The explanation of why the fact that rationality requires you to F is a reason for you to F would be derived from other normative requirements beyond rationality. It would be that rationality is part of the best means of achieving many of the things other normative sources require you to achieve.

But this is all pie in the sky. The argument does not go through. We are assuming you ought to have a rational disposition. The next step is to derive the conclusion that you have a reason to satisfy each individual requirement of rationality. But that conclusion just does not follow.

The relation between a disposition and satisfying individual requirements is causal. If you have the disposition, it will cause you to satisfy many individual requirements. But 'You ought to F; if you F, your Fing will cause you to G; so you have a reason to G' is not a valid pattern of deduction. This is obvious. Suppose you ought to take some drug to cure your serious disease. Suppose the drug has the side effect of causing you to feel unsteady. It does not follow that you have a reason to feel unsteady.

To be sure, if you take the drug and as a result feel unsteady, we might say there is a reason why you feel unsteady. That would simply be another way of saying there is an explanation of why you feel unsteady. 'The reason why' in this context has a non-normative meaning equivalent to 'the explanation of why'. There is no reason, in any normative sense, for you to feel unsteady.

In general, normativity is not transmitted from something to a causal effect of that thing. So we simply cannot conclude, from the fact that you ought to have a rational disposition, that you have a reason to satisfy any of the particular requirements of rationality.

The indirect strategy through the property of rationality

Now the alternative way of implementing the indirect strategy. Instead of starting by attaching normativity to a rational disposition, we start by attaching it to the property of rationality.[17] This is the property you have when you satisfy all the individual requirements of rationality. (Remember that by 'rational' I mean fully rational.) The connection between the property and satisfying individual requirements is not causal but logical. Logically necessarily, if you are rational, you satisfy each particular requirement. The problem with the previous implementation is that there is only a causal connection between a rational disposition and satisfying individual requirements. Could we found a better argument on a logical connection?

Suppose we could demonstrate on derivative grounds that you ought to be rational. Then we would be able to apply a different pattern of deduction to derive the conclusion that you have a reason to satisfy a particular requirement. We could apply the pattern: 'You ought to F; logically necessarily, if you F, you G; so you have a reason to G'. We could substitute 'be rational' for 'F' and 'satisfy a particular rational requirement' for 'G'. This would give us a different argument for Normativity of Rationality.

I see two difficulties with this parallel argument. First, the new pattern of deduction is questionable, for the same reason as End to Means Transmission on page 126 is questionable. Suppose you ought to buy a can of paint and decorate your kitchen. It follows by this pattern of deduction that you ought to buy a can of paint. But suppose you are not going to decorate your kitchen; you have no intention of doing so, and you will not do it. Then it seems obvious that there may be no reason for you to buy a can of paint. If you are not going to decorate your kitchen, it may be entirely pointless to buy one. This example suggests the pattern of deduction is invalid.

Perhaps that difficulty can be overcome. The other is more severe. I can see no satisfactory way of arguing for the premise that you ought to be rational. The argument is supposed to be on derivative grounds, so it would depend on showing that being rational is effective at satisfying requirements that stem from other sources. How could that be shown?

To make the corresponding argument that you ought to have a rational disposition, I assumed that having this disposition is part of the best means of achieving much of what you ought to achieve. By 'best' I meant best among those means that are psychologically possible for you. Granted that assumption, it is plausible that you ought to have a rational disposition.

But being rational is not even psychologically possible for you; no one could be entirely rational. And once we are looking into psychologically impossible properties, being rational would not be the most effective among them. To be rational is to satisfy each of the individual requirements of rationality. But the example of selling your car shows it is more effective for you to fail to satisfy a few of those requirements. By doing so, you will achieve more of what you ought to achieve. Given all this, I do not see how one could argue that you ought to have the psychologically impossible property of being rational.

But could we not run the argument differently? Maybe it is not the case that you ought to be rational. But being rational entails satisfying a number of individual requirements of rationality that you have derivative reasons to satisfy. Surely you have some reason to have a property that entails your satisfying some requirements that you have a reason to satisfy. So could we not conclude that you have a reason to be rational?

This is a weaker claim than the claim that you ought to be rational. It might be more defensible. And perhaps we could still derive from it the conclusion we want: that you have a reason to satisfy each individual requirement. We could do so through the pattern of deduction: 'You have a reason to F; logically necessarily, if you F, you G; so you have a reason to G'. That seems plausible.

But this argument would be simple trickery. To have the property of rationality is just to satisfy each of the individual requirements of rationality. To say you have a reason to have the property of rationality is just to say you have a reason to satisfy each of the individual requirements: you have a reason to satisfy R_1 and to satisfy R_2 and to satisfy R_3 and so on.

The first step of the argument is to derive this conclusion from the premise that you have a reason to satisfy some, but not all, of the individual requirements. Let them include R_2 and R_3, but not R_1. So the first step is to derive from:

You have a reason to satisfy R_2 and you have a reason to satisfy R_3 and you have a reason to satisfy. . . .

the conclusion that:

You have a reason to satisfy R_1 and to satisfy R_2 and to satisfy R_3 and to satisfy. . . .

The next stage is to derive from this the conclusion that you have a reason to satisfy each of the individual requirements. In particular:

You have a reason to satisfy R_1.

So in two steps we derive the conclusion that you have a reason to satisfy R_1 from the premise that you have a reason to satisfy some other requirements that do not include R_1. Obviously that cannot be done. So the argument must be invalid.

In sum, I have found no successful argument for the conclusion that rationality is derivatively normative. It remains possible that it is so nonetheless, and

I have missed the argument. But my own opinion is that rationality is not derivatively normative.

11.4 Is rationality non-derivatively normative?

Rationality might nevertheless be normative, though not derivatively so. If it is, when rationality requires you to F, this fact is a reason for you to F, but no explanation of why it is a reason stems from a source of requirements other than rationality itself. Then rationality is non-derivatively normative.

That there is no explanation that stems from another source does not mean there is no explanation at all.[18] A metaphysical account of normativity might provide one; it might be a consequence of the account that rationality is normative. Or an account of the nature of rationality might imply that rationality is normative. For instance, it is plausible that rationality is constitutive of agency, so that if we were not rational we would not be agents. It may be that, being the acting creatures we are, we cannot help taking rationality as normative. If so, an argument might be built on that fact for the conclusion that rationality actually is normative.[19] I shall not attempt any such argument in this book because I do not know one that convinces me.[20]

So I am without a argument for the normativity of rationality. Yet I believe rationality is non-derivatively normative. This is an uncomfortable position to be in, but I share it with others. H. A. Prichard claims that morality is non-derivatively normative,[21] and that all we can say by way of explanation is that it just is. We are naturally drawn to cast around for something better to say. According to Prichard, this tendency draws moral philosophy into a mistake. We start trying to explain the normativity of morality on derivative grounds, which is bound to fail.

The problem for rationality is worse than it is for morality. Most of us take it for granted that morality is normative, although we wonder why. The Normative Question for morality – have you a reason to do as morality requires? – is not a question that many philosophers ask for real. There are few genuine philosophical sceptics about the normativity of morality. But the Normative Question about rationality is often asked for real, and there are genuine sceptics. Indeed, in 'Why be rational?', Niko Kolodny goes so far as to deny the normativity of rationality. I rejected his negative argument against it on pages 144–6, but that merely leaves the question open. So I am not just looking for an explanation of something we already know to be true. I am looking for a demonstration that it is true. So long as I have no explanation, it remains a real question whether rationality is normative.[22]

I therefore do not rely on Normativity of Rationality in this book. The higher-order account of reasoning, which I shall discuss in chapter 12, implicitly assumes it. But for quite separate reasons I shall reject that account. My own account of reasoning is developed from chapter 13 onwards, and it does not assume Normativity of Rationality. Perhaps rationality is our 'plight', to use Christine Korsgaard's word.[23] Perhaps we find ourselves inescapably rational creatures who reason and strive to reason correctly. My account is consistent with that possibility.

Notes

1 See p. 27. I take the name 'Normative Question' from Christine Korsgaard's *The Sources of Normativity*, lecture 1.
2 See p. 53.
3 Jacob Ross in 'Rationality, normativity, and commitment' is one example.
4 Andrew Reisner persuaded me to change my practice, because Strong Normativity is not very plausible. He makes this point in his *Conflicts of Normativity*.
5 See section 4.1.
6 Two examples are Bernard Williams in 'Internal and external reasons', p. 110, and Michael Smith in 'Humean rationality'.
7 *Treatise*, book 2, part 3, section 3.
8 Mark Johnston in 'Dispositional theories of value', p. 161, Derek Parfit in *On What Matters*, vol. 2, pp. 453–5, and others. J. L. Mackie, on p. 79 of *Ethics*, also confuses the count noun with the mass noun in his interpretation of Hume's remark, though Mackie was not shocked.
9 *Treatise*, book 3, part 1, section 1.
10 Thanks to Sophie Botros for comments on this point.
11 *Treatise*, book 2, part 3, section 3.
12 The main argument is in 'Humean doubts', pp. 38–42.
13 'Humean doubts', p. 29.
14 'Humean doubts', p. 42.
15 In 'Reason-giving and the law', David Enoch says the law 'triggers' a reason. He says the law is not normative, but that is only because he does not count derivative normativity as a sort of normativity.
16 Carsten Nielsen helpfully reminded me of this difficulty.
17 This approach was suggested to me by Philip Pettit.
18 This point was urged on me by Nadeem Hussain, who makes it in his paper 'The requirements of rationality'.
19 An argument of this sort is to be found in Christine Korsgaard's *Self-Constitution*. There is a criticism of it in David Enoch's 'Agency, Schmagency'.
20 A different explanation appears in Nicholas Southwood's 'Vindicating the normativity of rationality'. I replied to it in my 'Replies to Southwood, Kearns and Star, and Cullity'.
21 'Does moral philosophy rest on a mistake?'. Each of Kent Hurtig, Nadeem Hussain, Christian Piller and Nicholas Southwood independently pointed out to me the parallel between rationality and morality as Prichard viewed it.
22 Jonathan Dancy finds himself in the same position at the end of his 'Reasons and rationality'.
23 'The normativity of instrumental reason', p. 244. This is Korsgaard's word, but she means something different by it.

12
Higher-Order Reasoning

12.1 The reasoning process

In chapter 9 I described various synchronic requirements of rationality. Rationality requires you not to have contradictory intentions, to believe what follows by modus ponens from what you believe, and so on. The more requirements you satisfy, the more rational you are. A fully rational person would satisfy all of them. But by what processes do you come to satisfy requirements of rationality in the first place?

Answering this question about processes is an important part of coming to understand our rationality. Indeed, Niko Kolodny suggests that all the requirements of rationality may be on processes rather than on states.[1] If that is right, all the requirements I listed in chapter 9 are mistaken. I do not think it is right, but I do think we need to understand the processes by which you come to satisfy requirements on states.

They must be causal processes of some sort. They constitute the working of your rational disposition, which I defined on page 200 as the disposition that causes you to satisfy many rational requirements. Very often your rational disposition works automatically, causing you to satisfy individual requirements without your doing anything about it. For instance, many of your intentions automatically persist so that, in many instances, you automatically satisfy Persistence of Intention, which is stated on page 178. For another example, when you intend to visit Glasgow, and believe you will not do so unless you buy a ticket, you just find yourself intending to buy a ticket. You automatically satisfy the Instrumental Requirement on page 159.

Another example again: automatic processes generally prevent you from having contradictory beliefs. Suppose you believe platypuses are not mammals, but then you learn from a radio programme that actually platypuses are mammals, so now you believe that platypuses are mammals. Normally, at that point you will automatically lose your belief that platypuses are not mammals. A great deal of our rationality is given us by automatic processes.

Although these are automatic causal processes, they nevertheless have semantic features. The causes and effects are attitudes that have contents with meaning. Moreover, when a process works properly, the semantic properties of the causes and effects are appropriately connected together. For instance, you stop having a belief whose content is the negation of the content of a belief you have acquired. It is an interesting and difficult question how an automatic causal process can have these semantic features. Fortunately, I do not need to answer it, since I am not concerned with these automatic processes.

Some ideally rational creatures such as angels may have a rational disposition that works infallibly in this automatic manner. They find themselves automatically satisfying every rational requirement they are under.[2] Even a mortal can improve the automatic operation of her rational disposition by cultivating it. Training is one way. You can train your memory, for instance, and then you will more often satisfy persistence requirements. By cultivating your rational disposition, you can make yourself more rational: you can bring yourself to satisfy more requirements of rationality in the future.

But we mortals will never match up to angels. Some requirements are too difficult for our automatic processes to cope with; I shall soon give the example of difficult Bayesian requirements. But when automatic processes let us down, our mortal rational disposition equips us with a further, self-help mechanism. We have another way of improving our score by our own efforts. We can do it through the mental activity of reasoning.[3]

You sometimes reason your way to satisfying a particular requirement of rationality. You believe it is raining and you believe that if it is raining you ought to take an umbrella. As you head for the door, thinking about what to pick up, you bring these beliefs together in your mind and end up believing you ought to take an umbrella. Going through this process is something you do. By doing it, you bring yourself to satisfy an instance of the Modus Ponens Requirement on page 157. You improve your rationality by satisfying one requirement that you did not previously satisfy. You do this yourself. It is part of the working of your rational disposition, but this part works through your own activity.

In sum, you have both an indirect and a direct means of improving your rationality: cultivating your rational disposition on the one hand, and reasoning on the other.

Reasoning is something we do that can bring us to satisfy requirements of rationality. (That is not all it can do for us; I shall explain on page 248 how reasoning can go beyond requirements.) The rest of this book investigates reasoning. More exactly, it investigates *active* reasoning, or reasoning as an activity, by which I mean reasoning that we do. Some automatic processes that happen in us might be classed as passive reasoning, but I am not interested in those. In this book, 'reasoning', unqualified, refers to active reasoning.

Philosophers' neglect of reasoning

Some philosophers who write on rationality seem to think they have finished their job when they have described requirements of rationality. But they have not. They would have done if they could rely on automatic processes to cause us to satisfy all the requirements we are under. But that is too hopeful. Sometimes we have to do some work for ourselves, in order to satisfy particular requirements.

Bayesian requirements provide a good example. Look at the one set out on page 175. It is a rather complicated requirement on your precise degrees of belief. It is not credible that automatic processes would bring you to satisfy this requirement, except by good luck on rare occasions. It could not happen that you satisfy it regularly, except by applying your mind to it. The same goes for other Bayesian requirements. So Bayesians owe us an account of the active reasoning process by which you can bring yourself to satisfy Bayesian requirements. In section 15.2 I shall outline a way this debt might be repaid.

A different, surprising example comes from Gilbert Harman's important book *Change in View: Principles of Reasoning*. Despite its subtitle, what this book principally does is specify some requirements of rationality. Harman's requirements are not the same as mine. One of his is (I quote):

> *Principle of Positive Undermining.* One should stop believing P whenever one positively believes one's reasons for believing P are no good.[4]

(Harman uses the normative word 'should' to describe a requirement of rationality. Evidently he assumes that rationality is strongly normative in the sense set out on page 192.)

For the sake of argument, let us suppose this is a genuine requirement of rationality. It requires a particular relation to hold among your mental states. But how can you actually achieve what it requires, and stop believing P under the conditions Harman specifies? Perhaps it will just happen, as part of the automatic operation of your rational disposition. But if it does not, you need to bring it about by reasoning, if you are to be rational. How would that reasoning go? Harman does not tell us, and in general his book does not tell us about processes of reasoning. For the Principle of Positive Undermining in particular, it is hard to see how any process of reasoning could bring you to satisfy it. It would have to conclude in a non-belief, and section 15.3 explains that it is hard to see how that could happen.

Why do Harman, the Bayesians, and many other writers on rationality, neglect to describe the process of reasoning? Why do they wind up their work once they have specified requirements? It must be because they see no further question. They must think it is obvious how, once you know what requirements there are, you can come to satisfy them.

They might think that, once you know what requirements there are, automatic processes will cause you to satisfy them. But this is not plausible for complex requirements such as Bayesian ones. In any case, we certainly do sometimes reason actively to bring ourselves to satisfy requirements, and we need an account of how.

So instead I think these authors must believe that, once you know what requirements there are, that knowledge directly supplies you with premises you can use in active reasoning. They must believe that, starting from knowledge of a particular requirement, you can reason your way actively to satisfying that requirement. They therefore need do no more than tell you what requirements there are.

Higher-order accounts of reasoning

Requirements of rationality are requirements on your attitudes. So, if you believe rationality requires you to F, that is a belief about your attitudes. That makes it a *higher-order belief*. These authors must think that a belief of this sort could, through a process of reasoning, bring you to F.

A belief of this sort could not achieve this result without at some point bringing you to believe you have a reason to F, or that you ought to F. If you believe merely that rationality requires you to F, but not that you have any reason to F, your belief is obviously not going to bring you to F by reasoning. So the process of reasoning must at some point involve a *normative* higher-order belief.

Many philosophers assume your belief about a rational requirement is already normative, because they assume that rationality is normative. Harman's statement of the Principle of Positive Undermining, quoted on page 208, implicitly reveals that assumption. In any case, many philosophers assume that a normative higher-order belief is essential to reasoning.

There are two ways in which this might be so. It might be that you must have one of these beliefs in the background in order to reason. I shall consider that possibility on page 228. Or the normative higher-order belief might be needed as part of the reasoning itself, with its content serving as a premise at some stage of the process. Any account of reasoning in which the content of a normative higher-order belief serves as a premise at some stage I call a 'higher-order account'. 'Higher-order account' is short for 'normative higher-order account'. This chapter considers higher-order accounts of reasoning.

Although this sort of account is implicit in the writings of many philosophers,[5] I do not know anywhere where one is worked out in detail. So I shall work out two alternative accounts for myself. Both may at first seem feasible, but I shall reject both. Indeed, the conclusion of this chapter is that the normative higher-order account of reasoning has to be rejected. I shall go on to present my own first-order account of reasoning starting in chapter 13.

12.2   Reasoning through an intention

The main challenge for a higher-order account of reasoning is to explain how a normative higher-order belief that you have a reason to F – or even the stronger belief that you ought to F – gets you to F. Remember that Fing in our context is having some attitude, or satisfying some condition on your attitudes. Suppose, say, that you believe you ought to believe something; how does that get you to believe it? One possibility is that it happens through an intention of yours to F. My first version of the higher-order account works that way; the second does not work through an intention. This section examines the first; section 12.3 the second. I shall conclude that both accounts fail.

The account

Suppose you have the higher-order belief that rationality requires you to F. How could reasoning get you from there to actually Fing? Here is one account of how it might happen.

As a first step, you derive the normative higher-order belief that you ought to F. You might do so on the basis of the principle of Strong Normativity from page 192. Or alternatively, on the basis of Weak Normativity from page 193, you might start by deriving the conclusion that you have a reason to F. You might believe this reason outweighs all contrary reasons in the particular case. On that basis, you could conclude that you ought to F.

Once you believe you ought to F, you have access to what seems at first to be a plausible process involving reasoning, which can bring you to F. Often when you believe you ought to F, this belief causes you to F, and it does so partly through reasoning. The process goes in two steps. First, your belief that you ought to F causes you to intend to F. Then your intention to F causes you to F. This last step is not reasoning, but the previous one may be. I, for one, believe there is a process of reasoning that takes you from believing you ought to F to intending to F. I call it 'enkratic reasoning'. I shall argue for its existence in chapter 16, and I do not need to describe its details here.

Now we have a higher-order account involving three steps. Your reasoning starts from a belief of yours that rationality requires you to F. Then – step one – from that you derive a belief that you ought to F. Next – step two – by enkratic reasoning you derive an intention to F. Finally – step three – this intention causes you to F. This process brings you to satisfy a requirement of reasoning, and it works through an intention of yours to satisfy that requirement.

It is difficult to make good sense of this story. First of all, it gives an intention a quite implausible role in reasoning. Intentions may be inputs into practical reasoning, or outputs from it, but it is implausible that an intention should be a part of the actual working of the reasoning. Moreover, particular difficulties arise at each step. I shall skip over the difficulties of step one, because many philosophers do not see this as a step at all. They do not even distinguish between the belief that rationality requires you to F and the belief that you ought to F. So they would not recognize a difficulty here. I therefore go on to step two.

Regress

If we ignore step one, step two is the only step of real reasoning in the whole process. So only step two entitles the whole process to count as reasoning. It is negotiated by enkratic reasoning. But on my own account of it in chapter 16, enkratic reasoning is not higher-order reasoning. It is a species of first-order reasoning. This higher-order account is consequently parasitic on a first-order account.

Actually, it is not strictly accurate to say in our context that enkratic reasoning is first-order reasoning on my account.[6] Enkratic reasoning takes you from believing you ought to F to intending to F. In our context, Fing is having some attitude or satisfying some condition on you attitudes. So the belief you start with – that you ought to F – is already a second-order normative belief. Enkratic reasoning in this context inevitably involves a second-order normative belief, therefore. But on my account it involves no belief that has an order higher than that one. It is not a higher-order account in that sense. It has the character of first-order reasoning, and I shall continue to call it that.

Enkratic reasoning brings you to satisfy the rational requirement Enkrasia, which is specified on page 170. Roughly, it says that rationality requires of you that, if you believe you ought to F, you intend to F. From chapter 13 onwards, I shall describe first-order accounts of various sorts of reasoning, which bring you to satisfy various other rational requirements as well as Enkrasia. If the first-order account is satisfactory for enkratic reasoning, it is satisfactory for these other sorts too. So if we once recognize first-order enkratic reasoning, higher-order reasoning becomes redundant. First-order reasoning is all we need.

To rescue higher-order reasoning, we could try and produce a higher-order account of enkratic reasoning. This account would have you reason your way to satisfying Enkrasia on the basis of a belief in Enkrasia itself. So you would need to start by believing that rationality requires of you that, if you believe you ought to F, you intend to F. In our context, this is actually a third-order belief: Fing is a relation among your attitudes, so believing you ought to F is a second-order belief, and a belief about believing you ought to F is a third-order belief.

According to the higher-order account, you reason your way from this third-order belief in a requirement to actually satisfying the requirement, via a third-order intention. Specifically, you form the intention that, if you believe you ought to F, you intend to F. You arrive at this intention by higher-order – now third-order – reasoning. How does that work? On our account of it, it involves enkratic reasoning. And we are now trying to treat enkratic reasoning as higher-order reasoning. That means we shall at this point have to call on a fourth-order belief and fourth-order reasoning involving a fourth-order intention, to explain how the third-order reasoning works. This whole story will repeat itself at the fourth order, and so on to higher and higher orders.

So if enkratic reasoning is to be treated as higher-order reasoning, we shall end up with an infinite hierarchy of beliefs, intentions and reasoning processes. Each process must take time. Consequently, the reasoning could never end.

To summarize, either the higher-order account depends on first-order reasoning, in which case it is redundant, or alternatively it requires a hierarchy of reasoning processes, which could never end.

Controlling beliefs by intentions

Another very serious difficulty afflicts the account at step three. This step is merely causal: an intention to F causes you to F. In more familiar contexts, that would be unproblematic. If you intend to get a newspaper, your intention normally causes you to get a newspaper. This is how enkratic reasoning normally achieves its purpose: by bringing you to intend to do what you believe you ought to do, it brings you to do what you believe you ought to do.

But in our context, Fing is having some attitude or satisfying some condition on your attitudes. And you do not control your attitudes in the way you control your acts. An intention to get a newspaper can easily cause you to get a newspaper. An intention to have some relation obtain among your attitudes does not so easily cause that relation to obtain.

It can sometimes. Sometimes you have a means available of altering your attitudes. Suppose you intend either to believe the window is open or to believe the end of the world is nigh. You can satisfy this intention by opening the window. That will cause you to believe the window is open.

When this banal sort of means is not available, means of a more exotic sort may be. You may be able to alter your attitudes by enlisting the help of a hypnotist or by undertaking a programme of self-persuasion. In science fiction, you can take a pill.

But we are trying to identify a process of *reasoning* that can bring you to have a pattern of attitudes that rationality requires of you. A process of reasoning cannot include such non-mental acts as opening a window, visiting a hypnotist or taking a pill. If the process is to be reasoning, your intention will have to cause your attitudes to change without using a means. As I shall put it, it will have to cause your attitudes to change *directly*.

You can do some things directly, without using a means. For example, you can raise your hand without using a means. Consequently, intending to raise your hand can directly bring you to raise your hand. For all I know, you may be able to change some of your attitudes directly by intending to. But I am concerned specifically with requirements on beliefs and intentions. Can you directly alter your beliefs and intentions by intending to?

For beliefs, the answer is straightforwardly 'No'. This is uncontroversial. It seems almost universally agreed among philosophers that you cannot directly bring yourself to believe p by intending to believe p. Nor can you bring yourself not to believe p by intending not to believe p. There is some dispute about whether these are contingent features of our psychology or necessary truths that stem from the nature of belief.[7] But there is no dispute over whether they are true. I take them for granted.

You cannot directly alter your beliefs by intending to. This by itself means that this account of reasoning, which works through an intention, cannot be a successful account of reasoning with beliefs.

Controlling intentions by intentions

For reasoning with intentions, the conclusion cannot be so quick. Several philosophers have claimed that you can never directly bring yourself to intend to F by intending to intend to F.[8] They make this claim largely on the grounds of intuition. My own intuition accords with theirs, but I am not as confident as they are. The following example casts doubt on their claim.

Suppose you are offered a large prize for intending, at some time between 12.00 and 12.01 today, to raise your arm between 12.00 and 12.01 today. To win the prize, you do not have to raise your arm. You just have to intend to. Moreover, you have no independent reason to raise your arm, and you know that.

In some circumstances you could not win this prize. For instance, you could not win it if your arm was tied down and you knew it was tied down. But in most circumstances you could win it. You only have to decide, sometime between 12.00 and 12.01, to raise your arm immediately. Deciding to raise it is forming the intention of raising it. So you win.

It is clear you could win. Moreover, it is clear that you could win even if you are fully rational. But how, in more detail, could you arrive at the intention you need? Here is one route.

First you form the belief that you ought to intend to raise your arm. You might rationally have this belief, because it is plausibly true. You can win a large prize by intending to raise your arm, and no harm is done by your having this intention, so it is plausible that you ought to have it.

Second, your belief that you ought to intend to raise your arm causes you to intend to intend to raise your arm. This might happen through enkratic reasoning. Alternatively, a process within you, in which you are not active, might bypass your reasoning and directly cause you to intend to intend to raise your arm.

Finally, your intention to intend to raise your arm directly causes you to intend to raise your arm. This is what several philosophers claim cannot happen. But if you can win the prize by this route, evidently it can.

You can win the prize. So if this was the only route by which you could do so, it would show those philosophers are wrong. To vindicate their view, we need to find another route to winning. Is there one?

One possibility is that your intention to intend to raise your arm might be cut out of the process. Once you believe you ought to intend to raise your arm, your belief might directly cause you to intend to raise your arm, without an intervening intention.

At first, this idea seems to be encouraged by T. M. Scanlon's notion of a judgement-sensitive attitude. In *What We Owe to Each Other*, Scanlon defines judgement-sensitive attitudes as 'attitudes that an ideally rational person would come to have whenever that person judged there to be sufficient reason for them'.[9] If you were ideally rational, you would come to have a judgement-sensitive attitude whenever you judged there to be sufficient reason to have it – whenever you believed you ought to have it, as I prefer to say. Your belief would directly cause you to have the attitude; no intention to have it need intervene in the process.

In the example, your intention to raise your arm might be a judgement-sensitive attitude. Nevertheless, actually Scanlon himself would not think your belief that you ought to intend to raise your arm would directly cause you to intend to raise your arm. Scanlon later made it clear that a judgement-sensitive attitude is sensitive to beliefs about object-given reasons, but not to beliefs about state-given reasons.[10] I formulated Scanlon's condition as I understand it on page 96, making this restriction explicit. I repeat it here:

> *Scanlon's Condition.* When *F*ing is having a particular attitude, necessarily, if you are rational then, if you believe your object-given reasons require you to *F*, you *F*.

An object-given reason to intend to raise your arm would be a reason actually to raise it, and you do not believe you have any such reason. Your belief that you ought to intend to raise your arm arises from a state-given reason only: a reason to be in the state of intending to raise your arm.

In agreement with Scanlon, I too argued in section 6.2 that a rational person's attitudes are more plausibly determined by her beliefs about object-given reasons than by her beliefs about state-given reasons. So it is not plausible that your intention to raise your arm would be directly caused by your belief that you ought to have this intention. This is not a plausible route to winning the prize.

I can think of no other possible routes. The first is the only plausible one. That route involves your directly bringing yourself to intend to raise your arm by intending to intend to raise your arm. It puts in doubt the claim that you can never directly bring yourself to intend to *F* by intending to intend to *F*.

I am therefore not confident in that claim. Nevertheless, on intuitive grounds I continue to believe it is largely true, despite exceptions such as the example I have just given. Generally, you cannot directly bring yourself to intend to *F* by intending to intend to *F*. If this is right, it means that doing so cannot be part of a process of reasoning. A reasoning process cannot rely on your doing something that you can only do in exceptional cases.

Conclusion

I conclude that the first higher-order account of reasoning, in which you reason through an intention, has to be rejected. First, it is implausible that intentions can play the role in reasoning that it attributes to them. Second, severe difficulties afflict the account in detail, at each step.

12.3   Reasoning with judgement-sensitive attitudes

That account of higher-order reasoning fails. It was never plausible anyway that reasoning works through an intention, so we need a new account that leaves the intention out. Once more, Scanlon's notion of a judgement-sensitive attitude suggests how we might find one. A rational person is causally disposed to satisfy Scanlon's condition. She is disposed to have a judgement-sensitive attitude whenever she believes her object-given reasons require her to have it. This happens without her forming any intention to have this attitude. Perhaps we can develop an account of higher-reasoning on this basis.

The snow example

It will be useful to have an example to work with.

One thing makes it difficult to create a simple, plausible example of active reasoning. All the theoretical requirements in Chapter 9 apart from the Bayesian one, are elementary. Few of us satisfy all instances of all of them, but if you do not satisfy one in a particular instance, you will normally come to satisfy it in a flash as soon as your attention settles on it. Because the requirements are so elementary, this is likely to happen automatically, without your doing any active reasoning. So it is hard to produce a plausible example that works through active reasoning.

To minimize this problem, I shall imagine your mind is slowed down by dopiness. Suppose you have just woken up and are gathering your wits. You hear dripping water, and come to believe it is raining. You are experienced enough to know that if it is raining the snow will melt. But you have not yet turned your mind to the snow, so you do not yet believe the snow will melt. However, because you plan to go skiing, you care about whether the snow will melt. So you do not satisfy the Modus Ponens Requirement on page 157 in this instance. You believe it is raining; you believe that if it is raining the snow will melt, you care about whether the snow will melt, but you do not believe the snow will melt.

How can you reason your way to satisfying the requirement? The higher-order account is supposed to provide an answer.

The account

Let us go back to the beginning, to the point on page 210 where I assumed you start with a belief in a particular requirement of rationality. You have the higher-order belief that rationality requires you to F for some F. In the example, you believe rationality requires of you that, if you believe it is raining, and you believe that if it is raining the snow will melt, then you believe the snow will melt. That is where we start. (Here I ignore the condition that you care about whether the snow will melt; I shall come back to it in section 12.4.)

Let us assume that, to satisfy the requirement of rationality to F, given the condition you are already in, you need to acquire a particular attitude A. Moreover, let us assume A is a judgement-sensitive attitude. In the example, to satisfy the Modus Ponens Requirement given your existing beliefs, you need to believe the snow will melt. So A is the belief that the snow will melt. This is judgement-sensitive because, according to Scanlon, beliefs are judgement-sensitive attitudes.

You believe rationality requires you to F; that is the starting point of the account. Starting from there, the first step of the reasoning process takes you to the normative belief that your object-given reasons require you to have the attitude A. In the example, you believe your object-given reasons require you to believe the snow will melt. According to the account, this happens in some way by reasoning.

The second step is that this normative belief causes you to have the attitude A. This happens just because, as a rational person, you are causally disposed to satisfy Scanlon's Condition. In the example, your belief that your object-given reasons require you to believe the snow will melt causes you to believe the snow will melt. So the reasoning is complete in two steps.

Problems for the first step of the account

This account meets problems at each step. At the first step, reasoning is supposed to lead you to the higher-order belief that your object-given reasons require you to have a particular attitude. There are problems over the content of this reasoning and over the nature of it.

Content first. You start from a belief in a requirement of rationality that has a wide scope. It is doubtful that a process of reasoning could take you from there to a normative belief about a single attitude. In the example, you believe these three propositions:

It is raining
If it is raining the snow will melt
Rationality requires of you that, if you believe it is raining and you believe that if it is raining the snow will melt, you believe the snow will melt.

These are your premises. From them, it just does not follow that your object-given reasons require you to believe the snow will melt. So it is doubtful that reasoning could bring you to believe that proposition.

Your higher-order premise is about your states – specifically your beliefs. It is therefore particularly doubtful that reasoning could bring you to believe that your object-given reasons, as opposed to your state-given reasons, require you to believe the snow will melt.

Next, problems about the nature of the reasoning. Suppose it is higher-order reasoning. Then, before you acquire the second-order belief that your object-given reasons require you to have attitude F, you must acquire the third-order belief that your object-given reasons require you to believe your object-given reasons require you to have attitude A. If this, too, is to happen by higher-order reasoning, you must previously acquire the fourth-order belief that your object-given reasons require you to believe your object-given reasons require you to believe your object-given reasons require you to have attitude A. And so on to infinity. The reasoning could not get going.

So you must acquire your belief at some level by a process that is not higher-order reasoning. It would be easy to explain how you can do that. Chapter 13 describes first-order reasoning, which could explain it. But first-order reasoning could also lead you directly to the first-order attitude A. In the example, it can lead you directly to believe the snow will melt. If a first-order account of reasoning is good enough at some higher level, it is good enough at the lowest level. The higher-order account is therefore redundant.

Problems for the second step of the account

Those are two problems at the account's first step. Now a problem at its second step. The account requires you to acquire a particular attitude by first believing that your object-given reasons require you to have that attitude. The problem is that this sort of higher-order belief is rare. As Scanlon recognizes,[11] you are more likely to have a first-order belief about the object of an attitude than a second-order belief about the attitude itself.

In the example, you believe two facts obtain: that it is raining and that if it is raining the snow will melt. If those facts did indeed obtain, they would together constitute conclusive evidence that the snow will melt. On the basis of your beliefs that they obtain, you are likely to arrive straight away at a belief that the snow will melt. Chapter 13 describes a process of first-order reasoning that can take you to that conclusion.

If you are sophisticated – if you have the concept of *evidence*, for one thing – you may arrive at a belief that the evidence shows conclusively that the snow will melt. Possibly – if you have the concepts of *requirement* and *belief* – you may also arrive at a belief that the evidence requires you to believe the snow will melt.

Only this last is a higher-order belief – a belief about an attitude. Described differently, it is the belief that your object-given reasons require you to believe the snow will melt. According to the higher-order account, the regular way for you to acquire, by reasoning, the first-order belief that the snow will melt is by first acquiring this higher-order belief.

That is implausible. It is intuitively clear that, to work out that the snow will melt, you need to attend to the state of the snow, not to the state of your mind. Even if you end up with the higher-order belief, you are much more likely to first have the first-order belief that the snow will melt. First-order reasoning can take you directly to it.

12.4 One more point

I have one more objection to the higher-order account of reasoning. The higher-order beliefs on which it is based are beliefs about requirements. They are about what rationality requires, what your object-given reasons require or about what state you ought to be in.

Yet intuitively, correct reasoning is governed by permissions of rationality, not by requirements of rationality. If it is correct to reason to some conclusion, that is because rationality permits you to reach that conclusion, not because it requires you to do so. In many cases, you commit no offence against rationality by failing to do a piece of reasoning that would have been correct had you done it.

For example the Modus Ponens Requirement contains the caring clause to register the fact that you are not required to believe all the trivial propositions that follow by modus ponens from things you believe. Yet if you do reason your way to believing one of them, your reasoning is correct. You are rationally permitted to reason to this conclusion even though you are not required to.

I do not see how higher-order reasoning could be based on beliefs about mere permissions as opposed to requirements. Suppose you believe it is permissible for you to believe p but not required. I cannot see how reasoning on the basis of this belief could bring you to believe p, since you equally believe that you need not believe p. This is one more problem for the higher-order account of reasoning. Section 13.7 explains how my own account of reasoning recognizes that correct reasoning is governed by permissions.

I have shown that the higher-order account of reasoning hits difficulties at every turn. I now turn to a better, first-order account.

Notes

1 'Why be rational?', p. 517.
2 In 'Practical reason and the possibility of error', Douglas Lavin investigates the question of whether these ideally rational creatures are truly governed by requirements of rationality. It does not matter here. There may also be a different species of ideally rational creature, which is not automatically rational but instead has an unerring ability to make itself rational by reasoning. This other species features in John Searle's *Rationality in Action*, particularly on p. 66.
3 The idea that there are these two ways of achieving rationality is recognized in psychology as 'dual process theory'. See Daniel Kahneman's 'A perspective on judgment and choice'. Nomy Arpaly and Timothy Schroeder make a similar point in 'Deliberation'.
4 *Change in View*, p. 39.
5 A good example in is Christine Korsgaard's 'The activity of reason'.
6 Thanks to Antonio Gaitán-Torres.
7 Among the many protagonists are: Jonathan Adler in *Belief's Own Ethics*, William Alston in 'The deontological conception of epistemic justification', Jonathan Bennett in 'Why is belief involuntary?', Richard Feldman in 'Voluntary belief in epistemic evaluation', Pamela Hieronymi in 'Controlling attitudes' and Bernard Williams in 'Deciding to believe'.
8 For example Pamela Hieronymi, 'Controlling attitudes', and Daniel Farrell's 'Intention, reason, and action', p. 287.
9 *What We Owe to Each Other*, p. 20.
10 Scanlon makes this clear in his 'Structural irrationality'.
11 'Structural irrationality', p. 91.

13

First-Order Reasoning

13.1 The reasoning process

Now a different account of reasoning. According to this account, reasoning is a process whereby some of your attitudes cause you to acquire a new attitude. Not just any such process is reasoning; to be reasoning the process must satisfy some particular conditions. In this chapter I shall identify what those conditions are.

My aim is actually more specific than that. First, I am concerned with active reasoning only. I suggested on page 208 that there may also be such a thing as passive reasoning. If there is, it is not the subject of this book. So I shall identify conditions that make a process specifically active reasoning. I shall also explain in section 13.4 how these conditions make the process an act – something you do.

Second, this chapter presents a particular account of reasoning: the first-order account. I rejected an alternative account in chapter 12, and I believe the first-order account is the correct one. The conditions I identify will ensure the reasoning takes place at the first order, as section 13.5 explains.

To understand reasoning, it is best to start with the most elementary sort, and I shall do that. Rather than dealing with, say, abductive reasoning and moral deliberation, my examples will include reasoning by modus ponens and end-means reasoning. These seem paradigmatic of reasoning. I assume that accounts of more complex reasoning can be built on this elementary basis, but this book does not undertake that task.

Some terminology. When some attitudes of yours cause you to acquire a new attitude through a process of reasoning, I call the initial attitudes the 'premise-attitudes' and the resulting attitude the 'conclusion-attitude'. I shall also use the more specific terms 'premise-belief', 'conclusion-intention' and so on. I use the terms 'premise' and 'conclusion' for the attitudes' contents.

I classify types of reasoning according to the nature of their conclusion attitude, as 'belief reasoning', 'intention reasoning' and so on. In introducing the first-order account of reasoning in this chapter, I shall apply it to belief reasoning only. I shall go on to other sorts in chapter 14. Still, most of the lessons I shall draw from this chapter extend to reasoning in general, and I shall express them in general terms as far as possible.

Belief reasoning is a sort of theoretical reasoning, but there may be other sorts of theoretical reasoning too. For instance there may be reasoning that concludes in your believing something to a degree that is less than full belief. Possibly, there may also be reasoning that concludes in your not believing something. I shall mention those possibilities in chapter 15.

To investigate belief reasoning, I shall use the example of snow that I introduced on page 216. You wake up believing it is raining, because you hear dripping water. You have a standing belief that if it is raining the snow will melt. As your pull your wits together, shaking off sleep, these two beliefs together cause you to acquire the belief that the snow will melt. What conditions must this process satisfy if it is to be active reasoning? This section and the next two aim to answer that question.

Conscious reasoning and explicit reasoning

I assume that active reasoning is conscious, just because we are normally conscious of what we do. There are exceptions to this rule; you might unconsciously put your mug down after drinking, and yet putting your mug down is something you do. There may also be such a thing as unconscious active reasoning. If there is, I exclude it from the subject-matter of this book. I shall concentrate on the core type of reasoning, which is active and conscious.

The attitudes you reason with must therefore be conscious ones. In the example, you need to believe consciously that it is raining, and that, if it is raining, the snow will melt. This is the first condition that is necessary for the process to be active reasoning.

For an attitude to be conscious means as a minimum that you are conscious of its content. (I shall consider further conditions on page 242.) One way of coming to be in a state of conscious belief is to call to mind the content of the belief. 'Calling to mind' means bringing it into your conscious mind. We all know from our experience that often this is extremely easy and occasionally it is difficult. One way of doing it is to express the content to yourself using a sentence. In the example, you might say to yourself the sentence 'If it is raining, the snow will melt'.

You might even utter this sentence out loud, but most of us most of the time speak to ourselves silently. I do not know just what silent inner speech is, and I shall not try to explain how we have the ability to do it. That is a topic for psychology, at least in part. But, however we do it, it is common experience that we do. Moreover, it is common experience that we do it in our natural language. Reciting poetry silently to yourself is a good example.

Speaking to yourself is only one means of bringing yourself to a state of conscious belief. No doubt a belief can be conscious in other ways too. In the example, your belief that it is raining may be conscious from the time you acquire it, and you might reason with it immediately. If so, you would not need to call its content to mind. You would therefore not need to express it to yourself for that purpose.

Even so, you might need to express this belief to yourself if you are to reason with it. The process of active reasoning itself might require you to express your attitudes to yourself, even though they might already be conscious without being expressed. Your reasoning might need to be *explicit*, as I shall say. It might need to be done in language.

If you were to reason explicitly in the snow example, you would say to yourself:

'It is raining.
If it is raining the snow will melt.
So the snow will melt.'

These sentences make your reasoning explicit by expressing the three beliefs that are involved in it. You do not have the third belief at the beginning of the process, but you acquire it by the end. The word 'so' marks the fact that you acquire this belief by reasoning.

One effect of calling to mind the contents of your beliefs is that it brings them together in your mind. Think of two television detectives, who have discovered different pieces of evidence. One says 'The murderer crossed the bridge after midnight'. The other says 'Hamish is the only person who crossed the bridge after midnight'. In that way they bring together in both their minds what they previously believed separately. Then together they say 'So Hamish is the murderer'. All this process is explicit reasoning involving two minds. It provides a model for explicit reasoning in a single mind.

A convenient method of describing a particular piece of active reasoning is to make it explicit, as I have just done for the snow example. When I use this method, I do not mean to imply that the reasoning actually has to be explicit. I do not assume that, to reason consciously, you must express to yourself in language the attitudes you reason with. That is not a premise in this book's argument.

Nevertheless, I am inclined to believe that active reasoning must be explicit: that to reason consciously, you must express your attitudes to yourself in language. Chapter 15 explores some of the consequences of this view. But since it is not essential to my argument, I shall not defend it vigorously. Chapter 15 offers some evidence in its favour; that is all.

Saying to yourself the sequence of sentences above may constitute a piece of explicit reasoning, but it may not. For one thing, you could recite those sentences to yourself without expressing any attitude. For instance, you could be working out what would be a correct conclusion to draw if you believed the two premises. Reasoning as I understand it is a process through which some attitudes you initially have cause you to acquire a new attitude. So, if you say to yourself the sequence of sentences above, they will express reasoning only if they express attitudes you have. I assume they express beliefs, which means they are assertions.

Possibly they might express some attitude other than belief. You may reason with other attitudes. For example, those sentences might express an attitude of make-believe. Section 14.4 explores the idea that hypothetical reasoning involves make-believe. If it does, the three sentences could be a piece of explicit hypothetical reasoning. But if, in saying those sentences to yourself, you express no attitude at all, you are not reasoning.

I said reasoning causes you to have an attitude you did not previously have, but that remark needs qualifying. Sometimes reasoning confirms an attitude you have already. In those cases, it would have caused you to have a new attitude if you had not already had it. To simplify my argument, I shall deal only with reasoning that causes you to acquire a new attitude. This will make no difference; reasoning that confirms an attitude could easily be added in.

My definition of reasoning excludes a lot of the thinking that commonly accompanies reasoning. Take a mathematician's thinking, for example. A mathematician might start a project by forming a plausible conjecture. That is not reasoning. Then she might go on to try and piece together a proof of the conjecture. No doubt there will be a lot of reasoning involved in the course of doing that. By means of pieces of hypothetical reasoning she is likely to come to believe some conditionals such as 'If that is so, then this is so'. But she will also do a lot of thinking that is not reasoning: she will choose which line of research to follow, she might be inspired by a sudden idea to try a particular move, or she might visualize part of the problem geometrically.

If this mathematician eventually finds a proof, she will be able to work through it, reasoning step by step. Starting from axioms that she believes, she will come to believe the next step through reasoning that follows the proof, and then the next step and so on, until she comes to believe the conclusion. This process projects her belief from the axioms to the conclusion. It is the way she will come to believe the conclusion in ideal cases.

Often in practice she will come to believe the conclusion earlier in her thinking process. She might come to believe it as supporting evidence accumulates, through some sort of inductive reasoning or possibly by a causal process that is not reasoning.

13.2   Necessary and sufficient conditions for reasoning

Reasoning is a process whereby some of your attitudes cause you to acquire a new attitude. In section 13.1 I added to this description only the condition that the attitudes are conscious. That is necessary if the process is to be active reasoning, but other conditions are necessary too. Suppose you believe that it is raining and that if it is raining the snow will melt. Suppose these beliefs are conscious, and suppose they cause you to believe you hear trumpets. That bizarre process is unlikely to be reasoning. (Page 233 mentions an exceptional case in which it is reasoning.) Yet it fits my description of reasoning so far.

In this section and the next I shall look for further necessary conditions. Indeed, I shall look for conditions that, when added to the description I gave in section 13.1, are also sufficient for a process to be reasoning.

In this section I shall review various ideas that turn out to be mistaken or incomplete. In the following section I shall give my own account.

Reliability

A first suggestion is that a process that satisfies the description in section 13.1 is not reasoning unless it also satisfies the criterion of correctness for reasoning. I shall give an account of correctness for belief reasoning in section 13.7, but in this section I need only an example of correct reasoning. Reasoning by modus ponens supplies one; it is obviously correct.

It cannot be true that a process must satisfy the criterion of correctness if it is to be reasoning. Sometimes you make mistakes in reasoning; you might mistake the scope of a quantifier, for instance. Even so, you are undoubtedly reasoning. We cannot insist that all reasoning is correct.[1]

What about a weaker condition of the same sort: that the process is of a type that typically satisfies the criterion of correctness? It is fairly reliably correct, as I shall put it. We cannot insist it is completely reliable, because that would preclude your making mistakes while reasoning, but we can insist it is fairly reliable. Call this 'the reliability condition'.

I shall argue on page 233 that it is not a necessary condition for a process to be reasoning. Here I shall argue that it is not a sufficient condition, even added to the description in section 13.1. I shall describe a type of process that meets the condition, and show it is not reasoning.

I said in section 12.1 that automatic processes within you can bring you to satisfy many of the requirements of rationality. For instance, they can bring you to satisfy the Modus Ponens Requirement. They can bring you to believe what follows by modus ponens from propositions you believe. When they do, they satisfy the criterion for correct reasoning. Because you are not ideally rational, these processes will not be correct every time, but let us suppose they are fairly reliably correct.

Calling to mind the contents of some of your beliefs might jog these automatic processes into action. For instance, in the snow example, suppose you consciously believe it is raining and then you call to mind that if it is raining the snow will melt. This might jog into action an automatic process that causes you to believe the snow will melt. This process meets the reliability condition, because we are assuming it is fairly reliable.

This gives us a putative account of reasoning; I call it the 'jogging account'. According to it, in reasoning you call to mind some of the premises, and doing so jogs into operation an automatic process that causes you to acquire a conclusion-attitude. The account assumes that this type of process is fairly reliably correct.

On the jogging account, reasoning is a bit like listening. Hearing is an automatic process through which you can acquire some beliefs: the belief that it is raining, for instance. Listening is something you can do to jog your hearing into operation on a particular occasion.

The jogging account is a poor account of active reasoning. If, when you call things to mind during the course of reasoning, all you do is jog into operation an automatic process, reasoning would scarcely be an act of yours. Most of it would not be done by you; all you would do is call the premises to mind. The core of reasoning would be a passive process, which sometimes needs a jog. But intuitively there is more to reasoning than that. Moreover, there are solid grounds for rejecting the jogging account, as I shall now explain.

Jogging may sometimes put you wrong. Suppose that, when you call some premises to mind, and doing so jogs into operation an automatic process that causes you to acquire a conclusion-belief, the process is generally correct. The jogging process is fairly reliable, that is to say. But suppose it sometimes goes wrong because of a quirk of your psychology. For instance, when you call to mind that it is raining and that if it is raining the snow will melt, this jogs into operation an automatic process that causes you to believe you hear trumpets.

Even when this happens, the jogging process in you satisfies the reliability condition. It is of a type that is fairly reliable. So when you call to mind that it is raining, and that if it is raining the snow will melt, and that causes you, by jogging, to believe you hear trumpets, you are reasoning according to the jogging account. But plainly you are not.

Moreover, once we recognize that psychological quirks can be jogged into action, as well as processes that might be properly a part of reasoning, we must recognize that sometimes a quirk may deliver a correct result. To put it differently, a correct conclusion-belief might be caused by your premise-beliefs through some deviant causal chain.[2] According to the jogging account, you would be reasoning, but actually you would not be.

We should therefore reject the jogging account as I have described it. It satisfies the reliability condition. So the reliability condition is not sufficient for reasoning, even when added to my description of reasoning in section 13.1.

Improving the jogging account

However, I am sure that a part of our rationality consists in jogging automatic processes. So I do not want to impugn the jogging account entirely. Let us see if we can improve it enough to overcome the glitch I described.

The glitch results from quirky automatic processes, which take you to a new belief by a process that could not count as reasoning. Suppose we could distinguish non-quirky processes from quirky ones in a way that is independent of their tendency to deliver the correct result. I do not know whether this is possible, but for the sake of argument suppose it is. For instance, suppose it turns out that processes that take place in some parts of your brain are not very reliable at causing you to believe a conclusion that follows from your premises, but those that take place in one particular part are especially reliable. Then we could think of that as a reasoning part of your brain, and we could identify processes that take place there as non-quirky ones.

These non-quirky processes would not be entirely reliable. Inevitably, complex causal processes in your brain can go wrong. But they are fairly reliable.

Now we can construct a better jogging account of reasoning. In reasoning, you call to mind your premises, and doing so jogs into operation an automatic non-quirky process that causes you to acquire a new attitude. On page 208 I suggested that some automatic processes could be classed as passive reasoning. For all I know, the improved jogging account may be a satisfactory account of these processes.

But it remains a poor account of active reasoning. On this account, reasoning is scarcely active at all. Moreover, it gives us no reason to doubt there are also processes of more truly active reasoning. I shall continue to look for a better account of active reasoning.

Higher-order linking belief

It is natural to think that, if a mental process of yours is to be reasoning, you must endorse it in some way. One way is to have what I call a 'linking belief'. You might have either a higher-order or a first-order linking belief.

A higher-order linking belief links your premise-attitudes with your conclusion-attitude. It may be the belief that some rational connection exists between these attitudes, or the belief that a normative connection exists between them.

In the snow example, it might be the belief that rationality requires you to believe the snow will melt if you believe it is raining and also believe that if it is raining the snow will melt. Or it might be the belief that rationality permits you to base a belief that the snow will melt on a belief of yours that it is raining and a belief of yours that if it is raining the snow will melt. Or it might be the belief that you ought to believe the snow will melt if you believe it is raining and also believe that if it is raining the snow will melt.

In chapter 12 I have already rejected the idea that a higher-order linking belief plays a part in reasoning as a premise. But a higher-order linking belief might instead play a part as a background condition of the process. It might be either a sufficient or a necessary condition for a process to be reasoning.

However, actually it is neither. First, a higher-order linking belief, added to the description in section 13.1, cannot be a sufficient condition for a process to be belief reasoning. This is because the linking belief might have nothing to do with any relation of implication that holds between the premises and the conclusion.

Here is an example. Suppose once again that you believe it is raining and that if it is raining the snow will melt. Suppose these beliefs cause you to believe you hear trumpets. Suppose next that you believe rationality requires you to believe you hear trumpets if you believe it is raining and that if it is raining the snow will melt. That is to say, you have a higher-order linking belief. Suppose however that you do not have this belief because you believe that the propositions that it is raining and that if it is raining the snow will melt implies the proposition that you hear trumpets. Instead your linking belief arises from some weird theory of rationality that you hold. For instance, suppose you believe that rationality requires you to have patterns of belief that are good for you, and you believe it is good for you to believe you hear trumpets when you believe it is raining and that if it is raining the snow will melt.

In this example, the bizarre process you go through is not reasoning. The presence of your weirdly-grounded linking belief is not sufficient to make it so.

Second, the presence of a higher-order linking belief is not necessary for reasoning either. This sort of belief has a sophisticated content that involves concepts such as *rationality, requirement, permit, ought* and *belief*. You do not need to have such sophisticated concepts in order to reason. A child could reason about rain and snow before she learns about rationality or about beliefs.

So a higher-order linking belief is neither necessary nor sufficient for reasoning.

First-order linking belief

A first-order linking belief does better. This is a belief that links together the contents of your attitudes, rather than the attitudes themselves. In the case of belief reasoning, it is specifically the belief that the premises imply the conclusion.[3] By that I mean simply that you believe a conditional proposition. When the premises are p, q, r and so on, and the conclusion is t, you believe that, if p, q, r and so on, then t.

I accept that a first-order linking belief is a necessary condition for reasoning. If you reason, you must think of your conclusion as arising somehow from your premises. So you must have a belief that links the premises and conclusion. In the case of belief reasoning, implication is the weakest relation between premises and conclusion that would allow you to think of the conclusion as arising from the premises.

The absence of a first-order linking belief provides a good explanation of why the bizarre process I described on page 225 is not reasoning. You presumably do not have the appropriate first-order linking belief; you presumably do not believe the conditional proposition that, if it is raining and if it is the case that if it is raining the snow will melt, you hear trumpets.

On pages 233–4, I shall add another argument in support of the view that a first-order linking belief is necessary for reasoning. For all these reasons I accept this view.

Let us turn to sufficiency. Is a first-order linking belief sufficient to make a process reasoning, when added to the description of reasoning in section 13.1? The answer is 'No'; we would need to add further conditions too. For one, we would need to add a causal condition. Suppose you arrive at a conclusion-belief in the way I described in section 13.1, and you have the linking belief, but it plays no causal role in the process. The mere existence of the linking belief is not enough to make the process reasoning.

The need for the linking belief to have a causal role creates a problem. In section 13.1 I described the process of reasoning as one where some attitudes of yours cause a new attitude. I have just said that your conclusion-belief is caused by your premise-beliefs together with your linking beliefs. So your linking belief is among the attitudes that cause a new attitude. This apparently makes it a premise-belief in the reasoning.

But a premise-belief is by definition not a linking belief. The content of a linking belief links the premises and conclusion of the reasoning; it cannot be one of the premises. So if, as I accept, the existence of a linking belief is a necessary condition for a process to be reasoning, something must distinguish linking beliefs from premise-beliefs.

This point is formally parallel to Lewis Carroll's point in 'What the tortoise said to Achilles'. Take the snow reasoning, made explicit on page 223. Your linking belief in this case is the belief that if (it is raining and if it is raining the snow will melt) then the snow will melt. You must have this belief for the process to be reasoning. But if it is a premise-belief, your reasoning, made explicit, would be:

> 'It is raining.
> If it is raining the snow will melt.
> If (it is raining and if it is raining the snow will melt) then the snow will melt.
> So the snow will melt.'

Granted the assumption that a linking belief is necessary for a process to be reasoning, this would be reasoning only if you had a linking belief that links the three premises to the conclusion. That would be the belief that if (it is raining and, if it is raining the snow will melt, and if (it is raining and if it is raining the snow will melt) then the snow will melt)) then the snow will melt. If this too was a premise-belief, you would have to have a yet more complicated linking belief. At some level, you must have a linking belief that is not a premise-belief.

So something must distinguish linking beliefs from premise beliefs. My description of reasoning so far offers just one possible way to make the distinction. In active reasoning, premise-beliefs are conscious. So if the linking belief is unconscious, it cannot be a premise-belief. If we made the distinction that way, the linking belief would have to be unconscious. But section 13.3 provides a better way to make the distinction, which does not require the linking belief to be unconscious. It is explained on page 234.

There is another question about sufficiency. Is a linking belief combined with a causal condition sufficient to make a process reasoning, when added to the description in section 13.1? The answer to this too is 'No'. We would need to add the further condition that the causal role of the linking belief is not deviant. Even if the linking belief plays a causal role, it might do so through some psychological quirk. Then its playing a causal role would not be enough to make the process reasoning.

How could we identify which causal processes are not deviant? The next section suggests an answer. If it is right, it turns out to give us directly a better sufficient condition for a process to be reasoning. We therefore do not need a first-order linking belief as a sufficient condition.

13.3   Operating on contents

In reasoning, you *operate* on the contents of your premise-attitudes to construct the content of your conclusion-attitude. When your reasoning is extended, this is obvious. You derive some beliefs, hold their contents in your mind, bring the contents of other beliefs to bear on them, and so on. All this is operating mentally on contents.

Suppose you consciously believe that there are 68 men in the room and that there are 57 women in the room. You operate on these two propositions following the rules of addition, and end up believing that there are 125 people in the room. Part of what you do is adding, which is an operation on numbers.

A simple, one-step process of reasoning is also an operation on contents. In any reasoning process, there is more than a contingent, causal connection between the premise-attitudes and the conclusion-attitude. There is also a semantic connection between the attitudes' contents. The proposition that constitutes the conclusion is derived in some way from the propositions that constitute the premises. When you reason actively, you make the derivation: you derive the conclusion by operating on the premises.

Take the snow example again. You consciously believe that it is raining and that if it is raining the snow will melt. Your first premise – that it is raining – is the antecedent of your second premise – the conditional proposition that if it is raining the snow will melt. You operate on these two propositions following the modus ponens rule. This rule tells you to construct the proposition that is the consequent of the second premise. You end up believing this consequent.

By contrast, take the bizarre example. You consciously believe that it is raining and that if it is raining the snow will melt. Then you find yourself believing you hear trumpets. You do nothing to derive this conclusion; the belief just comes upon you. At least, that is what I have been assuming about this example. That is why the bizarre process is not reasoning.

When I say you construct the conclusion, I do not mean it literally. That would imply the conclusion did not previously exist. But the conclusion is a proposition, which exists independently of your thinking. You construct it in the sense in which you construct a number by an algebraic operation, in the course of a proof. It would be more accurate to say you pick the number out from other numbers; you identify it. In your reasoning about snow, by operating on the premises, you identify the conclusion that the snow will melt. That is what you come to believe.

Your operation is computational or algorithmic. These terms might suggest it is an operation on symbols, but I do not mean that. You operate on meanings, not on symbols that represent meanings. In the example, you operate on the propositions that are the contents of your beliefs and not on sentences.

It is plain that in reasoning you do not operate on sentences in our natural language. You might reason explicitly

> 'If it rains, I shall get wet
> It will rain
> So I shall get wet.'

This does not express modus ponens reasoning applied to sentences, because the sentence 'It rains', which denotes the antecedent of the conditional, is not the same as the sentence 'It will rain' that denotes the second premise. However, given their grammatical setting, these sentences denote the same proposition. So your explicit reasoning is modus ponens reasoning applied to propositions.

It is an essential feature of reasoning that the operation is rule-governed. In reasoning you follow – are guided by – a rule. The rule may be expressed by a schema. The rule for modus ponens reasoning is 'from p and (If p then q) to derive q'. (This is a simplified version; the rule is stated more fully on page 252.) I assume in the example that you follow this rule, but you might alternatively follow the meteorologically specific rule 'from (It is Fing) and (If it is Fing the snow will G) to derive (the snow will G)', or some other rule.

In order to follow a rule, you do not need to know explicitly what the rule is. You follow the rule, but you may do so in the way in which you often follow rules of grammar. You may compose grammatical sentences without knowing explicitly what grammatical rules you follow in doing so. Similarly, you may reason by modus ponens without knowing explicitly what the modus ponens rule is.

Further conditions?

A necessary condition for you to reason is that you operate on the contents of your attitudes following a rule, in the way I have described. Do we need to add any further necessary conditions to arrive at sufficient conditions for reasoning?

First, should we add the condition that the rule you apply is a correct basis for reasoning?[4] We should not, since this is not a necessary condition for reasoning. You can reason following an incorrect rule. Suppose you go through a process in which you operate on some propositions you believe following the fallacious rule of affirming the consequent, and this causes you to acquire a new belief. This process is reasoning, just because it is an operation on contents that follows a rule.

You might regularly reason incorrectly. When reasoning with conditionals, you might always apply the rule of affirming the consequent. Each time you would be reasoning, though incorrectly. For you, the process of reasoning with conditionals would not be even fairly reliably correct. I said on page 225 that being fairly reliably correct is not a necessary condition for a process to be reasoning. This is why.

Second, should we impose some weaker limit on the rules you apply? For example, should we exclude this bizarre rule: from the proposition that it is raining and the proposition that if it is raining the snow will melt, to derive the proposition that you hear trumpets. Following this rule would lead you to believe you hear trumpets when you believe it is raining and believe that if it is raining the snow will melt. If you did this, should we count you as reasoning?

I think we should. If you derive this conclusion by operating on the premises, following the rule, we should count you as reasoning. That is not how I have imagined the bizarre process up to now; I have been assuming you just find yourself believing you hear trumpets. I think we should not impose a limit on rules.

Third, should we add the condition that you endorse the rule you apply? We should not. We cannot require you to endorse the rule explicitly, since you may not explicitly know the rule you are applying. And when you apply a rule in reasoning, you automatically give it a sort of endorsement. No further endorsement is needed.

You automatically endorse the rule by coming to have the attitude it takes you to. In belief reasoning, you come to believe the conclusion. True, believing the conclusion is not by itself enough of an endorsement to make a process reasoning. In the bizarre example as I first imagined it, you end up believing you hear trumpets. But in that example you do not endorse any rule, because you do not follow a rule; the belief just comes to you. When you arrive at your conclusion by operating on the premises to derive a conclusion, following a rule, then believing the conclusion is a sufficient endorsement of the rule.

In this case, we may say you believe that the premises imply the conclusion. You would not believe the conclusion if you did not believe the premises imply it. You may not believe this consciously. If you do not, we may treat your disposition to derive the conclusion from the premises – where deriving it includes actively operating on the premises following a rule and coming to believe the conclusion – as itself constituting an unconscious, implicit belief that the premises imply the conclusion.[5]

On page 229 I called the belief that the premises imply the conclusion a first-order linking belief. Now we see that, if you reason, you must have a first-order linking belief, at least implicitly; I accepted that view on page 229. Having this belief is a necessary condition for you to reason. However, we need not add it as a further necessary condition, since it is entailed by the condition that you come to believe the conclusion by operating on the premises in the way I have described.

On page 230 I explained that something must distinguish a linking belief from a premise-belief. We now have a good way to make the distinction. Reasoning is an operation on the contents of the premise-beliefs, whereas the content of the linking belief is not operated on. The distinction does not have to be made in terms of consciousness, so the linking belief may be either conscious or unconscious.

Fourth, should we add a condition that the process does not involve deviant causation? There must indeed be no deviant causation if the process is to be reasoning. But again, this condition is automatically satisfied. The condition that you operate on contents by applying a rule actually specifies the causal process by which you arrive at your conclusion. The process is that you operate on the contents of your beliefs. There is no room left for the causal process to be deviant.

You might see one chink where a deviant process might creep in: between the end of your operation and your coming to believe the conclusion. Suppose you construct a proposition by operating on your premises, and this causes you to believe the proposition you construct. There might be room for that last bit of causation to be deviant.

But there is no real gap there. We cannot split reasoning into two processes: first forming a conclusion and then coming to believe it. On page 243 I shall stress this point. You believe the conclusion as you form it by applying the rule; the process is imbued with belief. So there is no room for a deviant causal chain.

So far as I can see, then, no further conditions need be added. I have arrived at necessary and sufficient conditions for a process to be active reasoning. Active reasoning is a particular sort of process by which conscious premise-attitudes cause you to acquire a conclusion-attitude. The process is that you operate on the contents of your premise-attitudes following a rule, to construct the conclusion, which is the content of a new attitude of yours that you acquire in the process.

Briefly: reasoning is a rule-governed operation on the contents of your conscious attitudes.

13.4   Reasoning as activity

Reasoning is a rule-governed mental operation, and a rule-governed mental operation is intuitively something you do. It is not merely a causal process that takes place in your mind. So my account of what reasoning is also serves to explain how reasoning is something you do. The task of this section is to develop this intuition into a fuller explanation.

For a contrast, compare the jogging account I described on page 226. On that account, what you do is limited to calling the contents of your attitudes to mind. This sets you up for reasoning, but your reasoning itself consists in an automatic process. On my account, it is an act.

True, like most acts, the act of reasoning includes parts that are not acts. One part of the act of diving is being propelled along a parabolic trajectory by gravity. When you operate on contents, your act is causally mediated through a mass of automatic processes that happen within you. Those are not acts. Any mental act is mediated by brain process that are not acts. Still, the operation of reasoning itself is an act.

When you reason your way to a new belief, your reasoning is an act. Since the reasoning is an act, and is the forming of a belief, the forming of the belief this way is an act. Acts of this sort are sometimes called 'judgements'.

Reasoning may be an intentional act, and may even be intended by you. You may intend to do an act of reasoning that is the forming of a new belief and you may intend to believe whatever conclusion emerges from the reasoning. You intend that, if p is the proposition that emerges, you believe p. However, you rarely intend to believe the specific proposition that emerges: there is rarely a proposition p such that you intend to believe p.[6] In the example, you do not intend to believe the snow will melt. Forming the belief that the snow will melt is like finding your glasses under the sofa, as a result of looking for them. You intend to find your glasses, but you do not intend to find them under the sofa.[7]

Critical and uncritical reasoning

Philip Pettit's explanation of why reasoning is an act depends on what he calls 'meta-propositional beliefs'.[8] A meta-propositional belief is a belief whose content ascribes a property to a proposition. One example is a belief that the Archbishop of Canterbury believes God exists; the content of this belief ascribes the property of being believed by the Archbishop of Canterbury to the proposition that God exists. Another example is a belief that it cannot be true both that it is cold in Iceland and that palm-trees grow in Iceland; the content of this belief ascribes the relation of incompatibility to the two propositions that it is cold in Iceland and that palm-trees grow in Iceland. Pettit argues that you cannot reason unless you have meta-propositional beliefs. I disagree.

Higher-order beliefs form one class of meta-propositional beliefs. These are the beliefs a person has about her own propositional attitudes. I have already argued in chapter 12 and on pages 228–9 that higher-order beliefs are not necessary for reasoning. But Pettit is not thinking of higher-order beliefs, and there are many sorts of meta-propositional beliefs besides those.

I recognize that, to reason, you must have the first-order linking belief that the premises imply the conclusion. But the content of a first-order linking belief is just the conditional proposition that, if p, q, r and so on, then t, where p, q, r and so on are the premises and t is the conclusion. So a first-order linking belief is not meta-propositional. I think a reasoner needs the concept of *if*, *then*, but nothing more sophisticated than that.

Pettit takes reasoning to be a more sophisticated process than I do. He says 'I reason whenever I set out to form meta-propositional beliefs and let them play out as checks on the process whereby my attitudes form'.[9] But on my account, a child can reason even before she has meta-propositional beliefs.

We need not think of these as rival accounts; we can say they describe different sorts of reasoning. Let us call Pettit's sort 'critical reasoning' and mine 'uncritical reasoning'.[10] I recognize that we sometimes reason critically. We sometimes regulate our first-order reasoning by reasoning about it – by 'metareasoning' as I call it. But I think we can also reason uncritically, and that we could reason uncritically even if we could not reason critically.

Pettit believes that, if your reasoning is to be something you do, it must be critical reasoning, or at least you must be able to reason critically. So uncritical reasoning is not something you do but something that happens to you. According to Pettit, your possession of meta-propositional attitudes marks the borderline between what happens to you and what you do.

But whatever borderline these attitudes mark, it is not that one. When you have finished eating, you generally put your knife and fork together. This is an operation on tableware. It is something you do, applying a rule of etiquette. It is not a process that just happens. You do it even if you do it uncritically, just because you have been taught to. You do it even if you have no metaetiquettish attitudes. In the case of tableware, this is obvious, and mental operations are no different.

Pettit aims to show that a robot does not reason, and his explanation is that it does not have meta-propositional attitudes. I agree that many robots do not reason, and perhaps no robot could reason, but my explanation is that a robot does not understand what it is doing. Reasoning is an operation on contents, which have meanings. A robot that does not understand meanings cannot operate on them. It operates on symbols. To us, those symbols have meanings, but not to this robot.

Following a rule: seeming right

Reasoning is something you do; it is not merely a causal process that takes place in your mind. To be sure, it *is* a causal process that takes place in your mind. When you reason, your premise attitudes cause your conclusion attitude. But reasoning is not *merely* a causal process. Somehow, you do it. How, exactly, is it something you do?

Working out what makes some processes acts is a notoriously difficult problem in the philosophy of action. Paul Boghossian has identified some special difficulties that exacerbate the problem for mental processes of reasoning.[11] I do not hope to provide a definitive solution, but I do hope to show how my account of reasoning (which is much the same as Boghossian's) contributes to a solution.[12]

Reasoning is an act because in reasoning you follow a rule. The rule does not merely cause you to behave in a particular way, as a program does to a computer. The rule *guides* you and you actively follow it. Being guided involves a notion of rightness or correctness. The rule determines a right thing to do. You are not guided by a rule unless there is such a thing as following the rule correctly and, conversely, such a thing as not following it correctly. I shall give an account of this sort of correctness.

It is different from the correctness of the rule itself. That will not be an issue until section 13.7 where we consider when reasoning is correct. Here we are considering what reasoning is, not when it is correct. The issue here is the distinction between following a rule correctly and not doing so. The correctness of the rule is irrelevant, since you may correctly follow an incorrect rule.

Let us start by returning to the bizarre example and compare the two versions of it that I have by now described. In both, you start by believing it is raining and believing that if it is raining the snow will melt. In both versions, a causal process takes you from these beliefs to a new belief that you hear trumpets. In the original version on page 225, the new belief just comes to you. In the new version on page 233, you acquire the new belief by reasoning, following a rule. The rule is incorrect, of course. It is the rule of deriving the proposition that you hear trumpets from the proposition that it is raining and the proposition that if it is raining the snow will melt.

What is the difference between the two versions of the example? One difference is that in the version where you reason the process *seems right* to you, as I put it, whereas in the original version it does not. I take the term 'seems right' from Wittgenstein's remark quoted at the top of page 239. It does not refer to a phenomenal state. Seeming right may be associated with a phenomenal state – perhaps a comfortable feeling – but it need not be. There are phenomenal seemings and non-phenomenal ones. When a journey seems normal to you, that seeming may be associated with the absence of any phenomenal state, in particular with the absence of the phenomenal states that would be associated with the journey's seeming abnormal. Or when a proof seems right to you, you need not be in any particular phenomenal state; it may simply be that you can find no fault with any of the proof's steps.

Seeming right in our context is an attitude of yours towards the mental process you go through when you reason. An essential part of it is being open to the possibility of correction.[13] When a process seems right to you, you are open to the possibility that the process might no longer seem right to you if a certain sort of event were to occur. We may call the event 'checking'.

Checking may consist simply in a repetition of the process, or it may consist in a different process. Here is an example. If you are asked 'Three fours?', you will probably spontaneously answer 'Twelve', and this will seem right to you. You may later check your conclusion by calling up a spontaneous response once again, or alternatively you may do the sum by counting on your fingers.

Your openness to correction is a disposition. You are disposed to lose the attitude of seeming right in particular circumstances – specifically if checking occurs and produces a different result. This is often a counterfactual disposition, since there may actually be no checking. You may not be disposed to check, perhaps because you are confident of your conclusion. Nevertheless, you have the counterfactual disposition to change your attitude if you were to check and if the checking produced a different result.

By contrast, when you just find yourself believing you hear trumpets, whatever attitude you have to the process, it is nothing like this one. It is not open to correction in the same way, and there is no such thing as checking.

A process's seeming right to you is a sort of personal endorsement from you. This is part of what makes the process yours: something you do.

Following a rule: being right

Seeming right is not being right. But from the attitude of seeming right, we can construct a notion of being right.

Taking their lead from Wittgenstein, many philosophers doubt that this is possible.[14] Wittgenstein describes an example where you try to establish a rule for yourself. It is the rule of assigning the name 'S' to occurrences of a particular sensation. You concentrate hard on the connection between the sensation and the sign 'S'. Wittgenstein says:

I impress on myself the connexion between the sign and the sensation. But 'I impress it on myself' can only mean: this process brings it about that I remember the connexion *right* in the future. But in the present case I have no criterion of correctness. One would like to say: whatever is going to seem right to me is right. And that only means that here we can't talk about 'right'.[15]

You feel a sensation and name it 'S'. Because you have impressed the connection on yourself, this seems right to you. But it does not follow that you are guided by a rule, because you have not established a criterion for correctly following the rule. That is Wittgenstein's argument.

It does not take account of the nature of the attitude of seeming right. This attitude is essentially open to correction – to the possibility of not being right. Since the attitude of seeming right might get corrected, it is just not true that whatever is going to seem right to you is right.

True, as Wittgenstein means us to understand the example, it is not easy to see how a correction could happen. He means the problem to be one of reidentifying a sensation when it occurs at different times. It is hard to see how your naming of a sensation at one particular instant could be checked, since that instant could not be revisited.

But we can make checking possible in the example by supposing that each instance of the sensation lasts for a while. Suppose the sensation has two characteristics. It tingles and it varies in intensity. Suppose you feel a sensation and because it tingles you name it 'S'. Doing so seems right to you. But then you notice it does not vary in intensity, so you think 'It is not S after all'. You correct your attitude; your naming the sensation 'S' no longer seems right to you. This version of the example reveals a difference between seeming right and being right.

What is being right, then, as opposed to seeming right? I propose that, for a process to be right is for you to have a steady disposition for it to seem right. By this I mean that, were you to check several times, the process would generally seem right. A process that seems right to you may not actually be right, because you may not have a steady disposition for it to seem right.

On this definition, being right is given by your own dispositions, rather than by some external criterion. Wittgenstein is not impressed by internal checking and an internal criterion of rightness. He says:

'Surely I can appeal from one memory to another. For example, I don't know if I have remembered the time of departure of a train right and to check it I call to mind how a page of the time-table looked. . . .' . . . This process has got to produce a memory which is actually *correct*. If the mental image of the time-table could not itself be *tested* for correctness, how could it confirm the correctness of the first memory?[16]

Here Wittgenstein demands an external sort of correctness. This would be appropriate if we were concerned with whether you follow a correct rule. You must follow a correct rule if you are to catch the train.

But we are concerned only with whether you follow some rule, whether or not it is correct. That is what is needed to ensure you are acting and not merely being caused. For you to be following some rule, an internal criterion suffices. The criterion does have to make a difference between correctly following a rule and not doing so. My internal criterion of rightness makes that difference successfully.

One more thing. Take a case where a process seems right to you, but where it is not right because you do not have a steady disposition for it to seem right. Because it seems right, we may fairly say it seems to you that you are following a rule. As I use the term 'following a rule', it is also true that you are actually following a rule. So you may follow a rule even if you do not do so correctly.

I could have chosen to use 'following a rule' the other way, so that you follow a rule only if you do so correctly. But I find my usage more convenient. It means that, if you make a mistake in following a rule, you count as following the rule, so long as what you do seems right to you. In particular, if you make a mistake in reasoning, you nevertheless reason, because you are operating on the contents of your attitudes, following a rule.

There are consequently two ways of going wrong in reasoning. You can reason according to an incorrect rule, or you can make a mistake in following a rule, whether it is a correct or an incorrect rule. So long as what you do seems right to you, you reason. Moreover, your reasoning is something you do.

The rule you follow

When you reason on some particular occasion, your steady disposition for the process to seem right determines what is right – what the rule demands – on that occasion. But the rules you follow are normally general rules that apply on many occasions. How do we identify what they are?

This question looks ahead to section 13.7, which is concerned with the correctness of reasoning. The answer to it does not matter for the question of whether reasoning is something you do. But reasoning is correct when it correctly follows a correct rule. Whether your reasoning is correct therefore depends on what rule you follow.

Suppose you are such that, if you were to go through a process of a type D and check it several times, it would generally seem right to you. Let us say you have a steady disposition to D. D may have any degree of generality or complexity. For example, it could be any of:

> You believe it is raining and you believe that if it is raining the snow will melt, and these two beliefs cause you to believe you hear trumpets.
>
> It is Tuesday and you believe it is raining and you believe that if it is raining the snow will melt, and these two beliefs cause you to believe you hear trumpets.
>
> You believe that p and you believe that if p then q, and these two beliefs cause you to believe that q.
>
> You are on Earth and you believe that p and you believe that if p then q, and these two beliefs cause you to believe that q, or you are elsewhere and you believe that p and you believe that if p then q, and these two beliefs cause you to believe that not q.

When you have a steady disposition to D, D is a rule of yours.

The examples above are external descriptions of rules governing mental processes. We can redescribe the same rules in terms of the contents of your mental attitudes, representing them as derivations:

> From the proposition that it is raining and the proposition that if it is raining the snow will melt, to derive the proposition that you hear trumpets.
>
> When it is Tuesday, from the proposition that it is raining and the proposition that if it is raining the snow will melt, to derive the proposition that you hear trumpets.
>
> From p and if p then q, to derive q.
>
> From p and if p then q, to derive q when you are on Earth, and to derive not q when you are elsewhere.

The last pair of examples illustrates a well-known difficulty about rules that is associated with Saul Kripke's interpretation of Wittgenstein.[17] Your steady dispositions may not be determinate. I assume you will never be away from Earth. It may therefore not be determinate whether you have a steady disposition in favour of deriving q from p and if p then q, or instead a steady disposition in favour of doing this when you are on Earth and deriving not q from p and if p then q when you are elsewhere. So when you reason, it may not be determinate whether you are following the third rule above or the fourth one. The third is the modus ponens rule, which is correct. The fourth rule is incorrect.

According to Kripke, it is never determinate whether or not you are following a correct rule. Does this matter for the arguments of this book? I think not. In this book I give an account of what rules are correct, and I claim that reasoning is correct if and only if it correctly follows a correct rule. So I make conditional statements: if you correctly follow this rule or that rule, you reason correctly. I do not consider, of any particular person, whether or not she reasons correctly or incorrectly. If Kripke is right, there will not be a determinate answer to this question. That would be disconcerting, but it would not affect my conclusions.

13.5   Reasoning at the first order

According to the account of reasoning I have given in this chapter, you reason with your attitudes. You do not reason about your attitudes. You reason about the contents of your attitudes. This is first-order reasoning.

I assume your reasoning is conscious. In order to reason consciously with an attitude, the attitude must be conscious. As a minimum, this requires you to be conscious of its content. You may even need to be conscious of the attitude itself, which is to say aware of it. This awareness is a higher-order attitude of a sort towards your attitude.[18]

I think you may be aware of an attitude without believing you have it. Awareness is a more inchoate attitude than belief. If a child does not have the concept of *belief*, we might be reluctant to attribute to her the belief that she has a particular belief. Nevertheless, she may have beliefs and be aware of them. Michael Bratman suggests that you might be able to reason with an attitude even if you do not possess the second-order belief that you have the attitude.[19] I do not disagree.

On the other hand, in 'Thinking that one thinks', David Rosenthal argues that to have a conscious attitude is to have the full higher-order belief that you have that attitude. I do not wish to deny this claim either; I shall take no stand on it.[20] If it is true, it means that, when you reason consciously, you must believe that you have the attitudes you reason with.

So first-order reasoning may be necessarily accompanied by second-order awareness and even second-order beliefs. But this does assimilate it to higher-order reasoning of the sort I rejected in chapter 12. The contents of these second-order attitudes are not premises in the reasoning. Nor are they normative. But in higher-order reasoning as I defined it on page 209, the content of a normative higher-order belief serves as a premise in the reasoning.

The central difficulty with the higher-order account of reasoning is that it is hard to work out a way in which higher-order normative beliefs about your attitudes can lead you to have appropriate first-order attitudes. The first-order account does not encounter this difficulty. A first-order process modifies your attitudes directly, because it works on the contents of attitudes. In the snow example, when you conclude that the snow will melt, you are directly acquiring a belief that the snow will melt.

This needs emphasis. There are two aspects to reasoning. One is working out a conclusion on the basis of the premises. The other is taking up an attitude towards the conclusion. It is tempting to try and divide the reasoning into two stages according to these two aspects: first the working out of a conclusion, then the acquisition of an attitude. It is even tempting to think the first stage is the reasoning proper and the second stage something else. Referring to Paul Boghossian's account of inference, Crispin Wright says:

> Inferring is a movement of thought between propositions which may, in special circumstances, result in the thinker coming to judge the proposition inferred to be true. But no particular attitude to that proposition is implicit in inference itself, in particular not judgement of its truth. What Boghossian is talking about is coming to believe a proposition *on the basis of* inference. That is not inference per se. Inference is rather, one would suppose, a proper ingredient in it.[21]

But if there were these two stages, at the end of the first stage the conclusion would be parked somewhere in your consciousness, without your having any particular attitude towards it. We would have to explain how you then come to take up the attitude. The explanation could not go through your believing you ought to have it, or your intending to have it. How would you come to acquire that belief or that intention? And if you did, how would it bring you to take up the attitude towards the conclusion? It is the higher-order account that claims you come to believe the conclusion this way, and I have rejected that account.

On the first-order account, reasoning is not split into the two stages. You adopt an attitude as you work out its content. Belief reasoning appears to you as the process of discovering a truth.

13.6   The direction of reasoning

My account of reasoning has so far been limited to one special, paradigmatic type of theoretical reasoning: reasoning by modus ponens. The account has to be broadened, and in broadening it we shall find a potential role for higher-order reasoning of a sort.

We must recognize that reasoning often does not proceed in the neat linear fashion of the snow example. There, your reasoning sets out from some initial beliefs and concludes with a new belief. But theoretical reasoning will often cause you to drop one or more of your initial beliefs, rather than acquire a new one.[22]

On page 207 I described reasoning as a way of bringing ourselves to satisfy requirements of rationality. In the snow example, your reasoning brings you to satisfy the Modus Ponens Requirement on page 157 by giving you a new belief. But dropping one of your initial beliefs would achieve the same end of satisfying the Modus Ponens Requirement. Can reasoning have this effect, instead of giving you a new belief?

Suppose you embark on reasoning of the sort I have described, but do not conclude it. Let us have a new example. You believe that platypuses are mammals. You also believe that no mammals lay eggs, and in particular that if platypuses are mammals they do not lay eggs. You call the contents of these beliefs to mind. You attempt to operate on them, following the modus ponens rule. But you find you do not end up believing that platypuses do not lay eggs. Perhaps nothing can make you believe this because you have seen a platypus laying eggs.

If you care about whether platypuses lay eggs, you remain in violation of the Modus Ponens Requirement. But you may yet be able to satisfy this requirement through reasoning, provided you believe the negation of the conclusion your reasoning would have arrived at – provided you believe platypuses do lay eggs, that is to say. (Section 15.3 shows it is doubtful you can do so if you believe neither that platypuses lay eggs nor that they do not.)

So let us assume you believe that platypuses lay eggs. Given that, you can continue your reasoning in another direction. You can take this as a new premise, and put your reasoning into reverse. If we make your reasoning explicit, it goes:

> 'Platypuses are mammals.
> If platypuses are mammals, platypuses do not lay eggs.
> . . .
> But platypuses lay eggs.
> So, platypuses are not mammals.'

(The three dots indicate a break in the reasoning process; not that something is omitted.) This is best regarded as two bits of reasoning rather than one: a failed attempt at reasoning by modus ponens, followed by a successful piece of reasoning by modus tollens. In any case, each sentences expresses a belief of yours. You end up believing that platypuses are not mammals.

That is not enough to put you in conformity with the Modus Ponens Requirement. For that, you must stop believing platypuses are mammals. Until you do, you now violate, not only the Modus Ponens Requirement, but also No Contradictory Beliefs on page 155.

But we can expect that coming to believe platypuses are not mammals will cause you to stop believing platypuses are mammals. If it does, it can only be through one of those automatic processes I mentioned in section 12.1, which often bring you to satisfy many of the requirements of rationality. At least, I shall argue in section 15.3 that no explicit process of reasoning can bring about this result. But provided the automatic process occurs, you will come to satisfy both No Contradictory Beliefs and the Modus Ponens Requirements. So reverse reasoning can bring you to satisfy the Modus Ponens Requirement indirectly. The final step must happen through an automatic process.

Metareasoning

Since reasoning is not necessarily linear, it might go in various possible directions. In the example, it could have gone forward and brought you to believe platypuses do not lay eggs, but actually it went backward and brought you to believe platypuses are not mammals. It might alternatively have brought you to believe it is not the case that, if platypuses are mammals they do not lay eggs. The existence of all these alternatives raises a new question. What controls the direction of your reasoning?

In the example, you start with inconsistent beliefs: you believe that platypuses are mammals, that if platypuses are mammals they do not lay eggs, and that platypuses lay eggs. The direction of your reasoning must be determined by the relative robustness, in some sense, of these beliefs. But this is saying little until we know the nature of robustness.

Robustness is a tendency of one belief to override others. The robustness of a particular belief is likely to be influenced by your other beliefs. It will probably be influenced by your beliefs about what evidence you have. It will also probably be influenced by your meta-propositional beliefs,[23] and specifically by your higher-order beliefs. For instance, it may be influenced by your beliefs about what you ought to believe, what you have a reason to believe, or what rationality requires you to believe.

These influences may themselves be mediated by reasoning. You may engage in metareasoning, which is reasoning about your first-order reasoning, and your metareasoning may influence the way you conduct your first-order reasoning. Metareasoning will involve reasoning with your meta-propositional beliefs and your higher-order beliefs. So your first-order reasoning may be influenced or even controlled by higher-order beliefs and higher-order reasoning.

This does not conflict with my rejection of the higher-order account of reasoning in chapter 12. The problem with the higher-order account is that it requires your higher-order attitudes to control your first-order beliefs in a way they cannot. For example, you cannot come to believe something just because you believe you ought to believe it. But reasoning, unlike believing, is an activity of yours; it is something you do. It is therefore under your control in a way your beliefs are not. If, say, you believe you ought to reason backwards rather than forwards, you can choose to do so.

Higher-order metareasoning does not replace first-order reasoning. It influences its direction. There has to be first-order reasoning, because that is the only sort of reasoning that can bring you directly to acquire a new belief.

13.7   Correct belief reasoning

What distinguishes correct from incorrect reasoning? On page 207 I described reasoning as a self-help process for improving our rationality. It is a way of bringing ourselves to satisfy requirements of rationality that we do not satisfy automatically. This suggests as a natural first thought that reasoning is correct if and only if it achieves that aim.

Notice as a preliminary that correctness for reasoning is not itself a requirement of rationality. Rationality does not require you to reason correctly, because you can be rational without reasoning at all. One sort of ideally rational being is entirely rational as a result of automatic processes, so it does not need to reason. Instead, what rationality requires of you is conditional in content: it requires that, if you reason, you reason correctly. To put it another way, it requires you not to reason incorrectly.

But reasoning can improve your rationality by bringing you to satisfy requirements of rationality that are not themselves requirements on reasoning. In particular, it can bring you to satisfy one or more synchronic requirements of rationality, of the sort I mentioned in chapter 9. The natural first thought is that reasoning is correct if and only if it brings you to satisfy one of those requirements. But actually that is not so. For a piece of reasoning to be correct, it is neither sufficient nor necessary that it brings you to satisfy a synchronic requirement of rationality.

First a counterexample to sufficiency. Suppose you believe p and you believe that if p then q. Suppose also that you believe r and you believe that if q then r. Suppose you care about whether q. Now suppose you reason by operating on the contents of the latter pair of your beliefs: you derive the conclusion that q by following the rule of affirming the consequent. You end up believing q. This means your reasoning brings you to satisfy an instance of the Modus Ponens Requirement on page 157: you believe p, and you believe that if p then q, and you now believe q. Nevertheless, your reasoning by affirming the consequent is not correct.

Next two counterexamples to necessity. First, suppose you believe p and you believe that if p then q, and you care about whether q. Suppose you reason by operating on the contents of these beliefs: you derive the conclusion that q by following the modus ponens rule. You end up believing q. But suppose that by the time you complete your reasoning, with this result, you have stopped believing p. Then your reasoning may not bring you to satisfy any synchronic requirement of rationality. Nevertheless, it is correct reasoning.

Second, suppose again that you believe p and you believe that if p then q. But this time suppose you do not care about whether q. Suppose again you reason by operating on the contents of your beliefs, and derive the conclusion that q by following the modus ponens rule. You end up believing q. But since you do not care about whether q, your reasoning does not bring you to satisfy the Modus Ponens Requirement, and it may not bring you to satisfy any synchronic requirement of rationality. Nevertheless, it is correct reasoning. Here correct reasoning goes beyond what is required by rationality.

So merely bringing you to satisfy a requirement of rationality is not the criterion of correctness for reasoning. Instead we need to look at the rule you follow when you reason. In reasoning you operate on the contents of your attitudes, following a rule. The reasoning is correct if and only if you correctly follow a correct rule. In the above counterexample to sufficiency, you follow the rule of affirming the consequent, which is incorrect. In the two counterexamples to necessity, you correctly follow the rule of modus ponens, which is correct.

Now the problem is to identify which rules are correct. Even though the correctness of reasoning is not directly determined by whether it brings you to satisfy a requirement of rationality, you might at first think that the correctness of rules for reasoning will be determined by requirements of rationality. But intuitively, correctness for reasoning is a matter of which ways it is rationally *permissible* to reason. Even if you do not have to reason in a particular way, so long as it is permissible to reason that way it is correct to do so. Our intuitive idea of correctness does not even rule out the possibility that there may be more than one correct way to reason on the basis of some particular premise-attitudes. There is an example on pages 263–4. Correctness is a matter of permission, not requirement. On page 258 I shall reinforce this intuitive thought with an argument, for one particular case.

The standard of correctness for reasoning is therefore set by basing permission of rationality. Each permission will determine a rule, and reasoning by correctly following that rule will be correct. The general formula for determining a rule from a permission is explained on page 255. But it is obvious anyway that the modus ponens rule set out on page 232 can be derived from Modus Ponens Permission on page 191. On the other hand, it is prohibited to base a belief that *p* on a belief that *q* and a belief that if *p* then *q*. So the rule of reasoning by affirming the consequent is not correct.

All we have to do now is work out what basing permissions there are. On page 190 I declined to give a general account of basing permissions for beliefs. That is a topic for epistemology, and too large for this book. I did say they include some logical deductions but not all. Modus Ponens Permission is one that is included.

Now another question arises. Since correctness is given by permission rather than requirement, it remains to be explained how correct reasoning promotes rationality. How does reasoning correctly tend to bring you to conform with synchronic requirements of rationality?

The answer must be that permissions of rationality are closely related to requirements. Modus Ponens Permission is closely related to the Modus Ponens Requirement. If you reason correctly about a topic you care about, following a rule that corresponds to Modus Ponens Permission, you will come to satisfy a particular instance of the Modus Ponens Requirement.

Permissible, correct reasoning may well go further than satisfying a requirement. Modus Ponens Permission provides an example. The Modus Ponens Requirement is limited by the clause that you care about the conclusion. The permission has no such limitation. It is permissible to reason by modus ponens whether you care about the conclusion or not. Reasoning may bring you to satisfy requirements of rationality, but it can also go far beyond requirements.

I shall say more about the relation between requirements and permissions in section 14.2.

Notes

1　In 'The normative force of reasoning', pp. 662–3, Ralph Wedgwood assumes that, to be reasoning, a process must be correct reasoning. This is an idealizing assumption, which he recognizes is strictly false. I shall account for both correct and incorrect reasoning.

2　For a discussion of deviant causal connections in the context of reasoning, see Ralph Wedgwood, 'The normative force of reasoning'.

3　In *The Structure of Justification*, Robert Audi uses the term 'connecting belief' for what I call a 'first-order linking belief'. My views are similar to those he expresses on pp. 240–54.

4　See section 13.7.

5　In *The Possibility of Altruism*, p. 31, Thomas Nagel says: 'If someone draws conclusions in accordance with a principle of logic such as *modus ponens*, it is appropriate to ascribe to him the belief that the principle is true.' Frank Jackson and Philip Pettit make a similar remark in 'Moral functionalism', p. 32. It is true only if the person actually follows the rule of modus ponens. Drawing conclusions in accordance with it is not enough.

6   Simon Robertson pointed out to me that sometimes you may aim to arrive at a particular belief by reasoning. When you suspect some conjecture is true, you may embark on a piece of reasoning that you expect to bring you to believe the conjecture.

7   Compare Pettit, *The Common Mind*, p. 59.

8   'Rationality, reasoning and group agency', pp. 498–500.

9   'Rationality, reasoning and group agency', p. 500, n. 4.

10   I take the term 'critical reasoning' from Tyler Burge in 'Reason and the first person', p. 260, but I do not mean to suggest that Pettit's account of reasoning is the same as Burge's. It is not.

11   Boghossian, 'What is inference?'. This section developed out of my 'Comments on Boghossian', which is an attempt to respond to the difficulties Boghossian raises.

12   Boghossian also takes reasoning to be following a rule. His account appears in 'Blind reasoning' and 'What is inference?'. My own account originally evolved independently, but I have subsequently learnt a great deal from Boghossian as a result of long discussions. I think my account has improved substantially as a result, and not just in this section. I am extremely grateful to him.

13   Thanks to Robert Audi for a useful discussion.

14   Boghossian in 'What is inference?' quotes Saul Kripke in *Wittgenstein on Rules and Private Language*, p. 24, who quotes Wittgenstein's *Philosophical Investigations*, remark 258, quoted below.

15   *Philosophical Investigations*, remark 258.

16   *Philosophical Investigations*, remark 264.

17   Kripke, *Wittgenstein on Rules and Private Language*.

18   My thanks to Josée Brunet for helpful discussions on this subject.

19   'Intention, belief, and practical rationality'.

20   One of the many alternative views appears in Peter Carruthers's 'Phenomenal concepts'.

21   Wright, 'Comment on Paul Boghossian'. The same claim is advanced by James Hearne in 'Deductivism and practical reason'. See the useful commentary on Hearne in Josée Brunet's 'Le double aspect du raisonnement pratique'.

22   Gilbert Harman particularly emphasizes this point in *Change in View*.

23   See p. 235.

14

Practical Reasoning

14.1 Reasoning with attitudes other than beliefs

In chapter 13 I described reasoning whose premise-attitudes and conclusion-attitude are beliefs. In this chapter I shall present a first-order account of reasoning with other sorts of attitudes. Like belief reasoning, reasoning in general is a process whereby some of your attitudes cause you to acquire a new attitude. Such a process is reasoning only if it satisfies some further conditions. I shall identify what those conditions are.

The conditions will apply to all sorts of reasoning. But I am particularly concerned with intention reasoning, which is reasoning that concludes in an intention. It is the central case of practical reasoning.[1] There may be other types of practical reasoning too. For instance, there may be reasoning that concludes in your intending something to a degree that is less than full intention. There may also be reasoning that concludes in your not intending something. I shall mention those possibilities in chapter 15.

When reasoning concludes in a belief about what you ought to do or what you have a reason to do, I do not count it as practical reasoning.[2] It is theoretical reasoning with a normative content. Nor does practical reasoning conclude in a physical action.[3] True, since the conclusion-state of practical reasoning is an intention, and since an intention often causes a physical action, practical reasoning will often cause a physical action. That is why I call it 'practical'. But reasoning is a mental process. Suppose you do some reasoning, and it causes you to perform a physical act. Say it causes you to raise your arm. It could have happened that you went through exactly the same mental process of reasoning but did not raise your arm, because your arm was unexpectedly paralysed. Your reasoning is the same in either case, but in one case you raise your arm and in the other case you do not. So your raising your arm is not any part of your reasoning. In particular, it is not its conclusion.

This chapter takes its main example from one specific sort of intention reasoning: reasoning that brings you to intend a means to an end that you intend. I call this 'instrumental reasoning'. There are other sorts of intention reasoning too; chapter 16 is about one of them.

Here is an example of instrumental reasoning. You intend to visit Venice, and you believe that you will not do so if you do not buy a ticket. Your intention and belief together cause you to acquire the intention of buying a ticket. This causal process is reasoning, provided it satisfies some further conditions. In chapter 13 I identified two further conditions that are necessary and sufficient for belief reasoning. Now I need to generalize those conditions a little.

I continue to be concerned with active reasoning only. The conditions identified in chapter 13 are conditions for active reasoning. First, in section 13.1, I said that the attitudes involved must be conscious. Second, in section 13.3, I said the process of reasoning is a rule-governed operation on the attitudes' contents. Only the second condition needs to be generalized. The first applies to all sorts of active reasoning.

Marked contents

Attitudes of the sort we reason with – beliefs and intentions, for instance – are relations between a person and a proposition. I call the proposition the 'content' of the attitude. Attitudes of different types may have the same content. For instance, if you intend to visit Venice, the content of your intention is the proposition that you will visit Venice. If you believe you will visit Venice, the content of your belief is that same proposition.

An intention to visit Venice and a belief that you will visit Venice obviously participate in your reasoning in different ways. For instance, an intention to visit Venice might be a premise-attitude in instrumental reasoning that would lead you to intend to buy a ticket to Venice. But suppose you merely believe you will visit Venice – perhaps you believe that your cultured aunt will eventually persuade you to go there. Your belief could not play the same role in instrumental reasoning as an intention, and bring you to intend to buy a ticket.

Yet the intention and the belief have the same content. It follows that, when you apply a rule in the course of reasoning with an attitude, the rule must take account of the attitude's type as well as its content.[4]

This means that the rule must be defined on the attitudes' contents and types taken together. That is to say, it must be defined on pairs, each consisting of a content and a type of attitude. Your reasoning is a rule-governed operation on pairs of this sort.

In the Venice reasoning I described, you derive the pair <I shall buy a ticket; intention> from <I shall visit Venice; intention> and <I shall not visit Venice if I do not buy a ticket; belief>. You are probably applying the rule:

From
    <p; intention> and
    <If p then q; belief>
to derive
    <q; intention>.

Alternatively, you may be applying the more specific rule

From
    <I shall F; intention> and
    <If I shall F, I shall G; belief>
to derive
    <I shall G; intention>.

For just the same reasons, the rule for theoretical reasoning too must be defined on pairs like this. The fact that the content is believed rather than, say, intended, has to be registered in the rule. For instance, the modus ponens rule must be understood as:

From
    <p; belief> and
    <If p then q; belief>
to derive
    <q; belief>.

When I was dealing with theoretical reasoning only, I took it for granted that all the contents were believed. So I could state the rule in a simpler version on page 232, which mentions the contents only. But now we must recognize that theoretical reasoning is also an operation on pairs of this sort.

For a reason that will appear on page 253, I call pairs consisting of contents with attitudes the 'marked contents' of your attitudes. The 'mark' is the type of the attitude: intention, belief or whatever it is.

Reasoning is a rule-governed operation on the marked contents of your attitudes. That is my generalization of the condition developed in section 13.3.

Markers and explicit reasoning

Now I return to the first condition for a process to be reasoning, which comes from section 13.1. To reason actively, the attitudes involved must be conscious. It is now clear what you must be conscious of: you must be conscious of the attitudes' marked contents, since those are what you operate on. You reason about the marked contents.

For example, in the snow reasoning of chapter 13, you must be conscious of the pair <It is raining; belief>. It is not enough to be conscious of the proposition that it is raining, and also of a belief. You must be conscious of the pair in a particular way that recognizes the connection between them. You must be conscious of the proposition *as* believed by you.

In the Venice example, you must be conscious of the pair <I shall visit Venice; intention>. (I have expressed the content as you would express it, in the first person.) You must be conscious of the proposition *as* intended by you.

I do not mean that, when an attitude is part of your reasoning, you must necessarily have a second-order belief that you have the attitude. It is enough to be conscious of the attitude's content in a particular way: a believing way or an intending way, for instance. The fact that a marked content includes the type of attitude does not by itself imply that you have a second-order attitude. The marked content is not itself the content of any separate attitude. When you intend to visit Venice, the marked content of your intention is <I visit Venice; intention>. You need have no attitude besides the intention; you need have no second-order attitude that has the intention as part of its content.

However, I mentioned on page 242 that, according to one theory of consciousness, to have a conscious attitude is to have a second-order belief that you have the attitude. I take no stand on this theory.

If an attitude is not already conscious, you can make it so by the act of calling to mind its marked content. One way of doing this is to express it to yourself using a sentence. Our language is equipped to express marked contents. It does so by means of what I shall call 'markers'. When you utter a sentence, you perform a speech-act of some sort. A marker is a linguistic feature of the sentence that identifies the sort of speech-act you perform when you say the sentence. It is often a grammatical mood. For instance, a marker for the speech-act of commanding is the imperative mood, and a marker for the speech act of questioning is the interrogative mood.

Often when you say a sentence, the speech-act you perform is the act of expressing an attitude of yours. When you do that, your sentence often contains a marker that is specific to the particular type of attitude you are expressing. I call this an 'attitude marker'. Unless I say otherwise, when I use the word 'marker' alone, I am always referring to an attitude marker. An attitude marker in a sentence in effect denotes a mark, which is the type of attitude that the sentence expresses.

I have created some artificial sentences in which the attitude markers are the names of the attitudes, such as 'intention' and 'belief', bracketed together with indicative sentences that express contents.

An example of an attitude marker in natural language is the optative mood. This marks the attitude of desire. When Robert Browning wrote 'Oh, to be in England now that April's there!', he expressed his attitude of desiring to be in England now it is April. This sentence is in the optative mood (or the nearest approximation to the optative mood that English possesses). His sentence denotes the marked content <I am in England now that April is there; desire>.

The marker in English for expressing belief is the indicative mood. Artificially, I use 'belief'. If I understand him right, Frege's 'judgement-stroke' is an artificial marker with exactly the same meaning.[5] Frege was interested, as I am, in the process of reasoning, in which existing attitudes give rise to a new attitude. He therefore needed a way to express the attitude of judgement (which I take to be belief).[6] Modern logic does not use the judgement-stroke because it is concerned with relations of consequence that hold between propositions or sentences and not between attitudes.

I shall say more about markers for intention in section 15.1. Here I need say only that an intention marker in English is often subtle or entirely silent. We often express intentions using the very same indicative sentences as express beliefs. You would express your intention of visiting Venice by saying 'I am going to visit Venice' or 'I shall visit Venice' or 'I will visit Venice'. Any of those sentences could equally well express a belief that you will visit Venice. So they could equally well denote the marked content <I shall visit Venice; intention> or <I shall visit Venice; belief>.

You may call to mind the marked contents of an attitude by saying to yourself a sentence that denotes this marked content. You could call to mind your intention to visit Venice by saying to yourself the sentence 'I shall visit Venice'. This would render your intention conscious, and available to be reasoned with.

You might not need to call an attitude to mind to make it conscious, because it might be conscious already. Even so, you may need to express it to yourself if you are to reason with it. It may be that active reasoning needs to be explicit. If you made it explicit in the way I described, your reasoning about Venice would be:

> 'I shall visit Venice.
> I shall not visit Venice if I do not buy a ticket.
> So I shall buy a ticket.'

The first and third of these sentences express intentions. They contain the silent marker for intention, but because the marker is silent they are indistinguishable from sentences that express beliefs. This can lead to confusion between practical and theoretical reasoning, which section 15.4 tries to clear up.

I do not insist that reasoning has to be explicit – that it has to be conducted in language. That is not a premise in the argument of this chapter or this book. Nevertheless, I am inclined to think it is true, and in chapter 15 I shall explore the consequences of assuming it is. In any case, I often find it convenient to describe reasoning by writing it out in explicit form.

14.2 Correctness

In section 13.7 I explained that reasoning is correct if and only if it correctly follows a correct rule, and a correct rule is one that corresponds to a basing permission of rationality. There I was dealing with belief reasoning only, but what I said applies to reasoning of all sorts. I now need to work out the wider consequences of this principle, in particular for practical reasoning.

First I should state formally the way in a which a rule can correspond to a basing permission. The general form of a basing permission appears on page 190. I reproduce it here:

> Rationality permits N that
> N has attitude A at some time and
> N has attitude B at some time and
> N has attitude C at some time and
> . . .
> N has attitude K at some time and
> N's attitude K is based on N's attitudes A, B, C . . .

Let the content of attitude A be a, and let the type of attitude A (belief, intention, desire or whatever) be A–type. Then the marked content of attitude A is $<a; A\text{–type}>$. Represent the marked contents of the other attitudes in the same way. Then the rule that corresponds to this basing permission is:

> From
> $\quad <a; A\text{–type}>$ and
> $\quad <b; B\text{–type}>$ and
> $\quad <c; C\text{–type}>$ and
> $\quad$ . . .
> to derive
> $\quad <k; K\text{–type}>$.

Requirement and permission

What basing permissions support practical reasoning? In particular, what basing permission supports instrumental reasoning? A natural place to start from in trying to figure this out is the Instrumental Requirement on page 159. I repeat it here in its more friendly form from page 169:

> *Instrumental Requirement.* Rationality requires of N that, if
> (1) N intends at t that e, and if
> (2) N believes at t that m is a means implied by e, and if
> (3) N believes at t that m is up to her herself then, then
> (4) N intends at t that m.

Instrumental reasoning is a way of bringing yourself to satisfy this requirement. So we can expect that the rule you follow in correct instrumental reasoning will be connected with this requirement.

You might think a basing permission could be derived directly from the requirement. For instance, the Instrumental Requirement might give us:

> ? *Narrow Instrumental Permission.* Rationality permits N that:
> N intends at some time that e, and
> N believes at some time that m is a means implied by e, and
> N believes at some time that m is up to her herself then, and
> N intends at some time that m, and
> N's intention that m is based on N's intention that e, and belief that m is a means implied by e, and belief that m is up to her herself then.

But this is not the permission that validates instrumental reasoning.

For one thing, I derived it from a requirement by a method that is plainly mistaken. It can lead to obvious falsehoods. The Instrumental Requirement can be put in various forms by means of contraposition. This is one of them:

> Rationality requires of N that, if
> N intends at t that e, and if
> N does not intend at t that m, and if
> N believes at t that m is up to her herself then, then
> N does not believe at t that m is a means implied by e.

Applying the same method as before to derive a basing permission would bring us to conclude that it is permissible not to believe that m is a means implied by e on the basis of intending e but not intending m, and believing that m is up to you now. But that obviously is not permissible. So we cannot derive a basing permission from a requirement in such a straightforward manner.[7]

Moreover, as Kieran Setiya pointed out to me, the Narrow Instrumental Permission cannot be the basis of instrumental reasoning. Suppose at some time t that you intend e, and believe m is a means implied by e, and believe that m is up to you yourself then. Spelt out, the content of your second belief is that, were you not then to intend m, because of that m would not be so. 'Up to you then' is defined this way on page 162. 'Then' refers to the time t when you have this belief.

Now suppose you do not at t intend m. But suppose that at t you start reasoning on the basis of your three attitudes, to arrive at an intention that m. Your reasoning takes a bit of time, so you do not have this intention till a while after t. This means that, by the time you have it, according to your own belief it is already too late to achieve m. You believe at t that, were you not *then* to intend m, m would not be so, and you do not then intend m.

Reasoning that followed the Narrow Instrumental Permission would therefore be peculiar at the very least. It would be unsuccessful according to one of its own premises. I do not certify it would be incorrect, and I do not certify that the Narrow Instrumental Permission is false, but our ordinary instrumental reasoning is certainly not peculiar in this way. The Narrow Instrumental Permission therefore does not support our ordinary instrumental reasoning.

In any case, it is obvious that we have this broader permission of rationality:

> *Instrumental Permission.* Rationality permits N that:
> N intends at some time that e, and
> N believes at some time that m is a means implied by e, and
> N believes at some time that m is up to her herself, and
> N intends at some time that m, and
> N's intention that m is based on N's intention that e, and belief that m is a means implied by e, and belief that m is up to her herself.

This formula differs from the Narrow Instrumental Permission in just one respect: the two occurrences of 'then' have been deleted. N's belief is that m is up to her herself, rather than up to her herself then. Spelt out, the third conjunct within the Instrumental Permission is:

> N believes at some time that, were she not at some time to intend m, because of that m would not be so.

The two occurrences of 'at some time' do not necessarily refer to the same time.

This modification is obviously correct. In order to correctly derive an intention to take a means from an intention to achieve an end, you do not have to wait until you believe a time has arrived when you must already intend the means if you are to achieve the end. That is obvious.[8]

Setiya's point makes one thing clear. Instrumental reasoning is made correct – 'validated' I shall say – by a permission of rationality rather than by a requirement of rationality. In the Instrumental Requirement (see page 159), the 'then' in clause (3) is essential. Until you believe that intending the means is up to you now, you may rationally not intend the means: you may wait till later to form the intention. However, it must be correct to do your instrumental reasoning before you believe the means is up to you now. If you left it to the time you have that belief, you would already believe the reasoning comes too late. So it cannot be the requirement that validates your reasoning. This argument reinforces the intuition I recognized on page 247, that correctness in reasoning comes from permission, not requirement.

I mean that correctness does not come *directly* from requirement. Basing permissions themselves may derive ultimately from requirements. Indeed, there is a reason to think they must. Reasoning is a means of coming to satisfy requirements of rationality. The only way you can come to satisfy the Instrumental Requirement through correct reasoning is by reasoning that is validated by the Instrumental Permission. So the requirement and the permission must be intimately connected together. Presumably the permission is derived in some way from the requirement, so that it is correct to reason according to the permission just because this is a way to satisfy the requirement.

However, the connection between the requirement and the permission is complicated. The permission is wider than the requirement in one way and narrower in another. It is wider in that clause (3) in the requirement contains the restriction to 'then', which is absent from the permission. It is narrower in that no permission corresponds to any contraposed version of the requirement, such as the one on page 256.

This complexity prevents me from describing any general rule for deriving permissions from requirements. Nevertheless, for each requirement of rationality we can expect there to be a corresponding basing permission.

It is a serious gap in this book's argument that I cannot explain in general how a permission is derived from a requirement. I could seem to be identifying basing permissions simply by the condition that they validate reasoning that is correct. That would introduce some circularity into my account of correctness for reasoning. When is reasoning correct? – when it is validated by a genuine basing permission. When is a basing permission genuine? – when it validates reasoning that is correct.

The circularity would not actually be quite as bad as that, since basing permissions serve other purposes besides validating reasoning. For example, this is obviously a genuine basing permission:

Rationality permits N not to believe not p on the basis of believing p.

But I shall argue on page 279 that there is no correct reasoning, or at least no correct explicit reasoning, that is validated by this permission. We have to rely on unconscious processes to make sure we do not have contradictory beliefs. If you believe not p, and then come to believe p, an unconscious processes will normally cause you to stop believing that not p. Your non-belief in not p is then based on your belief in p. This permission above tells us that this is permissible, even though no reasoning is involved.

Still, it is important to recognize that basing permissions have an independent grounding in requirements of rationality.

Enthymematic instrumental reasoning

From the Instrumental Permission on page 257, following the procedure set out on page 255, we obtain this rule for correct instrumental reasoning:

From:
  <e; intention> and
  <m is a means implied by e; belief> and
  <m is up to me; belief>
to derive
  <m; intention>

Go back to the Venice example of instrumental reasoning I described on pages 251–2. You intend to visit Venice, and you believe that you will not visit Venice if you do not buy a ticket. You derive an intention of buying a ticket. Only one belief figures in this example, and its marked content is <I shall not visit Venice if I do not buy a ticket; belief>. So according to my account of correct instrumental reasoning, the reasoning in that example is incorrect.

And indeed, it certainly is incorrect as I have described it. Your belief that you will not visit Venice if you do not buy a ticket is not strong enough to make it correct. You could have this belief even if you did not believe that buying a ticket is a means of visiting Venice. For instance, you might believe that your visiting Venice and your buying a ticket are effects that share a common cause, so that if one happens so does the other. If that is what you believe, you could not correctly derive an intention to buy a ticket from your intention to visit Venice.

Moreover, if the reasoning is to be correct, you must believe that buying a ticket is up to you. Suppose instead that you believe you have delegated all your ticket-buying to your travel agent. Again it would be incorrect to derive an intention to buy a ticket from your intention to visit Venice.

The Venice reasoning on pages 251–2 is correct only if it is understood as enthymematic. Some premise-beliefs must be implicit. Fully spelt out and made explicit, correct reasoning would be:

> 'I shall visit Venice.
> My buying a ticket is a means implied by my visiting Venice.
> My buying a ticket is up to me.
> So I shall buy a ticket.'

Logic of marked contents?

Basing permissions of rationality generate rules of correct reasoning. These rules specify when it is correct to derive one marked content from others. In a sense, they constitute a logic for marked contents. However, the logic is very thin because it has no place for logical compounds of marked contents. In general a rule has the form:

> From
> <a; A–type> and
> <b; B–type> and
> <c; C–type> and
> . . .
> to derive
> <k; K–type>.

The words 'from', 'and' and 'to derive' all belong to the metalanguage in which the rule is described. They cannot be absorbed into the object language. For instance, the object language contains no sentence such as: 'if <a; A–type> and <b; B–type> and <c; C–type> and . . . then <k; K–type>'. That is nonsense.

There is a history of much more ambitious attempts to develop a logic of marked contents.[9] They have generally had a very different purpose from mine. They have generally been constructed in support of an expressivist metaethics. Their authors claim that what appear to be beliefs having normative contents are not truly beliefs, but instead attitudes of some other, noncognitive sort. They need a logic for the marked contents of those noncognitive attitudes.

Expressivists recognize that they will not successfully replace beliefs with noncognitive attitudes unless the marked contents of those attitudes possess a logic that mirrors the logic of the contents of beliefs. Their logic must mirror propositional logic, that is to say. Propositional logic allows for compound propositions such as conjunctions and conditionals, in which one proposition is embedded inside another. So the mirror logic of marked contents also has to allow embedding.

Embedding raises the so-called Frege–Geach problem for these logics.[10] Most fundamentally, the problem is to explain what it means to embed the marked content of one attitude inside the marked content of another. Since I do not embed, I am not faced with the Frege-Geach problem. Frege himself avoided the problem in the same way: he did not allow sentences marked with the judgement-stroke to be embedded in other sentences.[11]

14.3   Choosing a means

Let us call reasoning of the sort that is validated by the Instrumental Permission 'paradigmatic instrumental reasoning'. The Venice reasoning, as fully spelt out on page 260, is an example of it. This sort of reasoning takes you from intending an end to intending a means that you believe is implied by the end. But if you believe there is a choice among alternative means to your end, you do not believe a particular means is implied by the end. Paradigmatic instrumental reasoning is then not available to you. If you believe there is a choice, you must make your choice before you can do this sort of reasoning.

So we need to consider how reasoning can help you choose among means.[12] Various routes are available to making a choice, and this section outlines some of them.

Often the process of choosing a means to an end has several steps. You start with the broad intention of achieving the end, and you believe you have a choice of means to do so. As time passes, and often step by step, you acquire progressively narrower intentions to take particular means to the end, means to those means, and so on. This can happen in various different ways. Not every step need involve reasoning, and various different sorts of reasoning might be involved.

When you intend an end, you may occasionally believe you can achieve it without taking any means to it. But normally you will believe you need to take a means, and that it is up to you to do so. Then you will intend a means if you are rational. You might have a very broad intention whose content is just that you take some means or other. Taking some means or other is a means implied by your end, according to my definition of an implied means on page

160. So paradigmatic instrumental reasoning could take you to this broad intention.

Often paradigmatic instrumental reasoning will take you to some narrower intention than that. Go back to the example on page 160, where you intend to get milk. You might get it from a shop, or you might steal it from a cow. But suppose you believe you would never steal a cow's milk, so that means of getting milk is knocked out even before you intend any means at all. You may believe that buying milk from a shop is a means implied by the end of getting milk, because you would never take another means. You do not believe you have a real choice of means at all. Paradigmatic instrumental reasoning can then bring you to intend to buy milk from a shop. This is a narrower intention than simply to take some means of getting milk.

It may alternatively happen that, when you intend some end, you believe you have a real choice but that one of the available means is better than the others. I take it that rationality requires you to intend what you believe is the best means to an end you intend. On page 170 I declined to try and specify this requirement precisely because I am not sure how to specify the notion of *best means*. Still, shelving this problem, we may assume there is a corresponding basing permission of rationality:

> Rationality permits N that:
> N intends at some time that e, and
> N believes at some time that m is the best means implied by e, and
> N believes at some time that m is up to her herself, and
> N intends at some time that m, and
> N's intention that m is based on N's intention that e, and belief that m
> is the best means to e, and belief that m is up to her herself.

For example, this piece of explicit reasoning:

> 'I shall collect the table.
> The best means of collecting the table is to hire a van.
> Hiring a van is up to me.
> So I shall hire a van.'

would be validated by the permission above. This is a second way in which reasoning can narrow your intention.

Often you will narrow your intention to take a means in a different way. Suppose you have formed the disjunctive intention of taking one of a number of available means. You intend to hire a van from Hertz or from Budget or from the local garage. You might form the belief that you ought not to take a particular one of those available means. You might arrive at this belief in various ways. You might do so through reasoning. If so, it would be theoretical reasoning since it concludes in a belief.

Say that, somehow, you form the belief you ought not to hire a van from Budget. From this belief you can derive the intention of not taking that means. You might do so through a process of 'enkratic' reasoning, which I shall describe in chapter 16. You will end up intending a smaller disjunction of means. You might get to that point by reasoning, which, made explicit, would go something like this:

> 'I shall hire a van from Hertz, or from Budget, or from the local garage.
> I shall not hire a van from Budget.
> So I shall hire a van from Hertz or from the local garage.'

This is practical reasoning, since it concludes in an intention. It is also surely correct. Moreover it brings you to satisfy a requirement of rationality. I shall not set out formally either the requirement or the permission that validates the reasoning.

One interesting case is when you believe there is nothing to choose between alternative means. You do not believe that a particular means is best, nor that you ought not to take a particular means. Nevertheless, you have to choose between them. At some point you will come to believe you will not achieve the end unless you now intend a specific one or other of the means. At that point, the Generalized Instrumental Requirement from page 170 applies to you. If you have not by then chosen a means, you are not rational.

For instance, suppose you intend to survive, and you believe you will not survive unless you go either to the left-hand bale of hay or the right-hand bale of hay. Suppose you believe this is the last moment before you become too weak to go either way. According to the Generalized Instrumental Requirement, you are not rational unless either you now intend to go left, or you now intend to go right.

Suppose next that you believe that going left is no worse a means than going right. Then you could come to satisfy the requirement by doing some reasoning before that last moment arrives. Made explicit, your reasoning might be:

> 'I shall survive.
> Going either left or right is a means implied by my surviving.
> Going left is no worse a means than going right.
> Going left is up to me.
> So I shall go left.'

This reasoning is intuitively correct. It would be validated by this basing permission, which seems intuitively plausible:

> Rationality permits N that:
> N intends at some time that e, and
> N believes at some time that either m or n or p or . . . is a means implied by e, and
> N believes at some time that m is no worse a means than n or p or . . .
> N believes at some time that m is up to her herself, and
> N intends at some time that m, and
> N's intention that m is based on N's intention that e, and belief that either m or n or p or . . . is a means implied by e, belief that m is no worse a means than n or p or . . ., and belief that m is up to her herself.

Since I am not sure how to formulate accurately the notion of the *goodness of a means*, this formula is not as tight as it should be.

The interesting thing about this permission is that it permits choice. In the example, suppose that, as well as believing that going left is no worse than going right, you believe that going right is no worse than going left. Then you might alternatively reason:

> 'I shall survive.
> Going either left or right is a means implied by my surviving.
> Going right is no worse a means than going left.
> Going right is up to me.
> So I shall go right.'

This is also intuitively correct reasoning, validated by the same basing permission.

It may seem surprising at first that there is room for choice in reasoning. There could have been no choice if reasoning were validated by requirements, but actually there is room for choice because it is validated by permissions.

14.4   Hypothesizing

This chapter is about reasoning with attitudes other than beliefs. I have concentrated on practical reasoning. But I need to mention briefly another sort of reasoning, because it is so important. We often need to reason with the attitude of hypothesizing.[13]

We can reason hypothetically. Here is an example. You hypothesize that Ben has been very busy today. You work out as a consequence that he will not have been shopping. You add into your reasoning your belief that food is short. You conclude that you will need to go to the supermarket tonight. Finally, as a result of this reasoning, you come to believe the conditional proposition that, if Ben has been very busy today, you will need to go to the supermarket tonight.

That way, you end up believing a conditional proposition. Your reasoning follows the method of conditional proof in logic. We have no other way of coming to believe a complicated conditional proposition such as the one in the example. So we have to be able to reason hypothetically.

In the course of hypothetical reasoning, you reason about several propositions that you do not believe. Yet you are genuinely reasoning; you are not merely saying empty sentences to yourself. You have some attitude to those propositions other than belief, and you express that attitude. It is the attitude of hypothesizing.

I shall not try to give a full account of reasoning with this attitude. I mention it simply to record the fact that theoretical reasoning can involve this further attitude. However, I shall make one speculative remark. It is an interesting fact that the reasoning you can correctly do with the attitude of hypothesizing is exactly the same as the reasoning you can correctly do with belief. Exactly the same rules are correct. This needs explaining, since other attitudes do not resemble belief so closely in this respect.

Here is a tentative explanation. I suggest that hypothesizing is *make believe*.[14] Hypothesizing a proposition is creating some sort of a fiction.

Notes

1   Gilbert Harman, *Change in View*, p. 77: 'I understand practical reasoning to be the reasoned revision of intentions'.
2   In *Practical Reasoning and Ethical Decisions*, pp. 91–2, Robert Audi takes practical reasoning to conclude in a judgement that has a normative content.
3   According to some commentators, Aristotle takes practical reasoning to conclude in a physical action. For instance, see Elizabeth Anscombe, *Intention*, pp. 57–62 or Alexander Broadie, 'The practical syllogism'. Other commentators disagree. For instance, see Robert Audi, *Practical Reasoning and Ethical Decision*, pp. 23–7.
4   Nadeem Hussain impressed on me the importance of this point long ago.
5   Frege, *'Begriffsschrift'*, pp. 1–2.
6   See Nicholas Smith's 'Frege's judgement-stroke'. I am very grateful to Nicholas Smith for drawing this feature of Frege's logic to my attention.
7   I am grateful to Sarah Stroud for making me see this point.
8   Though it took Geoff Brennan to remind me of it. I am very grateful to him.
9   For example: Hector-Neri Castañeda, 'Practical thinking'; Allan Gibbard, *Thinking How to Live*; Paul Grice, *Aspects of Reason*; Richard Hare, *Practical Inferences* and *The Language of Morals*.

10   See Peter Geach, 'Ascriptivism' and 'Assertion'. There is a valuable account of the Frege-Geach problem in Susan Hurley's *Natural Reasons*, chapter 9.
11   See Nicholas Smith, 'Frege's judgement-stroke', p. 658. Nicholas Smith has pointed out to me the parallel between Frege's 'judgement-stroke' and my marker 'belief'. They differ in that the judgement-stroke marks the act of assertion, whereas 'belief' marks the attitude of belief.
12   In this section, I owe a special thanks to James Morauta.
13   Thanks to Margaret Gilbert here.
14   Dan Sperber made this suggestion to me.

15

Explicit Reasoning

15.1 Markers

Chapters 13 and 14 propounded the first-order account of active reasoning. They assumed that active reasoning is necessarily conscious, but they did not assume it is necessarily explicit. Explicit reasoning is reasoning that is expressed in language. Most often it is expressed in silent inner speech, but occasionally we may reason out loud. I have no doubt we can express our reasoning in language, but I did not assume we have to.

Nevertheless, it is plausible to think that active reasoning has to be explicit. I shall not try to defend this view, since it is not required by this book's argument. But I can say something to make it plausible. In active reasoning, you operate on the marked contents of your conscious attitudes, following a rule. These marked contents are complex. They have a syntactic structure, and the rules you apply in operating on them depend on their structure. In operating on them, you have to hold them in your consciousness, maintaining an awareness of their syntactic structure. Language is well suited to doing that. It has a meaning that can represent the semantic elements of the marked contents, and it has a syntax that can represent their syntactic structure. It is plausible that, without the help of language, you could not keep the marked contents properly organized in your consciousness.

If it is true that active reasoning has to be explicit, that makes a lot of difference to the reasoning we can actively do. It means that the processes of reasoning available to us are constrained by the resources that our language provides. Those resources are contingent, and reasoning would be constrained by the same contingencies. We might even be debarred by our language from doing some sorts of reasoning that would have been correct had we done them. There will be examples in section 15.3.

This is presumably not a significant limitation on how we manage our lives.[1] No doubt our language has evolved the resources for any reasoning that we actually need to do. Reasoning is only a self-help mechanism that allows us mortals to overcome one of our contingent deficiencies. We do not satisfy every requirement of rationality automatically, so we have to employ reasoning to do better. Where automatic processes work satisfactorily, we do not need reasoning.

This chapter explores the constraints that are imposed on explicit reasoning by English. If active reasoning has to be explicit, these are also constraints on the active reasoning of English speakers. But I do not assert they are.

To reason explicitly, we need to express the marked contents of the attitudes we reason with. A marked content consists of the content of an attitude, which is a proposition, together with a mark that is the nature of the attitude. We need to express both the content and the mark.

I shall assume for the sake of argument that the content – any proposition we need to reason with – can always be expressed by an English sentence. There is evidence even in this book that that is not entirely true; I have occasionally been forced to depart from English grammar to express some of the propositions I needed to express. But that was only in sophisticated philosophical argument. Here, I am trying to explain only the most elementary sorts of reasoning, and I think this is a safe assumption in that context.

But although English imposes no constraints on the content that can be expressed, constraints appear with expressing the mark. I explained on page 253 that a mark is expressed by a linguistic feature of a sentence that I call an 'attitude marker', or just a 'marker'. English offers only a limited range of markers. This limits its expressive power.

This section surveys the markers we have available in English. Later sections in the chapter examine the reasoning we can do using these markers.

Moods

The best recognized markers in natural language are the moods of sentences. The standard marker for a belief is the indicative mood. When we reason explicitly with beliefs, we use indicative sentences. So far as I can tell, the expressive power of English does not constrain our reasoning with beliefs, using indicative sentences – at least, not our elementary, unphilosophical reasoning. But it may constrain our reasoning with attitudes of other sorts.

On page 254 I mentioned the optative mood as a marker for desire. I am not convinced there is any correct reasoning to be done with desires, but there may be correct reasoning with preferences, using a different sort of optative construction.[2]

Suppose you prefer it to be sunny rather than snowing. Jonathan Dancy pointed out to me that you might express your preference with the sentence 'Rather sunny than snowing'. It is fair to count this as an optative construction, since a preference is a comparative desire. It is an attitude to two propositions together – in this case the proposition that it is sunny and the proposition that it is snowing.

Plausibly rationality requires you to have transitive preferences. (I do not insist on this; it is only a useful example.) That is:

> *Transitivity Requirement.* Rationality requires of N that, if
> N prefers p to q and
> N prefers q to r, then
> N prefers p to r.

Moreover, plausibly correct reasoning can bring you to satisfy this requirement. Plausibly, this is a correct rule of reasoning:

> From
>   <p, q; preference> and
>   <q, r; preference>
> to derive
>   <p, r; preference>.

It is plausibly validated by the basing permission:

> *Transitivity Permission.* Rationality permits N that
> N prefers p to q and
> N prefers q to r and
> N prefers p to r and
> N's preference for p over r is based on N's preference for p over q and
> preference for q over r.

Suppose you prefer it to be sunny rather than snowing, and you also prefer it to be snowing rather than raining. Then a piece of reasoning could bring you to acquire a new preference for its being sunny rather than raining. You could do this reasoning explicitly using the English sentences:

> 'Rather sunny than snowing.
> Rather snowing than raining.
> So rather sunny than raining'.

This is plausibly correct reasoning, but I do not insist it is. I mention it only as a simple illustration of reasoning with markers.

Some philosophers treat the imperative mood as a marker for intention. They think intentions are expressed in first-person imperative sentences. This is certainly not true in English. We use an imperative sentence when we think a person does not have a particular intention, and hope to induce her to have it. You say 'Take the next left!' when you think the driver does not intend to take the next left and you hope to induce her to intend to take it. When you say an imperative sentence to yourself, it serves the same purpose. I say to myself 'Stop staring out of the window and get on with writing!' in the hope of inducing myself to intend to do what I tell myself to do. If I already had that intention I would not issue the command. I form most of my intentions without this palaver, so I rarely need to use the imperative mood in speaking to myself.

I shall come to genuine markers for intentions next. The markers I shall mention from here on are not moods. They occur in indicative sentences.

Silent markers

Some markers are silent. We often issue a command or ask a question using the indicative mood. You say 'You will not do that again!' meaning the same as 'Do not do that again!', or 'She is coming at seven?' meaning the same as 'Is she coming at seven?'. 'You will not do that again!' and 'She is coming at seven?' contain silent markers. In truth, the markers may not be completely silent; they may be audible inflexions of intonation. Either by intonation or in some other way, the presence of a silent marker is conveyed from the speaker to the hearer. On paper, it is conveyed by a punctuation mark.

Markers for commanding or questioning do not mark attitudes. But now I come to a silent attitude marker. It is one we use constantly. It is the ordinary marker for intention. The ordinary way of expressing an intention is to use an indicative sentence. Suppose you intend to be awake by five; you have set your alarm-clock because you plan to be on the river before the mayflies start to rise. The marked content of your intention is <I shall be awake by five; intention>. You may express this intention by saying 'I shall be awake by five'.

You can express a belief in exactly the same way, using an indicative sentence. Suppose you believe you will be awake by five because you expect the guns to have started firing by then and woken you. The marked content of your belief is <I shall be awake by five; belief>. You could express your belief by saying the same indicative sentence 'I shall be awake by five'.

The difference between a belief and an intention may sometimes be signalled by subtle grammatical inflexions within an indicative sentence. For instance, according to the Fowlers, the first person singular 'I will' is more coloured than 'I shall', and may be used to indicate the presence of will or intention.[3] If they are right, the use of 'will' rather than 'shall' is an audible marker for intention. But I doubt what the Fowlers say. Perhaps in their day it was true of English English. (They do not claim it was ever true of all British English.) But in modern English the very same sentence may express either an intention or a belief. Only a silent marker distinguishes an expression of intention from an expression of belief.

The fact that the marker for intention is silent has an important consequence. When you express an intention, you utter a sentence in the indicative mood, and the consequence is that you make an assertion. That is the common rule when uttering an indicative sentence. Asking a question and issuing a command using the indicative are exceptions to this rule. When you command a child 'You will not do that again!', you do not assert that the child will not do that again. The silent marker in your sentence cancels out the normal assertoric effect of saying the sentence. So does the silent marker in the question 'She is coming at seven?'. But it is rare for a marker to cancel an assertion in that way.

You may use indicative sentences to perform many sorts of speech-act besides commanding and enquiring. When you do, what you say almost always retains its force as an assertion. For instance, a judge can sentence a criminal to prison by saying 'I sentence you to prison'. When she does, she also asserts that she sentences the criminal to prison.

Expressing an intention follows the common rule. The silent marker for intention does not cancel the assertoric effect of what you say. When you say 'I shall be awake by five', expressing an intention, you also assert that you will be awake by five. To assert something is to express a belief in it. So you express two attitudes at once: an intention and a belief. A burglar overhearing you will know that burgling after five is unsafe. To the burglar, it makes no difference whether your sentence expresses an intention or only a belief that you will be awake by five. What matters to the burglar is that it expresses a belief.

Intentions and beliefs

It is a striking linguistic fact that a belief and an intention can be expressed in the same sentence. It means that whenever you are able to express an intention sincerely in the ordinary way, you must have the corresponding belief. When you sincerely express your intention by saying 'I shall be awake by five', you must believe you will be awake by five. How can that be explained?

I explain it like this.[4] You normally fulfil your intentions: generally, when you intend something, you do what you intend. Consequently, when you intend to F, the fact that you intend to F constitutes evidence that you will F. If your intention is conscious, you are conscious of evidence that you will F. Provided the evidence is sufficiently strong, it will make you believe you will F. You will then be in a position to express the intention in the normal way, by saying 'I shall F', which also expresses the corresponding belief.

When an intention is conscious and constitutes strong enough evidence to make you believe you will do what you intend, let us call it an 'ordinary intention'. You can express an ordinary intention in the ordinary way.[5]

Many philosophers inspired by Elizabeth Anscombe explain the striking linguistic fact differently.[6] Both David Velleman and Kieran Setiya claim that an intention to F actually *is* a particular sort of belief that you will F.[7] Rae Langton points out that this claim raises a puzzle.[8] When you form an intention to F, you form a belief that you will F, but at the time you have no evidence that you will F. Once you have formed the intention, it will constitute evidence that you will F. But that evidence exists only once you have formed the belief, since the belief is the intention. How can you rationally form a belief without any evidence? That is the puzzle. My explanation raises no such puzzle.

Adverbial markers

Consider the indicative sentence 'Hopefully, the wind will veer'. If you uttered this sentence, you would not be expressing a belief in the proposition that hopefully the wind will veer. There is no such proposition. There is a proposition that the wind will veer hopefully, but that is not it. The adverb 'hopefully' used this way does not denote any part of your attitude's content. Instead, it is an attitude marker. This sentence expresses an attitude of hope towards the proposition that the wind will veer. It denotes the marked content <The wind will veer; hope>.

Writers of taste refuse to use 'hopefully' in this way, as a marker. But other adverbial markers are well accepted. Take 'maybe'. Saying 'Maybe the wind will veer' might be doing either of two things. It could be expressing a belief in the proposition that maybe the wind will veer. But according to Bayesians at least, there is no such proposition. According to Bayesians, you are expressing a partial belief in the proposition that the wind will veer. The marked content of your attitude is <The wind will veer; partial belief>. 'Maybe' is the marker for partial belief.

That example illustrates how there is room for alternative interpretations of attitudes and markers. In the example, it is questionable whether 'maybe' is a marker. But take another use of 'maybe'. Suppose you are thinking of setting your alarm for five, but you have not yet firmly made up your mind. To express your state of intention, you might say 'Maybe I shall be awake at five'. It is clear in this case that you are not expressing an attitude of intention towards the proposition that maybe you will be awake at five, if there is such a proposition. In this context of intention, 'maybe' is clearly an attitude marker. Your sentence expresses an attitude of partial intention towards the proposition that you will be awake at five. It denotes the marked content <I shall be awake at five; partial intention>.

As indicative sentences usually do, this one also expresses a belief. Here there is once again room for alternative interpretations. It may express a full belief that maybe you will be awake at five, or a partial belief that you will be awake at five.

Descriptive markers

You sometimes express an attitude using a sentence that, taken literally, asserts that you have the attitude. Someone asks you 'What is the plural of "mongoose"?'. You answer 'I believe it is "mongeese"'. Literally, you assert that you believe the plural of 'mongoose' is 'mongeese'. But if that is all you do, you are not answering the question. The question is about grammar, and you do not answer it by saying something about your state of mind.

Actually, you do answer the question, and what you say has another meaning. The words 'I believe' can serve as a marker for the attitude of belief. Taken this way, what you say expresses your belief that the plural of 'mongoose' is 'mongeese'.

Then why not answer simply 'It is "mongeese"'? Probably because your belief is partial, so you do not want to assert flatly that the plural is mongeese. 'I believe' generally marks a partial belief rather than a full one.

However, you use the indicative mood, and you cannot turn off the literal meaning of your sentence. What you say retains its assertoric force. In saying it, you assert that you believe the plural of 'mongoose' is 'mongeese'. That is to say, you express a belief that you believe the plural of 'mongoose' is 'mongeese'. You express two attitudes at once: your partial belief that the plural of 'mongoose' is 'mongeese', and your full belief that you have this partial belief.

Here is another example of a similar type of marker. Someone asks you 'What are you doing tomorrow?' You answer 'I intend to work out my taxes'. Literally, you assert that you intend to work out your taxes. But what you say has another meaning too. The words 'I intend' can serve as a marker for the attitude of intention. Taken this way, what you say expresses your intention to work out your taxes.

Why not express your intention in the ordinary way by answering simply 'I shall work out my taxes'? Why instead use a sentence that describes your state of mind? The answer is probably that you are not sure you will work out your taxes, so you do not want to assert that you will. However, you do assert that you intend to work them out.

I shall call markers of this type 'descriptive markers'. They are very common.[9] You can express a desire to be in England by saying 'I want to be in England'; you can express a hope that you will soon be home by saying 'I hope I shall soon be home'; and so on. The descriptive marker for belief tends to express partial beliefs, and the descriptive marker for intention tends to express partial intentions. But other descriptive markers are often used to express attitudes that are not partial. There need be nothing partial about your desire or your hope.

In principle, we can use descriptive markers to express any attitude, including what I called 'negative attitudes' on page 188. A negative attitude is the absence of an attitude, such as the absence of an intention.

You are asked 'Will you be at the conference?' You answer 'I do not intend to be'. If this was merely a description of the state of your mind, it would not answer the question. But it does seem to answer the question. You seem to be expressing your non-intention of being at the conference. If that is right, 'I do not intend' is serving as a descriptive marker for not intending. Your sentence seems to denote the marked content <I shall be at the conference; non-intention>. If we are to express a negative attitude in language, a descriptive marker is the only means we have of doing so.

It is a questionable means. When you say 'I do not intend to be at the conference', you may well not be expressing a non-intention. In English, we often position a 'not' inaccurately. The sentence 'I do not believe the train will be on time' often has the meaning of 'I believe the train will not be on time'. So you may mean to say that you intend not to be at the conference. Indeed, you may even be using a descriptive marker to express an intention not to be at the conference.

Descriptive markers are ways of making all sorts of attitudes explicit. In principle they make these attitudes available to be reasoned with explicitly. But in practice, sentences containing descriptive markers do not work well in reasoning. When you use them, you cannot shake off their literal meanings, so you find yourself making assertions about your attitudes. When you say 'I do not intend to be at the conference', you assert that you do not intend to be at the conference. This feature of reasoning with descriptive markers makes it hard to avoid seeing your reasoning as reasoning with beliefs, rather than what it is intended to be. Section 15.3 provides examples. There I shall consider explicit reasoning with negative attitudes, which will turn out to be unconvincing. Another example appears at the end of section 15.4.

15.2   Bayesian and expressivist reasoning

I have surveyed the various markers that English makes available for express-ing our attitudes. Now I come to the explicit reasoning we can do with these markers. On page 269 I described some reasoning with optative sentences. But from here on I shall consider only reasoning that uses indicative sentences. Most of the markers I mentioned in section 15.1 occur in indicative sen-tences, including all the markers for intention. Almost all the significant explicit reasoning I know uses indicative sentences.

I explained on page 271 that nearly all indicative sentences express beliefs, even if they express other attitudes as well. When you use an indicative sen-tence with a marker, you express two attitudes at once. This turns out to be an important constraint on explicit reasoning.

My first pair of examples is chosen just to illustrate this constraint. These examples come from controversial theories about markers. I do not endorse these theories. But they can teach us a useful lesson about markers in reasoning.

The first comes from the Bayesian theory of probability.[10] I do not know of a worked-out Bayesian account of reasoning, so my account is an extrapola-tion of recognized Bayesian thinking. Take the sentence 'The probability that there will be an explosion is twenty per cent'. On the face of it, to say this sentence is to express a belief in the proposition that the probability that there will be an explosion is twenty per cent. But Bayesians think instead that saying this sentence expresses a particular attitude towards the proposition that there will be an explosion: the attitude of believing it partially, to a degree of twenty per cent. The marker for this attitude is the words 'The probability . . . is twenty per cent'. The marked content of the attitude is <There will be an explosion; twenty-per-cent belief>.

The second example comes from expressivist metaethics. Take the sentence 'People ought not to waste water'. On the face of it, if you say this sentence, you express a belief in the proposition that people ought not to waste water. But expressivists think instead that you express some sort of a favouring attitude, or – in Allan Gibbard's version of the theory[11] – some sort of a con-ditional planning attitude, towards the proposition that people do not waste water. The marker for this attitude is the word 'ought'. The marked content of your attitude is <People do not waste water; favour> or <People do not waste water; plan> or something of the sort.

According to Bayesians and expressivists, then, sentences such as 'The prob-ability that there will be an explosion is twenty per cent' and 'People ought not to waste water' express attitudes that are not beliefs, or at least not full beliefs.[12] I shall call them 'Bayesian and expressivist attitudes'. Those sentences make it possible to reason explicitly with these attitudes.

Taken at face value, each of those sentences denotes a proposition. Neither Bayesians nor expressivists think that is what they actually do. However, it turns out in both theories that the reasoning we can do with the sentences exactly corresponds to the reasoning we would be able to do with them if we took them at face value. Furthermore, it is correct reasoning exactly when the corresponding face-value reasoning would be correct. Reasoning that corresponds to propositional logic is correct, for example. Also, in the case of Bayesian theory, reasoning is correct if the corresponding face-value reasoning conforms to the ordinary calculus of probability. We may say that reasoning is correct exactly when it looks correct.

For instance, suppose you say to yourself the sentences:

'The probability that there will be an explosion is twenty per cent.
So the probability that there will not be an explosion is eighty per cent.'

At face value, you operate on the marked content <The probability that there will be an explosion is twenty per cent; belief> and derive <The probability that there will not be an explosion is eighty per cent; belief>. This is correct reasoning by the probability calculus. From the Bayesian point of view, you operate on the marked content <There will be an explosion; twenty-per-cent belief> and derive <There will not be an explosion; eighty-per-cent belief>. This is correct reasoning according to Bayesian theory.

Or suppose you say to yourself the sentences:

'People ought not to waste water.
If people ought not to waste water, people ought not to grow lawns in the desert.
So people ought not to grow lawns in the desert.'

At face value, this is correct reasoning by modus ponens. On the expressivist theory, it is correct reasoning of a different sort.

Why is there this match between correct face-value reasoning and correct reasoning according to Bayesian or expressivist theories? There just has to be. Long before Bayesianism and expressivism were invented, people already knew how to reason about probabilities and oughts. Any philosophical theory about reasoning in these areas has to conform to what we already know. We know we must apply logic and probability calculus, so Bayesians and expressivists have to recognize that correct reasoning conforms to logic and probability calculus.

How come we already know how to reason about these things? Because, whatever the truth may be about the nature of our attitudes, we express the marked contents of our attitudes in the form of indicative sentences. The indicative mood is a marker for the speech-act of assertion and the attitude of belief. I think that, in saying these sentences, we take ourselves to be making assertions and expressing beliefs. I am not sure that all Bayesians and expressivists would agree, though some would.[13] But in any case, whether or not that is so, if we are to reason using these indicative sentences, we cannot escape the rules of correct reasoning that go with their indicative form. Those rules are given us by ordinary inference. They include logic and probability calculus.

That sets a challenge for Bayesians and expressivists. They have to explain why reasoning is correct just when it looks correct at face value. To meet this challenge, they start by explaining just what non-belief attitudes are expressed by sentences with particular structures. For instance, expressivists explain what attitude is expressed by the conditional sentence 'If people ought not to waste water, people ought not to grow lawns in the desert' in the reasoning above.[14] Then they give an account of correctness that starts from rational requirements on Bayesian and expressivist attitudes. These rational requirements are explained in some way that is specific to their theory. For each requirement, there will be corresponding basing permissions that validate particular patterns of reasoning. Then these theorists aim to demonstrate in detail how those patterns match the patterns of correct reasoning with indicative sentences.

For instance, Bayesians think that rationality requires of you that, if you believe to degree twenty per cent that there will be an explosion, you believe to degree eighty per cent that there will not be an explosion. This is an instance of the Bayesian Requirement set out on page 175. The corresponding basing permission validates reasoning that takes you from the first of these attitudes to the second.

Why does the requirement hold, according to Bayesians? Not because the proposition that the probability that there will be an explosion is twenty per cent entails the proposition that the probability that there will not be an explosion is eighty per cent. Bayesians think there is no such entailment. Instead, the requirement holds because of a 'Dutch book argument'.[15] Briefly, they argue that satisfying the requirement is beneficial in some way, and that is why rationality requires it. Dutch book arguments can be elaborated to the point of supporting all of probability calculus. That is to say, they give us enough requirements of rationality to ensure that any reasoning that corresponds to the probability calculus is correct.

I do not need to assess how successfully Bayesians and expressivists have met their challenge. The lesson I draw from their work is simply that they accept the challenge. They accept that, whatever our attitudes may be, if we express them in indicative sentences, the reasoning we can do with them is constrained by the logic of those sentences. The sort of reasoning we can do with our attitudes is constrained by the vehicle we use to express them. Any theory about how we reason with attitudes has to respect this constraint. Correct reasoning has to look correct.

15.3   Reasoning with absences

Reasoning can bring you to satisfy requirements of rationality. But satisfying requirements can often be achieved by not having an attitude rather than by having one. Indeed, some requirements can only be satisfied by not having an attitude. Can correct reasoning bring you to satisfy a requirement in this way?

Intuitively, the answer seems to be 'No'. It seems intuitively implausible that reasoning could conclude in the absence of an attitude or (to use the term I adopted on page 188) in a negative attitude. This section gives some support to this intuition. It argues at least that explicit reasoning cannot conclude in an absence.

Consistency

Take the requirement from page 155

> *No Contradictory Beliefs.* Rationality requires of N that N does not believe at t that p and also believe at t that not p.

Suppose you violate this requirement; you believe p and also believe not p. Could correct reasoning bring you to satisfy it?

Your reasoning would have to take you from your belief that p serving as premise-attitude to a non-belief that not p as conclusion-attitude, or vice versa. If you could achieve this by reasoning, it would be correct. It would be validated by the obvious basing permission of rationality that

> Rationality permits N not to believe not p on the basis of believing p,

which supports the rule:

> From
>   <p; belief>
> to derive
>   <not p; non-belief>.

I am considering only active reasoning in this book, and in this chapter I am pursuing the consequences of assuming that active reasoning is explicit. To do this reasoning explicitly, you would have to express the conclusion-attitude in language. So you would have to employ a marker for non-belief. The only available marker in English is the descriptive marker 'I do not believe'. On page 274 I raised a question about descriptive markers for absences of attitudes. But for the sake of argument, let us assume you can use one.

Then your explicit reasoning (in a particular instance) would go:

> 'The climate is not warming.
> So I do not believe the climate is warming.'

The first sentence would express a belief; the second a non-belief.

But you would meet a problem. This reasoning does not look correct. The second sentence expresses a non-belief. But, as an indicative sentence, it also expresses the belief that you do not believe the climate is warming. When you reason with indicative sentences, you cannot cancel their assertoric effect. Your reasoning therefore takes you from a belief that the climate is not warming to a belief that you do not believe the climate is warming.

A process that takes you from the first of these beliefs to the second cannot be correct reasoning. Rationality prohibits you from basing a belief that you do not believe the climate is warming on a belief that the climate is not warming. This is not a correct rule:

> From
> <p; belief>
> to derive
> <I do not believe not p; belief>

When you reason explicitly, using those sentences, this is not the rule you are supposed to be following. You are supposed to be following a correct rule that takes you to the absence of a belief that the climate is warming rather than to the belief that you do not believe the climate is warming. But it is difficult to understand the reasoning that way. It is especially difficult to do so because the sentence 'I do not believe the climate is warming' expresses a belief much more readily than it expresses the absence of a belief.

I conclude, hesitantly, that the absence of a belief cannot be the conclusion-attitude of correct explicit reasoning. If active reasoning has to be explicit, the absence of a belief cannot be the conclusion-attitude of correct active reasoning.

Automatic processes will normally prevent you from having contradictory beliefs. I have concluded that you cannot use explicit reasoning as a self-help mechanism to achieve this result. This conclusion can be generalized. If you have any set of inconsistent beliefs, you could bring yourself to consistency only by dropping one of them. To achieve this by reasoning, the conclusion would have to be a non-belief. But a non-belief cannot be the conclusion of explicit reasoning. So you cannot achieve consistency among your beliefs by explicit reasoning.

This is no loss so long as you can rely on automatic processes to achieve consistency.

Deduction

Now another example of potential reasoning with absences. Suppose you believe p and you believe that if p then q, and suppose you do not believe q, although you care about whether q. At present you violate the Modus Ponens Requirement on page 157. In chapter 13 I described some processes of reasoning that can bring you to satisfy it. One is straightforward modus ponens reasoning, which is validated by Modus Ponens Permission on page 191. Modus ponens reasoning could be explicit; I gave an example on page 223.

In section 13.5 I also described backwards reasoning that is available to you if you believe not q. By reasoning backwards, you can end up either believing not p or believing it is not the case that if p then q. There are obviously basing permissions of rationality that would validate reasoning that concludes in either belief; I do not need to set them out. These processes of reasoning could be made explicit.

However, they do not alone bring you to satisfy the Modus Ponens Requirement. For that, you must give up either your belief that p or your belief that if p then q. We can expect that result to follow through automatic processes: once you believe not p, automatic processes will cause you to stop believing p, and once you believe it is not the case that if p then q, they will cause you to stop believing that if p then q. I have just argued that this process cannot be conducted through explicit reasoning.

Neither of the processes of backwards reasoning I described is available to you unless you believe not q. Yet if you merely do not believe q, there are still three ways you can come into line with the Modus Ponens Requirement: you can come to believe q, you can stop believing p or you can stop believing that if p then q.

You can achieve the first of these results by modus ponens reasoning in a forward direction. Could you achieve either of the others by backwards reasoning of some sort? If you could, it would be correct reasoning, because it would be supported by a basing permission of rationality. For instance, this is a genuine permission:

> Rationality permits N that
> N does not believe q, and
> N believes that if p then q, and

N does not believe p, and

N's not believing p is based on N's not believing q and N's believing that if p then q.

However, I do not think that either of those results could be achieved by backwards reasoning – at least, not by explicit backwards reasoning. Any backwards reasoning you did would have to take your non-belief in q as a premise-state and also have a non-belief as its conclusion-state. If the reasoning is to be explicit, you would have to express those attitudes to yourself in language. You would need to employ a marker for non-belief, and the only one available is a descriptive marker.

To use an example again, your reasoning might go:

'I do not believe platypuses do not lay eggs.

If platypuses are mammals, platypuses do not lay eggs.

So I do not believe platypuses are mammals.'

The first and last sentences of this putative piece of reasoning express non-beliefs.

Like the example on page 279, this piece of reasoning is supposed to conclude in a non-belief. For the same reason as before, I do not think we can understand it as correct reasoning. The only way to understand it seems to be as a piece of incorrect belief reasoning.

One consequence is that explicit reasoning has only a limited power to bring you to satisfy the Modus Ponens Requirement. It can do so in only one out of the three ways that should be available in principle, unless you happen to believe the negation of the conclusion.

15.4   Theoretical and practical reasoning

On page 254, I set out this example of explicit instrumental reasoning:

'I shall visit Venice.

I shall not visit Venice if I do not buy a ticket.

So I shall buy a ticket.'

On page 260 I said this is not correct practical reasoning unless it is enthymematic and set out the correct reasoning explicitly and in full:

'I shall visit Venice.

My buying a ticket is a means implied by my visiting Venice.

My buying a ticket is up to me.

So I shall buy a ticket.'

In either version of this reasoning, the first and last sentences express intentions. They do so in the ordinary way: they are indicative sentences, containing a silent marker for intention. This means the intentions they express are ordinary intentions as I defined them on page 272.

The ordinary assertoric force of those sentences is not cancelled, so they express beliefs as well as intentions. The same sequences of sentences could express theoretical reasoning, therefore. In this respect, intention reasoning resembles the examples in section 15.3. But it differs crucially in another respect. In the examples of section 15.3 the reasoning is incorrect if interpreted as theoretical reasoning, whereas either version of the Venice reasoning would be correct if it was interpreted as theoretical reasoning. There would be some redundancy among the premises of the second version, but that does not prevent it from being correct.

So if correct instrumental reasoning is made explicit, it seems to be closely parallel to correct theoretical reasoning. This section investigates the parallel.

The independence of practical reasoning

I shall concentrate on the first version of Venice reasoning above. It is a sequence of three sentences that can express practical reasoning but could also express an unimpeachably correct piece of theoretical reasoning by modus tollens. Furthermore, it is better suited to expressing theoretical rather than practical reasoning, since it expresses correct practical reasoning only if it is enthymematic. Given that, it is easy to get the impression that the theoretical reasoning in some way drives the corresponding practical reasoning. That thought gives some intuitive support to the doctrine of cognitivism, which I introduced in section 9.4. Even if it is not the driver, the theoretical reasoning may seem very much entangled with the practical reasoning.

For many years I thought that was so, but now I realize I was mistaken.[16] Despite appearances, the practical reasoning is independent of the theoretical reasoning. Practical reasoning can bring you to acquire a new intention, but theoretical reasoning can never do so.

To explain why, I shall examine the working of theoretical reasoning in various different cases. Start with cases in which the theoretical Venice reasoning is available to you but the parallel practical reasoning is not. These will be cases where at least one of the following is true: (1) although you believe you will visit Venice, you do not have an ordinary intention to do so; (2) although you believe your buying a ticket is implied by your visiting Venice, you do not believe it is a *means* implied by your visiting Venice; (3) You do not believe your buying a ticket is up to you. It is easy to make up stories for each of these cases. For example, (1) would be true if you do not intend to visit Venice but you believe your cultured aunt will eventually persuade you to do so.

In any of these cases, you might be able to reason theoretically to a belief that you will buy a ticket. If you do, your reasoning need not in any way incline you to intend to buy a ticket. For instance, it may lead you to believe your aunt will eventually persuade you to buy a ticket.

Alternatively, your theoretical reasoning might be prevented from going forward to a belief that you will buy a ticket. Theoretical reasoning may always be blocked in this fashion. For example, you might already believe the opposite – that you will not buy a ticket. Perhaps you believe you cannot afford one. In that case your beliefs are initially inconsistent with each other: you believe that you will visit Venice, that you will not visit Venice if you do not buy a ticket, and that you will not buy a ticket.

In this situation, you may be able to reason in reverse, in the way I described in section 13.5. If so, you may come to the conclusion that you will not visit Venice. If you do that, passive processes will probably cause you to drop your belief that you will visit Venice. Which direction your reasoning takes you – forwards or backwards – depends on the relative robustness of your conflicting beliefs, as I explained in section 13.5.

An interesting situation arises when (1) and (2) are false and (3) is true. To fill out this story: suppose you have an ordinary intention to visit Venice and that is why you believe you will visit Venice. Suppose you believe that your buying a ticket is a means implied by your visiting Venice. But suppose you do not believe that your buying a ticket is up to you; you believe your ticket-buying has been delegated to your agent, whom you cannot now contact.

Now assume you robustly believe you will not buy a ticket – say you are sure you have not made enough money available to your agent for you to do so. Suppose that by backwards reasoning from this belief, you come to believe you will not visit Venice. If passive processes work as they should, and bring you to satisfy the requirement of No Contradictory Beliefs, you will stop believing you will visit Venice. But you cannot do that while maintaining your ordinary intention of visiting Venice. So you will drop that intention.

This is striking. Your reasoning causes you to change the state of your intentions – specifically to drop one of them. This is a practical effect. Yet it is brought about by purely theoretical reasoning. You reason on the basis of beliefs only: the belief that you will not buy a ticket and the belief that, if you do not buy a ticket you will not visit Venice. No relevant practical reasoning is available to you. It may seem surprising at first that theoretical reasoning can have a practical effect, but it is so.

Indeed this is a very common occurrence. You intend an end and believe some means is implied by the end. But then you realize the means is not going to happen, so you drop the intention. This can occur whether or not you believe the means is up to you.

That is all I have to say about cases where only theoretical reasoning is available to you. Now I come to cases where both theoretical and practical reasoning are available. (1), (2) and (3) are all false. You believe you will visit Venice, and have an ordinary intention of doing so. You believe buying a ticket is a means implied by doing so, and you believe that buying a ticket is up to you.

Among these cases are ones where, before you do any theoretical reasoning, you believe you will buy a ticket. That might be because you have already done your practical reasoning, and reasoned your way to intending to buy a ticket, or there might be some other explanation. In these cases there is no work for theoretical reasoning to do.

So let us concentrate on cases where initially you do not believe you will buy a ticket. In some of these cases, you might be able to take your theoretical reasoning forward to arrive at a belief that you will buy a ticket. Arriving at this belief has no tendency to make you intend to buy a ticket if you do not already intend to do so. For instance, you might believe the time has not yet arrived when you need to have this intention in order to buy a ticket. You believe that your buying a ticket is up to you, but this means only that you believe you would not buy one were you not to intend sometime to do so. You might believe you do not need to have this intention yet.

I suppose alternatively that you might do forward theoretical reasoning simultaneously with practical reasoning. Your practical reasoning would bring you to an ordinary intention to buy a ticket. This would make you believe you will buy a ticket. But perhaps you might simultaneously arrive at the same belief by theoretical reasoning. Perhaps simultaneous reasoning is possible; I take no view on that.

Alternatively again, you might find your forward theoretical reasoning blocked, because you cannot acquire the conclusion-belief that you will buy a ticket. Perhaps you believe you cannot afford one. Then you might reverse your theoretical reasoning, and perhaps arrive at the conclusion that you will not visit Venice. This might cause you to drop your belief that you will visit Venice, and with it your intention of visiting Venice. In that case, theoretical reasoning will have the practical effect that I have already described of causing you to drop an intention.

That concludes my review of cases. In none of them does your theoretical reasoning supplant practical reasoning by bringing you to acquire an intention. Nor does it drive your practical reasoning in any way. The idea that it might do one or the other arose from the parallel between theoretical reasoning and instrumental reasoning using a silent marker. But we have discovered that this idea is mistaken. Theoretical reasoning cannot bring you to acquire an intention. However, we have discovered that it can cause you to drop one, even when practical reasoning cannot.

15.5   Intention reasoning with other markers

I have been assuming that, when instrumental reasoning is made explicit, intentions are expressed using the silent marker. But there are other ways of expressing intentions. One is the descriptive marker mentioned on page 273. The Venice reasoning described in chapter 14 could be made explicit like this:

> 'I intend to visit Venice.
> I shall not visit Venice if I do not buy a ticket.
> So I shall buy a ticket.'

This is the enthymematic version. The full explicit reasoning is:

> 'I intend to visit Venice.
> My buying a ticket is a means implied by my visiting Venice.
> My buying a ticket is up to me.
> So I shall buy a ticket.'

These are plausible examples of correct instrumental reasoning.

When reasoning is expressed this way, it cannot be confused with theoretical reasoning. This fact helps to cement the conclusion of section 15.4 that practical reasoning is independent of the parallel theoretical reasoning.

In neither version of the reasoning did I use the descriptive marker in the conclusion-sentence. It appears only in a premise-sentence. This is because, so far as I can tell, a descriptive marker cannot be used in the conclusion-sentence of explicit reasoning. Take this putative piece of reasoning:

> 'I intend to visit Venice.
> I shall not visit Venice if I do not buy a ticket.
> So I intend to buy a ticket.'

I could not understand this as instrumental reasoning, but only as incorrect theoretical reasoning. It appears to conclude in the belief that you intend to buy a ticket. It seems impossible for a sentence that stands at the conclusion of a piece of explicit reasoning to contain a descriptive marker. The sentence can only be understood as describing an attitude. I cannot explain this phenomenon; I mention it as an interesting feature of English.

So far as I can tell, then, if the conclusion-state of a piece of explicit reasoning is an intention, it cannot be expressed using a descriptive marker. This would pose a problem if the only alternative marker were the silent one. The silent marker cannot be used for an intention that is not strong enough to make you believe you will do what you intend. Yet it should be possible for instrumental reasoning to conclude in a less strong intention. If this reasoning is to be explicit, how can it be expressed?

Take an example of Michael Bratman's. You intend to go round by the library on the way home. However, you know you are absent-minded, and so you do not fully believe you will carry out your intention. Presumably you can nevertheless reason your way to intending a means of getting to the library, such as turning at the crossing, and presumably your reasoning could be explicit. Suppose that, because you know you are absent-minded, you cannot fully believe you will carry out the conclusion-intention either. So you cannot express your conclusion by saying 'I shall turn at the crossing'. How can you reason explicitly, then?

You could use an adverbial marker from pages 272–3. You could reason:

'Maybe I shall go to the library.
I shall not go to the library if I do not turn at the crossing.
So maybe I shall turn at the crossing.'

This is enthymematic, but it seems to me correct explicit instrumental reasoning.

Notes

1   Thanks to Derek Parfit for this point.
2   For a fuller discussion, see my 'Reasoning with preferences?'
3   *The King's English*, chapter 2. Interestingly, Robert Brandom adopts exactly the opposite convention in *Making It Explicit*, p. 245.
4   The evidential account that follows of the relation between intending to F and believing you will F is set out in much more detail by Sarah Paul in 'Knowing what we're doing'.
5   In 'Practical knowledge' Kieran Setiya calls this a 'hopeless' manouevre. It makes only a contingent connection between intending to F and believing you will F, whereas Setiya believes the connection is necessary.
6   Anscombe, *Intention*.
7   Velleman, *The Possibility of Practical Reason*, p. 26. Setiya, 'Practical knowledge'.
8   Langton, 'Intention as faith'.
9   Thanks to Henry Richardson for this point.
10   For example, see Richard Jeffrey's *The Logic of Decision*.
11   Gibbard, *Thinking How to Live*.

12   The parallel between Bayesianism and expressivism is explored in detail in Seth Yalcin's 'Bayesian expressivism'.
13   For example, Simon Blackburn in *Ruling Passions* and Allan Gibbard in *Thinking How to Live*.
14   See, for instance, Simon Blackburn's *Spreading the Word*, p. 195.
15   See Susan Vineberg, 'Dutch Book Arguments'.
16   In past writings, I gave the wrong account of the relation between practical and theoretical reasoning. My first account appeared in my 'Instrumental reasoning'. It was improved as a result of some accurate criticism I received from Jay Wallace in his 'Normativity, commitment, and instrumental reason', particularly pp. 18–19. A better version appeared in my 'The unity of reasoning?' But that version too was wrong. It was still too vulnerable to Michael Bratman's objections, expressed particularly in his 'Intention, belief, and practical rationality'. I am grateful to Bratman for showing me my mistake. My present theory first appeared in my 'Practical reasoning and inference'. This section has also benefited from the advice of James Morauta and Nicholas Shackel.

16
Enkratic Reasoning

16.1 Enkratic reasoning

Enkrasia is the requirement of rationality that, roughly, you intend to do what you believe you ought to do. I set it out in full detail on page 170, and in this slightly more friendly form on page 171:

> *Enkrasia.* Rationality requires of N that, if
> N believes at t that she herself ought that p, and if
> N believes at t that it is up to her herself then whether or not p, then
> N intends at t that p.

On many occasions you satisfy Enkrasia automatically, as you satisfy many other requirements of rationality automatically. Suppose that, after staring at your computer screen for a while, you come to realize you ought to take a break. As you do that, you may automatically acquire the intention of taking a break. If you do, automatic processes have brought you to satisfy Enkrasia. (I assume you believe it is up to you whether or not you take a break.)

But once again, automatic processes might let you down. And once again, you have a self-help device. You might reason by saying to yourself:

> 'I ought to take a break.
> So I shall take a break.'

The first sentence expresses a belief of yours. The second expresses an intention. You do not initially have this intention, but you acquire it by your reasoning. This bit of explicit reasoning might be a way of getting yourself to take a break.

I call a process of this sort 'enkratic reasoning'. I find it intuitively plausible that it is reasoning. Moreover, it satisfies the necessary and sufficient conditions for reasoning that I laid out earlier in this book.

On page 234 I said

> Active reasoning is a particular sort of process by which conscious premise-attitudes cause you to acquire a conclusion-attitude. The process is that you operate on the contents of your premise-attitudes following a rule, to construct the conclusion, which is the content of a new attitude of yours that you acquire in the process.

I claimed that this describes necessary and sufficient conditions for a process to be reasoning. On page 252 I amended this remark by altering 'content' to 'marked content'. Enkratic reasoning satisfies the amended description.

Your premise-attitude is a belief whose marked content, described as you would describe it, is:

<I ought to take a break; belief>.

You operate on this marked content following a rule, to get:

<I take a break; intention>.

This is the marked content of an intention to take a break, which you acquire during the reasoning.

So if I was right to say that those conditions are necessary and sufficient for the process to be reasoning, enkratic reasoning is indeed reasoning.

Correctness

It had better be correct reasoning. Is your reasoning about taking a break correct? This depends on what rule you follow and whether it is a correct rule.

I have not yet said what rule you follow. It might be this:

From
    <I ought that *p*; belief>
to derive
    <*p*; intention>.

If so, your reasoning is not correct. This rule does not correspond to a permission of rationality. It would correspond to this permission if it was one:

> * Rationality permits N that
> N believe at some time that she herself ought that p, and
> N intends at some time that p, and
> N's intention that p is based on N's belief that she herself ought that p.

But actually this is not a genuine permission. Suppose, say, that you believe you ought to know the President's name. But suppose you believe it is not up to you (in the special sense defined on page 162) whether or not you know the President's name, because you already know it. Intending to know it will make no difference one way or the other. Then you could not rationally base an intention to know the President's name on your belief that you ought to know it.

The relevant permission is:

> *Enkratic Permission.* Rationality permits N that
> N believe at some time that she herself ought that p, and
> N believes at some time that it is up to her herself whether or not p
> N intends at some time that p, and
> N's intention that p is based on N's belief that she herself ought that p
>   and belief that it is up to her herself whether or not p.

This is derived from Enkrasia. The corresponding rule is:

> From
>   <I ought that p; belief> and
>   <It is up to me whether or not p; belief>
> to derive
>   <p; intention>.

Your reasoning about taking a break is correct only if it is enthymematic and follows this rule. Fully spelt out and made explicit, correct enkratic reasoning would be

> 'I ought to take a break.
> It is up to me whether or not I take a break.
> So I shall take a break.

16.2   Humean objections

In Book 2 of the *Treatise*, David Hume declared that

Reason alone can never be a motive to any action of the will'.[1]

Enkratic reasoning concludes in your acquiring an intention, which is to say it is an action of the will. It does not do so on the basis of reasoning alone; it sets out from a normative belief. But Hume places beliefs as well as reasoning within the domain of reason, so in effect his remark flatly denies the possibility of enkratic reasoning.

If enkratic reasoning is impossible, it seems unlikely that Enkrasia could be a genuine requirement of rationality. We could not come to satisfy Enkrasia by reasoning; we would have to rely on automatic processes. It seems unlikely it could be a genuine requirement if those processes were the only way we could come to satisfy it. So Hume's denial is likely also to entail a denial of Enkrasia. But since his argument concerns processes, I consider it here rather than in chapter 9.

In Book 2, Hume offers just one argument for his claim that reason alone can never be a motive to any action of the will. It rests on the premise that:

The understanding exerts itself after two different ways, as it judges from demonstration or probability; as it regards the abstract relations of our ideas, or those relations of objects, of which experience only gives us information.[2]

In Book 3, Hume repeats the same argument in a different form. There, he expresses the premise more succinctly as:

Reason is the discovery of truth or falsehood.[3]

The fuller version above mentions the two routes by which reason goes about discovering truth or falsehood: 'demonstration' refers to a priori reasoning and 'probability' to empirical investigation.

To say that reason is the discovery of truth or falsehood is simply to deny the possibility of all practical reasoning, whether instrumental reasoning or enkratic reasoning. It begs the question badly. I hope I have shown in chapter 14 that practical reasoning is possible, and I shall not reopen that question here. I reject Hume's premise, and so his argument.

The rest of the relevant section of Book 2 aims to show that 'reason alone . . . can never oppose passion in the direction of the will'.[4] In his defence of this claim, Hume takes it for granted that reason alone can never be a motive to any action of the will, which he believes he has already demonstrated. So this part of the section does not contribute any argument against enkratic reasoning. Still, one point is worth mentioning.

According to Hume, if it is to oppose passion, reason must prevent a volition that is caused by passion. Hume says:

> 'Tis impossible reason cou'd have the . . . effect of preventing volition, but by giving an impulse in a contrary direction to our passion; and that impulse, had it operated alone, wou'd have been able to produce volition.[5]

That is to say, if reason can have the effect of preventing volition, it can produce volition. Hume believes he has already demonstrated that reason cannot produce volition. It follows that reason cannot have the effect of preventing volition.

This argument can be reversed, since actually reason can have the effect of preventing volition. Even Hume should recognize this. I explained on page 283 that theoretical reasoning, which Hume would accept as part of reason, may make you give up an intention you have. Here is a simple example. You intend to do something, but then by theoretical reasoning you come to believe you cannot do it. You will give up your intention, since you cannot intend to do something you believe you cannot do. It follows from Hume's sentence quoted above that reason is able to produce volition.

I do not believe that sentence of Hume's, so this is only an ad hominem remark rather than a real argument in favour of enkratic reasoning. However, it does suggest that Hume has let himself be carried away by his metaphor of impulses. He supposes that volition can be produced only by a sort of push. He concludes that, since reason cannot push, it cannot produce volition. But the metaphor does not really prove anything.

Motivation-out – motivation-in

Hume's own argument begs the question, but nevertheless his conclusion that reason can never motivate any action of the will is accepted by many philosophers. There is a vast body of literature on this subject.[6] I shall not review it here. My aim in this book has been to provide a new way of looking at this issue, which will have to stand or fall on its own merits.

However, I need to mention one very direct objection to enkratic reasoning. Let us call a disposition to act a 'motivation'. Many Humean philosophers think a motivation could not be derived by reasoning from an attitude that does not in some way already incorporate a motivation. They believe in the principle of 'motivation-out – motivation-in' – to adapt a nice expression from

Jay Wallace.[7] In 'Internal and external reasons', Bernard Williams seems to take this principle for granted. He says that an anti-Humean would make

> the claim that if the agent rationally deliberated, then, whatever motivations he originally had, he would come to be motivated to φ. But if this is correct, there does seem to be great force in Hume's basic point. . . . For, *ex hypothesi*, there is no motivation for the agent to deliberate *from*, to reach this new motivation.[8]

Williams seems to assume that if no motivation goes into the agent's deliberation, no motivation can come out. This is an amplification of Hume's view that reason alone cannot be a motive to any action of the will.

The premise-attitude of enkratic reasoning is a belief. The conclusion-attitude is an intention, which is a sort of motivation. So enkratic reasoning violates motivation-out – motivation-in, unless the premise-belief in some way incorporates a motivation.

There is a complication. If there is such a thing as enkratic reasoning, the premise-belief does incorporate a motivation of a sort. Suppose your premise-belief is that you ought to take a break, and suppose you are rational. Being rational, you are disposed to reason enkratically. Therefore you are disposed to reason your way from your belief to an intention to take a break. This intention is itself a sort of disposition to take a break. So your belief that you ought to take a break constitutes a sort of disposition to take a break. And a disposition to take a break is a motivation to take a break. So if enkratic reasoning exists and we understand motivation this way, the principle of motivation-out – motivation-in is automatically true for a rational person. If enkratic reasoning exists, it does not violate the principle.

If the principle is to provide an objection to enkratic reasoning, we must therefore restrict the notion of motivation. The disposition I described works through enkratic reasoning itself. We must exclude a disposition of that sort. Then we may take it that your premise-belief does not incorporate a motivation. Enkratic reasoning does now violate the principle of motivation-out – motivation-in.

I see no reason to accept this principle. Why should we think that a motivation cannot be derived by reasoning from an attitude that does not incorporate a motivation? Specifically, why should we think that an intention cannot be derived by reasoning from a belief? I know no argument why we should, and it is an implausible principle.

It is implausible because, without doubt, a belief can cause an intention. Intentions can be caused in all sorts of ways. You can wake up with a new intention, and you can get a new intention by hypnosis or a knock on the head. It is easy to construct a story in which a genuine belief causes an intention through a mental process. Here is one. Your habit is to walk the dog at 11 o'clock every day. You now believe it is 11 o'clock, and this causes you to intend to fetch the lead. This process is automatic. You need have no desire to walk the dog. Perhaps you know the dog is away for the day – something you remember after you have fetched the lead.

So a belief can cause an intention through a mental process. The Humean objection to enkratic reasoning has to be that any mental process through which this happens cannot be reasoning. But why not? Why should reasoning not be able to accomplish what other mental processes can? I can see no reason why not.

Perhaps I am misinterpreting the principle of motivation-out – motivation-in.[9] The claim may be that a motivation cannot come out of *correct* reasoning unless a motivation goes in, not that one cannot come out of any reasoning at all unless a motivation goes in. The Humean objection may not be to the possibility of enkratic reasoning but to the claim that enkratic reasoning is correct.

Enkratic reasoning is validated – made correct – by the Enkratic Permission on page 290, which is derived from Enkrasia. Understood this way, the Humean objection is not to a process of reasoning, but to the requirement of rationality Enkrasia. I have done what I can to defend Enkrasia in section 9.5, and I shall not repeat that argument here.

16.3 Conclusion

I conclude that enkratic reasoning is genuinely correct reasoning. If I am right, enkratic reasoning offers a very attractive explanation of how we are motivated by a normative belief. I argued in Section 13.4 that reasoning is something we do. In enkratic reasoning we are active: we actively bring ourselves to intend to do what we believe we ought to do. We motivate ourselves.

That completes the argument I promised in Chapter 1.

Notes

1 *Treatise*, book 2, part 3, section 3.
2 *Treatise*, book 2, part 3, section 3.
3 *Treatise*, book 3, part 1, section 1.
4 *Treatise*, book 2, part 3, section 3.
5 *Treatise*, book 2, part 3, section 3.
6 Among the highlights are Bernard Williams's 'Internal and external reasons' and Michael Smith's *The Moral Problem*.
7 Wallace, 'How to argue about practical reason'. Wallace's expression is 'Desire-out – desire-in'.
8 'Internal and external reasons', p. 109.
9 This useful point comes from Nicholas Southwood.

Bibliography

Adler, Jonathan, *Belief's Own Ethics*, MIT Press, 2002.

Alston, William P., 'The deontological conception of epistemic justification', *Philosophical Perspectives*, 2 (1988), pp. 257–99.

Anscombe, Elizabeth, *Intention*, Blackwell, 1957.

Arpaly, Nomy, *Unprincipled Virtue*, Oxford University Press, 2003.

Arpaly, Nomy and Timothy Schroeder, 'Deliberation and acting for reasons', *Philosophical Review*, 121 (2012), pp. 209–39.

Audi, Robert, *The Architecture of Reason*, Oxford University Press, 2001.

Audi, Robert, 'Dispositional beliefs and dispositions to believe', *Noûs*, 28 (1994), pp. 419–34.

Audi, Robert, *Practical Reasoning and Ethical Decision*, Routledge, 2006.

Audi, Robert, *The Structure of Justification*, Cambridge University Press, 1993.

Bennett, Jonathan, 'Why is belief involuntary?', *Analysis*, 50 (1990), pp. 87–107.

Binkley, Robert, 'A theory of practical reason', *Philosophical Review*, 74 (1965), pp. 423–48.

Blackburn, Simon, *Ruling Passions*, Oxford University Press, 1998.

Blackburn, Simon, *Spreading the Word*, Oxford University Press, 1984.

Boghossian, Paul, 'Blind reasoning', in his *Content and Justification*, Oxford University Press, 2008, pp. 266–87.

Boghossian, Paul, 'What is inference?', *Philosophical Studies*, 2012, DOI 10.1007/s11098-012-9903-x.

Bovens, Luc, and Stephan Hartmann, *Bayesian Epistemology*, Oxford University Press, 2003.

Brandom, Robert, *Making It Explicit*, Harvard University Press, 1994.

Bratman, Michael, 'Cognitivism about practical reason', in his *Faces of Intention*, Cambridge University Press, 1999, pp. 250–64.

Bratman, Michael, 'Intention, belief, and instrumental rationality', in *Reasons for Action*, edited by David Sobel and Steven Wall, Cambridge University Press, 2011, pp. 13–36.

Bratman, Michael, 'Intention, belief, practical, theoretical', in *Spheres of Reason*, edited by Simon Robertson, Oxford University Press, 2009, pp. 29–61.

Bratman, Michael, *Intention, Plans, and Practical Reason*, Harvard University Press, 1987.

Broadie, Alexander, 'The practical syllogism', *Analysis*, 29 (1968), pp. 26–8.

Broome, John, 'Are intentions reasons? And how should we cope with incommensurable values?', in *Practical Rationality and Preference: Essays for David Gauthier*, edited by Christopher Morris and Arthur Ripstein, Cambridge University Press, 2001, pp. 98–120.

Broome, John, 'Comments on Allan Gibbard's Tanner Lectures', in *Reconciling Our Aims: In Search of Bases for Ethics*, by Allan Gibbard, edited by Barry Stroud, Oxford University Press, 2008, pp. 102–19.

Broome, John, 'Comments on Boghossian', *Philosophical Studies*, 2012, DOI 10.1007/s11098-012-9894-7.

Broome, John, 'Normative requirements', *Ratio*, 12 (1999), pp. 398–419. Reprinted in *Normativity*, edited by Jonathan Dancy, Blackwell, 2000, pp. 78–99.

Broome, John, 'Practical reasoning', in *Reason and Nature: Essays in the Theory of Rationality*, edited by José Bermúdez and Alan Millar, Oxford University Press, 2002, pp. 85–111.

Broome, John, 'Practical reasoning and inference', in *Thinking About Reasons: Essays in Honour of Jonathan Dancy*, edited by David Bakhurst, Brad Hooker and Margaret Little, Oxford University Press, 2013, pp. 286–309.

Broome, John, 'Reasoning with preferences?', in *Preferences and Well-Being*, edited by Serena Olsaretti, Cambridge University Press, 2006, pp. 183–208.

Broome, John, 'Reasons', in *Reason and Value: Themes from the Moral Philosophy of Joseph Raz*, edited by R. Jay Wallace, Michael Smith, Samuel Scheffler and Philip Pettit, Oxford University Press, 2004, pp. 28–55.

Broome, John, 'Replies to Southwood, Kearns and Star, and Cullity', *Ethics*, 119 (2008), pp. 96–108.

Broome, John, 'Requirements', in *Homage à Wlodek: Philosophical Papers Dedicated to Wlodek Rabinowicz*, edited by Toni Rønnow-Rasmussen, Björn Petersson, Jonas Josefsson and Dan Egonsson, 2007, www.fil.lu.se/hommageawlodek.

Broome, John, 'The unity of reasoning?', in *Spheres of Reason*, edited by Simon Robertson, Oxford University Press, 2009, pp. 62–92.

Broome, John, *Weighing Goods: Equality, Uncertainty, and Time*, Blackwell, 1991.

Broome, John, *Weighing Lives*, Oxford University Press, 2004.

Broome, John, 'Williams on *ought*', in *Luck, Value, and Commitment: Themes from the Ethics of Bernard Williams*, edited by Ulrike Heuer and Gerald Lang, Oxford University Press, 2012, pp. 247–65.

Brunet, Josée, 'Le double aspect du raisonnement pratique', *Revue Philosophique de Louvain*, 101 (2003), pp. 479–500.

Burge, Tyler, 'Reason and the first person', in *Knowing Our Own Minds*, edited by Crispin Wright, Barry C. Smith and Cynthia MacDonald, Oxford University Press, 1998, pp. 243–70.

Bykvist, Krister, 'Objective versus subjective moral oughts', in *Logic, Ethics, and All That Jazz: Essays in Honour of Jordan Howard Sobel*, edited by L.-G. Johansson, R. Sliwinski and J. Osterberg, Uppsala Philosophical Studies 57, 2009, pp. 39–65.

Carroll, Lewis, 'What the tortoise said to Achilles', *Mind*, 4 (1895), pp. 278–80.

Carruthers, Peter, 'Phenomenal concepts and higher-order experiences', *Philosophy and Phenomenological Research*, 68 (2004), pp. 316–35.

Castañeda, Hector-Neri, 'On the logic of attributions of self-knowledge to others', *Journal of Philosophy*, 65 (1968), pp. 439–56.

Castañeda, Hector-Neri, 'Practical thinking, reasons for doing, and intentional action: the thinking of doing and the doing of thinking', *Philosophical Perspectives*, 4 (1990), pp. 273–308.

Chisholm, Roderick, 'The ethics of requirement', *American Philosophical Quarterly*, 1 (1964), pp. 147–53.

Chisholm, Roderick, 'Practical reasoning and the logic of requirement', in *Practical Reason*, edited by S. Körner, Blackwell, 1974, pp. 2–13. Reprinted in *Practical Reasoning*, edited by Joseph Raz, Oxford University Press, 1978, pp. 118–27.

Chrisman, Matthew, 'On the meaning of "ought"', in *Oxford Studies in Metaethics*, Volume 7, edited by Russ Schafer-Landau, Oxford University Press, 2012, pp. 304–32.

Cullity, Garrett, 'Decisions, reasons, and rationality', *Ethics*, 119 (2008), pp. 57–95.

Dancy, Jonathan, 'Enticing reasons', in *Reason and Value: Themes from the Moral Philosophy of Joseph Raz*, edited by R. Jay Wallace, Michael Smith, Samuel Scheffler and Philip Pettit, Oxford University Press, 2004, pp. 91–118.

Dancy, Jonathan, *Ethics Without Principles*, Oxford University Press, 2004.

Dancy, Jonathan, 'The logical conscience', *Analysis*, 37 (1977), pp. 81–4.

Dancy, Jonathan, 'Reasons and rationality', in *Spheres of Reason*, edited by Simon Robertson, Oxford University Press, 2009, pp. 93–112.

Danielsson, Sven, 'What shall we do with deontic logic?', *Theoria*, 66 (2000), pp. 97–114.

Dreier, James, 'Humean doubts about categorical imperatives', in *Varieties of Practical Reasoning*, edited by Elijah Millgram, MIT Press, 2001, pp. 27–48.

Enoch, David, 'Agency, schmagency: why normativity won't come from what is constitutive of action', *Philosophical Review*, 115 (2006), pp. 169–98.

Enoch, David, 'Reason-giving and the law', in *Oxford Studies in Philosophy of Law*, Volume 1, edited by Leslie Green and Brian Leiter, Oxford University Press, 2011, pp. 1–38.

Farrell, Daniel M., 'Intention, reason, and action', *American Philosophical Quarterly*, 26 (1989). pp. 283–95.

Feldman, Richard, 'Voluntary belief and epistemic evaluation', in *Knowledge, Truth, and Duty*, edited by M. Steup, Oxford University Press, 2001, pp. 77–92.

Fine, Kit, 'Essence and modality', *Philosophical Perspectives*, 8 (1994), pp. 1–16.

Fink, Julian, 'A constitutive account of "rationality requires"', forthcoming.

Foot, Philippa, *Natural Goodness*, Oxford University Press, 2001.

Forrester, James William, *Being Good and Being Logical: Philosophical Groundwork for a New Deontic Logic*, M. E. Sharpe, 1996.

Fowler, H. W. and F. G., *The King's English*, Second edition, Oxford University Press, 1908.

Frege, Gottlob, '*Begriffsschrift*: a formalized language of pure thought modelled upon the language of arithmetic', in *Translations from the Philosophical Writings of Gottlob Frege*, edited by Peter Geach and Max Black, Blackwell, 1970, pp. 1–20.

Geach, Peter, 'Ascriptivism', *Philosophical Review*, 69 (1960), pp. 221–5.

Geach, Peter, 'Assertion', *Philosophical Review*, 74 (1965), pp. 449–65.

Geach, Peter, 'Whatever happened to deontic logic?', *Philosophia*, 11 (1982), pp. 1–12.

Goble, Lou, 'Normative conflicts and the logic of "ought"', *Noûs*, 43 (2009), pp. 450–89.

Gibbard, Allan, *Thinking How to Live*, Harvard University Press, 2003.

Gibbard, Allan, *Wise Choices, Apt Feelings: A Theory of Normative Judgment*, Oxford University Press, 1990.

Greenspan, Patricia, 'Conditional oughts and hypothetical imperatives', *Journal of Philosophy*, 72 (1975), pp. 259–76,

Grice, Paul, *Aspects of Reason*, Oxford University Press, 2001.

Hare, R. M., *The Language of Morals*, Oxford University Press, 1952.

Hare, R. M., *Practical Inferences*, Macmillan, 1971.

Harman, Gilbert, *Change in View: Principles of Reasoning*, MIT Press, 1986.

Harman, Gilbert, Review of *The Significance of Sense: Meaning, Modality and Morality* by Roger Wertheimer, *Philosophical Review*, 82 (1973), pp. 235–9.

Hearne, James, 'Deductivism and practical reason', *Philosophical Studies*, 45 (1984), pp. 205–8.

Hieronymi, Pamela, 'Controlling attitudes', *Pacific Philosophical Quarterly*, 87 (2006), pp. 45–74.

Horty, John F., *Agency and Deontic Logic*, Oxford University Press, 2001.

Horty, John F., 'Reasoning with moral conflicts', *Noûs*, 37 (2003), pp. 557–605.

Horty, John F., and Nuel Belnap, 'The deliberative stit: a study of action, omission, ability, and obligation', *Journal of Philosophical Logic*, 24 (1995), pp. 583–644.

Humberstone, Lloyd, 'Two kinds of agent-relativity', *Philosophical Quarterly*, 41 (1991), pp. 144–66.

Hume, David, *A Treatise of Human Nature*, edited by L. A. Selby-Bigge and P. H. Nidditch, Oxford University Press, 1978.

Hurley, Susan, *Natural Reasons*, Oxford University Press, 1989.

Hursthouse, Rosalind, *On Virtue Ethics*, Oxford University Press, 1999.

Hussain, Nadeem, 'The requirements of rationality', forthcoming.

Jackson, Frank, 'Decision-theoretic consequentialism and the nearest and dearest objection', *Ethics*, 101 (1991), pp. 461–82.

Jackson, Frank, and Philip Pettit, 'Moral functionalism and moral motivation', *Philosophical Quarterly*, 45 (1995), pp. 20–40.

Jeffrey, Richard, *The Logic of Decision*, Second Edition, University of Chicago Press, 1983.

Johnston, Mark, 'Dispositional theories of value', *Proceedings of the Aristotelian Society*, Supplementary Volume 63 (1989), pp. 139–74.

Joyce, Richard, *The Myth of Morality*, Cambridge University Press, 2001.

Kahneman, Daniel, 'A perspective on judgment and choice: mapping bounded rationality', *American Psychologist*, 58 (2003), pp. 697–720.

Kamm, Francis, 'The doctrine of triple effect and why a rational agent need not intend the means to his ends', *Proceedings of the Aristotelian Society*, Supplementary Volume 74 (2000), pp. 21–39.

Kant, Immanuel, *Groundwork of the Metaphysic of Morals*, translated by H. J. Paton under the title *The Moral Law*, Hutchinson, 1948.

Kavka, Gregory, 'The toxin puzzle', *Analysis*, 43 (1983), pp. 33–6.

Kearns, Stephen, and Daniel Star, 'Reasons: explanation or evidence?', *Ethics*, 119 (2008), pp. 31–56.

Kiesewetter, Benjamin, 'Instrumental normativity', forthcoming.

Kolodny, Niko, 'How does coherence matter?', *Proceedings of the Aristotelian Society*, 107 (2007), pp. 229–63.

Kolodny, Niko, 'Instrumental reasons', in *The Oxford Handbook of Reasons and Normativity*, edited by Daniel Star, Oxford University Press, forthcoming.

Kolodny, Niko, 'The myth of practical consistency', *European Journal of Philosophy*, 16 (2008), pp. 366–402.

Kolodny, Niko, 'Why be disposed to be coherent?', *Ethics*, 118 (2008), pp. 437–63.

Kolodny, Niko, 'Why be rational?', *Mind*, 114 (2005), pp. 509–63.

Korsgaard, Christine, 'The activity of reason', *Proceedings and Addresses of the American Philosophical Association*, 83 (2009), pp. 23–43.

Korsgaard, Christine, 'The normativity of instrumental reason', in *Ethics and Practical Reason*, edited by Garrett Cullity and Berys Gaut, Oxford University Press, 1997, pp. 215–54.

Korsgaard, Christine, *Self-Constitution: Agency, Identity, and Integrity*, Oxford University Press, 2009.

Korsgaard, Christine, *The Sources of Normativity*, Cambridge University Press, 1996.

Kratzer, Angelika, *Morals and Conditionals*, Oxford University Press, 2012.

Kripke, Saul, *Wittgenstein on Rules and Private Language*, Blackwell, 1982.

Krogh, Christen, and Henning Herrestad, 'Getting personal: some notes on the relationship between personal and impersonal obligation', in *Deontic Logic, Agency, and Normative Systems*, edited by Mark Brown and José Carmo, Springer–Verlag, 1996, pp. 134–53.

Langton, Rae, 'Intention as faith', in *Agency and Action*, edited by John Hyman and Helen Steward, Cambridge University Press, 2004, pp. 243–58.

Lavin, Douglas, 'Practical reason and the possibility of error', *Ethics*, 114 (2004), pp. 424–57.

Lewis, David, 'Causal explanation', in his *Philosophical Papers*, Volume 2, Oxford University Press, 1986, pp. 214–40.

Lewis, David, 'Semantic analyses for dyadic deontic logic', in *Logical Theory and Semantic Analysis*, edited by S. Stendlund, Reidel, 1974, pp. 1–14.

Mackie, J. L., *Ethics: Inventing Right and Wrong*, Penguin, 1977.

McNamara, Paul, 'Agential obligation as non-agential personal obligation plus agency', *Journal of Applied Logic*, 2 (2004), pp. 117–52.

McNamara, Paul, 'Deontic logic', *Stanford Encyclopedia of Philosophy*.

Moore, G. E., *Principia Ethica*, Cambridge University Press, 1903.

Morauta, James, *Evaluating Intentions*, DPhil Thesis, University of Oxford, 2006.

Nagel, Thomas, *The Possibility of Altruism*, Oxford University Press, 1970.

Parfit, Derek, *On What Matters*, Oxford University Press, 2012.

Parfit, Derek, *Reasons and Persons*, Oxford University Press, 1984.

Paul, Sarah, 'How we know what we're doing', *Philosopher's Imprint*, 99 (2009), pp. 1–24.

Persson, Ingmar, 'A consequentialist distinction between what we ought to do and ought to try', *Utilitas*, pp. 348–55.

Pettit, Philip, *The Common Mind: an Essay on Psychology, Society and Politics*, Oxford University Press, 1993.

Pettit, Philip, 'Rationality, reasoning and group agency', *Dialectica*, 51 (2007), pp. 495–519.

Piller, Christian, 'Normative practical reasoning', *Proceedings of the Aristotelian Society*, Supplementary Volume 75 (2001), pp. 195–216.

Price, A. W., *Contextuality in Practical Reason*, Oxford University Press, 2008.

Prichard, H. A., 'Does moral philosophy rest on a mistake?', *Mind*, 21 (1912), pp. 21–37, reprinted in his *Moral Writings*, edited by Jim MacAdam, Oxford University Press, 2002, pp. 7–20.

Priest, Graham, Koji Tanaka and Zach Weber, 'Paraconsistent logic', *Stanford Encyclopedia of Philosophy*.

Rawls, John, *A Theory of Justice*, Harvard University Press, 1972.

Raz, Joseph, *Engaging Reason: On the Theory of Value and Action*, Oxford University Press, 1999.

Raz, Joseph, 'The myth of instrumental rationality', *Journal of Ethics and Social Philosophy*, 1 (2005).

Raz, Joseph, *Practical Reason and Norms*, edition published by Oxford University Press, 1999. (Originally published in 1975.)

Reisner, Andrew, *Conflicts of Normativity*, DPhil thesis, University of Oxford, 2004.

Reisner, Andrew, 'Unifying the Requirements of Rationality', *Philosophical Explorations*, 12 (2009), pp. 243–60.

Rosenthal, David, 'Thinking that one thinks', in his *Consciousness and Mind*, Oxford University Press, 2005, pp. 46–70.

Ross, Alf, 'Imperatives and logic', *Theoria*, 7 (1941), pp. 53–71.

Ross, Jacob, 'How to be a cognitivist about practical reason', *Oxford Studies in Metaethics*, Volume 4, edited by Russ Shafer-Landau, Oxford University Press, 2009, pp. 243–82.

Ross, Jacob, 'The irreducibility of personal obligation', *Journal of Philosophical Logic*, 39 (2010), pp. 307–23.

Ross, Jacob, 'Rationality, normativity, and commitment', in *Oxford Studies in Metaethics*, Volume 7, edited by Russ Shafer-Landau, Oxford University Press, 2012.

Salmon, Nathan, 'Being of two minds: belief with doubt', *Noûs*, 29 (1995), pp. 1–20.

Scanlon, T. M., 'Reasons: a puzzling duality?', in *Reason and Value: Themes from the Moral Philosophy of Joseph Raz*, edited by R. Jay Wallace, Michael Smith, Samuel Scheffler and Philip Pettit, Oxford University Press, 2004, pp. 231–46.

Scanlon, T. M., 'Structural irrationality', in *Common Minds: Themes from the Philosophy of Philip Pettit*, edited by Geoffrey Brennan, Robert Goodin, Frank Jackson and Michael Smith, Oxford University Press, 2007, pp. 84–103.

Scanlon, T. M., *What We Owe to Each Other*, Harvard University Press, 1998.

Scheffler, Samuel, *Human Morality*, Oxford University Press, 1992.

Schroeder, Mark, 'The scope of instrumental reason', *Philosophical Perspectives*, 18 (2004), pp. 337–64.

Schroeter, Laura and François Schroeter, 'Reasons as right-makers', *Philosophical Explorations*, 12 (2009), pp. 279–96.

Searle, John, *Rationality in Action*, MIT Press, 2001.

Sellars, Wilfred, 'Language as thought and as communication', *Philosophy and Phenomenological Research*, 29 (1969), pp. 506–27.

Setiya, Kieran, 'Cognitivism about instrumental reason', *Ethics*, 117 (2007), pp. 649–73.

Setiya, Kieran, 'Knowledge of intention', in *Essays on Anscombe's* Intention, edited by Anton Ford, Jennifer Hornsby and Frederick Stoutland, Harvard University Press, 2011.

Setiya, Kieran, 'Practical knowledge', *Ethics*, 118 (2008), pp. 388–409.

Shackel, Nicholas, 'Two kinds of normativity', forthcoming.

Sidgwick, Henry, *The Methods of Ethics*, Seventh edition, Macmillan, 1907.

Skorupski, John, *The Domain of Reasons*, Oxford University Press, 2010.

Smith, Michael, *Ethics and the A Priori*, Cambridge University Press, 2004.

Smith, Michael, 'Humean rationality', in *The Oxford Handbook of Rationality*, edited by Alfred R. Mele and Piers Rawling, Oxford University Press, 2004, pp. 75–92.

Smith, Michael, 'Internal reasons', *Philosophy and Phenomenological Research*, 55 (1995), pp. 109–31.
Smith, Michael, *The Moral Problem*, Blackwell, 1994.
Smith, Nicholas, 'Frege's judgement stroke and the conception of logic as the study of inference not consequence', *Philosophy Compass*, 4 (2009), pp. 639–65.
Southwood, Nicholas, 'Vindicating the normativity of rationality', *Ethics*, 119 (2008), pp. 9–30.
Tännsjö, Torbjörn, *From Reasons to Norms: On the Basic Question in Ethics*, Springer, 2010.
Tenenbaum, Sergio, 'Minimalism about intention: a modest defence', forthcoming.
Thomson, Judith Jarvis, *The Realm of Rights*, Harvard University Press, 1990.
Van Fraassen, Bas C., 'Values and the heart's command', *Journal of Philosophy*, 70 (1973), pp. 5–19.
Velleman, David, 'Deciding how to decide', in *Ethics and Practical Reason*, edited by Garrett Cullity and Berys Gaut, Oxford University Press, 1997, pp. 29–52.
Velleman, David, *The Possibility of Practical Reason*, Oxford University Press, 2000.
Vineberg, Susan, 'Dutch Book Arguments', in *The Stanford Encyclopedia of Philosophy*.
Von Wright, G. H., 'A note on deontic logic and derived obligation', *Mind*, 65 (1956), pp. 507–9.
Vranas, Peter, 'New foundations for imperative logic I: logical connectives, consistency, and quantifiers', *Noûs*, 42 (2008), pp. 529–72.
Wallace, R. Jay, 'How to argue about practical reason', *Mind*, 99 (1990), pp. 355–85.
Wallace, R. Jay, 'Normativity, commitment, and instrumental reason', *Philosophers' Imprint*, 1 (2001).
Way, Jonathan, 'The symmetry of rational requirements', *Philosophical Studies*, 155 (2011), pp. 227–39.
Wedgwood, Ralph, 'Internalism explained', *Philosophy and Phenomenological Research*, 65 (2002), pp. 349–69.
Wedgwood, Ralph, 'The meaning of "ought"', in *Oxford Studies in Methaethics*, Volume 1, edited by Russ Shafer-Landau, Oxford University Press, 2006, pp. 127–60.
Wedgwood, Ralph, *The Nature of Normativity*, Oxford University Press, 2007.
Wedgwood, Ralph, 'The normative force of reasoning', *Noûs*, 40 (2006), pp. 660–86.
Williams, Bernard, 'Deciding to believe', in his *Problems of the Self: Philosophical Papers 1956–1972*, Cambridge University Press, 1973, pp. 136–51.
Williams, Bernard, 'Ethical consistency', in his *Problems of the Self: Philosophical Papers 1956–1972*, Cambridge University Press, 1973 pp. 166–86.
Williams, Bernard, *Ethics and the Limits of Philosophy*, Fontana, 1985.
Williams, Bernard, 'Internal and external reasons', in his *Moral Luck*, Cambridge University Press, 1981, pp. 101–13.
Williams, Bernard, '*Ought* and moral obligation', in his *Moral Luck*, Cambridge University Press, 1981, pp. 114–23.
Wittgenstein, Ludwig, *Philosophical Investigations*, Blackwell, 1968.
Woods, Michael, 'Reasons for action and desires', *Proceedings of the Aristotelian Society*, Supplementary Volume 46 (1972), pp. 189–201.
Wright, Crispin, 'Comment on Paul Boghossian: "The nature of inference"', *Philosophical Studies*, 2012, DOI 10.1007/s11098-012-9892-9.
Yalcin, Seth, 'Bayesian expressivism', *Proceedings of the Aristotelian Society*, 112 (2012), pp. 123–60.

Žarnić, Berislav, 'A logical typology of normative systems', *Journal of Applied Ethics and Philosophy*, 2 (2010), pp. 30–40.

Zimmerman, Michael, 'Is moral obligation objective or subjective?', *Utilitas*, 18 (2006), pp. 329–61.

Zimmerman, Michael, *Living With Uncertainty: the Moral Significance of Ignorance*, Cambridge University Press, 2008.

Zimmerman, Michael, *Reconsidering the Moral Significance of Ignorance*, Hägerström Lectures, 2011.

Index

Printed and bound by CPI Group (UK) Ltd, Croydon, CR0 4YY

09/06/2025

14686100-0002